Stranded Assets and the Environment

T0298446

Drawing on the work of leading researchers and practitioners from a range of disciplines, including economic geography, economics, economic history, finance, law, and public policy, this edited collection provides a comprehensive assessment of stranded assets and the environment, covering the fundamental issues and debates, including climate change and societal responses to environmental change, as well as its origins and theoretical basis.

The volume provides much-needed clarity as the discourse on stranded assets gathers further momentum. In addition to drawing on scholarly contributions, there are chapters from practitioners and analysts to provide a range of critical perspectives. While chapters have been written as important standalone contributions, the book is intended to systematically take the reader through the key dimensions of stranded assets as a topic of research inquiry and practice. The work adopts a broad-based social science perspective for setting out what stranded assets are, why they are relevant, and how they might inform the decision making of firms, investors, policy makers, and regulators. The topic of stranded assets is inherently multi-disciplinary, cross-sectoral, and multi-jurisdictional, and the volume reflects this diversity.

This book will be of great relevance to scholars, practitioners, and policy makers with an interest in economics, business and development studies, climate policy, and environmental studies in general.

Ben Caldecott is the Founding Director of the Oxford Sustainable Finance Programme at the University of Oxford, UK. He is a leading authority on sustainable finance and investment with a considerable international reputation. He has pioneered key concepts in his field, including the concept of 'stranded assets'.

Routledge Explorations in Environmental Studies

A Green History of the Welfare State
Tony Fitzpatrick

The Governance of Green Urban Spaces in the EU
Social Innovation and Civil Society
Judith Schicklinski

NGO Discourses in the Debate on Genetically Modified Crops
Ksenia Gerasimova

Sustainability in the Gulf
Challenges and Opportunities
Edited by Elie Azar and Mohamed Abdelraouf

Environmental Human Rights
A Political Theory Perspective
Edited by Markku Oksanen, Ashley Dodsworth and Selina O'Doherty

African Philosophy and Environmental Conservation
Jonathan O. Chimakonam

Domestic Environmental Labour
An Eco-feminist Perspective on Making Homes Greener
Carol Farbotko

Stranded Assets and the Environment
Risk, Resilience and Opportunity
Edited by Ben Caldecott

Society, Environment and Human Security in the Arctic Barents Region
Edited by Kamrul Hossain and Dorothée Cambou

www.routledge.com/Routledge-Explorations-in-Environmental-Studies/book-series/REES

Stranded Assets and the Environment

Risk, Resilience and Opportunity

Edited by Ben Caldecott

LONDON AND NEW YORK

First published 2018
by Routledge

2 Park Square, Milton Park, Abingdon, Oxfordshire OX14 4RN
52 Vanderbilt Avenue, New York, NY 10017

Routledge is an imprint of the Taylor & Francis Group, an informa business

First issued in paperback 2020

British Library Cataloguing-in-Publication Data
A catalogue record for this book is available from the British Library

Library of Congress Cataloging-in-Publication Data
Names: Caldecott, Ben, author.
Title: Stranded assets and the environment : risk, resilience and
    opportunity / edited by Ben Caldecott.
Description: Abingdon, Oxon ; New York, NY : Routledge, 2018. |
    Series: Routledge explorations in environmental studies | Includes
    bibliographical references.
Identifiers: LCCN 2017058518 | ISBN 9781138120600 (hardback) | ISBN
    9781315651606 (ebook)
Subjects: LCSH: Global environmental change—Economic aspects. | Sunk
    costs. | Infrastructure (Economics) | Investments.
Classification: LCC HC79.E5 S757 2018 | DDC 333.7—dc23
LC record available at https://lccn.loc.gov/2017058518

ISBN: 978-1-138-12060-0 (hbk)
ISBN: 978-0-367-45897-3 (pbk)

Typeset in Times New Roman
by Apex CoVantage, LLC

Contents

Figures

Tables

Box

Contributors

In order of appearance in the book:

Ben Caldecott is the Founding Director of the Oxford Sustainable Finance Programme at the University of Oxford Smith School of Enterprise and the Environment. The Oxford Sustainable Finance Programme is a multidisciplinary research centre working to be the world's best place for research and teaching on sustainable finance and investment. He is concurrently an Academic Visitor at the Bank of England, a Visiting Scholar at Stanford University, a Senior Advisor at Highmore LLC, and a Senior Associate Fellow at Bright Blue. Ben specialises in environment, energy, and sustainability issues and works at the intersection between finance, government, civil society, and academe, having held senior roles in each domain. Ben holds a doctorate in economic geography from the University of Oxford. He initially read economics and specialised in development and China at the University of Cambridge and the School of Oriental and African Studies, University of London.

Dimitri Zenghelis is Principal Research Fellow at the Grantham Research Institute at the LSE. In 2014 he was acting chief economist for the Global Commission on the Economy and Climate. He was recently senior economic advisor to Cisco's long-term innovation group and an Associate Fellow at the Royal Institute of International Affairs, Chatham House. Previously, he headed the Stern Review Team at the Office of Climate Change, London, and was a senior economist on the Stern Review on the Economics of Climate Change, commissioned by then-Chancellor Gordon Brown. Before working on climate change, Dimitri was Head of Economic Forecasting at HM Treasury.

Roger Fouquet is Associate Professorial Research Fellow at the Grantham Research Institute on Climate Change and the Environment at the London School of Economics. Over the last twenty-five years, he has been investigating the long-run relationship between economic development, energy and transport use, and its environmental impacts, publishing more than thirty books and articles in leading international journals. In 2006, his joint article was chosen for the Campbell Watkins Award for Best Paper in *The Energy Journal*. In 2010, his book *Heat, Power and Light* was selected by *Choice Magazine* as one of its Outstanding Academic Titles.

Ralph Hippe is Research Fellow at the European Commission's Joint Research Centre (JRC). He has previously worked for the London School of Economics, Sciences Po Strasbourg, and University of Tübingen and has been a consultant for the World Bank and a Visiting Researcher at IDDRI/Sciences Po Paris. He holds a PhD in economics from University of Strasbourg, BETA/CNRS, and University of Tübingen (summa cum laude). He was awarded four dissertation awards for his PhD thesis, among others, by Franco-German University.

Alexander Pfeiffer holds a Doctor of Philosophy from the University of Oxford, where his research focused on stranded carbon assets and their effects on climate and energy policy. He also holds a Master of Science from the University of Mannheim in Germany, where he studied management with a focus on corporate finance, asset valuation, and financial markets. Between 2011–2014 he worked for McKinsey & Company, Inc. in Germany, where he specialised in distressed companies in the renewable energies and energy efficiency sector. He has further relevant work experience from occupations at KPMG (transaction advisory), UBS Investment Bank (fixed income sales), and as a research assistant for the New Climate Economy Project of the Global Commission on the Economy and Climate.

Elizabeth Harnett is a Research Assistant for the Sustainable Finance Programme at the Oxford Smith School. She is also studying for a DPhil within the Oxford Smith School, researching the economic geographies of responsible investment in the UK, Australia, and the USA. She holds an MPhil in geography and the environment (with distinction) and a BA in geography from the University of Oxford. She is a postgraduate fellow of the Royal Geographical Society (with the Institute of British Geographers).

Jakob Thomä is Director of 2° Investing Initiative Germany. He co-founded the 2° Investing network in New York and Berlin and manages the think tank's research on 2°C scenario analysis for financial institutions and companies. Jakob led the development of the first 2°C scenario analysis tool for financial portfolios, now applied by more than 200 financial institutions worldwide. Jakob also leads the organisation's partnerships with financial supervisors and governments in Europe.

Daniel J. Tulloch is a Senior Adviser at the Electricity Authority, New Zealand, and an Honorary Research Associate at the Smith School of Enterprise and the Environment of the University of Oxford. His research focuses on energy policy, carbon markets, sector restructuring, empirical finance, and econometrics. Daniel holds a PhD in finance from the University of Otago, New Zealand. His thesis examined the impact of risk factors and regulatory changes on the return profile of European energy utilities. He also holds an MSc (with distinction) in international accounting and financial management from the University of East Anglia, Norwich. The views and opinions of Daniel J. Tulloch are his own and do not reflect those of the Electricity Authority.

Kevin Muldoon-Smith is a Lecturer in Real Estate Economics and Building Adaptation and co-founder of R3intelligence. His research, teaching and practice combines expertise in real estate development, international finance, and public policy. He has delivered projects, lectures and presentations across regional, national and international scales on these topics – most recently advising the House of Commons Communities and Local Government Select Committee, British Council for Offices and Royal Institution of Chartered Surveyors. His most recent research tracks the impact of public policy on property – specifically in relation to energy, tax, and public finance.

Paul Greenhalgh is Associate Professor in Real Estate and Head of Built Environment at Northumbria University. He is a chartered surveyor (MRICS) with expertise in commercial property markets, valuation and development appraisal. His PhD evaluated the impact of real estate development on property markets using an occupier chaining technique. Paul is founder of the URBaNE research network, co-founder of R3intelligence consultancy and his current research explores the potential of spatial modelling of commercial real estate data to inform investment strategies and analyse the impact of business rate reform in the UK.

Michael Wilkins is a Managing Director at S&P Global Ratings based in London, where he has global responsibility for the firm's infrastructure and environmental and climate risk research. He is a non-executive director on the board of the International Project Finance Association (IPFA). He is also a member of the FSB Taskforce on Climate Related Financial Disclosures (TCFD), the G20 Green Finance Study Group (GFSG), the advisory council of the Oxford Sustainable Finance Programme, and the Climate Bonds Initiative. Michael has a Bachelor of Arts degree within modern languages at Bristol University. He also holds an MBA in finance from the Cass Business School and additionally has a Certificate of Carbon Finance & Analytics from the London Business School.

Sarah Barker is a Special Counsel at the Asia-Pacific's largest commercial law firm, MinterEllison. She has two decades' experience as a corporate lawyer, advising Australian and multi-national clients on governance, compliance, misleading disclosure, and competition law (antitrust) issues. Sarah is also an experienced director, with current board roles including the Emergency Services & State Superannuation Fund and the Responsible Investment Association of Australasia. She is recognised as one of the world's leading authorities on ESG (environmental, social, and governance) in financial services and investment and their relationship to fiduciary duties.

Sandra Batten is a Senior Economist in the Monetary Analysis Directorate of the Bank of England. Before joining the Bank, she worked for the UK government as an economic advisor. She received her PhD in economics from the London School of Economics. Her research interests include economic growth, technological innovation, international trade, and climate change.

Rhiannon Sowerbutts is a Senior Economist in the Macroprudential Strategy and Support Division of the Bank of England. She received her PhD in economics from Universitat Pompeu Fabra. Her research interests include macroprudential policy, regulatory arbitrage, international banking flows, banking, and banking crises.

Misa Tanaka is the Head of Research at the Bank of England. She joined the Bank in 2002 after completing a D.Phil in economics at Nuffield College, University of Oxford. She has held a number of positions across monetary analysis, financial stability, and prudential policy areas of the Bank. Misa has previously published articles in *Journal of Money, Credit and Banking*, *Journal of Financial Intermediation*, and *Economic Journal*, amongst others.

Christopher R. Kaminker is Head of Sustainable Finance Research and a Senior Advisor at Skandinaviska Enskilda Banken (SEB). Prior to SEB, Christopher held an appointment as economist and policy advisor at the OECD, where he led the OECD's sustainable finance work, producing more than publications and policy recommendations. He represented the OECD as delegate to the G20 and Financial Stability Board and currently represents SEB on the Green Bond Principles Executive Committee. Christopher worked in investment banking at Société Générale and Goldman Sachs earlier in his career. He holds a doctorate from the University of Oxford and degrees from Columbia University and the University of London.

Foreword

While the promise of the Paris climate agreement is one of long-term sustainability, for some the transition away from fossil fuels and other carbon-heavy development paths could prove costly as so-called stranded assets are left to waste. Yet experience has shown that, through appropriate measures, these losses can be offset by the economic gains of a green economy.

Challenges in de-carbonization

Rapid, economywide de-carbonization has social and financial implications. Changes in the market and regulatory environment when transitioning to a zero-carbon economy will result in certain technology and infrastructure investments that no longer earn an economic return, thus 'stranding' these assets well ahead of their originally predicted economic life.[1] According to a recent IRENA report,[2] early action on policies to achieve the Paris Agreement decreases the chances of stranding assets; a delayed response, however, could double the total value of stranded assets to US$20 trillion or 4 percent of the global wealth in 2015.[3]

But the history of technology revolutions suggest that the long-term winners will be those technologies that realize their competitive advantage early on, help to advance the technology shift, and reduce their adjustment period by adapting ahead of their competitors.

Seizing the green economy momentum

Through the global commitments of the Paris Agreement and the momentum spurred by more affordable and more efficient energy options, countries now have a unique opportunity to mitigate the losses of high-value stranded assets through a quick and decisive transition towards a green economy. Three elements are key to this: **technological advancement**, **greener policy choices**, and **financial incentives**.

First, technological advancements, particularly around renewable energies, are key to reducing carbon emissions and mitigating the losses associated with stranded assets. Goldman Sachs investment research[4] confirms that zero-carbon technologies have the potential to transform our societies. Four technologies – LEDs, solar power, wind power, and electric vehicles – show competitive growth patterns.[5] They could lead a capital shift away from carbon-intensive to zero-carbon investments.

Second, in order to accelerate innovation and investment, ambitious regulatory measures have to increase pressure on companies, investors, and civil society while also becoming more consistent and predictable. Examples of interlinked policy measures include tax incentives, carbon markets, energy performance regulations, and building standards, as well as legislation for energy-efficiency retrofits and concessional finance for zero-carbon technologies.

Third, it is important that financial institutions make corrections quickly and recognize the link between investment and environmental impacts, thereby providing the necessary financial incentive for companies to make green business decisions. Banks can introduce new lending practices that incentivise mitigation outcomes through lower interest rates. In immature markets in which low-cost financing and longer loan tenors are not available, structured finance will be needed. In these markets, public finance and insurance will need to cater for financial de-risking measures such as loan guarantees, first loss tranches, credit risk insurance or lower-cost refinancing through bonds to overcome investment barriers and increase the efficiency of capital deployment for zero-carbon technologies.

Promisingly, dozens of countries, companies, and organisations are rapidly moving towards the green economy. China is leading the world on renewables. India is putting in place new policies to expand clean electricity use. Countries from Tunisia to South Africa are re-working policy environments to encourage investment in renewable energies. For the UN, our role can and should be to support this effort and to act as a facilitator and convener, offering policy and technical support where it is needed. This will help countries expedite their transition and mitigate the impact of economic losses associated with stranded assets.

Achim Steiner, UNDP administrator

Notes

1 Carbon Tracker Initiative. 2015. *The $2 Trillion Stranded Assets Danger Zone: How Fossil Fuel Firms Risk Destroying Investor Returns.* Available at: www.carbontracker.org/wp-content/uploads/2015/11/CAR3817_Synthesis_Report_24.11.15_WEB2.pdf
2 IRENA. 2017. *Stranded Assets and Renewables: How the Energy Transition Affects the Value of Energy Reserves, Buildings and Capital Stock.* Abu Dhabi: International Renewable Energy Agency (IRENA).
3 Credit Suisse Research Institute. 2015. *Global Wealth Report.*
4 Goldman Sachs Group, Inc. 2016. The Low Carbon Economy. In *Economy Equity Research.* Goldman Sachs.
5 In fact, financial analysts have already outlined promising figures: "In 2016, electric vehicles delivered the fourth year in a row more than 50% of volume growth, the lighting industry will have shifted to almost exclusively LEDs in the 2020s, and by 2020, wind and solar energy will exceed today's share of ecommerce in global retail globally. Thermal coal use has already peaked and if current share losses continue in the US and China, consumption will cease by 2039 in the US and 2055 in China".

Foreword

This is an important and timely book. It is the first book published on stranded assets since the topic began its rapid ascent in the early 2010s. The concept has since been recognised, and rightly so, as of great relevance for a whole manner of different policy, regulatory, financial, and corporate priorities internationally. This success has, in part, been shaped by many of the contributors to this volume.

The book helps to strengthen the academic foundation for analyses of stranded assets and provides a much-needed review of key issues. The book also reflects on how and why the concept has become such an important vehicle for helping to bring core changes related to the environment, particularly with financial institutions, into the mainstream. It identifies exciting potential areas for future research and analysis.

As the book makes clear, market shifts in our environment and associated societal responses will have profound implications for the global economy. Climate risks threaten to transform how and where humanity lives, to reverse recent gains in development and mass poverty reductions, and to increase the likelihood and scale of migration and conflict. The next two decades will be critical in bringing about the immense transformations of the global economy, including the ways in which goods and services are produced, distributed, and consumed, that are necessary to avoid dangerous climate change. Done well, these changes could lead to a very attractive new path of growth and development.

The global economy is still overwhelmingly dependent on oil, gas, and coal. Fossil carbon emissions have to be reduced to zero if global temperature is to be stabilised. The potential for the mass stranding of productive assets if the transition is not well managed is clear.

Actual or expected changes in policy, technology, and physical risks as well as the threat of litigation could prompt a rapid reassessment of the value of a large range of assets as changing costs and opportunities become apparent. The speed and nature of such re-pricing are uncertain and could be decisive for financial stability. If the transition is orderly, then financial markets will likely cope. But as Mark Carney, governor of the Bank of England, recently noted, "there have already been a few high-profile examples of jump-to-distress pricing because of shifts in environmental policy or performance" (Carney 2015).

The world is set to invest about US$90 trillion in infrastructure over the next 15 years (NCE 2014). That means infrastructure investment will increase from about US$3 to $4 trillion per year to about US$6 trillion. Most of this investment will be in developing and emerging market countries. If this infrastructure is not sustainable, and instead locks-in polluting activities, the world will lose its chance of meeting the Paris (COP21) climate change target (holding global temperature increase to 'well-below 2°C') and of achieving the Sustainable Development Goals. This scenario would be deeply dangerous to lives and living standards across the world, and in the process would also entail significant stranding of assets.

This book shows us that it is entirely possible to avoid such lock-in and associated stranded assets. There are changes to existing corporate, investor, and government behaviour and practice that can align decision making throughout society with sustainable outcomes and ensure that the transition happens smoothly and not late and abruptly.

Getting this right will deliver tremendous opportunities; we can see a dynamic few decades of innovation, creativity, and growth. We can create cities in which we can move and breathe and develop ecosystems that have a chance of flourishing. We can rise to the two defining challenges of the century, overcoming poverty and managing climate change.

We can make this the best of centuries, but it could be the worst of centuries if we make the wrong decisions. This book successfully maps out, at both micro and macro levels, how we can avoid these costly delays and mistakes. It is essential reading for current and future decision makers alike.

Lord Nicholas Stern, CH, Kt, FBA, FRS
IG Patel Professor of Economics and Government at the LSE and Chair of the
Grantham Institute on Climate Change and the Environment
17.1.2018

References

Carney, M. 2015. *Breaking the Tragedy of the Horizon – Climate Change and Financial Stability*. Available at: www.bankofengland.co.uk/publications/Documents/speeches/2015/speech844.pdf.

NCE. 2014. *Better Growth, Better Climate: The New Climate Economy Report*. Washington, DC: New Climate Economy. Available at: http://static.newclimateeconomy.report/TheNewClimateEconomyReport.pdf.

Preface

'Stranded assets' caused by environmental change and societal responses to environmental change has now achieved significant importance since the discourse gained momentum in the early 2010s. Yet despite its prominence there remains a great deal of confusion about what stranded assets are, what assets might be affected, what drives stranding, how financial institutions and companies can manage the risk of stranded assets, what it means for policy makers and regulators, and how it links to climate change policy.

The motivation for *Stranded Assets and the Environment: Risk, Resilience and Opportunity* is to create an accessible advanced primer for researchers, scholars, and practitioners so they can quickly understand and navigate the main issues within this rapidly developing area. This has proven to be somewhat of a moving target given the pace of new research related to stranded assets. The result is that for each chapter, we have focused on core principles and concepts that will be relevant and applicable well into the future. The authors have also identified forward-looking research questions and issues to ensure this volume remains relevant over the long term. The volume also makes recommendations for researchers and practitioners to further develop work on stranded assets.

The main audience for this volume is expected to lie in academia, particularly graduate students, advanced undergraduates, and university teachers in fields that include economics, geography, management, public policy, and development studies, especially where there is a climate- and environment-related dimension to their work. We also expect it to be of strong interest to the following groups:

- practitioners in the financial services industry, especially those working on environmental, social, and governance (ESG) issues and risk management;
- policy makers in government departments and agencies, parliamentarians, and multilateral institutions such as the World Bank and UN agencies;
- company executives interested in long-term corporate strategy, social responsibility, and investor relations;
- regulators, particularly those involved in financial and utility regulation;
- members of non-profit civil society, where environmental groups have already taken a keen interest in the topic; and
- consultants serving and providing thought leadership to these varied groups.

In addition to drawing on scholarly contributions from academic researchers, we also have chapters from practitioners and analysts to provide a range of critical perspectives. While chapters have been written as important standalone contributions, the volume is intended to systematically take the reader through the key dimensions of stranded assets as a topic of research inquiry and practice.

Acknowledgements

There are inevitably very many people to be recognised and thanked as part of such a project. First, I would like to thank the contributors to this volume for taking time from their often very gruelling schedules to produce their chapters. Second, I would like to thank my various co-authors, research collaborators, post-docs, and students who have worked with me on stranded assets–related topics. They have each helped to shape my views and provided invaluable probing and questioning of emerging ideas. Third, I would like to thank Sir David King, James Cameron, Ian Temperton, and Professor Gordon Clark, all of whom encouraged me to explore these issues and enabled me to end up at Oxford. Fourth, Professor Dariusz Wójcik, Steve Waygood, and Paul Jepson each provided particularly important guidance at key stages of my work on stranded assets. Fifth, I would like to thank Elizabeth Harnett, who, in addition to contributing a chapter to this volume, has acted as a brilliant editorial assistant to it, playing a key instrumental role in the endeavour.

This project would not have been possible without support from various funders of my research over the years. I would like to thank them all for engaging to help solve the problems raised in this volume and for stumping up the cash and in-kind support that enabled the work to take place.

Finally and on a more personal note, I would like to thank Louise Hanson for all of her patience and encouragement. Without it this volume and much of the work underpinning it would not have been produced.

Ben Caldecott
Oxford, November 2017

1 Introduction

Stranded assets and the environment

Ben Caldecott

1. Introduction to the volume

Asset stranding caused by environmental changes, in particular physical climate change impacts and societal responses to climate change, is now a topic of significant interest to scholars and practitioners alike.

The concept of 'stranded assets' has been endorsed by significant international figures, including former UN Secretary-General Ban Ki-moon (McGrath 2014); US President Barack Obama (Friedman 2014); Jim Yong Kim, President of the World Bank (World Bank 2013a, 2013b); Mark Carney, governor of the Bank of England and chair of the G20 Financial Stability Board (Carney 2015); Angel Gurría, secretary-general of the OECD (Gurría 2013); Christiana Figueres, former executive secretary of the UNFCCC (Figueres 2013); Lord Stern of Brentford (London School of Economics 2013); and Ben van Beurden, CEO of Shell plc (Mufson 2014).

The idea that environment-related risk factors can result in stranded assets is directly relevant to a wide range of critically important topics that face investors, companies, policy makers, regulators, and civil society today. For example:

- Measuring and managing the exposure of investments to environment-related risks across sectors, geographies, and asset classes so that financial institutions can avoid stranded assets (for example, see Financial Stability Board 2015; Caldecott et al. 2013; Generation Foundation 2013; Carbon Tracker Initiative 2011; Caldecott 2011).
- Financial stability implications of stranded assets and what this means for macroprudential regulation, microprudential regulation, and financial conduct (for example, see Kruitwagen et al. 2016; Bank of England 2015b; Carbon Tracker Initiative 2011; Caldecott 2011).
- Reducing the negative consequences of stranded assets created as societies transition to more environmentally sustainable economic models by finding ways to effectively address unemployment, lost profits, and reduced tax income that are associated with asset stranding (for example, see Caldecott 2015a).
- Internalising the risk of stranded assets in corporate strategy and decision making, particularly in carbon intensive sectors susceptible to the effects of

societal action on climate change (for example, see Rook and Caldecott 2015; Carbon Tracker Initiative 2013; Ansar et al. 2013).

- Underpinning arguments by civil society campaigns attempting to secure rapid economy-wide decarbonisation in order to reduce the scale of anthropogenic climate change (for example, see Ansar et al. 2013).
- Keeping track of progress towards emission reduction targets and understanding how 'committed emissions'[1] should influence decarbonisation plans developed by governments, as well as companies and investors (for example, see Pfeiffer et al. 2016; Davis and Socolow 2014; Davis et al. 2010).

These are some of the most important topics in policy, investor, industry, and civil society discourses on the environment and will remain so for as long as societies continue to transition towards greater environmental sustainability.

Drawing on the work of leading researchers and practitioners from a range of disciplines, including economic geography, economics, economic history, finance, law, and public policy, this volume is an attempt to create the essential advanced primer on stranded assets and the environment by covering the fundamental issues and debates, as well as its origins and theoretical basis. The volume provides much-needed clarity as the discourse on stranded assets gathers further momentum.

We have adopted a broad-based social science perspective for setting out what stranded assets are, why they are relevant, and how they might inform the decision making of firms, investors, policy makers, and regulators. The topic of stranded assets is inherently multi-disciplinary, cross-sectoral, and multi-jurisdictional, and the volume reflects this diversity.

This introductory chapter sets out what stranded assets are and their theoretical origins, how the literature on stranded assets has developed, the rationale for work on stranded assets and the environment, and where we are in terms of 'mainstreaming' the topic, particularly among financial institutions.

The second chapter, *Stranded assets: then and now*, by Dimitri Zenghelis, Roger Fouquet, and Ralph Hippe, examines the issue of stranded assets from a macro-economic perspective. It compares past macro-economy drivers of change and rates of asset stranding with those observable today and forecasted for the future. The following questions are addressed: what pace of asset stranding can be expected normally and during economywide transitions? What could be an optimal rate of asset stranding? Could environment-related factors be generating a different rate and scale of asset stranding? Could stranded assets be seen as an opportunity – refreshing capital stocks, reducing pollution, and moving closer to technological frontiers.

The third chapter, *The 'decarbonisation identity': stranded assets in the power generation sector*, by Alexander Pfeiffer, introduces a new theoretical framework – the *decarbonisation identity* – to analytically describe the choices policy makers have available to avoid asset stranding caused by carbon budget constraints. These choices are (1) protecting and enhancing remaining carbon budgets (e.g. by early and decisive action on non-CO_2 pollutants); (2) retrofitting carbon capture and storage (CCS) to operating capital stock; (3) making sure that additions to the capital stock are clean (non-emitting); (4) large-scale stranding of capital stock; or (5) creating additional carbon budget through the development and implementation of net–negative-emission technologies. With the decarbonisation identity, this chapter introduces for the first time a mutually exclusive and collectively exhaustive framework that makes these choices, especially the choice to strand assets, explicit.

The fourth chapter, *Stranded assets: an environmentally driven framework of sunk costs*, by Elizabeth Harnett, explores the relationship and comparisons between stranded assets and sunk costs. The chapter proposes a new spatial-temporal framework through which to view stranding risk in different geographies and time horizons, building on literatures pertaining to sunk costs, relational economic geography, and behavioural finance. This could help investors recognise the immediate and long-term investment implications of stranded assets, as investors are used to dealing with risk over varied geographical and time horizons with regards to investment costs.

The fifth chapter, *The stranding of upstream fossil fuel assets in the context of the transition to a low-carbon economy*, by Jakob Thomä, disentangles what stranded assets mean for the different upstream fossil fuels: oil, gas, and coal. It also sets out how to distinguish the economic stranding of assets (i.e. the stranding of the fossil fuels themselves) from the financial risks (i.e. changes in valuation and credit default driven by economic risks) and what this might mean for different actors across the investment chain.

The sixth chapter, *Examining stranded assets in power generation: coal, gas and nuclear*, by Daniel J. Tulloch, examines stranded assets in the electricity industry, with a focus on coal, gas, and nuclear generation technologies. The chapter provides an overview of the various environment-related risk factors which can strand generation assets and some responses to stranded asset risks. This chapter aims to assist researchers in accurately identifying stranded asset risks for a specific asset. The chapter provides a flexible framework which can be applied to a variety of global electricity industries which, themselves, differ in structure, regulation and operating environments.

The seventh chapter, *Understanding climate-related stranded assets in the global real estate sector*, by Kevin Muldoon-Smith and Paul Greenhalgh, introduces stranded assets into the heterogeneous global real estate asset class. Real estate is taken to mean, broadly, all residential, commercial, and operational property. The chapter observes that stranded assets are not new in real estate; the changing consumer demand of occupiers has regularly rendered property assets redundant or obsolete. However, what is new is the influence and systemic reach of climate change and associated environmental policy on some property assets and related capital markets. At the same time, the global real estate sector is going through its own set of structural growing pains in response to dynamic changes in residential and business practices – potentially coalescing with and exacerbating the issue of stranded assets.

The eighth chapter, *Knowing the risks: how stranded assets relate to credit risk assessment and the debt markets*, by Michael Wilkins, examines how stranded assets pose a serious risk to companies' creditworthiness – the crucial measure of their ability to meet financial obligations, service debt, or make the necessary investments to manage or respond to risks. As environmental regulation grows, the threat of cash-flow attrition due to unmitigated environmental risks becomes more acute. The chapter sets out how these risks can be reflected in credit risk assessment and how developments in disclosure and data, as well as new debt products, could help financial institutions manage their exposure to stranded asset risks.

The ninth chapter, *An introduction to directors' duties in relation to stranded asset risks*, by Sarah Barker, explores the emerging liability exposures for the directors of listed, for-profit corporations who fail to adequately assess and/or disclose the impacts of climate change-related issues on corporate risk and strategy. The analysis focuses, in particular, on directors' statutory and fiduciary duties to govern with regard to stranded asset risk exposures. The chapter proposes general principles that may act as the starting point for further detailed application in individual jurisdictions.

The tenth chapter, *Climate change: what implications for central banks and financial regulators?*, by Sandra Batten, Rhiannon Sowerbutts, and Misa Tanaka, outlines the ways that stranded assets impact on the financial stability objectives of central banks. It identifies areas where central banks and financial regulators could contribute in mitigating the financial risks associated with climate change and climate-related policies. These could also likely mitigate financial stability risks arising from stranded assets.

The eleventh chapter, *Diversifying stranded asset risks by investing in "green": mobilising institutional investment in green infrastructure*, by Christopher R. Kaminker, reviews how institutional investors are investing in green infrastructure, how this is changing, and how this creates opportunities to manage or hedge against stranded asset risks in investor portfolios.

The twelfth chapter, *Stranded assets as economic geography: the case for a disciplinary home?*, argues for stranded assets to have a more explicit disciplinary basis to ensure its development and longevity as a topic of both 'real-world' interest and sufficient academic rigour. This chapter makes the case for economic geography. It can help stranded assets to both develop firmer foundations and also explore new areas by providing relevant ideas, concepts, and methodologies that can be usefully adapted. Importantly, economic geography is a discipline supportive of producing research that interacts with and speaks to a range of practitioner audiences and one that is suitably adaptable so as to encourage multi-disciplinary research.

The concluding chapter, *Next steps for stranded assets and the environment*, discusses some of the limitations in the current literature and how this should inform research priorities on stranded assets over the next decade.

2. What are stranded assets?

There are various definitions of stranded assets that have been proposed or are used in different contexts. Accountants have measures to deal with the impairment of assets (e.g. IAS16) which seek to ensure that an entity's assets are not carried at more than their recoverable amount (Deloitte 2016). In this context, stranded assets are assets that have become obsolete or non-performing but must be recorded on the balance sheet as a loss of profit (Deloitte 2016). The term 'stranded costs' or 'stranded investment' is used by regulators to refer to 'the decline in the value of electricity-generating assets due to restructuring of the industry' (Congressional Budget Office 1998). This was a major topic for utilities regulators as power markets were liberalised in the United States and the United Kingdom in the 1990s.

In the context of upstream energy production and from an energy economist's perspective the International Energy Agency (IEA) (2013) defines stranded assets as 'those investments which have already been made but which, at some time prior to the end of their economic life (as assumed at the investment decision point), are no longer able to earn an economic return' (IEA 2013, p. 98). The Carbon Tracker Initiative also use this definition of economic loss but says they are a 'result of changes in the market and regulatory environment associated with the transition to a low-carbon economy' (Carbon Tracker Initiative n.d.). The Generation Foundation (2013) defines a stranded asset 'as an asset which loses economic value well ahead of its anticipated useful life, whether that is a result of changes in legislation, regulation, market forces, disruptive innovation, societal norms, or environmental shocks' (Generation Foundation 2013, p. 21).

Different definitions for economists ('economic loss'), accountants ('impairment'), regulators ('stranded costs'), and investors ('financial loss') make it difficult for different disciplines and professions to communicate with each other about very similar and overlapping concepts. Caldecott et al. (2013) proposed a 'meta' definition to encompass all of these different definitions: 'stranded assets are assets that have suffered from unanticipated or premature write-downs, devaluations, or conversion to liabilities' (Caldecott, Howarth, et al. 2013, p. 7). This is the definition used throughout this volume and the definition most widely used in the literature.

While the environmental discourse appropriated the term in the 2010s and is focused on the environment-related risk factors that can strand assets, asset stranding in fact occurs regularly as part and parcel of economic development. As such it is not a novel phenomenon. Schumpeter (1942) coined the term 'creative destruction', and implicit in his 'essential fact about capitalism' (Schumpeter 1942, p. 83) is the idea that value is created, as well as destroyed, and that this dynamic process drives forward innovation and economic growth. Schumpeter built on the work of Kondratiev (1926) and the idea of 'long waves' in the economic cycle (Perez 2010).

Neo-Schumpeterians have attempted to understand the dynamics of creative destruction, particularly how and why technological innovation and diffusion results in technological revolutions. This gave rise to the idea of 'techno-economic paradigms' (TEPs), a term coined by Perez (1985), which captures the idea of overlapping technological innovations that are strongly inter-related and interdependent, resulting in technological revolutions. Perez (2002) finds five such TEPs: the Industrial Revolution (1771–1829); the Age of Steam and Railways

(1829–1875); the Age of Steel, Electricity, and Heavy Engineering (1875–1908); the Age of Oil, the Automobile, and Mass Production (1908–1971); and the Age of Information and Telecommunications (1971–present).

Each TEP was accompanied by the emergence of new sectors and stranded assets in redundant ones. For example, the Industrial Revolution ushered in mechanised cotton production in England that eclipsed India's cottage textile industry (Broadberry and Gupta 2005); the Age of Steam and Railways introduced railway networks that replaced canals and waterways (Bagwell and Lyth 2002); the Age of Steel, Electricity, and Heavy Engineering saw the end of sailing ships and the dominance of steam ships (Grübler and Nakićenović 1991); the Age of Oil, the Automobile, and Mass Production resulted in the rise of the automobile and the decline of railways (Wolf 1996); and our Age of Information and Telecommunications has seen the widespread adoption of digital communication and an information revolution, making analogue communication redundant and technologies from typewriters to telegraphs entirely obsolete. Within each TEP, specific companies and brands, physical infrastructure, plant and machinery, and human capital, among other things, have become stranded.

Clearly then, stranded assets can be caused by many factors related to innovation and commercialisation, and these are part of the process of creative destruction articulated in Perez's TEPs and conceived by Schumpeter. Recent research on stranded assets has, however, sought to explore the idea that some of the causes of asset stranding are increasingly environment related. In other words, a combination of physical environmental change and societal responses to this environmental change might be qualitatively and quantitatively different from previous drivers of creative destruction we have seen in past TEPs. Moreover, such environment-related factors appear to be stranding assets across all sectors, geographies, and asset classes simultaneously and perhaps more quickly than in previous TEPs, and this trend is accelerating – something that could be unprecedented.

2.1 Carbon budgets and stranded assets

From the late 1980s individuals and organisations working on climate and sustainability issues began to acknowledge the possibility that environmental policy and regulation could negatively influence the value or profitability of fossil fuel companies to the point that they could become impaired (Krause et al. 1989; IPCC 1999, 2001; IEA 2008). With the concept of a global 'carbon budget' – the amount of cumulative atmospheric CO_2 emissions allowable for certain amounts of anthropogenic climate change – there was a way to determine when impairments ought to begin given a certain climate change target (Allen et al. 2014). When the amount of fossil fuels combusted plus the amount of carbon accounted for in reserves yet to be burned exceeded the carbon budget, either the climate or the value of fossil fuel reserves would have to give. This concept was dubbed 'unburnable carbon' by the Carbon Tracker Initiative (2011) and was popularised by the US environmentalist Bill McKibben (2011), among others, in the early 2010s.

Unburnable carbon quantified the disconnect between the current value of the listed equity of global fossil fuel producers and their potential commercialisation under a strict carbon budget constraint (Carbon Tracker Initiative 2011; Caldecott 2011). The idea that 'unburnable' fossil fuel reserves could become stranded assets sparked a significant discussion on the risk of investing in fossil fuels (Ansar et al. 2013). It has also helped to spur the development of the fossil fuel divestment campaign (Ansar et al. 2013).

Conjoined with and in parallel, the idea of a 'carbon bubble' also gained traction. This is the hypothesis that unburnable carbon would mean that upstream fossil fuel assets were significantly overvalued, potentially creating a financial bubble with systemic implications for the global economy (Carbon Tracker Initiative 2011; Caldecott 2011). This has inspired divergent responses – from qualified support to outright opposition (for example, see Royal Dutch Shell PLC 2014; Exxon Mobil Corporation 2014; Weyzig et al. 2014; EAC 2014; Caldecott 2012; King 2012).

Unburnable carbon and the carbon bubble were considered to be derived from work conducted and produced in the early 2010s. However, unknown to the proponents of this discourse in the early 2010s, these ideas actually originated much earlier. This only became clear in 2013–2014 and was confirmed by interviews with authors of previously published work.[2]

Krause et al. (1989) were the first to explicitly make the case for unburnable carbon when they said, 'The mere fact that remaining allowable global carbon emissions are so limited means that any economic infrastructures built up mainly on the basis of fossil fuels risk early obsolescence. In effect, the tight carbon budgets implied by climate stabilisation greatly reduce the long-term value of fossil fuels' (Krause et al. 1989, p. 164).

Krause et al. (1989) were also the first to make the explicit link between carbon budgets, fossil fuel obsolescence, and implications for financial markets (i.e. the carbon bubble):

> capital owners in the fossil industries would have to bear an indirect cost that is, die risks and uncertainties of having to diversify into other business activities. For example, even a well-planned retrenchment [from fossil fuels] could create impacts on the value of stocks in the financial markets. Government financial incentives could be required to make these risks acceptable to capital owners.
>
> (Krause et al. 1989, pp. 172–173)

Krause et al. (1989) made another significant contribution by highlighting how unburnable carbon is in complete contrast to assumptions used in the energy industry.

> [a carbon budget] means major restrictions on the use of global fossil resources . . . [our carbon budget] figures clash with the conventional assumption that all conventional oil and gas resources would probably be consumed

before a major shift away from fossil fuels would occur. Our analysis suggests that climate stabilisation requires keeping significant portions of even the world's conventional fossil resources in the ground. Such a requirement is a stark contradiction to all conventional energy planning and illustrates the magnitude of the greenhouse challenge.

(Krause et al. 1989, p. 144)

The points are made in exactly the same way in publications more than twenty years later (for example, see Carbon Tracker Initiative 2011, 2013). Unfortunately, these novel ideas from the late 1980s were largely ignored and then forgotten. One can only speculate as to why this happened and why later work has managed to achieve greater traction, but it must inevitably have something to do with the fact that climate change is now an imperative for contemporary policy makers, businesses, and financial institutions, whereas it simply was not in the late 1980s and early 1990s.

2.2 *From unburnable carbon towards environment-related risk*

One tension within the 2010s discourse of stranded assets is the scope of risks that can cause asset stranding. Early on, some preferred to focus on the idea of scientifically derived carbon budgets being *directly* enforced top-down by governments in a coordinated way (in particular, see Carbon Tracker Initiative 2011). Others have been much more sceptical of coordinated international action and saw carbon budgets being introduced *indirectly* bottom-up through a panoply of different local and national policies, technological change and innovation, and social pressure, among other things (in particular, see Caldecott et al. 2013). The views of individuals and organisations has trended towards the latter view over time (see Hedegaard 2015), including those that originally preferred the 'direct top-down' model over the 'indirect bottom-up' one (for example, see Carbon Tracker Initiative 2015).

Relatedly, another tension has been the relative status of climate change versus the environment more broadly. Some have been more concerned with stranded assets created by international climate change policy (Carbon Tracker Initiative 2011), others have been more interested in the range of societal responses to physical climate change impacts that extend beyond unburnable carbon (Bank of England 2015b), and others have been concerned with both physical environmental change and societal responses to such environmental change (Bank of England 2015a; Caldecott et al. 2013). Again, the views of individuals and organisations has trended towards the latter view, which is more comprehensive and expansive, and has allowed for a wider range of interests to be engaged on the topic, such as those concerned with water risk and stranded water assets (see Lamb 2015) or in sectors that might be affected beyond fossil fuels, such as agriculture (see Rautner et al. 2016; Morel et al. 2016; Caldecott et al. 2013). To underpin a more expansive interpretation Caldecott et al. (2013) proposed a typology for different environment-related risks that could cause stranded assets, and this is set out in Figure 1.1.

	Class	Description
PHYSICAL	Environmental challenges and change	For example, climate change, water stress, and biodiversity loss.
	Changing resource landscapes	Price and availability of different resources, such as oil, gas, coal, and other minerals and metals. For example, peak oil and the shale gas revolution.
SOCIETAL	New government regulations	Introduction of carbon pricing (via taxes and trading schemes), subsidy regimes (e.g. for fossil fuels and renewables), air pollution regulation, disclosure requirements, the 'carbon bubble', and international climate policy.
	Technological change	For example, falling clean technology costs (e.g. solar PV, onshore wind), disruptive technologies, and GMO.
	Evolving social norms and consumer behaviour	For example, fossil fuel divestment campaign, product labelling and certification schemes, consumer preferences.
	Litigation and changing statutory interpretations	For example, court cases, compensation payments, and changes in the way existing laws are applied or interpreted.

Figure 1.1 Typology of environment-related risk

Source: Caldecott et al. (2013)

Recent developments very clearly illustrate that environment-related risks, and not just those related to unburnable carbon, can have a significant impact on assets today, and these are likely to increase in significance over time (Caldecott, Dericks, et al. 2016). If anything, the evidence suggests these are much more material, particularly in the short to medium term, than the risk of unburnable carbon or the carbon bubble (Caldecott, Dericks, et al. 2016). For example, air pollution and water scarcity in China threatens coal-fired power generation and has changed coal demand and affected global coal prices (Caldecott et al. 2013); the shale gas revolution in the US has put downward pressure on coal prices in Europe, stranding new high-efficiency gas plants (Caldecott and McDaniels 2014); and the fossil fuel divestment campaign threatens to erode the social licence of some targeted companies and could increase their cost of capital (Ansar et al. 2013).

2.3 The stranded assets straw man

It is worth noting that there is a particular straw man argument that has been used in an attempt to dismiss the idea of stranded assets, and it contains two parts (Caldecott 2015b). The first part is to raise doubts about the idea that there is unburnable carbon and then to conflate unburnable carbon with stranded assets.

The second part is to argue that markets already price stranded assets risks effectively. These arguments have been made by Royal Dutch Shell PLC (2014), Exxon Mobil Corporation (2014), Butler (2015), and Helm (2015).

We should not rely on the assumption that the world will stick to a 1.5°C (or 2°C) carbon budget, objectors point out, so we should not be so sure that fossil fuel reserves that would take us beyond that limit will become stranded assets. These objectors may be right to be sceptical about the 1.5°C constraint, but when it comes to stranded assets, they entirely miss the point.

This straw man is a conflation of 'stranded assets' with 'unburnable carbon', the latter being one potential driver of asset stranding, but as we have already discussed, not the only one. The straw man argument suits those who want to discredit concerns about stranded assets (for example, some fossil fuel companies), as it is easier for them to secure traction attacking an effective 1.5°C policy commitment as unlikely than say falling costs of renewables, electricity storage, air pollution regulations, or water stress. The reason for this is that the former has yet to happen, but as we have seen, the latter factors are already transforming markets and stranding assets. It is easier to attack an unprecedented scenario than facts on the ground.

Even the claim that a 1.5°C pathway is impossible is not true. Though probably quite unlikely, a 1.5°C pathway is not something you can discount entirely. If it did come to pass, it would have significant implications for investors, companies, and governments. Given that 1.5°C is a stated objective in the Paris Agreement, it makes sense as a useful analytical starting point.

But 2, 3, 4, 5, or 6°C pathways could also have significant and systemic implications (Dietz et al. 2016; Economist Intelligence Unit 2015). Not achieving 1.5°C will itself have significant impacts on asset values across the global economy. Whichever way you look at it, action or inaction on climate change will strand assets. You may think that a 1.5°C policy-induced carbon constraint is unlikely, but this does not mean stranded asset issues vanish.

The second line of objection is that investors and companies have levels of foresight and analysis that mean they are already pricing in these risks and so we need not worry. But the idea that investors and companies know about these risks and have a better understanding of them than anyone else is also wrong.

Even at the best of times, relatively simple risks can be mispriced by markets and known risks can be left ignored. As we shall see in this volume, this is often because of biases, misaligned incentives, and endemic short-termism (Carney 2015; Caldecott and Rook 2015; Kay 2012). These problems are also exacerbated when the risks in question are novel and where the data, analytical tools, and methodologies are missing (Caldecott and Rook 2015). Add to the mix a lack of viable options to hedge risk (Cambridge Institute for Sustainability Leadership 2015), and there is plenty of scope for markets to be getting risk management wrong.

3. The work begins

The research agenda of stranded assets in an environmental context was motivated by the failure of the international climate change negotiations in Copenhagen at the end of 2009 ('COP15'). This is when I began to articulate ideas related to stranded assets and began to discover and collaborate with people of like mind working on similar and related issues. It is worth reflecting briefly here on the rationale for this and why its wider appreciation and adoption of the concept can help support the transition towards global environmental sustainability.

Almost all the work that groups concerned about tackling anthropogenic climate change had been conducting in the first decade of the twenty-first century was focused on the 'opportunity' side of the equation. That is, making the case for and working on the implications of new investment in cleaner technologies, whether renewable energy, energy efficiency, clean tech, and so on. This reached fever pitch in the run up to and during COP15.

The rationale for focusing on opportunity made (and still makes) a lot of sense: it is seen to be more exciting and more optimistic (Futerra 2006). The narrative was essentially that tackling climate change and going 'green' would create lots of new jobs, new companies, and new industries, as well as save the environment. This story, brimming with positivity as it does, did not have much space for anything that might induce pessimism – all mention of cost, risk, and difficulty was closed down, and closed down quickly.

This framing ultimately impacted the priorities of those working on or in areas related to the environment and climate change. Study after study was commissioned focusing on trying to estimate how many new 'green' jobs would be created by building windfarms and solar parks or through ambitious energy efficiency programmes (for example, see Greenpeace UK 2004; Bird and Lawton 2009; Board 2010). This relentless focus on 'upside' was unbalanced and is problematic.

The problem with the opportunity framing is that it can only get you so far. The environmental challenges we face mean that we cannot continue to pursue two different strategies simultaneously: support for greener, low-carbon technologies, while continuing with business as usual in polluting sectors.

In the case of climate change it is perfectly simple – the stock of cumulative emissions causes physical climate change impacts, and the stock of emissions continues to expand unless we switch off the flow (Allen et al. 2014). My concern with how an unbalanced approach focusing only on the 'green' and ignoring the phase out of 'brown' was compounded in my mind by three other related worries.

First, the transition to a more sustainable global economy is likely to be a complex and challenging process, with significant value lost throughout the economy, as well as created. The implications of value destruction could be considerable – in terms of lost jobs and industries and the concomitant social pressures they generate. If the community of actors working on environmental issues continued to ignore them, then policy makers would be unprepared and would not put in place policies to minimise or manage such social pressures. Instead such pressures would be left unmanaged or only be addressed *ex post*, resulting in a political backlash against environmental policies, undermining the transition to sustainability. To me this seemed like a very serious medium- to long-term threat to achieving environmental outcomes, and I have been surprised at how reluctant environmentalists were to talk about these social and political-economy issues.

Second, the same process of value creation and destruction would impact the value of assets across a wide range of sectors, and this would have implications for investors. It was quite clear to me working at a financial institution at the time of COP15, where we were speaking to and advising a very wide range of different types of financial institution and investing ourselves, that these factors were not being factored into decision making or being priced appropriately. If they were, the risk premium for assets exposed to these factors would be higher, and these would most likely be assets that were environmentally unsustainable. Shifting the cost of capital in favour of 'green' and away from 'brown' would benefit environmental outcomes and aid risk management, as well as attract capital into 'green'. This would necessitate significant changes in investment practice, require better-aligned incentives, and probably also require changes in the governance of financial institutions.

Third, a successful transition to environmental sustainability resulting in over-valued and overcapitalised polluting assets becoming impaired could have financial stability implications given significant exposure to these assets throughout financial markets. In 2010–11 financial markets and policy makers were still working through (and arguably are still working through) the causes and consequences of the global financial crisis, or GFC). The causes of the GFC (e.g. overvalued sub-prime mortgages and irrational exuberance) seemed to me to be analogous with the scenario I was contemplating here: (i) polluting assets being overvalued because valuation did not take account of environmental sustainability and (ii) evidence of 'frothiness' in some asset markets that would be affected – the ever-larger investments and valuations in upstream oil, gas, and coal driven by the 'commodities super cycle' looked like a bubble that would burst, and one that must do so if you believed that society would take action to tackle climate change.

It is perhaps easy to see why the 2010–2011 period was fertile ground to be cogitating on these four related insights: (i) phasing out 'brown' has been neglected by environmentalists at the expense of promoting 'green', and this needs to be rebalanced; (ii) pre-emptively managing the consequences of phasing out 'brown' is essential if the transition to sustainability is to succeed and sustain political support; (iii) shifting capital away from 'brown' supports environmental outcomes and helps investors to manage risks that are currently mispriced; and (iv) there could be financial stability implications associated with a sudden readjustment in the value of polluting assets, and while on the face of it this might be good for the environment, it could have severe negative implications that ought to be managed. These four concerns and insights are linked together and laid the foundation for the work that we would now call 'stranded assets'.

Ructions in the world of climate change policy and environmentalism due to the collapse of Copenhagen in 2009 helped people to question current approaches of trying to make the case for environmental action. This was happening at the same time as the GFC and its devastation were creating space for a more profound re-evaluation of financial and economic systems, with topics related to systemic risk and the role of finance in society gaining traction. This manifested itself across the social sciences and in politics and policy in a variety of different ways (see Wolf 2014). The idea that finance and investment had a significant role in shaping the environment and vice versa, while clearly pre-dating the GFC, was certainly 'turbo-charged' after the GFC.

The policy response to the GFC meant that financial regulation was in a state of flux, with new regulatory arrangements being drawn up and revised internationally. The one that caught my imagination and prompted me to consider the links between environmental factors destroying value and ultimately affecting financial stability was the creation of the Bank of England's Financial Policy Committee (FPC). The FPC was established in order to, 'contribute to the Bank's financial stability objective by identifying, monitoring, and taking action to remove or reduce systemic risks with a view to protecting and enhancing the resilience of the UK financial system' (Bank of England 2016a). The FPC was established as part of the Financial Services Act 2012 and was formally constituted on 1 April 2013. Prior to that, however, an interim FPC was created in February 2011 and the press coverage associated with that was a catalyst for me to start thinking and writing about systemic risk and climate change.

4. Towards mainstreaming

Since 2010 stranded assets has become a topic of interest to many financial institutions and finance practitioners. Stranded assets arguments have underpinned developments in practice that are successfully shifting capital away from 'brown' and towards 'green' based on an enhanced understanding of environment-related risk (for example, see Caldecott et al. 2016). It has also provided the basis for the fossil fuel divestment campaign, the fastest-growing divestment campaign in history (Ansar et al. 2013), with the movement currently claiming that 534 institutions with \$3.4 trillion of assets have committed to partially or fully divest from fossil fuels (Go Fossil Free 2016). These strides have been significant, but to what extent has stranded assets become 'mainstreamed'?

Mainstreaming, when ideas, practices, or norms become regarded as normal, has unquestionably been an explicit priority of my work on stranded assets. It is undoubtedly an objective shared by others working on stranded assets too. But there are two main challenges of tracking progress towards this goal.

First, the definition of mainstreaming that I and others have has been too ambiguous. It is not just a question of the term or idea entering the lexicon, which I think stranded assets has achieved among specialist and many non-specialist audiences. Mainstreaming is also about changing practice – both improving best practice and the 'state of the art', as well as ratcheting up the quality of what could be called 'routine practice'. The threshold for the achievement of mainstreaming, whatever that threshold is, also needs to be irreversibly reached across multiple parts of the investment chain in a wide range of different markets. It is not sufficient for the threshold to be fleetingly met in one or two parts of the investment chain and in one or two parts of the world – it is permanently mainstreaming a topic across the financial system with its inherent breadth, depth, and complexity. Finally, it should also be about outcomes, in terms of capital being more likely to flow in the direction we would expect if stranded asset risks were appropriately understood and then integrated into decision making. If these different criteria have to be met to achieve mainstreaming, and I think they probably should be, then this is a very high bar indeed.

Second, detecting progress towards the achievement of mainstreaming is difficult, not least because of the aforementioned lack of definition, but also because of the 'echo chamber'. For those of us working within a domain or field it is hard to differentiate change among 'usual suspects' versus change in the 'real world'. While it can be very comforting to attend one of the many conferences organised on stranded assets and meet with people I know already and hear about the progress they are making, it can provide a lopsided and entirely unrealistic impression of what is actually going on outside. In the case of stranded assets, this is exacerbated by press coverage. The quantity of references in newspapers, magazines, and other media to stranded assets has increased dramatically (see Harnett 2018 forthcoming), but a lot of this coverage is consumed by the same usual suspects and written by correspondents who write on the environment and climate change. This can further reinforce an impression of rapid change and mainstreaming, when actual real-world progress has been much slower.

Nonetheless, I have detected a perceptible shift among financial institutions over the 2010–2018 period that is real and meaningful, although perhaps still some way from the achievement of mainstreaming. These include the following changes:

First, the fact that the Bank of England and other central banks (see Chapter 10), by showing sustained interest in stranded assets at the highest levels, have forced functions within financial institutions that were not previously engaged on anything to do with stranded assets to now become engaged. For example, Solvency II requires every insurance and reinsurance firm to conduct its own risk and solvency assessment (ORSA) and to submit this to the regulator for approval in order to be licensed to operate (Bank of England 2016b). After the Bank of England's pronouncements on stranded assets it is likely to be the view of insurers and reinsurers that their ORSAs should include some reference to these risks to avoid the possibility of their ORSAs being rejected or further interrogated. This moves stranded assets from the category of being entirely optional into something that is now fundamental to securing regulatory approval to operate.

Second, the aforementioned involvement of central banks and regulators has also helped to shift the terms of the dialogue within financial institutions. It has been the norm in many institutions for ESG specialists or those with a direct interest in stranded assets topics to 'sell upwards' to their senior management. This means they identify topics or ideas that are likely to be approved by their superiors – which inevitably means that some topics or ideas are rejected and that the ambition of what is sold up is lower than they might want in order to secure internal support. In most organisations this inevitably places a premium on low-cost, uncontroversial, and non-disruptive proposals. These may also be the least effective proposals for the integration of stranded assets into investment decision making.

This situation may now be changing. One thing that I have noticed recently, particularly in the run-up to the Paris climate change negotiations in December 2015 and in the two years after it, has been CEO- and CIO-level engagement from many more institutions than has previously been the case. The involvement of the central bank, for example in convening meetings at these levels, means that there are new opportunities for CEOs and CIOs to be more ambitious and also be competitive with each other in person. They can then instruct downwards and get their teams to implement what they have committed to voluntarily with their peers and with the regulator. This is a new dynamic for many firms, though its implications and durability are yet to be seen. Moreover, whether the central bank, which has the necessary convening power, will continue to deploy finite resources into these efforts is also uncertain.

Third, developments in practice are starting to catch up with the theory. Unfortunately, the tools available to manage exposure to stranded assets created by environment-related risks have been rather limited to date. As Caldecott, Dericks, et al. (2016) point out, the vast majority of analysis that is undertaken is usually done 'top down', where financial institutions look at company-level voluntary reporting and focus on measures of carbon emissions and intensity to differentiate between companies. Even if company-level reporting is accurate and up-to-date (in many cases it is not), this is an overly simplistic approach that attempts to measure a wide range of environment-related risk factors (often with widely varying degrees of correlation) through one proxy metric (carbon emissions). While this might be a useful exercise, more sophisticated 'bottom-up' approaches can yield improved insights for asset performance and, if appropriately aggregated, company performance (Caldecott, Kruitwagen et al. 2016).

There are also significant new analytical possibilities. Existing data can be analysed using techniques involving artificial intelligence and machine learning, while new data can be made accessible from sources previously unavailable, such as remote sensing and 'big data' (Caldecott, Kruitwagen, et al. 2016). These new frontiers are complemented with extant international efforts to enhance and improve the consistency of disclosures that can support the management of stranded assets (for example, see Task Force on Climate-Related Financial Disclosures 2016 and Sustainability Accounting Standards Board 2013, as well as efforts to improve integrated and narrative reporting; for example, see Eccles and Krzus 2015).

In addition to these developments, new products are being launched regularly, such as indices that are weighted away from the risk of stranded assets (Fossil Free Indexes 2016), exchange traded funds that employ such indices (State Street Global Advisors 2016), and credit ratings integrating stranded asset risks (Standard and Poor's 2014; Center for International Environmental Law 2015). These examples do not fully capture the rapid innovation taking place across the investment chain in relation to environmental risk and opportunity, of which stranded assets has been a disproportionately important part.

While this innovation across the investment chain is exciting, it is too early to tell whether this will result in successful mainstreaming. The innovation is largely limited to pockets of excellence in Northern Europe (particularly the UK, France, the Netherlands, Norway, Sweden, and Denmark) and parts of the United States (particularly the Bay Area). The conversations in Asian financial centres are much less mature, and in many emerging economies this is simply not an issue of concern. While initiatives such as the UNEP Inquiry into the Design of Sustainable Financial System are promoting these topics internationally and are placing particular emphasis on building awareness in less developed economies, the reality is that innovation in terms of practice has been incredibly lopsided, and perhaps understandably so given that innovation usually has to begin somewhere before spreading outwards (see Breschi and Malerba 2001).

Another issue is that key intermediaries along the investment chain, particularly investment consultants, are hindering the uptake of these new practices, and this could yet be a major blockage to mainstreaming stranded assets (Caldecott and Rook 2015). Unpicking the causes of this, which are unfortunately both complex and diverse, will not be straightforward and requires a degree of asset owner coordination that has so far been lacking (Caldecott and Rook 2015).

4.1 Stranded assets in the context of a broader reform agenda

One of the things that has become clear to me is that it is very hard, if not impossible, to disentangle what needs to happen for financial institutions to take account of stranded assets from broader reforms to finance and investment. If financial institutions could only just extend their time horizons, many of the factors that make stranded assets a knotty issue would be addressed (Carney 2015).

Clarifying fiduciary duty and addressing some of the perverse incentives of liquidity requirements would each go some way towards encouraging this long-termism. Asset owners also need to have the courage and conviction necessary to create longer-term mandates for asset managers, and this should be more natural given the long tail of future liabilities that many asset owners have (Investec Investment Institute 2016). Ultimately the paradigm of getting to long-term results via a series of short-term positions will need to change (Investec Investment Institute 2016).

Developments and innovations in the practice of analysing stranded asset risk can only achieve so much if they must operate in an institutional environment that is endemically short term. Stranded assets work should therefore not just be about innovation in practice but also about understanding and ensuring that changes in governance, fiduciary duty, and incentives promote a form of long-termism that properly takes account of the environment.

5. Conclusion

This introductory chapter has set out what stranded assets are and their theoretical origins, how the literature on stranded assets has developed, the rationale for work on stranded assets and the environment, and where we are in terms of 'mainstreaming' the topic, particularly among financial institutions.

Stranded assets created by environment-related risk factors, including physical climate change impacts and societal and regulatory responses to climate change, have become increasingly prominent. The emergence of the topic should be of significant interest to scholars and practitioners alike, as it has arguably influenced a number of pressing issues facing investors, companies, policy makers, regulators, and civil society in relation to global environmental change.

While the environmental discourse appropriated the term in the 2010s and is focused on the environment-related risk factors that can strand assets, asset stranding in fact occurs regularly as part and parcel of economic development. As such it is not a novel phenomenon and is implicit in Schumpeterian creative destruction.

Unburnable carbon and the carbon bubble, one set of environment-related drivers of asset stranding, were considered to be derived from work conducted and produced in the early 2010s. However, these ideas actually originated much earlier from the late 1980s, and it is important to reflect on why this was the case. Climate change is now an imperative for contemporary policy makers, businesses, and financial institutions, whereas it simply was not in the late 1980s and early 1990s.

This elevation of climate change and wider sustainability issues has meant there is now a broad audience for arguments and analysis related to stranded assets. This has resulted in the topic achieving a form of modest mainstreaming among important audiences internationally. However, this remains concentrated in certain geographies and sectors, and there is much more to do to properly 'operationalise' the concept of stranded assets into decision making.

The prize of success is significant. Avoiding stranded assets means, among other things: avoiding carbon lock-in; less capital available for assets that are the most polluting; resilient financial institutions and a more resilient financial system; corporations not wasting capital on activities that harm society and making longer-term decisions for their benefit and the benefit of others; and policy makers proactively helping communities to adjust as our economy transitions and backing the sectors of the future not the industries of the past. In short, appreciating and integrating stranded assets into decision making is a necessary condition for a cleaner, safer, and more productive future. We will not meet the Paris Climate Change Agreement or the Sustainable Development Goals without doing so.

Notes

1 Defined as the future emissions expected from all existing fossil fuel-burning infrastructure worldwide (Davis et al. 2010).
2 These were conducted by the author and took place in March–April 2016 at Stanford University.

References

Allen, M., et al. 2014. *IPCC Fifth Assessment Synthesis Report-Climate Change 2014 Synthesis Report*. Available at: www.citeulike.org/group/15400/article/13416115 [Accessed August 9, 2016].

Ansar, A., Caldecott, B. and Tibury, J. 2013. Stranded Assets and the Fossil Fuel Divestment Campaign: What Does Divestment Mean for the Valuation of Fossil Fuel Assets? *Smith School of Enterprise and the Environment, University of Oxford*, October.

Bagwell, P. and Lyth, P. 2002. *Transport in Britain: From Canal Lock to Gridlock*. Available at: https://books.google.co.uk/books?hl=en&lr=&id=1JdCtWuaQhcC&oi=fnd&pg=PR7&dq=railway+networks+replaced+canals+and+waterways+england&ots=W-YkMrbBVF&sig=ywv87TQiCFWx1P4D5UqYsqBYe2M [Accessed August 15, 2016].

Bank of England. 2015a. *One Bank Research Agenda*. London: Bank of England.

Bank of England. 2015b. *The Impact of Climate Change on the UK Insurance Sector a Climate Change Adaptation Report by the Prudential Regulation Authority*. London: Bank of England.

Bank of England. 2016a. *Financial Policy Committee*. London: Bank of England.

Bank of England. 2016b. *Solvency II Management and Governance*. Available at: www.bankofengland.co.uk/pra/Pages/supervision/insurance/mangov.aspx [Accessed August 7, 2016].

Bird, J. and Lawton, K. 2009. *The Future's Green: Jobs and the UK Low-Carbon Transition*. Available at: www.ippr.org/files/images/media/files/publication/2011/05/future green_1737.pdf [Accessed August 9, 2016].

Board, R. 2010. *Value Breakdown for the Offshore Wind Sector*. Available at: www.gov.uk/government/uploads/system/uploads/attachment_data/file/48171/2806-value-breakdown-offshore-wind-sector.pdf [Accessed August 9, 2016].

Breschi, S. and Malerba, F. 2001. The Geography of Innovation and Economic Clustering: Some Introductory Notes. *Industrial and Corporate Change*. Available at: http://icc.oxfordjournals.org/content/10/4/817.short [Accessed August 9, 2016].

Broadberry, S. and Gupta, B. 2005. *Cotton Textiles and the Great Divergence: Lancashire, India and Shifting Competitive Advantage 1600–1850*, pp. 23–25. Available at: www.iisg.nl/hpw/factormarkets.php [Accessed August 15, 2016].

Butler, N. 2015. Climate Change and the Myth of Stranded Assets. *The Financial Times*.

Caldecott, B. 2011. Why High Carbon Investment Could Be the Next Sub-Prime Crisis. *The Guardian*.

Caldecott, B. 2012. *Review of UK Exposure to High Carbon Investments*. London: Climate Change Capital.

Caldecott, B. 2015a. *Stranded Assets and Multilateral Development Banks*. Washington, DC: Inter-American Development Bank.

Caldecott, B. 2015b. *Why Stranded Assets Matter and Should Not Be Dismissed*. Available at: https://theconversation.com/why-stranded-assets-matter-and-should-not-be-dismissed-51939.

Caldecott, B., Dericks, G., et al. 2016. *Stranded Assets: The Transition to a Low Carbon Economy*. Lloyd's of London Emerging Risk Report.

Caldecott, B., Howarth, N. and McSharry, P. 2013. Stranded Assets in Agriculture: Protecting Value from Environment-Related Risks. *Smith School of Enterprise and the Environment, University of Oxford*. Available at: www.smithschool.ox.ac.uk/research-programmes/stranded-assets/Stranded Assets Agriculture Report Final.pdf.

Caldecott, B., Kruitwagen, L., et al. 2016. Stranded Assets and Thermal Coal: An Analysis of Environment-Related Risk Exposure. *Smith School of Enterprise and the Environment, University of Oxford*.

Caldecott, B. and McDaniels, J. 2014. Stranded Generation Assets: Implications for European Capacity Mechanisms, Energy Markets and Climate Policy. *Smith School of Enterprise and the Environment, University of Oxford*. Available at: www.smithschool.

ox.ac.uk/research-programmes/stranded-assets/Stranded Generation Assets – Working Paper – Final Version.pdf.

Caldecott, B. and Rook, D. 2015. Investment Consultants and Green Investment: Risking Stranded Advice? *Smith School of Enterprise and the Environment, University of Oxford.*

Caldecott, B., Tilbury, J. and Ma, Y. 2013. Stranded Down Under? Environment-Related Factors Changing China's Demand for Coal and What This Means for Australian Coal Assets. *Smith School of Enterprise and the Environment, University of Oxford.* Available at: www.smithschool.ox.ac.uk/research-programmes/stranded-assets/Stranded Down Under Report.pdf [Accessed December 2, 2015].

Cambridge Institute for Sustainability Leadership. 2015. Unhedgeable Risk: How Climate Change Sentiment Impacts Investment. *Cambridge Institute for Sustainability Leadership*, p. 64. Available at: www.cisl.cam.ac.uk/publications/publication-pdfs/unhedgea ble-risk.pdf [Accessed September 9, 2016].

Carbon Tracker Initiative. 2011. *Unburnable Carbon – Are the World's Financial Markets Carrying a Carbon Bubble?* London: Carbon Tracker Initiative.

Carbon Tracker Initiative. 2013. *Unburnable Carbon 2013: Wasted Capital and Stranded Assets.* London: Carbon Tracker Initiative.

Carbon Tracker Initiative. 2015. *Lost in Transition: How the Energy Sector Is Missing Potential Demand Destruction.* Available at: www.carbontracker.org/report/lost_in_ transition/.

Carbon Tracker Initiative. *Carbon Tracker Initiative's Definition of Stranded Assets.* Available at: www.carbontracker.org/resources/ [Accessed August 23, 2016].

Carney, M. 2015. *Breaking the Tragedy of the Horizon – Climate Change and Financial Stability.* Speech given by Mark Carney at Lloyd's of London. Available at: www. bankofengland.co.uk/publications/Pages/speeches/default.aspx [Accessed August 8, 2016].

Center for International Environmental Law. 2015. *(Mis)Calculated Risk and Climate Change: Are Rating Agencies Repeating Credit Crisis Mistakes?* Available at: www.ciel. org/wp-content/uploads/2015/10/ciel-rpt-credits-10.15-webv2smaller.pdf [Accessed August 7, 2016].

Christiana Figueres. 2013. *Keynote Address by Christiana Figueres, Executive Secretary UNFCCC at the World Coal Association International Coal & Climate Summit.* Available at: www.unep.org/newscentre/Default.aspx?DocumentID=2754&ArticleID=9703.

Congressional Budget Office. 1998. Electric Utilities: Deregulation and Stranded Costs. *CBO Paper.*

Davis, S. J., Caldeira, K. and Matthews, H. D. 2010. Future CO2 Emissions and Climate Change From Existing Energy Infrastructure. *Science*, 329(5997), 1330–1333. Available at: www.sciencemag.org/cgi/doi/10.1126/science.1188566 [Accessed August 14, 2016].

Davis, S. J. and Socolow, R. H. 2014. Commitment Accounting of CO2 Emissions. *Environmental Research Letters*, 9(8), 84018. Available at: http://stacks.iop.org/1748-9326/9/i=8/a=084018?key=crossref.b7c8701dfa5d89a68f45f1956e8793b9.

Deloitte, 2016. *IAS 16 – Property, Plant and Equipment.* Available at: www.iasplus.com/en/standards/ias/ias16.

Dietz, S., et al. 2016. 'Climate Value at Risk' of Global Financial Assets. *Nature Clim. Change*, 6(7), 676–679. Available at: http://dx.doi.org/10.1038/nclimate2972.

EAC. 2014. Green Finance E. A. Committee, ed.

Eccles, R. G. and Krzus, M. P. 2015. *The Integrated Reporting Movement: Meaning, Momentum, Motives, and Materiality.* Hoboken, NJ: Wiley.

Economist Intelligence Unit. 2015. *The Cost of Inaction: Recognising the Value at Risk From Climate Change*. A Report From the Economist Intelligence Unit.

Exxon Mobil Corporation. 2014. *Letter on to Shareholders and NGOs Carbon Asset Risk*.

Financial Stability Board. 2015. *FSB to Establish Task Force on Climate-Related Financial Disclosures*.

Fossil Free Indexes, Research & Responsible Investing. 2016. Available at: http://fossil freeindexes.com/ [Accessed August 7, 2016].

Friedman, T. L. 2014. Obama on Obama on Climate. *The New York Times*. Available at: www.nytimes.com/2014/06/08/opinion/sunday/friedman-obama-on-obama-on-climate.html?smid=tw-TomFriedman&seid=auto&_r=2 [Accessed June 7, 2014].

Futerra, 2006. *The Rules of the Game – Evidence Base for the Climate Change Communications Strategy*.

Generation Foundation. 2013. *Stranded Carbon Assets*, p. 26. Available at: http://gen found.org/media/pdf-generation-foundation-stranded-carbon-assets-v1.pdf.

Go Fossil Free. 2016. *Fossil Free – Commitments*. Available at: http://gofossilfree.org/ commitments/ [Accessed August 7, 2016].

Greenpeace UK. 2004. *Offshore Wind Onshore Jobs – a New Industry for Britain*.

Grübler, A. and Nakićenović, N. 1991. Long Waves, Technology Diffusion, and Substitution. *Review (Fernand Braudel Center)*, 14(2), 313–343. Available at: www.jstor.org/ stable/40241184.

Gurría, A. 2013. *The Climate Challenge: Achieving Zero Emissions*. Lecture by OECD Secretary-General. Available at: www.oecd.org/about/secretary-general/the-climate-challenge-achieving-zero-emissions.htm.

Harnett, E. 2018. *Geographic Diffusion of the Stranded Asset Discourse 2010 to 2015*. Oxford: University of Oxford.

Hedegaard, C. 2015. Divestment and Stranded Assets in the Low-Carbon Transition – Chair's Summary. *OECD's 32nd Roundtable on Sustainable Development*, October 28.

Helm, D. 2015. Stranded Assets – a Deceptively Simple and Flawed Idea. *Energy Futures Network*, (15).

IEA. 2008. *World Energy Outlook 2008*. Paris, France: International Energy Agency.

IEA. 2013. *Redrawing the Energy Climate Map*. World Energy Outlook Special Report, p. 134. Available at: www.worldenergyoutlook.org/media/weowebsite/2013/energycli matemap/RedrawingEnergyClimateMap.pdf.

Investec Investment Institute. 2016. *Avoiding Long-Term Value Destruction: A Conversation Between Ben Caldecott and Roger Urwin*.

IPCC. 1999. Economic Impact of Mitigation Measures. *Proceedings of IPCC Expert Meeting on Economic Impact of Mitigation Measures: The Hague, the Netherlands, May 27–28, 1999*, CPB.

IPCC. 2001. *IPCC Third Assessment Report – Climate Change 2001*. Geneva, Switzerland: Intergovernmental Panel on Climate Change.

Kay, J. 2012. *The Kay Review of UK Equity Markets and Long-Term Decision Making*.

King, S. M. 2012. *Reply to Your Recent Letter on UK Exposure to High Carbon Investments C. C. Capital*, ed.

Kondratiev, N. 1926. *The Long Waves in Economic Life*. Eastford: Martino Publishing.

Krause, F., Bach, W. and Koomey, J. 1989. *Energy Policy in the Greenhouse*. El Cerrito, CA: International Project for Sustainable Energy Paths,.

Kruitwagen, L., MacDonald-Korth, D. and Caldecott, B. 2016. Summary of Proceedings: Environment-Related Risks and the Future of Prudential Regulation and Financial Conduct – 4th Stranded Assets Forum, Waddesdon Manor, October 23, 2015. *Smith School of Enterprise and the Environment, University of Oxford*.

Lamb, C. 2015. *Drying and Drowning Assets — How Worsening Water Security Is Stranding Assets.*

London School of Economics. 2013. $674 Billion Annual Spend on 'Unburnable' Fossil Fuel Assets Signals Failure to Recognise Huge Financial Risks. *Press Release.* Available at: www.lse.ac.uk/GranthamInstitute/news/674-billion-annual-spend-on-unburnable-fossil-fuel-assets-signals-failure-to-recognise-huge-financial-risks-2/.

McGrath, P. 2014. Ban Ki-Moon Urges Pension Funds to Dump Fossil Fuel Investments. *ABC.*

McKibben, B. 2011. Global Warming's Terrifying New Math. *Rolling Stone.*

Morel, A., et al. 2016. Stranded Assets in Palm Oil Production: A Case Study of Indonesia About the Sustainable Finance Programme. *Smith School of Enterprise and the Environment, University of Oxford.*

Mufson, S. 2014. *CEO of Royal Dutch Shell: Climate Change Discussion 'Has Gone Into la-la Land'.* Available at: www.washingtonpost.com/news/wonk/wp/2014/09/10/ceo-of-royal-dutch-shell-climate-change-discussion-has-gone-into-la-la-land/.

Perez, C. 1985. Microelectronics, Long Waves and World Structural Change: New Perspectives for Developing Countries. *World Development*, 13(3), 441–463. Available at: http://linkinghub.elsevier.com/retrieve/pii/0305750X85901408 [Accessed August 15, 2016].

Perez, C. 2002. *Technological Revolutions and Financial Capital.* Edward Elgar. Available at: www.amazon.co.uk/Technological-Revolutions-Financial-Capital-Dynamics/dp/1843763311.

Perez, C. 2010. Technological Revolutions and Techno-Economic Paradigms. *Cambridge Journal of Economics*, 34(1), 185–202. Available at: http://cje.oxfordjournals.org/content/34/1/185.abstract.

Pfeiffer, A., et al. 2016. The '2°C Capital Stock' for Electricity Generation: Committed Cumulative Carbon Emissions From the Electricity Generation Sector and the Transition to a Green Economy. *Applied Energy*, 179(1), 1395–1408.

Rautner, M., Tomlinson, S. and Hoare, A. 2016. Managing the Risk of Stranded Assets in Agriculture and Forestry. *Chatham House Research Paper.*

Rook, D. and Caldecott, B. 2015. Cognitive Biases and Stranded Assets: Detecting Psychological Vulnerabilities Within international Oil Companies. *Smith School of Enterprise and the Environment, University of Oxford.*

Royal Dutch Shell PLC. 2014. *Letter to Shareholders – Stranded Assets.* Available at: http://s02.static-shell.com/content/dam/shell-new/local/corporate/corporate/downloads/pdf/investor/presentations/2014/sri-web-response-climate-change-may14.pdf [Accessed May 16, 2014].

Schumpeter, J. A. 1942. *Capitalism, Socialism and Democracy.* Routledge. Available at: http://aulavirtual.tecnologicocomfenalcovirtual.edu.co/aulavirtual/pluginfile.php/520365/mod_resource/content/1/TEORIAS DEL EMPRENDIMIENTO.pdf [Accessed August 14, 2016].

Standard & Poor's. 2014. *Climate Change Is a Global Mega-Trend for Sovereign Risk.* Available at: www.globalcreditportal.com/ratingsdirect/renderArticle.do?articleId=1318252&SctArtId=236925&from=CM&nsl_code=LIME&sourceObjectId=8606813&sourceRevId=1&fee_ind=N&exp_date=20240514-20:34:43.

State Street Global Advisors. 2016. *SPYX – SPDR S&P 500 Fossil Fuel Free ETF.* State Street Global Advisors (SSGA). Available at: www.spdrs.com/product/fund.seam?ticker=spyx.

Sustainability Accounting Standards Board. 2013. *Conceptual Framework of the Sustainability Accounting Standards Board.* Available at: www.sasb.org/wp-content/

uploads/2013/10/SASB-Conceptual-Framework-Final-Formatted-10-22-13.pdf [Accessed August 7, 2016].

Task Force on Climate-Related Financial Disclosures. 2016. *Phase I Report of the Task Force on Climate-Related Financial Disclosures*. Available at: www.fsb-tcfd.org/wp-content/uploads/2016/03/Phase_I_Report_v15.pdf [Accessed August 7, 2016].

Weyzig, F., et al. 2014. *The Price of Doing Too Little Too Late the Impact of the Carbon Bubble on the EU Financial System*.

Wolf, M. 2014. *The Shifts and the Shocks: What We've Learned – and Still Have to Learn – From the Financial Crisis*. London\ : Penguin Books.

Wolf, W. 1996. *Car Mania: A Critical History of Transport*. Available at: https://books.google.co.uk/books?hl=en&lr=&id=DD0samQuijgC&oi=fnd&pg=PR1&dq=rise+of+the+automobile+and+the+end+of+the+steam+railway+&ots=DmO5Le-Z7W&sig=WuYG9kiWjsWptp6C9-toB1shc40 [Accessed August 15, 2016].

The World Bank. 2013a. *Toward a Sustainable Energy Future for All: Directions for the World Bank Group's Energy Sector*.

The World Bank. 2013b. *World Bank Group Sets Direction for Energy Sector Investments*. Available at: www.worldbank.org/en/news/feature/2013/07/16/world-bank-group-direction-for-energy-sector [Accessed July 16, 2013].

2 Stranded assets

Then and now

Dimitri Zenghelis, Roger Fouquet
and Ralph Hippe[1]

1. Introduction

This chapter examines the issue of stranded assets and the likely energy transition from a macro-economic perspective. Given the lack of historical evidence on this issue, it will compare past macro-economy drivers of change and rates of asset stranding with those observable today and forecasted for the future. It will ask what pace of asset stranding can be expected normally and during economywide transitions. What could be an optimal rate of asset stranding? Could environment-related factors be generating a different rate and scale of asset stranding? It will also discuss why stranded assets can be seen as an opportunity – refreshing capital stocks, reducing pollution, and moving closer to technological frontiers.

The first two sections look at how economies change, using the period running up to and after the Industrial Revolution in the UK as a case study in how embracing change can lead to technological and structural transformation and rapid growth and development. The subsequent sections look at the historical limitations to resource-based development and the importance of managing change effectively before introducing the risks associated with a more rapid and contagious shift to a low-carbon network, which can leave companies, sectors, and regions caught out with stranded and unproductive assets. The next sections will examine how the main barriers to yielding the opportunities and limiting the risks from transformative change are mainly institutional and come from vested interests seeking to delay change and propagate inertia. The final section concludes and offers policy recommendations drawn from this historical analysis.

2. Economies always change

The structure of any economy is subject to continual flux. Possibilities for production evolve as new technologies, techniques, and materials are discovered while demands also shift in line with evolving tastes, preferences, and behaviours. Institutions and cultures will then reflect and reinforce these changes. These so-called disruptive changes can happen surprisingly quickly in historical terms.

Joseph Schumpeter (Schumpeter 1942, p. 82) described an economic structure "incessantly destroying the old one, incessantly creating a new one. The process of Creative Destruction is the essential fact about capitalism." Throughout history, economies have suffered from major phases of economic stagnation and decline interrupting periods of strong growth (Fouquet and Broadberry 2015). This chapter shows that these periods of decline have been associated with a lack of inclusive institutions, failure to adapt to changing markets while allowing vested interests to delay vital structural transformations (Olson 1983).

Governance structures that are most resilient to inevitable change are those that recognise and plan for it. In particular, economies which allow resources to be reallocated from old, declining, low-productivity sectors to new, fast-growing, high-productivity sectors are likely to be more resilient. A hundred years ago, several haircuts, a holiday weekend, or a seven-course gourmet meal might have been exchanged for an accurate water resistant watch. Today such a watch can be picked up across the world often for less than the price of a cup of coffee, while the relative price of labour-intensive services has gone up. Meanwhile internet-enabled devices have only recently been conceived and invented. VHS recorders and analogue cameras have gone from non-existent to near saturation and back again in a matter of decades. These shifts are part of the diversity and innovation associated with economic dynamism. Indeed, changes happen faster and faster in the era of mass communications and rapid global diffusion of knowledge capital. It took 25 years for the fixed-line telephone and 30 years for electricity to penetrate 10% of the US market and decades more to reach 50% saturation (DeGusta 2012). By contrast, tablets, smartphones, and the internet are reaching such penetration rates in years. More recent innovations are being adopted more quickly in a readily connected globalised communication and trading environment (see Figure 2.1).

For the most part, such shifts cause little economic strain. Resources are re-allocated from sector to sector; people are reskilled and retrained; capital depreciates and is replaced. This is part of a healthy dynamic economy; half of the companies listed in the fortune 500 in 2000 no longer exist (Nanterme 2016). However,

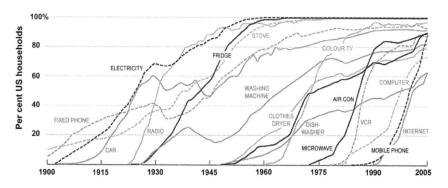

Figure 2.1 Diffusion/adoption rates

Source Nicholas Felton, *The New York Times* www.nytimes.com/imagepages/2008/02/10/opinion/
10op.graphic.ready.html

every so often the shift is so large or so sudden (or both) that substantial economic assets are rendered stranded. Most vulnerable to such changes are goods and services that rely on integrated networks, more especially mass transport, communication, and energy. Decisions on long-lived capital investment and the adoption of new integrated networks affect a country's wealth for decades or even centuries.

For instance, over the space of 150 years, canals in Britain experienced rapid success, then stagnation, and eventually major decline. From the mid-18th century, canals played an important role in the supply of heavy goods, such as coal and iron, between strategic economic centres. As the network of canals expanded between the 1780s and the 1820s, the cost of freighting heavy goods fell substantially. Canal barges increasingly supplied lighter goods and carried passengers, too. However, competition from railways meant that, by the mid-19th century, only the heaviest goods were profitable to freight using canal barges (Jackman 1960).

The growing success of railway companies and the declining value of canals meant that the former began to own the latter's assets. During the 'Railway Mania' of the 1840s, canal owners, anticipating the stranding of their assets, offered their waterways at low prices (Bagwell 1974). Railway operators seeking to integrate services were happy to snap them up. Concern about the monopolistic powers of the railways led to the creation of the Canal Carriers Act in 1845, which stipulated that only existing canal companies were allowed to acquire or lease waterways. The next year, before the Act was in force, railway companies bought almost 20% of the whole canal network. Many railway companies changed their names to reflect their business on the waterways, expanding their ownership of an increasingly unattractive business – by 1865, they owned one-third of the canal network. In 1873, mergers were forbidden except by Parliament's consent (Bagwell 1974).

However, ultimately, this protectionism accelerated the demise of the canals. Because railway owners struggled to acquire certain stretches of canals, they were unable to integrate their distribution networks effectively. This barrier encouraged them to concentrate their distribution through the railways. Over time, they failed to maintain their canals, which often needed repair due to ice damage. This made them less usable and drove up the cost of freight along the canals. The overall level of freighting activity on the waterways remained broadly the same during the second half of the 19th century and then declined after the First World War (Bagwell 1974).

This chapter seeks to investigate the likelihood and impact of a rapid transition to new energy and transport networks. The risk is big oil companies become the canal companies, Kodaks, and Blockbusters of the next century, with significant stranding of physical, human, and knowledge assets.

3. UK case study: structural transformation the key to growth and development

In this section we turn to a classic case study of how structural transformation is crucial to economic growth and development. It is the story of the Industrial Revolution in the UK. After the decline of the Roman Empire, Britain lost a great deal of its economic structure and, over the subsequent centuries, became the subject of a number of invasions that redefined it (Dyer 2002). Then, from the 12th century, England, in particular, transformed itself from an economic backwater to the leading global economy by the 19th century. Lessons will be drawn from this section throughout the remainder of this chapter.

The early periods of growth in England were associated with its development of a cloth industry. For centuries, England had manufactured its own woollen cloth, which was considered of high quality but relatively expensive (van der Wee 2003). However, by the 13th century, England had become a major exporter of wool, especially to Flanders, which was very efficient in the production of textiles, and then importing much of its demand for manufactured woollen textiles (Carus-Wilson 1950). Following a series of wars, in the second half of the 14th century, the English woollen textile manufacturers began regaining their market and even started exporting textiles, particularly to Gascony, which sold wine in return (Carus-Wilson and Colman 1963). By the 16th century, England had fully converted to a cloth-manufacturing and -exporting economy. Increases in England's per-capita GDP around the 1370s and the 1480s can be discerned from Figure 2.2.

The 16th century saw the expansion of two other sectors of the English economy, iron and coal, which would become the pillars of economic growth. In the 1490s, a number of French Huguenot families, escaping religious repression, were welcomed and settled in the Weald in Sussex. They introduced the furnace, which produced faster, cheaper, and generally better quality iron. Pig iron

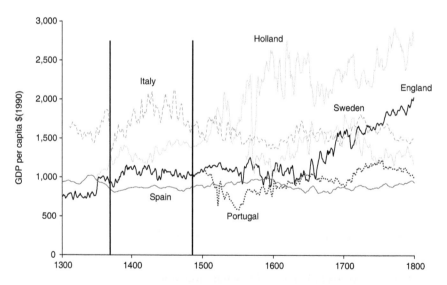

Figure 2.2 GDP per capita in selected European economies, 1300–1800[2, 3]

Note: *3-year average; Spain: 11-year average

Source: Fouquet and Broadberry (2015). Original sources: Broadberry et al. (2011), Malanima (2011), van Zanden and van Leeuwen (2012), Schön and Krantz (2012), Alvarez-Nogel and Prados de la Escosura (2013), Palma and Reis (2014).

production in the Weald, which centred on meeting military demands for cannons and cannon balls, increased 28-fold between 1530 and 1590.[4] Furnace pig iron production outside the Weald, which provided tools and smaller items, took off, and, throughout England, pig iron production increased 30-fold between 1540 and 1620 (King 2005). Since the 16th century, many ironmasters had tried to use coal-based fuels to smelt iron but failed until Abraham Darby's invention in the early 18th century and, still, the fuel needs made coke iron too expensive except for specific purposes (King 2011). Then improvements in the efficiency of coke-iron furnaces transformed the industry in the second half of the 18th century, reducing variable costs of production and increasing the incentive to build coke iron furnaces – between 1755 and 1760, coke pig iron production tripled, and it more than doubled again between 1760 and 1780 (King 2005).

The main pillar, which fuelled the iron industry and the cotton industry during the Industrial Revolution, was the coal industry. Yet the introduction of mineral fuels reduced the burden imposed by land constraints resulting from a growing population with rising standards of living since the 16th century (Allen 2009). As the price of woodfuels rose in London, shipments down the East coast grew substantially throughout the 16th century. With rising incomes, as well as improvements in the grates and fireplaces necessary to burn coal in homes, demand grew rapidly (Fouquet 2008). From the 15th century to the end of the 17th century, the coal mining industry expanded from a niche business to the main generator of wealth in the North-East of England (Hatcher 1993). Despite only a few technical improvements in production methods, large and accessible reserves, a diversity of types and qualities of coal, a big labour force to draw from, and improving means of transportation enabled coal supply to expand in line with the growing demand (Church 1986). This ensured that real prices remained relatively stable from the 15th to the 19th century. The ability to meet highly elastic demands for energy-intensive products and energy services over hundreds of years was arguably Britain's source of ascendency (Allen 2009).

Thus, the Industrial Revolution in Britain was driven by coal. But Britain was not the only country with an ample and readily accessible supply of fossil fuels. What drove the rapid development and industrialisation in the UK was a political system limiting the absolute rule of monarchy with legally enshrined political rights, which allowed the free flow of ideas and the ownership of ideas. The search for profits and new markets drove the British development, and the development of new and flexible institutions propelled change and drove forward innovation. Although still influenced by powerful groups, successive British governments tended to be less directed by these vested interests than in other countries, particularly in policies related to industrial activities (Moe 2007).

4. Resource-based development; curse or blessing?

The UK story suggests that managing change is the key to economic success. However, shifting comparative advantages and climbing the economic value chain is harder when the bulk of an economy's production is already tied up in low-skilled, low-technology sectors extracting rent from selling natural resources. Since the Industrial Revolution, increasing economic dependence on natural resource exploitation as a source of income appears to often have been a hindrance to economic development in low- and mid-income countries in the world (Barbier 2005). There is considerable evidence for a negative relationship between GDP per-capita growth and measures of non-renewable natural capital – known as the 'resource curse' (Sachs and Warner 1995; Auty 2001).[5] However, there are a number of conflicting forces influencing the likelihood of a 'resource curse'.

Badia-Miró et al. (2015) propose numerous factors that influence how resource availability might affect economic performance – either positively or negatively. The curse can manifest itself through changes in the productive structure of the economy, including the crowding out of more productive sectors and a less dynamically efficient allocation of factor endowments and institutions. On the other hand, resources can be a 'blessing'. In many situations, trade has developed as a means to generate wealth and economic growth from unexploited natural resources (Barbier 2005). The quality of institutions is seen as central to whether resource abundance has a positive or negative effect on economic performance.

For instance, Wright and Czelusta (2007) have shown how, in the US, resource and, in particular, coal abundance led to the establishment of a number of major educational institutions and knowledge for other sectors of the economy. Norway (Sanders and Sandvic 2015) and Botswana (Hillbom 2015) are other examples in which resource abundance led to favourable outcomes, in large part due to prudent state management. Indeed, natural resources have been a blessing when the increasing tax revenue following the associated booms has been used carefully (Badia-Miró and Duciong 2015).

However, there is ample historical evidence of the vulnerability of resource-based development (supported by theory – Lundahl 1998) – indeed, resource-based development is often likely to be successful initially but not in the long run (Badia-Miró et al. 2015). For instance, in the late 19th and early 20th centuries, a number of economies specialised in primary exports. During this period, global economic expansion led to a boom in the demand for primary products, and prices reflected this. As a consequence, resource-dependent economies grew considerably. However, these economies were vulnerable to economic contractions (as triggered by the First World War and later the Great Depression), as well as competition from new producers of natural resources and substitutions to alternatives stimulated by high prices.

These economies were highly vulnerable to the decline in international commodity prices relative to manufactured goods and the introduction of cheaper sources or substitutes. As Willebald et al put it,

> This form of economic life, which is typical of 'new' economies, was able to offer high standards of living but only for as long as supplies and world demand remained dynamic. Declines in demand or increases in supply would have severe consequences for internal political economy, leaving it weakly positioned to react to the challenge of finding a new basic product to trade.

> These economies face the risks of the 'staple' trap . . . where the export orientation of some economies presents lock-in effects whereby the main primary specialisation blocks structural change and impedes economic growth.
>
> (Willebald et al. 2015, pp. 10–11)

For instance, during the 19th century, the Amazonian region was one of the wealthiest parts of Brazil (Leff 1997), because it produced 90% of the world's rubber (Barham and Coomes 1994). Given the increasing value placed on rubber in the global economy, by the end of the century, international competitors (especially from today's Malaysia and Indonesia) began to enter the market, developing more intensive and cheaper methods of producing rubber. However, Amazonia failed to adapt to new market pressures or alter its production methods (Barham and Coomes 1994). Following the drop in demand associated with the First World War, the Brazilian rubber industry never recovered. Thus, the whole Amazonian region, which was once the greatest source of wealth in the country, went into decline.

Similarly, Malaysia would eventually face declining demand for its rubber and needed to transform its economy to develop. In the 1920s and 1930s, it was the wealthiest economy in Asia due to its key role in rubber production. However, during the Second World War, the US managed to develop synthetic rubber, which captured close to 50% of the global market by 1960 and 70% of the market by 1980. While improving productivity, Malaysia could no longer rely on rubber revenue for economic growth and development. Instead, it diversified, becoming the world's leader in palm oil production, and, in the 1970s and 1980s, expanded its oil and natural gas industry. There were also developments in manufacturing, such as electronics and textiles (Drabble 2000). Despite modest growth in domestic rubber production until the mid-1970s, Malaysia would have experienced major economic decline without its structural transformation. Indeed, the important increases in GDP per capita occurred only after diversification.

Furthermore, in the late 19th and 20th centuries, numerous countries, such as Mexico, Venezuela, Chile, and Indonesia, failed to shift away from their specialisation in primary exports and manufacture.[6] Bertola (2015) shows how an economy can become unable to invest returns in more dynamic and productive sectors. In the long run, this inability led to stagnation and decline of these economies.

> History teaches us that 'curses' and 'blessings' are constructions – they are the result of the socioeconomic system – . . . Thus, successful experiences of economic development in countries like Australia and Canada highlights the fact that institutions promoting interaction between enabling and receiving sectors are fundamental to science-based and innovation-driven growth in resource-based economies. It is crucial, therefore, to develop institutional structures to support knowledge capabilities in the growth of natural resource–based industries.
>
> (Willebald et al. 2015, p. 24)

Asset diversification, it turns out, matters more to the success of an economy than output diversification and export diversification. The results mentioned suggest that what matters for development is not so much what a country makes at home and sells abroad but how it goes about making those goods and services. World Bank analysis shows a strong correlation between economic performance – measured as an index of productivity growth, job creation, and output stability – and a country's assets – measured as an index of natural resources, built capital, and public institutions (World Economic Forum 2017). Building strong public institutions at an early stage of development is particularly important. For example, Gelb (2010) argues that Algeria struggled to diversify away from oil-based activities due to a lack of rules-based institutions and a poor business environment. By contrast, Botswana's economy has performed well despite limited export diversification. He attributes this in part to the meritocratic government and strong institutions which governed the use of rents associated with diamond extraction.

5. Low-carbon transition risks stranding assets

The chapter now turns to the future, looking at the likely scale and impact of global decarbonisation and the mounting risks of asset stranding. The reason for this is that greenhouse gases (GHGs) stay in the atmosphere for tens and in some cases hundreds of years. Thus, it is the stock of GHGs that drives temperature change, not the annual flows or emissions. In other words, fossil carbon emissions have to be reduced to zero if global temperature is to be stabilised – no matter what the temperature at which we seek to stabilise (whether two degrees warmer or a disastrous six degrees). Climate modelling by the Intergovernmental Panel on Climate Change (IPCC) shows that to have a likely chance of holding warming to 2°C, carbon emissions must be cut to net zero by 2065–2085 (IPCC 2014).

This will require a fundamental structural transformation in all economies. Carbon from fossil fuels has powered most of the world's economic activity for more than 200 years, since the use of coal to fire steam engines generated the Industrial Revolution. Oil, gas, and coal currently make up almost 80% of global primary energy use (International Energy Agency 2016). It is impossible to foresee every technology or process that will be involved in the future, but we are beginning to understand the outlines of how such a transformation might evolve.[7] Fossil fuels for energy will have to be more or less phased out (with some role for carbon capture and storage) and replaced by nuclear and renewable energy combined with electricity storage. In transport, this will mean almost complete electrification of vehicles and/or the widespread use of hydrogen fuel cells.

To accommodate much higher energy demand, the efficiency of energy consumption in all its uses will have to increase dramatically, which will require using digital and information technologies to manage energy demand in 'real time' and 'dematerialise' economic output. The design and functioning of cities as a whole will have to change very significantly. As Carlota Perez recently described, this is a technological revolution on a par with those which have disrupted and transformed economic systems in the past (Jacobs and Mazzucato 2016). In the same volume, Mariana Mazzucato showed that the direction of innovation is not pre-ordained. The challenge of shifting the fossil fuel-based infrastructure of present production and consumption to low-carbon forms will require strong government direction, what Mazzucato describes as "mission-oriented" policy.

To decarbonise, economies, nation states, and the private sector need to build new energy, transport, industrial, agricultural, and urban systems, which are likely to be more expensive in the short term. In doing so, they will inevitably cause current assets and activities based on fossil energy to decline in value and profitability. The likely resistance encountered shall be discussed in what follows. Because carbon is so central to the global economy it is a much larger task, involving a fundamental reshaping not just of individual technologies but of entire systems of production, distribution, and consumption. For this to be a practical reality, it is necessary to understand not just the latest technical innovations but the underlying drivers of innovation, not just in technologies but in institutions and behaviours, and the role of path dependence in system transformation. To do this one must draw on the history of economic development and the dynamics of change in economic systems.

6. The low-carbon transition may reflect a gear change

History shows that innovation activity tends to be focussed towards the dominant technologies in which returns on incremental improvements are easily observed and understood. Acemoglu et al. (2012) provide empirical evidence both for geographical knowledge spillovers (a firm's decision to innovate in clean technologies is influenced by the presence of associated researchers and inventors in their local region) and for path dependence (firms tend to direct innovation towards what they are already good at – see also Aghion et al. 2011).

Nevertheless, disruptive innovation can manifest itself in tipping points where new networks rapidly displace old. There is a risk of a rapid process of decarbonisation being triggered by policies, technologies, or litigation generating a change in the demand and supply of goods and services and leading to a rapid revaluation of assets. The recent signing of the Paris Climate Accord can be seen as early evidence of such risks materialising as policy makers agree to national decarbonisation plans (many of these driven by an enhanced perception of national self-interest, for example from managing economic transitions, benefiting from associated gains in efficiency and reductions in air pollution, and opportunities in developing low-cost renewable technologies).

There is no way to estimate the optimal rate of asset stranding, but we know it is not zero. The future is unpredictable, and mistakes will inevitably be made when planning for decades ahead. Occasional redundancy has to be expected. Kielder Water (McCulloch 2006) in Northumberland, England, is the biggest manmade reservoir in Northern Europe. It was built in the 1970s on the expectation of ever-expanding industrial demand for water in the north of England. By the time it opened in 1982, the recession had markedly reduced the demand for water, and permanent changes in the structure of the UK economy meant industrial demand never recovered. The reservoir was almost immediately stranded as an asset, but that does not mean it should not have been built. It's in the nature of infrastructure projects that some forecasts will be wrong.

Yet some stranding is predictable, when it comes to technological transitions, and can be guarded against. It is increasingly clear that only a small proportion of existing fossil fuel reserves can be commercially exploited if global climate goals are to be realised. A paper published in *Nature* shows that a third of global oil reserves, half of gas reserves, and more than 80% of current coal reserves should remain in the ground from 2010 to 2050 (McGlade and Ekins 2015). Carbon-intensive infrastructure also risks being stranded. Pfeiffer et al. (2016) analyse concentrations of greenhouse gases in the atmosphere and conclude that in order to meet the two-degree target (with 50% probability) no new emitting-electricity infrastructure can be built after 2017, unless other electricity infrastructure is retired early or retrofitted with carbon capture technologies. This highlights the gap between what politicians have signed up to in Paris and what markets and fossil fuel companies are assuming. This gap should alarm policy makers and central bankers: it suggests either asymmetric information or a lack of credibility in policies.

The speed at which such re-pricing occurs is uncertain and could be decisive for economic and financial stability. If the transition is orderly then financial markets will likely cope. But as Bank of England governor Mark Carney recently noted "there have already been a few high profile examples of jump-to-distress pricing because of shifts in environmental policy or performance" (Bank of England 2015). Moreover, it is clear that the risks of a transition to a low-carbon economy co-vary and indeed are mutually reinforcing. Most obviously, a focused policy effort can lead to enhanced deployment of new technologies whose costs would be expected to come down as a result.

The potential for unit costs to fall as new technologies are developed and benefit from learning and experience, and as engineers learn how to cheaply install, connect, and repair technology, is higher for many new technologies than for long-established incumbents. This has already allowed solar photovoltaic and onshore wind technologies to become competitive with gas and coal in a number of global locations, even without a strong carbon price. As planning guidelines are updated and new networks are built, and especially if consumers change behaviour and demand support for resource efficiency, recycling and pedestrianisation, then it is possible that the costs of new energy systems will fall further, closing the gaps with conventional energy sources.[8]

Strong policy can set in train a new positive dynamic. For example, the EU in 2008 required all member states to adopt renewable energy targets, amounting to 20% of primary energy demand by 2020. German subsidies were required for the installation of photovoltaic (PV) solar power, initially at very high cost, in the early 1990s. But as demand rose, prices fell, and incentives were created for further technical innovation in addition to 'learning by doing' as new firms entered the market. Mass manufacture – in China as well as Europe – pushed costs down further, leading to higher global demand. The result was a 90% reduction in the cost of PV modules in just six years from 2009 to 2015. Installed solar power is now at cost parity with fossil fuels in many parts of the world and close to it even in parts of northern Europe. Consumer behaviour has correspondingly changed, with solar power now a relatively normal household investment. Having attained such momentum, PV subsidies have radically declined and are on their way to being unnecessary.

Lower technology costs in turn make the application of decarbonisation policies more politically and economically palatable. New lobbies for climate policy among both businesses and consumers have been created. Positive feedback loops in the innovation chain interact across the economy, prompting institutional and behavioural change and the emergence of new scale economies. The trigger could come from climate policies or from a breakthrough technology (such as cheap and effective energy storage) or something else; the point being that policies, institutions, and technologies reinforce each other in a positive feedback that leads to rapid step-changes.

Conceptually, a variety of studies have identified that innovation and deployment of new technologies at times of structural change is 'path dependent'.[9] This means that at first, innovation and research tend to focus on further improving technologies and networks that are already established. However, if change is pushed, say, by technological breakthroughs (the shift from horses to combustion engines, canals to railways, kerosene to electricity) or credible and deliberate mission-orientated policy, feedback loops in the innovation process interact across the economy, prompting institutional and behavioural change and the possible emergence of new scale economies (Aghion et al. 2014). If few people own electric cars, charging stations will be rare and few will want to buy electric cars. But if most cars are electric, petrol stations will be rare and few will want to buy petrol-fuel cars. This is the network effect.

Tipping dynamics further result from the fact that the perceived payoff to action to decarbonise by any single agent will be a function of what others are expected to do. Once a critical mass of players shifts, for example in markets such as China, the US, and the EU, the rest will quickly follow. The US–China agreement to reduce emissions signed by Xi Jinping and Barack Obama in 2014 paved the way for a successful international agreement at the Paris Accord the following year.[10] Technology and finance costs are expected to fall, while markets are expected to grow. This is why such risks are often termed 'transition risks,' which is intended to portray a sense of the dynamic process in which paths become reinforcing.

However, the alignment or anchoring of expectations on the likely shape of future energy networks and innovations can lead to a 'tipping point' where the nature and direction of mainstream innovation activity can switch quickly. This becomes self-reinforcing through new network effects: so long as one network technology is dominant, products and services linked to the use of that network will receive the bulk of innovation activity, and there will be less effort committed to developing an alternative; but if a new technology network becomes dominant, then innovation activity can shift quickly. The recent rapid development of energy storage technologies in the wake of the growth of renewables – storage being a principal means to cope with the intermittency of solar and wind power – provides a powerful example. This revolution has only just begun and has yet to play out.

The gains from disruptive innovation can be widespread and extend beyond the sector in question. A striking finding of recent research is that the potential spillovers from low-carbon innovation to other sectors – one of the factors which help to drive overall growth – may be higher than for other technologies.[11] Using data on 1 million patents and 3 million citations, Dechezleprêtre et al. suggest that spillovers from low-carbon innovation in the energy production and transportation sectors are more than 40% greater than in conventional technologies (Dechezleprêtre et al. 2013) At the same time Acemoglu et al. provide a powerful theoretical case to suggest that once systems of clean innovation have been switched on, they may be more productive than conventional alternatives based on existing technologies (Acemoglu et al. 2012).

The point here is not that such tipping dynamics are about to happen, they might or might not. But if they do, change could be rapid. This provides an accelerated risk of asset stranding in a range of assets from infrastructure to human skills, knowledge capital, and institutions. Investors will rightly demand that firms make appropriate contingency plans for such potential rapid changes, even if such changes remain one scenario among many. Put another way, it is becoming increasingly risky to pin all strategies on the assumption that extensive decarbonisation will not happen, for example, on the basis of (mostly backward-looking) lack of political will.

7. Social norms – another tipping point?

Tipping points apply to social norms as much as to institutions and technologies, and these are already forming a key part of the propagating dynamics. Formal institutions struggle to enforce collectively desirable outcomes without popular support. Social norms are defined as the predominant behaviour within a society, supported by a shared understanding of acceptable actions and sustained through social interactions (Ostrom 2000). Social feedbacks help make norms self-reinforcing and therefore stable, but when norms change, that can happen abruptly.

Permitting slavery, denying voting rights to women, mining asbestos, smoking in public places, not wearing seatbelts, and driving after consuming alcohol were all once considered normal practices. Today, robust *global moral norms* socially condition many states and their citizens to see these practices as morally wrong and to regulate them accordingly.[12] Policy can modify prevalent self-reinforcing feedbacks. For example, regulations, taxes, subsidies, or infrastructure investment such as cycle lanes or dense housing and public transport can aid the process of shifting norms. When people prefer to behave like others, changed expectations can abruptly change behaviour. Thus a potential powerful role for policy is to provide reasons for people to change their expectations and behaviours (Young 2015).

Emitting carbon with full knowledge of the damage it causes is increasingly seen in the same light (Green forthcoming). This applies in particular to fossil fuels (especially coal and unconventional oil and gas) and/or particular activities in fossil fuel supply chains (especially investment, production, and large-scale consumption, for example in coal-fired power stations). The concept of 'unburnable carbon'[13] has become widely acknowledged along with civil society actions targeting the exploitation of new fossil fuel deposits.[14] The concept of fossil fuel divestment aimed at major institutional investors has also garnered traction.[15]

Anti–fossil fuel norms are already concentrating moral pressure on the largest culprits of climate change (Collier and Venables 2015). Following pressure by the Obama administration, 34 member states of the OECD agreed to end state subsidies for financing the export of technologies to build coal-fired power plants.[16] Following pressure from divestment campaigners, the Norwegian Parliament voted to require Norway's sovereign wealth fund to divest from coal companies (defined as companies that generate more than 30% of their revenue from coal – Carrington 2016). The leaders of 14 Pacific Island countries agreed in July 2016 to consider a proposed Pacific Climate Treaty, which would ban new coal mines, the expansion of existing coal mines, and the provision of fossil fuel production and consumption subsidies (Slezak 2016). In 2016, the United States imposed a three-year moratorium on the allocation of new coal mining leases on federal land, and the Chinese central government also imposed three-year moratoria on new coal mines and coal-fired power stations.

These actions suggest that we are in fact already starting to see the emergence of an anti-coal norm in the international community. The implementation of norms is likely to be influenced by the ease with which norm-compliance can be monitored by third parties, since third-party verification makes it harder for responsibilities to be sidestepped (Bell et al. 2012). Effective disclosure of carbon emissions at the company and public jurisdiction levels (cities, countries, and regions) is vital. Actual or expected changes in policy, technology, and physical risks – as well as the threat of litigation – could prompt a rapid reassessment of the value of a large range of assets as changing costs and opportunities become apparent (Stern and Zenghelis 2016). This enhances the risk of early yet avoidable financial loss and the locking in to stranded assets.

The presence of low-cost alternatives to emitting greenhouse gases is facilitating the spread of changing social norms and forms another part of the feedback mechanism that could yield a rapid transition. The availability of low-cost solar PV and wind power has enabled anti-coal campaigns to point to economically affordable – often superior – energy alternatives. Normative political interventions affect institutions, interests, power relations, capabilities, identities, and ideas.[17] Even legalised global norms are reliant on states implementing them 'voluntarily,' the likelihood of which increases with pressure from civil society and from other states (Dai 2010). This virtuous spiral helped form the basis of the Paris Agreement.

8. Inertia, politics, and resistance to change

History suggests that if an alternative technology is superior, players will tend to move towards the new technologies and new networks as the comparative advantages shift (Fouquet 2010). But the costs of shifting from an existing network can also delay transitions for some time. For example, some countries may continue to commit to fossil fuel infrastructure while others move entirely to renewables.

Many incumbent producers, investors, workers, and institutions have strong incentives to impart inertia on the system to preserve markets and influence. There is a wide range of historical examples in which the success or failure of overcoming vested interests has proved crucial to facilitating appropriate asset-allocation decisions. For example, the Ottoman Empire banned the use of the printing press in part for fear of loss of control (partly having observed its effects in Europe – Hippe 2015). In contrast, European cities in which printing presses were used grew 60% faster than those without presses between 1500 and 1600 (Dittmar 2011).

The success story of the UK in the Industrial Revolution also reflected economic and institutional flexibility. In 1774, the British government's ability to overcome pressures from the textile industry and repeal the protectionist Calico Act spurred the mechanisation of the cotton industry, which kick-started the First Industrial Revolution (Broadberry and Gupta 2009). In 1846, the British government's repeal of the Corn Law and abolishment of tariffs on many manufacturing goods, which land owners had blocked for decades, ushered in a new era of free trade and the first wave of globalization (Chang 2002).

Similarly, land owners lobbied in many European countries for keeping the status quo and against growth-inducing policies, in particular the provision of mass education, which they considered a threat.[18] The successful lobbying for protection of the landed elites to deter industrialisation has also been considered as an important factor in explaining the lower economic performance of Argentina vis-à-vis Canada in the 20th century (Adamopoulos 2008).

Mancur Olson (1983) and more recently Acemoglu and Robinson (2012) have stressed the importance of powerful extractive or rent-seeking institutions. They have argued that vested interests limited the potential for economies to transform and are a likely source of stagnation. During the status quo, they are in a position of primacy. Change, especially structural change, may put their position of power in jeopardy. Thus, one could propose that incumbents tend to impose (for want of a better word) a 'dynamic' externality upon the economy – equivalent to the divergence between the actual and potential levels of economic development (for the duration of the divergence). For example, Moe (2007) explored the role of governments in influencing long run economic performance since the Industrial Revolution. Looking at Britain, France, Germany, the United States, and Japan, he found that the most successful economies had governments that did not prioritise excessively the demands of powerful incumbent interest groups.

Other economies, such as the Northern and Central Italian States, Flanders, and Holland (as well as Spain and Portugal), failed to build on their early successes and transform their economies. The relatively modest periods of growth from the mid-14th century and from the mid-15th century in England were associated with the growth of the raw wool trade and then the woollen cloth trade. In a sense, the woollen cloth manufacturers were allowed to grow and gain power from the raw wool industry, possibly because it also could benefit the incumbents, the raw wool business. Then, in the 17th century, England experienced a more substantial period of growth and structural change. The change may well have been, in part, stimulated by the Tudor government's Big Push, identified by Joan Thirsk (1976), in which the government coordinated the expansion of a number of industries simultaneously to generate the increase in aggregate demand necessary to ensure a market for the higher industrial production and create synergies between industries. In the 18th century, woollen cloth manufacturers sought to protect their market share of the textile industry from Indian cotton through protectionism, and instead created an even more powerful competitor, the Lancashire cotton mills. So the history of English economic development shows how vested interests at times were open to change and at other times were not (although the incumbent may not necessarily manage to impose permanent 'dynamic' externalities).

Another example is Britain's ban on slave trading in 1807 (slavery, however, continued to exist throughout the British Empire until the 1830s). The eventual end to slavery did not mean that owners had to bear the entire financial cost of emancipation, as the British government paid compensation to slave owners. As Draper (2007) outlines, the compensation scheme and thus a financial incentive was key to ending the system of slavery. The Slavery Abolition Act in 1833 set up a total of £20 million for 'slave property' in the colonies, which was close to 10% of British government expenditure (Draper 2007, p. 79). In addition, former slaves had to work unpaid for an 'apprenticeship' period of several years at their former owner's plant. In other words, this period was also intended to provide some necessary education and skills to 'cope' with the subsequent freedom. Overall, while government policy was successful, it was a costly financial burden for the state.

The history of the slave trade also shows us that bans in particular countries tend to lead to initially reduced demand and supply. However, other markets emerge. While prices for slaves significantly fell in British-dominated West Africa due to depleted demand after the 1807 ban, prices in other African areas such as Portuguese-controlled Angola remained stable and even increased over time (Fenske and Kala 2014; Richardson 1995). Thus, for several decades, the total slave trade was higher after 1807 than before (see Figure 2.3). Indeed, the Portuguese took up much of the slack, and the Spanish, who did not trade slaves before, became major traders afterwards. However, as Acemoglu, Johnson, and Robinson's (Acemoglu et al. 2002) study suggests, this did not imply that those economies did better. In fact, they find that those that were stuck in an old paradigm were going to experience a reversal of fortunes.

The history of container shipping offers additional aspects on the impact of new technologies on local, regional, and national competitiveness. The ports of New York and London both struggled to respond to the new technology in the 1950s and 1960s and ultimately met with decline (Levinson 2006). In this example, resistance to change also meant wasted sunk investments, which could have been spent in managing the structural change and providing opportunities for other industries. This fact highlights the importance of comprehending the fundamentals underlying changing economic conditions, which is not an easy task,

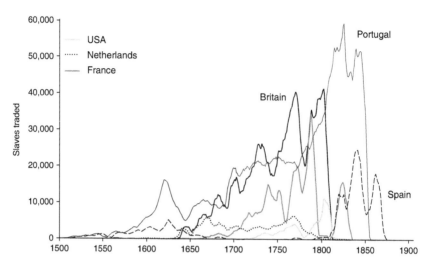

Figure 2.3 Number of slaves traded by selected countries, 1500–1900

Note: *10-year average

Source: Emory University

but long-term analysis may offer some clues. The success of newly emerging technologies and more efficient industries shows the need for sufficiently flexible regulation. It also highlights that major investments in new infrastructure for a novel technology – constructing specialized ports (and railways) for containers – can pay off in the medium and long run.

Political risk will apply more to the losses of incumbents than to the equally valuable opportunities of new entrants. This is because, in any representative political system, the losers will be more effective at lobbying politicians than potential winners (Baldwin and Robert-Nicoud 2007). From the perspective of overall economic and financial risks, winners and losers should be treated equally, with the valuation of new sectors exploiting opportunities offsetting the decline in value of less productive and slow-growing sectors. This crucial political economy aspect will be revisited in the sections on institutions and policies.

Incumbents often claim, in particular, that stronger climate policy will put them at a competitive disadvantage relative to those in other countries or even cause them to relocate elsewhere: the result, it is argued, will be the transfer ('leakage') of emissions from the more strongly regulated economy to the weaker one, with no net reduction in total. But the evidence does not support these fears. Recent studies of European climate policy, particularly of the EU emissions trading system, suggest that the impacts have thus far been small, whether in terms of carbon leakage, economic growth, employment, or consumer prices, with only a few energy-intensive sectors (such as steel and cement) at risk of significant adverse effects even if policy is strengthened (Bassi and Zenghelis 2014). Policy makers should largely resist giving in to incumbent lobbies.

Indeed, this is not just a problem of distribution between winners and losers. Even those who perceive themselves as losers may in fact be acting against their own interests by opposing or delaying change. Policies and regulations which affected firms complain will damage them can turn out to incentivise innovation once implemented (Combes and Zenghelis 2014). For example, EU fuel efficiency targets for cars helped induce technological improvements which have improved the global competitiveness of European cars. In 2009 the EU introduced a fleet average target of 130 g/km by 2015. This was widely opposed by the motor industry, but it was met two years early. In the US, by contrast, car- and consumer-industry pressures kept gasoline taxation low such that improvements in fuel efficiency have been slower. As a consequence, the US car industry was much less prepared for higher oil prices and the global financial crisis, an important but largely unheralded factor in the bankruptcies of Chrysler and General Motors in 2009 (Bassi and Zenghelis 2014).

Perhaps the single most important feature of climate policy is consistency. Switching to lower-carbon forms of production requires investment in heavily regulated markets; but investment and finance requires confidence on the part of businesses and investors that the policy framework will be implemented and sustained (Romani et al. 2011). There is now considerable evidence that environmental policy uncertainty is associated with negative effects at both firm level, in terms of lower investment and hiring, and country level in terms of lost GDP and unemployment (Baker et al. 2012). Maintaining credible and consistent policy signals over time maximises the cost effectiveness of decarbonisation.

Credibly steering expectations is key to a cost-effective transition. No player wants to move early into new technologies when they are expensive, subject to expensive niche financing, and the market has yet to evolve, let alone mature. Risks are high and profitable opportunities few. But if whole markets are expected to move at scale, then technology and financing costs will be expected to fall and profits rise. Investment will breed investment and expectations will become self-fulfilling. A virtuous circle is therefore possible; but it requires policy makers to set clear goals and to hold their nerve when temporary political resistance is encountered. Changing policy too late and in response to events only increases risk and raises costs. A leading economic historian concludes,

> What matters is the state['s. . .] ability to and willingness to pursue policies of structural change. And hence, what matters is whether or not the state is in possession of sufficient political consensus and social cohesion for political elites to be able to go against powerful vested interests resisting change.
>
> (Moe 2007, p. 268)

Rapid decarbonisation also generates negative economic feedback effects which serve to slow down adjustment. Lower demand for fossil fuels reduces the price, making burning these fuels more attractive in countries which have not invested in alternatives. The knowledge that fossil fuels may not be burnt also provides incentives to owners of reserves to pump as much out and sell it as quickly as they can, before the stocks become stranded as policies tighten and alternative technologies become competitive (the so-called green paradox – Sinn 2008). There is the further risk that the kind of normative interventions outlined in the previous section might stigmatise fossil fuels and alienate some of the constituencies (e.g. workers, unions, communities in fossil fuel–dependent regions). These groups will need to be brought 'onside' in order to deliver an effective and just transition away from fossil fuels.

A current example of the difficulty in overcoming such lock-in is the challenge of developing electric vehicle infrastructure (Eberle and Von Helmolt 2010). For electric vehicle infrastructure to become established, the incentives to conduct research and development on electric cars must increase substantially relative to fuel cell or combustion engine vehicles. Since the Industrial Revolution, firms have been routinely exploiting path dependence in technology adoption and network effects in order to diffuse their innovations and create new markets (Bessen 2014). For instance, realising that fossil-driven networks are hard to dislodge, in June 2014 Tesla Motors announced they would make their electric vehicle patents public. Toyota followed. Urban development provides another example of how feedback loops can interact. For example, dense urban development based on public transport will breed political support for pedestrianisation, congestion charging, cycle lanes, and investment in public transport.

9. Institutions make the difference

Adaptable institutions can ease a shift in economic activity in a country following the onset of a global transformation by applying necessary changes to regulatory frameworks and the rule of law and provision of sound competition policy. The World Bank defines institutions as "the mechanisms to manage resource rents, administer social services, and regulate economic production" (Gill et al. 2014, p. 9) and identifies that the strengths or weaknesses of these mechanisms are crucial for long-term economic performance. This is because high-quality institutions are crucial for making the right decisions over the quantity and mix of assets in which the economy invests. Indeed, institutions themselves can be thought of as assets: their development requires policy makers to devote time and monetary resources to ensure that these rules and mechanisms exist and are adhered to, but with the pay-off from this effort primarily seen in the future. The UN's Sustainable Development Goals recognise the role of strong institutions in countries across the world, calling for 'effective, accountable and inclusive institutions at all levels' by 2030 (United Nations 2015).

Strong institutions can help to overcome opposition to structural change. Vested interests are less likely to emerge and block structural change when competition between firms and technologies is promoted. For instance, Crafts (2012) argues that England only lost its economic and technological leadership when it failed to enforce its competition policies, leading to the formation of cartels and low rates of competition. Another example is gas market liberalisation. While the advent of shale gas in the US, a highly disruptive energy technology, can be attributed to a number of factors, it is notable that in the last decades of the 20th century, the US actively regulated and promoted competition in a market that is often character-ised by the existence of natural monopolies. This led to a wide variety of smaller and larger companies and competitive markets. By contrast, in the EU, despite regulatory rules by the European Commission, the gas sector is dominated by large and integrated 'national champions' with wide political influence.

10. Inertia or tipping point – what next for the low-carbon economy?

Recent decades have witnessed much inertia and resistance to the transition to a low-carbon economy, along familiar historical lines. But a pertinent question is whether the global economy is about to reach or already has reached a tipping point. The costs of key low-carbon technologies have been falling sharply. Mean-while, the impact of policy action on the behaviour of producers and consumers is likely to grow, with incentives to develop and scale up low-carbon technologies increasing. As the United Nations Framework Convention on Climate Change (UNFCCC) negotiations are advancing, climate policies are being enacted at an accelerating pace. Forty countries and 24 sub-national regions covering 13% of global GHG emissions have adopted or are planning to adopt carbon pricing (World Bank 2016). In the 2016 Global Climate Legislation Study, 850 pieces of national legislation relevant for climate change were analysed across 99 coun-tries (both developing and developed) which, taken together, account for 93% of global emissions. According to the study, the number of climate laws has approxi-mately doubled every four to five years: there were 50 in 1997 (at the time of the Kyoto agreement) and 400 in 2009 (at the time of the Copenhagen Accord) and more than 800 in 2016 (Nachmany et al. 2015).

This includes action by some of the largest economies. For example, China embraced high-technology, low-carbon growth in its outline for the 12th five-year plan which sets strong targets, identifying seven 'Magic Growth sectors' of which three are low-carbon industries: clean energy, energy efficiency, and clean-energy vehicles. Germany, Europe's leading economy, is set on a path to zero net carbon by mid-century. Global cities are actively adopting decarbonisation plans of their own, through organisations such as the C40. Norway's Sovereign Wealth Fund has recently declared its intention to entirely divest coal, while divestment of US coal also gathers pace (Grunwald 2015). Share prices of heavily fossil fuel–dependent sectors have lagged the S&P500 average, while sustainable companies have outperformed their peers by 9.1% over the past four years (New Climate Economy 2015). The evidence suggests the prospect of a rapidly propagating tip-ping set to a low-carbon economy cannot be dismissed, and those that place their bets on a linear and steady transformation or no transformation at all potentially stand to lose.

11. Managing country risks and opportunities

A low-carbon transition puts the business models of different countries, sectors, and regions at risk and threatens the value they generate as new technologies and networks undercut incumbents. Across the globe, primary energy exporters are concerned that their major export markets will curb consumption of carbon-based fuels. Other countries with carbon-intensive assets in energy generation and industry worry that revenues of these sectors may suffer if importers decide to impose some border tax adjustments related to the carbon content of manufacturing products. There is the prospect of a permanent loss of demand for fossil fuels or carbon-intensive goods and services. This can have an impact at the national level. It can lead to a loss of production and fiscal challenges as existing spending programs are increasingly difficult to finance and require a rapid reorganisation of physical and human capital. The future of climate policies and disruptive technology and social transformations is therefore characterised by deep uncertainty.

Coal is already undergoing substantial transition, while the low-carbon transition has the potential to put intense pressure on oil and gas markets. The IEA expects oil demand to contract by 21% in 2040 relative to current levels in the 450 scenario but gas demand to increase by 28% (International Energy Agency 2016), but a more rapid transition cannot be ruled out. Refineries, steel, cement, chemicals, and other high-carbon sectors are also at risk if they do not adjust their business models.

Firms that are fixed in their processes and seek to repeat a former recipe for success that no longer works are less likely to endure (Van Rooij 2014). For example, the brewing industry in Britain experienced a rapid boom in the last 20 years of the 19th century. Companies boosted by new developments in stock markets raised large amounts of capital and invested heavily in expected future revenue associated with continued rising demand. However, many companies failed to anticipate the slow-down in demand at the turn of the century and the emergence of the temperance movement as a reaction against the social impacts of this earlier growth, which led to a decline in consumption. Many companies, heavily indebted, went bankrupt only a couple of decades after a period of record growth (Acheson et al. 2016).

The ability to anticipate changes in market dynamics and adapt to the new circumstances is critical. European luxury industries, such as fashion and watch-makers, faced major contractions in the 1970s but instead underwent dramatic structural transformations which enabled them to enter the Japanese markets in the 1980s and 1990s and then Chinese markets from the beginning of the 21st century (Donzé and Fujioka 2015). Similarly, recent experiences in the paper and pulp industry reflect the influence of corporate governance and long-term strategies in its ability to transform, particularly related to adapting production to new social and environmental demands. While the US paper and pulp companies were technologically locked in, Swedish firms took a more proactive approach to environmental research and development (R&D) and collaborative relationship with national policy makers associated with developing integrated abatement technology. Today, Swedish firms are technological leaders in the industry (Bergquist and Söderholm 2015). The ability to change and transform is a typical feature of the world's longest-surviving companies (Napolitano et al. 2015).

As with all structural transformations, the implications from any transition to a low-carbon future are impossible to fully predict. Fundamental uncertainties persist in relation to the speed of the transition, the technologies that will emerge, which countries are best able to harness those technologies, and how effectively any declining industries can be managed. Nonetheless, it is possible to identify characteristics that would make some countries more vulnerable to the challenges of the global low-carbon transition than others.

One way to do this is to look at countries' exposure and resilience to these shocks. *Exposure* indicates the share of the current activities of a country's economy that might be threatened by external climate policy or technology shocks. It represents the likely direct impact associated with low-carbon transition. A second criterion is *resilience/flexibility*. This captures how well positioned an economy is to respond to the threats posed by external climate policy and technology shocks. It describes its capacity to adjust to the risks and challenges associated with structural transformation. A country may be able to avert the potential negative impacts of structural change and realise the potential upsides if it is well positioned to adapt its economy in response to that shock.

The two are linked. Countries with a diverse structure to their economy dependent on a variety of sectors, together with a well-balanced and developed economic asset portfolio, tend to be better able to adapt to a new state of the world by generating new productive knowledge. This productive knowledge expresses itself in innovation and new capabilities to produce and export goods and services. A country will be able to re-allocate factor resources and may discover new comparative advantages, enabling further economic growth and development. Within the asset portfolio, a number of key elements have a particularly strong influence on the capacity of an economy to develop in accordance with its comparative advantage – and, as such, its economic resilience (Lin 2012) – such as macroeconomic stability without external account problems, fiscal deficits, debt burdens, and financial fragility accumulate (IMF 2015). Countries must provide a set of appropriate conditions for technology transfer so that they can continuously upgrade their industry–technology structure and be open to international trade.

Economic diversification and flexibility will work in the interests of making any country resilient to change. However, climate change brings an additional layer of challenges to carbon-intensive countries, heavily dependent on the exports of fossil fuels and carbon-intensive goods and services. In many cases, they have faced challenges of using the resource rents smartly to diversify their products and exports. International efforts to reduce greenhouse gas emissions, amplified by disruptive technological changes, can trigger significant shifts in demand for fossil fuels and carbon-intensive commodities facilitating deep economic transformations. Unlike many cyclical economic shocks, such low-carbon transition impacts may be large scale, structural, and permanent.

The World Bank (Peszko et al. forthcoming) will use these criteria to identify the most vulnerable countries and suggest policies. A number of countries such as Venezuela, Russia, and Iran remain very vulnerable by these criteria. These countries may face a loss of production and export revenues, leading to fiscal challenges with access to external finance constrained. As a consequence, domestic poverty and inequality may increase, as the rich will be better able to adapt to new shocks, for example by transferring their accumulated wealth abroad. In addition, such countries may be challenged by political turmoil, conflicts, and migration, which will generate international contagion effects.

The clear and unambiguous lesson from history is that there always has been and will continue to be change. Indeed, the world economy appears to follow the dynamics of creative destruction that Joseph Schumpeter proposed (Klimek et al. 2012). The ability to change and transform is a typical feature of long-surviving firms (Napolitano et al. 2015). Conversely, companies that are fixed in their processes and try to repeat former recipes for success are less likely to endure (Van Rooij 2014). Critical is the ability to anticipate changes in market dynamics. This ability to adjust is also crucial at a regional and national level. In the late 19th century, substantial differences in their per-capita income existed between the states in the US, but, by the late 20th century, they had largely vanished. The ability to catch up with leading states was based on the ability to transform the structure of the economy (Caselli and Coleman 2001). Ultimately, economies manage to grow and develop by upgrading the products they produce and export. "It is quite difficult for production to shift to [radically different] products . . . and therefore policies to promote large jumps are more challenging. Yet it is precisely these long jumps that generate subsequent structural transformation, convergence, and growth" (Hidalgo et al. 2007, p. 487).

Transformations will occur in all sectors and industries, including revolutions in the energy systems (Fouquet 2008). For policy makers, the task is to identify the likely direction and nature of changes and align policies with them (or at least not in opposition to them). Ultimately, declining demand for a resource implies that all the producers and suppliers are competing for a shrinking market. Prices will fall, which will help keep some of the buoyancy in the demand, but wherever possible, consumers will be shifting to ever-cheaper renewable energy sources. The implication of declining prices for producers and suppliers is declining revenue. Thus, only the most efficient and competitive fossil fuel opportunities will survive.

Fossil fuel–rich economies should see climate change as a blessing in disguise. Economies that have benefitted from natural resources need to see them as opportunities for transformation. Over-reliance on a single industry is a very unstable form of economic development. Climate change should act as a warning or a reminder that (i) they should not depend excessively on their fossil fuels and (ii) they should be using rents carefully to invest in the expansion of new skills, technologies, infrastructure, and industries.

12. Conclusion and policy recommendations

The transition to a low-carbon economy associated with falling technology and network costs and ambitious policy support could be rapid when it comes. This is especially true in heavily regulated policy-driven sector networks, such as energy and transport, where reinforcing mechanisms can rapidly bring about change. This enhances the risk of locking into and eventually stranding assets. Some countries are vulnerable because the structure of their economies is reliant on the extraction of high-carbon commodities or production activities requiring their use, others because of the inflexibility and vulnerability of their institutional structures.

The historical evidence suggests a general approach to economic policy that encourages flexibility is important to economic resilience and development. Open trade, good governance, competition, and well-regulated labour markets facilitate the flow of resources from declining, high-carbon sectors to growing and more productive low-carbon activities more easily. The biggest risk to economic flexibility tends to be vested interests capturing institutions and generating economic inertia. Strong and credible policies backed by public support are often prerequisites to overcoming such obstacles. This in turn requires a common understanding of the opportunities associated with a transition and a recognition of where action is in the self-interest of individuals. History suggests the following key policies are requirements for economic resilience in the face of change, lowering the risks associated with asset stranding:

1 **Openness to international markets makes a country more sensitive to global transformational change through export sensitivity to shifts in demand for its products and services.** However, it also facilitates structural economic change through the diffusion of technology embedded in imports. Despite being politically contentious, this ultimately renders a country's industry more competitive. Increased trade in accordance with an economy's comparative advantage is therefore conducive to growth, development, and poverty reduction. However, as many countries still have distortive policies in place, trade liberalisation often needs to be managed carefully to avoid adverse effects on certain actors in the economy.

2 **Policies to promote both the quantity and quality of human capital are strongly linked to economic growth and development.** Education is a core component of a human resource development strategy, but it also encompasses policies for promoting skill formation and retraining across age groups. Flexible institutions allow the government and the private sector to work closely together to anticipate or respond to the skills needs in the labour market.

3 **Productive, low-carbon infrastructure is key to economic resilience.** Poor infrastructure including roads, ports, and utilities can be a major impediment to business success, while efficient infrastructure which is resilient to the low-carbon transition can facilitate a business-led transition to new economic activity. Thinking ahead and locking into future-proof networks will allow an economy room to best manage a transition and limit the risk of asset stranding.

4 **Financial deepening is a key lubricant of any investment-led transition.** Previous empirical studies point to a causal relationship between financial deepening and economic growth. Lack of access to finance is a key constraint to capital accumulation, which is essential for building up new industries in response to shocks.

5   **Recognising and addressing distributional issues is crucial for political and economic traction.** Structural change has adverse effects on some industries, workers, and communities – notably those in high-carbon sectors such as coal, but also in production sectors such as steel, cement, and chemicals, which will need heavy investment to move towards lower-carbon production activities. Transitional support can enable investment through the reskilling and redeployment of labour to new sectors helping smooth the transformation process, both economically and politically.[19]

6   **Successful climate policy making requires a willingness to take on entrenched interests.** There is a well-established asymmetry in political economy which favours incumbents. Incumbents often claim, in particular, that stronger climate policy will put them at a competitive disadvantage relative to those in other countries, but the evidence in most cases does not support these fears. Policy makers should largely resist giving in to incumbent lobbies and spell out clearly the net costs and benefits to society.

7   **Policy must be believable and credible to lower risk premiums on low-carbon investment**. As noted, policy can modify or accelerate prevalent self-reinforcing feedback mechanisms and change expectations which drive transformation. Climate policy making is in this sense much to do with the creation and management of economic expectations through clear leadership. The greater the belief among economic actors that the world is shifting towards a low-carbon trajectory, the more likely it is to happen – and the more cost effective it will be. Anticipated returns to a business contemplating investment in, say, renewables or energy efficiency will depend on its expectations about how others are going to behave. If few others are expected to invest likewise, the markets will be smaller, the technologies more expensive, and the cost of capital higher.

8   **Support of innovation will be vital to maximise future economic returns.** The lesson for policy makers and economists here is an important one. The direction of innovation is not pre-ordained, and the challenge of shifting the fossil fuel-based infrastructure of present production and consumption to low-carbon forms will require strong government direction. In many cases this will need to overcome early high costs, which are likely to breed political resistance. But if a tipping point in investment and policy can be reached, feedback loops and network effects may kick in and accelerate the process of change, with positive spill-overs to the rest of the economy. The long-run costs may therefore be far less than some anticipate, and indeed negative. Learning the lessons from history and managing the transition could accelerate growth, boost profits, and enhance well-being, leaving the world wealthier and more resilient than ever before.

Notes

1   The views expressed are purely those of the author and may not in any circumstances be regarded as stating an official position of the European Commission.

2　Carus-Wilson, E. M. and Coleman, D. C. 1963. *England's Export Trade, 1275–1547.* Oxford: Oxford University Press.

3　Carus-Wilson, E. M. and Coleman, D. C. 1963. *England's Export Trade, 1275–1547.* Oxford: Oxford University Press.

4　Data is from Fouquet and Broadberry (2015). The original data sources are England: Broadberry et al. (2011, 2015); Holland: van Zanden and van Leeuwen (2012); Italy: Malanima (2011); Spain: Alvarez-Nogal and Prados de la Escosura (2013); Schön and Krantz (2012); Palma and Reis (2014).

5　See also Gylfason (2001).

6　See Badia-Miró and Ducoing (2015), Rubio-Varas (2015) and van der Eng (2015).

7　A useful account of some of the major transformations required can be found in Global Commission on the Economy and Climate. 2014. *Better Growth, Better Climate.* New Climate Economy. See also: *World Energy Outlook Special Report 2015: Energy and Climate Change.* International Energy Agency.

8　See, for example, Bloomberg New Energy Finance (BNEF). 2011. Onshore Wind Energy to Reach Parity With Fossil-Fuel Electricity by 2016. *Press Release,* November 10. [pdf] London: BNEF. Available at: www.bnef.com/Downloads/pressreleases/172/pdffile/ or European Photovoltaic Industry Association (EPIA). 2011. *Solar Photovoltaics Competing in the Energy Sector – On the Road to Competitiveness.* [pdf]. Brussels: EPIA. Available at: www.epia.org/index.php?eID=tx_nawsecuredl&u=0&file=fileadmin/ EPIA_docs/publications/epia/Competing_Full_Report.pdf&t=1348056379&hash=e4 1a327fa13247bb3125bb2e79e41389

9　Seminal work includes Romer 1990; Aghion and Howitt 2009; Solow 1994; Krugman 1991; Matsuyama 1991.

10　See *U.S.-China Joint Announcement on Climate Change.* 2014. The White House, Office of the Press Secretary https://obamawhitehouse.archives.gov/the-press-office/ 2014/11/11/us-china-joint-announcement-climate-change

11　See Smulders 2005 and Popp 2002 which provides some evidence that these returns may be diminishing

12　At its most general, a norm can be defined as *a standard of behaviour expected of an agent in a particular situation*; see Finnemore, Martha and Sikkink, Kathryn. 1998. International Norm Dynamics and Political Change. *International Organization,* 52(4), 887–917.

13　See Carbon Tracker Initiative 2011, Griffin et al. 2015 and McGlade and Ekins 2015.

14　See Bradshaw 2015; Denniss 2015 and Hodges et al. 2016.

15　Accounts include Ansar, Atif et al. 2013; Apfel 2015; Ayling and Gunningham 2015; Grady-Benson and Sarathy 2015; Kiyar and Wittneben 2015; and Tollefson 2015.

16　An exception was made for so-called ultra super critical plants, but the OECD ban was estimated by the Obama administration to cover about 85% of coal power plants; see Sink, Justin and Nussbaum, Alex. 2015. In Coal Setback, Rich Nations Agree to End Export Credits. *Bloomberg,* November 18. Available at: www.bloomberg. com/news/articles/2015-11-18/in-latest-blow-to-coal-rich-nations-agree-to-end-export-credits.

17　For a discussion on "policy feedbacks" see Jordan et al. 2014; Lockwood 2013; Patashnik 2008; Pierson 1993 and Urpelainen 2013.

18　See Hippe 2015, Baten and Hippe 2017 and also Galor et al. 2009.

19　The concept of a 'just transition' has been used to promote policies designed to make decarbonisation more equitable for sectors and communities adversely affected.

References

Acemoglu, D., Aghion, P., Bursztyn, L. and Hemous, D. 2012. The Environment and Directed Technical Change. *American Economic Review,* 102(1), 131–166.

Acemoglu, D., Johnson, S. and Robinson, J. 2002. Reversal of Fortune: Geography and Institutions in the Making of the Modern World Income Distribution. *Quarterly Journal of Economics*, 117, 1231–1294.

Acemoglu, D. and Robinson, J. 2012. *Why Nations Fail? The Origins of Power, Prosperity and Poverty*. New York: Crown Business.

Acheson, G., Coyle, C. and Turner, J. D. 2016. Happy Hour Followed by Hangover: Financing the UK Brewery Industry, 1880–1913. *Business History*, 58(5), Special Issue: Beer, Brewing, and Business History, 725–751.

Adamopoulos, T. 2008. Land Inequality and the Transition to Modern Growth. *Review of Economic Dynamics*, 11(2), 257–282.

Aghion, P., Boulanger, J. and Cohen, E. 2011. Rethinking Industrial Policy. *Breugel Policy Brief* 04, June.

Aghion, P., Hepburn, C., Teytelboym, A. and Zenghelis, D. 2014. *Path Dependence, Innovation and the Economics of Climate Change*. Available at: http://2014.newclimateecon omy.report/wp-content/uploads/2014/11/Path-dependence-and-econ-of-change.pdf.

Aghion, P. and Howitt, P. 2009. *The Economics of Growth*. Cambridge, MA: Massachusetts Institute of Technology (MIT) Press. Available at: http://discovery.ucl.ac.uk/17829/

Allen, R. C. 2009. *The British Industrial Revolution in Global Perspective*. Cambridge: Cambridge University Press.

Alvarez-Nogal, C. and Prados de la Escosura, L. 2013. The Rise and Fall of Spain (1270–1850). *Economic History Review*, 66(1), 1–37.

Ansar, A., Caldecott, B. and Tilbury, J. 2013. Stranded Assets and the Fossil Fuel Divestment Campaign: What Does Divestment Mean for the Valuation of Fossil Fuel Assets? *Smith School of Enterprise and the Environment, University of Oxford*.

Apfel, D. C. 2015. Exploring Divestment as a Strategy for Change: An Evaluation of the History, Success, and Challenges of Fossil Fuel Divestment. *Social Research*, 82(4), 913–1050.

Auty, R. M. 2001. *Resource Abundance and Economic Development*. Oxford: Oxford University Press.

Ayling, J. and Gunningham, N. 2015. Non-State Governance and Climate Policy: The Fossil Fuel Divestment Movement. *Climate Policy*, 17, 131–149. doi: 10.1080/14693062. 2015.1094729

Badia-Miró, M. and Ducoing, C. A. 2015. Long-Run Development in Chile and Natural Resource Curse: Linkages, Policy and Growth, 1850–1950. In Badia-Miró, M., Willebald, H. and Pinilla, V. (eds.), *Natural Resources and Economic Development: Learning From History*. New York: Routledge, pp. 204–225.

Badia-Miró, M., Willebald, H. and Pinilla, V. (eds.). 2015. *Natural Resources and Economic Development: Learning From History*. New York: Routledge.

Bagwell, P. S. 1974. *The Transport Revolution From 1770*. London: B.T. Batsford, pp. 157–163.

Baker, S. R., Bloom, N. and Davis, S. J. 2012. Measuring Economic Policy Uncertainty. *Working Paper*. See also Etsy, D. C. and Porter, M. E. 2005. *National Environmental Performance: An Empirical Analysis of Policy Results and Determinants*. Cambridge: Cambridge University Press.

Baldwin, R. E. and Robert-Nicoud, F. 2007. Entry and Asymmetric Lobbying: Why Governments Pick Losers. *London School of Economics and Political Science Political Science and Political Economy Working Paper No. 3*. Available at: www.lse.ac.uk/gov ernment/research/resgroups/pspe/pdf/pspe_wp3_07.pdf

Bank of England. 2015. *Breaking the Tragedy of the Horizon – Climate Change and Financial Stability.* Speech by Mark Carney, September 29, 2015 at Lloyds of London. www.bankofengland.co.uk/publications/Pages/speeches/2015/844.aspx

Barbier, E. B. 2005. Natural Resource-Based Economic Development in History. *World Economics*, 6(3), 103–152.

Barham, B. and Coomes, O. 1994. Wild Rubber: Industrial Organisation and the Microeconomics of Extraction During the Amazon Rubber Boom (1860–1920). *Journal of Latin American Studies*, 26(1), 37–72.

Bassi, S. and Zenghelis, D. 2014. Burden or Opportunity? How UK Emissions Reductions Policies Affect the Competitiveness of Businesses. *Policy Paper*, Centre for Climate Change Economics and Policy and Grantham Research Institute on Climate Change and the Environment. Available at: www.lse.ac.uk/GranthamInstitute/publication/burden-or-opportunity-how-uk-emissions-reductions-policies-affect-the-competitiveness-of-businesses/

Baten, J. and Hippe, R. 2017. Geography, Land Inequality and Regional Numeracy in Europe in Historical Perspective. *Journal of Economic Growth*, 2017, 23(1), 79–109.

Bell, R. G., Ziegler, M. S., Blechman, B., Finlay, B. and Ziegler, M. S. 2012. *Building International Climate Cooperation: Lessons From the Weapons and Trade Regimes for Achieving International Climate Goals.* Washington, DC: World Resources Institute.

Bergquist, A. and Söderholm, K. 2015. Transition to Greener Pulp: Regulation, Industry Responses and Path Dependency. *Business History*, 57(6), 862–884.

Bértola, L. 2015. Welfare States and Development Patterns in Latin America. In Badia-Miró, M., Willebald, H. and Pinilla, V. (eds.), *Natural Resources and Economic Development: Learning From History*. New York: Routledge, pp. 140–159.

Bessen, J. 2014. History Backs Up Tesla's Patent Sharing. *Harvard Business Review Blog*, June 13. [online] Available at: http://blogs.hbr.org/2014/06/history-backsup-teslas-patent-sharing/

Bradshaw, E. A. 2015. Blockadia Rising: Rowdy Greens, Direct Action and the Keystone XL Pipeline. *Critical Criminology*, 23, 433–448. http://dx.doi.org/10.1007/s10612-015-9289-0

Broadberry, S. N., Campbell, B., Klein, A., Overton, M. and van Leeuwen, B. 2011. *British Economic Growth, 1270–1870: An Output-Based Approach.* Available at: http://www2.lse.ac.uk/economicHistory/whosWho/profiles/sbroadberry.aspx.

Broadberry, S. N., Campbell, B., Klein, A., Overton, M. and van Leeuwen, B. 2015. *British Economic Growth, 1270–1870.* Cambridge: Cambridge University Press.

Broadberry, S. N. and Gupta, B. 2009. Lancashire, India, and Shifting Competitive Advantage in Cotton Textiles, 1700–1850: The Neglected Role of Factor Prices. *Economic History Review*, 62(2), 279–305.

Carbon Tracker Initiative. 2011. *Unburnable Carbon – Are the World's Financial Markets Carrying a Carbon Bubble?* Available at: http://www.carbontracker.org/wpcontent/uploads/downloads/2011/07/Unburnable-Carbon-Full-rev2.pdf.

Carrington, D. 2016. Norway Confirms $900bn Sovereign Wealth Fund's Major Coal Divestment. *The Guardian*, June 5. Available at: www.theguardian.com/environment/2015/jun/05/norways-pension-fund-to-divest-8bn-from-coal-a-new-analysis-shows.

Carus-Wilson, E. M. 1950. Trends in the Export of English Woollens in the Fourteenth Century. *Economic History Review*, 3(2), 162–179, 164.

Carus-Wilson, E. M. and Coleman, D. C. 1963. *England's Export Trade, 1275–1547.* Oxford: Oxford University Press.

Caselli, F. and Coleman, W. J. 2001. Cross-Country Technology Diffusion: The Case of Computers. *American Economic Review*, 91(2), 328–335.

Chang, H. J. 2002. *Kicking Away the Ladder*. London: Anthem Press, p. 23.

Church, R. 1986. *The History of the British Coal Industry. Vol. 3. 1830–1913*. Oxford: Clarendon Press.

Collier, P. and Venables, A. J. 2015. Closing Coal: Economic and Moral Incentives. *Oxford Review of Economic Policy*, 30(3), 492–512.

Combes, B. and Zenghelis, D. 2014. *Tough Love*. London: MacroPlus Comment, Llewellyn Consulting.

Crafts, N. 2012. British Relative Economic Decline Revisited: The Role of Competition. *Explorations in Economic History*, 49(1), 17–29.

Dai, X. 2010. Global Regime and National Change. *Climate Policy*, 10(6), 622–637. Available at: www.tandfonline.com/doi/abs/10.3763/cpol.2010.0146 [Accessed October 27, 2014].

Dechezleprêtre, A., Martin, R. and Mohnen, M. 2013. Knowledge Spillovers From Clean and Dirty Technologies: A Patent Citation Analysis. *Grantham Research Institute on Climate Change and the Environment Working Paper No. 135*, September.

DeGusta, M. 2012. Are Smart Phones Spreading Faster than Any Technology in Human History? *MIT Technology Review*, May 9. Available at: www.technologyreview.com/s/427787/are-smart-phones-spreading-faster-than-any-technology-in-human-history/

Denniss, R. 2015. When You're in a Hole – Stop Digging! The Economic Case for a Moratorium on New Coal Mines. *Discussion Paper*. The Australia Institute.

Dittmar, J. E. 2011. Information Technology and Economic Change: The Impact of the Printing Press. *The Quarterly Journal of Economics*, 126(3), 1133–1172.

Donzé, P-Y. and Fujioka, R. 2015. European Luxury Big Business and Emerging Asian Markets, 1960–2010. *Business History*, 57(6), 822–840.

Drabble, J. H. 2000. *An Economic History of Malaysia, c.1800–1990: The Transition to Modern Economic Growth*. London: Macmillan.

Draper, N. 2007. 'Possessing Slaves': Ownership, Compensation and Metropolitan Society in Britain at the time of Emancipation 1834–40. *History Workshop Journal*, 64 (1): 74–102.

Dyer, C. 2002. *Making a Living in the Middle Ages: The People of Britain 850–1520*. London: Yale University Press, pp. 7–11.

Eberle, U. and Von Helmolt, R. 2010. Sustainable Transportation Based on Electric Vehicle Concepts: A Brief Overview. *Energy and Environmental Science*, 3, 689–699.

Emory University. 2013. *Slave Voyages*. Available at: www.slavevoyages.org/assessment/estimates

Fenske, J. and Kala, N. 2014. *1807: Economic Shocks, Conflict and the Slave Trade* (No. 2014–02). Centre for the Study of African Economies, University of Oxford.

Finnemore, M. and Sikkink, K. 1998. International Norm Dynamics and Political Change. *International Organization*, 52(4), 887–917.

Fouquet, R. 2008. *Heat, Power and Light: Revolutions in Energy Services*. Cheltenham, UK and Northampton, MA: Edward Elgar Publications.

Fouquet, R. 2010. The Slow Search for Solutions: Lessons From Historical Energy Transitions by Sector and Service. *Energy Policy*, 38(11), 6586–6596.

Fouquet, R. and Broadberry, S. 2015. Seven Centuries of European Economic Growth and Decline. *The Journal of Economic Perspectives*, 29(4), 227–244.

Galor, O., Moav, O. and Vollrath, D. 2009. Inequality in Landownership, the Emergence of Human-Capital Promoting Institutions, and the Great Divergence. *The Review of Economic Studies*, 76(1), 143–179.

Gelb, A. 2010. *Economic Diversification in Resource Rich Countries*. Drawn from a Lecture at a High-Level Seminar on Natural Resources, Finance and Development: Confronting Old and New Challenges, Organised by the Central Bank of Algeria and the IMF Institute in Algiers, November 4–5, pp. 1–23.

Gill, I. S., Izvorski, I., van Eeghen, W. and De Rosa, D. 2014. *Diversified Development: Making the Most of Natural Resources in Eurasia*. Washington, DC: World Bank, February, pp. 1–42. http://dx.doi.org/10.1596/978-1-4648-0119-8_ov.

Grady-Benson, J. and Sarathy, B. 2015. Fossil Fuel Divestment in US Higher Education: Student-Led Organising for Climate Justice. *Local Environment*, 21(6), 661–681.

Green, R. F. Forthcoming. Anti-Fossil Fuel Norms. *Working Paper Grantham Research Institute on Climate and the Environment*, London School of Economics and Political Science.

Griffin, P. A., Jaffe, A. M., David, H. L. and Dominguez-Faus, R. 2015. Science and the Stock Market: Investors' Recognition of Unburnable Carbon. *Energy Economics*, 52, 1–12.

Grunwald, M. 2015. Inside the War on Coal. *Politico.com*. Available at: www.politico.com/agenda/story/2015/05/inside-war-on-coal-000002?utm_term=0_876aab4fd7-d7a965efd7-303449629&utm_content=bufferbaeab&utm_medium=social&utm_source=facebook.com&utm_campaign=buffer

Gylfason, T. 2001. Natural Resources, Education, and Economic Development. *European Economic Review*, Elsevier, 45(4–6), 847–859.

Hatcher, J. 1993. *The History of the British Coal Industry*. Volume I. Oxford: Clarendon Press. *The Journal of Economic Perspectives*, 29(4), 227–244.

Hidalgo, C. A., Klinger, B., Barabási, A-L. and Hausmann, R. 2007. The Product Space Conditions the Development of Nations. *Science*, 317(5837), 482–487.

Hillbom, E. 2015. Botswana: Caught in a Natural Resource Trap. In Badia-Miró, M., Willebald, H. and Pinilla, V. (eds.), *Natural Resources and Economic Development: Learning From History*. New York: Routledge, pp. 77–99.

Hippe, R. 2015. Why Did the Knowledge Transition Occur in the West and Not the East? ICT and the Role of Governments in Europe, East Asia and the Muslim World. *Economics and Business Review*, 1, 9–33.

Hodges, H. E. and Stocking, G. 2016. A Pipeline of Tweets: Environmental Movements' Use of Twitter in Response to the Keystone XL Pipeline. *Environmental Politics*, 25(2), 223–247.

IMF. 2015. *Topic 5: Financial Deepening for Macroeconomic Stability and Sustained Growth*. Available at: www.imf.org/external/np/res/dfidimf/topic5.htm

International Energy Agency. 2016. *World Energy Outlook*. Paris: IEA.

IPCC. 2014. Summary for Policymakers. In *Climate Change 2014: Impacts, Adaptation, and Vulnerability. Part A: Global and Sectoral Aspects. Contribution of Working Group II to the Fifth Assessment Report of the Intergovernmental Panel on Climate Change*. Available at: www.ipcc.ch/report/ar5/wg2/.

Jackman, W. T. 1960. *The Development of Transportation in Modern England*. London: Frank Cass, p. 728.

Jacobs, M. and Mazzucato, M. 2016. *Rethinking Capitalism: Economics and Policy for Sustainable and Inclusive Growth*. London: Wiley-Blackwell. ISBN: 978-1-119-12095-7. Available at: http://eu.wiley.com/WileyCDA/WileyTitle/productCd-1119120950.html

Jordan, A. and Matt, E. 2014. Designing Policies That Intentionally Stick: Policy Feedback in a Changing Climate. *Policy Sciences*, 47(3), 227–247.

King, P. 2005. The Production and Consumption of Bar Iron in Early Modern England and Wales. *Economic History Review*, 58(1), 1–33.

King, P. 2011. The Choice of Fuel in the Eighteenth-Century Iron Industry: The Coalbrook-dale Accounts Reconsidered. *Economic History Review*, 64(1), 132–146, 139.

Kiyar, D. and Wittneben, B. B. F. 2015. Carbon as Investment Risk – the Influence of Fossil Fuel Divestment on Decision Making at Germany's Main Power Providers. *Energies*, 8(9), 9620–9639.

Klimek, P., Hausmann, R. and Thurner, S. 2012. Empirical Confirmation of Creative Destruction from World Trade Data. *Harvard Kennedy School Faculty Research Working Paper Series and CID Working Papers* (RWP12-022 and 238), May.

Krugman, P. 1991. History Versus Expectations. *Quarterly Journal of Economics*, 106(2), 651–667.

Leff, N. H. 1997. The Economic History of Brazil, 1822–1914. In Haber, F. (ed.), *Why Latin America Fell Behind?* Stanford: Stanford University Press.

Levinson, M. 2006. Container Shipping and the Decline of New York, 1955–1975. *Business History Review*, 80, 49–80.

Lin, J. Y. 2012. *New Structural Economics: A Framework for Rethinking Development*. Washington, DC: The World Bank.

Lockwood, M. 2013. The Political Sustainability of Climate Policy: The Case of the UK Climate Change Act. *Global Environmental Change*, 23(5), 1339–1348.

Lovejoy, P. E. and Richardson, D. 1995. British Abolition and Its Impact on Slave Prices Along the Atlantic Coast of Africa, 1783–1850. *The Journal of Economic History*, 55(1), 98–119.

Lundahl, M. 1998. Staples Trade and Economic Development. In Lundahl, M. (ed.), *Theories of International Economics*. Boston, MA: Ashgate Publishing, pp. 45–68.

Malanima, P. 2011. The Long Decline of a Leading Economy: GDP in Central and Northern Italy, 1300–1913. *European Review of Economic History*, 15, 169–219.

Matsuyama, K. 1991. Increasing Returns, Industrialization, and Indeterminacy of Equilibrium. *Quarterly Journal of Economics*, 106(2), 617–650.

McCulloch, C. S. 2006. *The Kielder Water Scheme: The Last of Its Kind?* (PDF). University of Oxford. Available at: www.britishdams.org/2006conf/papers/Paper%2010%20Mcculloch.PDF

McGlade, C. and Ekins, P. 2015. The Geographical Distribution of Fossil Fuels Unused When Limiting Global Warming to 2 °C. *Nature*, 517(7533), 187–190. Available at: www.nature.com/doifinder/10.1038/nature14016\npapers2://publication/doi/10.1038/nature14016.

Moe, E. 2007. *Governance, Growth and Global Leadership: The Role of the State in Technological Progress, 1750–2000*. Aldershot: Ashgate.

Nachmany, M., Fankhauser, S., Davidová, J., Kingsmill, N., Landesman, T., Roppongi, H. and Townshend, T. 2015. *The 2015 Global Climate Legislation Study: A Review of Climate Change Legislation in 99 Countries: Summary for Policymakers*. Available at: www.lse.ac.uk/GranthamInstitute/wp-content/uploads/2015/05/Global_climate_legislation_study_20151.pdf and also The Global Climate Legislation Study Summary of key trends 2016 www.lse.ac.uk/GranthamInstitute/wp-content/uploads/2016/11/The-Global-Climate-Legislation-Study_2016-update.pdf

Nanterme, P. 2016. Digital Disruption Has Only Just Begun. *World Economic Forum*, January. Available at: www.weforum.org/agenda/2016/01/digital-disruption-has-only-just-begun/

Napolitano, M. R., Marino, V. and Ojala, J. 2015. In Search of an Integrated Framework of Business Longevity. *Business History*, 57(7), 955–969.

New Climate Economy. 2015. *Top 10 Signs That Momentum is Building for a New Climate Economy*. Available at: http://newclimateeconomy.net/content/top-10-signs-momentum-building-new-climate-economy

Olson, M. 1983. *The Rise and Fall of Nations*. New Haven, CT: Yale University Press.

Ostrom, E. 2000. Collective Action and the Evolution of Social Norms. *Journal of Economic Perspectives*, 14, 137–158.

Palma, N. and Reis, J. 2014. Portuguese Demography and Economic Growth, 1500–1850. Paper for *Accounting for the Great Divergence* Conference, The University of Warwick in Venice, May 22–24. Available at: http://www2.warwick.ac.uk/fac/soc/economics/research/centres/cage/events/conferences/greatdivergence14/portuguese_demography_and_economic_growth_1500-1850_-_may_19th_2014.pdf

Patashnik, E. 2008. *Reforms at Risk: What Happens after Major Policy Changes Are Enacted*. Princeton: Princeton University Press.

Peszko, G., Golub, A., van der Mensbrugghe, D., Rogers, J. A., Mukhi, N., Schopp, C., Ward, J. and Zenghelis, D. Forthcoming. *Stranded Wealth of Nations? Diversifying Assets of Carbon-Intensive Countries Under Uncertainty (Climate Change and Development)*. Washington, DC: World Bank Group Publications. ISBN-10: 1464807825, 13: 978-1464807824

Pfeiffer, A., Millar, R., Hepburn, C. and Beinhocker, E. 2016. The '2°C Capital Stock' for Electricity Generation: Committed Cumulative Carbon Emissions From the Electricity Generation Sector and the Transition to a Green Economy. *Applied Energy*. ISSN: 0306-2619. Available at: http://dx.doi.org/10.1016/j.apenergy.2016.02.093 [Accessed March 24].

Pierson, P. 1993. When Effect Becomes Cause: Policy Feedback and Policy Change. *World Politics*, 45(4), 595–628.

Popp, D. 2002. Induced Innovation and Energy Prices. *American Economic Review*, 92(1), 160–180.

Richardson, D. 1995. British Abolition and Its Impact on Slave Prices Along the Atlantic Coast of Africa, 1783–1850. *The Journal of Economic History*, 55(1), 98–119.

Romani, M., Stern, N. and Zenghelis, D. 2011. *The Basic Economics of Low-Carbon Growth in the UK*. London: Grantham Research Institute on Climate Change and the Environment and Centre for Climate Change Economics and Policy, LSE.

Romer, P. 1990. Endogenous Technological Change. *Journal of Political Economy*, 98(5), S71–S102.

Rubio-Varas, M. 2015. Oil Illusion and Delusion: Mexico and Venezuela Over the Twentieth Century. In Badia-Miró, M., Willebald, H. and Pinilla, V. (eds.), *Natural Resources and Economic Development: Learning From History*. New York: Routledge, pp. 160–183.

Sachs, J. D. and Warner, A. M. 1995. Natural Resource Abundance and Economic Growth. *NBER Working Papers 5398*, National Bureau of Economic Research.

Sachs, J. D. and Warner, A. M. 2001. The Curse of Natural Resources. *European Economic Review*, 45(4–6), 827–838.

Sanders, A. R. D. and Sandvik, P. T. 2015. Avoiding the Resource Curse? Democracy and Natural Resources in Norway Since 1900. In Badia-Miró, M., Willebald, H. and Pinilla, V. (eds.), *Natural Resources and Economic Development: Learning From History*. New York: Routledge, pp. 313–338.

Schön, L. and Krantz, O. 2012. The Swedish Economy in the Early Modern Period: Constructing Historical National Accounts 1560–2000. *European Review of Economic History*, 16, 529–549.

Schumpeter, J. A. 1942. *Socialism, Capitalism and Democracy*. New York: Harper and Brothers, p. 82.

Sink, J. and Nussbaum, A. 2015. In Coal Setback, Rich Nations Agree to End Export Credits. *Bloomberg*, November 18. Available at: www.bloomberg.com/news/articles/2015-11-18/in-latest-blow-to-coal-rich-nations-agree-to-end-export-credits.

Sinn, H-W. 2008. Public Policies against Global Warming: A Supply Side Approach. *International Tax and Public Finance*, 15(4), 360–394.

Slezak, M. 2016. Pacific Islands Nations Consider World's First Treaty to Ban Fossil Fuels. *Guardian*, July 14. Available at: www.theguardian.com/world/2016/jul/14/pacific-islands-nations-consider-worlds-first-treaty-to-ban-fossil-fuels.

Smulders, S. 2005. Endogenous Technological Change, Natural Resources and Growth. In Simpson, R. D., Toman, M. A. and Ayres, R. U. (eds.), *Scarcity and Growth Revisited: Natural Resources and the Environment in the New Millennium*. Washington, DC: Resources for the Future.

Solow, R. M. 1994. Perspectives on Growth Theory. *Journal of Economic Perspectives*, 8(1), 45–54.

Stern, N. and Zenghelis, D. 2016. *The Importance of Looking Forward to Manage Risks: Submission to the Task Force on Climate-Related Financial Disclosures*. Policy paper by the Grantham Research Institute on Climate Change and the Environment, London School of Economics, June. Available at: www.lse.ac.uk/GranthamInstitute/wp-content/uploads/2016/06/Zenghelis-and-Stern-policy-paper-June-2016.pdf

Thirsk, J. 1976. *Economic Policy and Projects: The Development of a Consumer Society in Early Modern England*. Oxford: Clarendon Press.

Tollefson, J. 2015. Reality Check for Fossil-Fuel Divestment. *Nature*, 521(7550), 16–17.

United Nations Open Working Group Proposal for Sustainable Development Goals. 2015. Available at: https://sustainabledevelopment.un.org/content/documents/1579SDGs%20Proposal.pdf

Urpelainen, J. 2013. A Model of Dynamic Climate Governance: Dream Big, Win Small. *International Environmental Agreements: Politics, Law and Economics*, 13(2), 107–125.

van der Eng, P. 2015. Mixed Blessings: Mining in Indonesia's Economy, 1870–2010. In Badia-Miró, M., Willebald, H. and Pinilla, V. (eds.), *Natural Resources and Economic Development: Learning From History*. New York: Routledge, pp. 226–247.

van der Wee, H. 2003. The Western European Woollen Industries, 1500–1750. In Jenkins, D. T. (ed.), *The Cambridge History of Western Textiles*. Cambridge: Cambridge University Press.

Van Rooij, A. 2014. Sisyphus in Business: Success, Failure and the Different Type of Failure. *Business History*, 57(2), 203–223.

van Zanden, J. L. and van Leeuwen, B. 2012. Persistent But Not Consistent: The Growth of National Income in Holland 1347–1807. *Explorations in Economic History*, 49, 119–130.

Willebald, H., Badia-Miró, M. and Pinilla, V. 2015. Introduction: Natural Resources and Economic Development – What Can We Learn From History? In Badia-Miró, M., Willebald, H. and Pinilla, V. (eds.), *Natural Resources and Economic Development: Learning From History*. New York: Routledge, pp. 1–25, 10–11.

World Bank. 2016. *State and Trends of Carbon Pricing*. Washington, DC, October. Available at: https://openknowledge.worldbank.org/bitstream/handle/10986/25160/9781464810015.pdf

World Economic Forum, 2017. *The Global Competitiveness Report 2017–2018*. Geneva: World Economic Forum.

Wright, G. and Czelusta, J. 2007. Resource-Based Growth Past and Present. In Lederman, D. and Maloney, W. F. (eds.), *Natural Resources: Neither Curse Nor Destiny*. Stanford: Stanford University Press, pp. 183–211.

Young, H. P. 2015. The Evolution of Social Norms. *Annual Review of Economics*, 7, 359–387.

3 The 'decarbonisation identity'

Stranded assets in the power generation sector

Alexander Pfeiffer

1. Net-zero emissions, human development and capital stock inertia

When, in December 2015, the gavel came down to end the 21st Conference of the Parties (COP) of the United Nations Framework Convention on Climate Change (UNFCCC), 196 parties had agreed jointly to address the global emissions of greenhouse gases (GHGs) in order to limit climate change to "well below 2°C (. . .) and pursuing efforts to limit the temperature increase to 1.5°C above pre-industrial levels" (UNFCCC 2015). The Paris Agreement is in many ways unique, not least because of its Article 4–1, in which the parties agree to "achieve a balance between anthropogenic emissions by sources and removals by sinks of greenhouse gases in the second half of this century." By acknowledging the need to balance residual emissions with the removal of CO_2 from the atmosphere, the parties acknowledged not only the need to fully decarbonise their economies in the second half of the 21st century but also the latest science in respect to CO_2 emissions and climate change.

In recent years, a growing body of literature has repeatedly emphasised that what is decisive for climate change is not the *annual* rate of emissions of long-lived climate pollutants (LLCPs), such as carbon dioxide (CO_2),[1] but rather the *cumulative* emissions of such pollutants (Allen et al. 2009; Meinshausen et al. 2009). Most LLCPs, once released into the atmosphere, will remain there for many decades or even centuries before being removed by natural processes (Archer et al. 2009; Clark et al. 2016). It is therefore the cumulative amount of these gases in the atmosphere that will have the biggest influence on the greenhouse effect that is warming our planet (Matthews et al. 2009). This means, however, that to stabilise the climate at any level, not only at 1.5 or 2°C above current temperatures but virtually any level, eventually, the emission of CO_2 and other GHGs will have to decrease to *near-* or *net-zero*. A balance between sustained emissions and removals by carbon sinks, for example oceans and biomass, must be achieved (Matthews and Caldeira 2008).

For humanity, this connection between cumulative carbon emissions and climate change constitutes a major trade-off. On the one hand, most economies around the world are built on and around the energy extracted from the burning of fossil fuels (IPCC 2014b). On the other hand, the burning of exactly these fossil fuels releases pollutants into our local environment and the atmosphere, which harms humans locally and, even more importantly, increases global temperatures, thereby posing a threat to humanity (IPCC 2014b).

While scientists may still disagree on the tolerable level of climate change, be it 1.5, 2, or even 3°C (Knutti et al. 2015), the international community has decided that efforts should be made to limit it to well below 2°C, and this decision has been confirmed with the Paris Accord. The implications are grave. To achieve the Paris goals, the global economy, which has been built around the consumption of fossil fuels, must be decarbonised in the second half of this century. For many reasons, this poses a serious and complex challenge that can be illustrated in a simplified way by the Kaya Identity in what follows (Kaya and Yokobori 1998).

$$CO_2 \text{ emissions} = Population * \frac{GDP}{Population} * \frac{Energy}{GDP} * \frac{CO_2}{Energy}$$

While the Kaya Identity certainly has its flaws, e.g. the assumption that its four parts are mutually independent, it still points towards an important issue: global population keeps growing and is expected to grow to ~10 billion individuals by mid-century (United Nations 2017). At the same time, many people still live in dire conditions and strive for economic development to lift themselves out of poverty (WBG 2016). Despite advances in poverty alleviation in recent decades, the average per-capita income in many developing parts of the world is still considerably lower than in developed nations. The necessary economic growth, however, will also increase the demand for energy by multiple times, a demand that cannot yet be met fully by means of clean, zero-carbon energy sources, such as solar or wind (see Figure 3.1).[2]

Acknowledging the technological, institutional and behavioural inertia in the global energy system (Seto et al. 2016), it is therefore likely that, despite the goal to decarbonise, the global economy will see additions to its *polluting capital stock* over the coming years (IEA 2016b) (see Figure 3.2). In the context of this chapter, the polluting capital stock denotes the aggregate of all currently operating anthropogenic sources of GHG emissions (Pfeiffer et al. 2016). Such assets often have a long lifetime. An economic lifespan of 20 to 60 years for power generators (EIA 2011; IEA 2016b), 10 to 50 years for industrial installations and 20 to 100 years for buildings is not unusual (Rozenberg et al. 2015). Airplanes that burn kerosene and ships that burn heavy bunker fuels are in service for 5 to 30 years, and even gasoline-fuelled cars are usually operated for more than 10 years before eventually being retired (Rozenberg et al. 2015). Many of these assets will still have a remaining lifetime by the time global emissions must reach net-zero. Their economic value, however, depends on their ability to operate and burn fossil fuels. If humanity is to reach its climate goals, these assets either must be retrofitted with carbon capture and storage[3] (CCS) or cease operations, thereby becoming stranded assets (Caldecott et al. 2014).

Defining stranded assets in this context is challenging: in this chapter asset stranding occurs when power plants operate below their target utilisation.

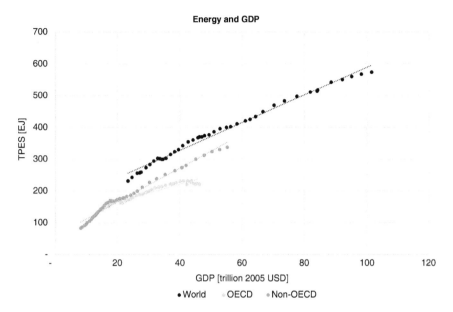

Figure 3.1 Correlation between GDP and total primary energy supply, 1971–2014

There are, however, many more factors that would influence asset stranding in this definition. Asset owners could, for example, decide to transform coal-to biomass-powered generators or retrofit generators with CCS. Both would reduce capacity of coal-fired pollution generation capital stock and hence constitutes stranding in the context of this chapter. The same applies for the decision to retire certain generators early, thereby increasing utilisation rates of the remaining generators, or to mothball capacity or change operating mode of a power plant but receive a compensation, e.g. in form of a capacity contract, for doing so. The general assumption in this chapter is, that deviating from full (expected) utilisation of a fossil fuel powered generator is not captured in the original asset value and hence essentially constitutes stranding. Mechanisms as described above can reduce or even completely offset the impact on the balance sheet and bottom line of the asset owner but do not change the general definition of asset stranding.

The decisions and investments that are made today can therefore commit humanity to many years of carbon-intensive economic activity. They affect our future ability to decarbonise our economy and achieve net-zero by the second half of this century, as well as the cost of achieving this (Unruh 2000; Erickson et al. 2015; Seto et al. 2016).

When decarbonisation, especially deep decarbonisation, overcomes carbon lock-in, *stranded carbon assets* are likely to occur (Goulder et al. 2010). According to the most common definition, an asset strands when it experiences an unanticipated or premature write-down, a devaluation or a conversion to a

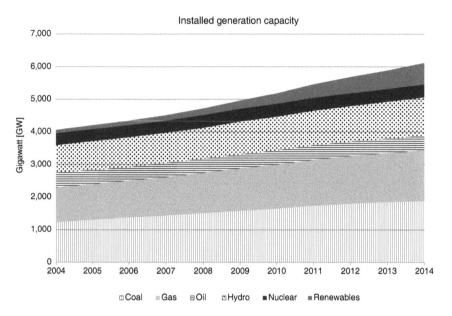

Figure 3.2 Development of global generation capacity, 2004–2014

liability (Caldecott et al. 2014). If carbon-emitting physical assets or related financial assets are affected by this form of stranding they are typically referred to as stranded carbon assets (Caldecott et al. 2015). In the narrower context of this chapter, carbon assets of the energy sector can strand when society gradually decides to stop the burning of fossil fuels in general or certain fossil fuels, for example coal, to generate energy.

This chapter introduces a new theoretical framework – the *decarbonisation identity* – to analytically describe all choices policy makers have available to avoid such asset stranding. These choices can be described as (1) protecting and enhancing remaining carbon budgets (e.g. by early and decisive action on non-CO_2 pollutants); (2) retrofitting CCS to operating capital stock; (3) making sure that additions to the capital stock are clean (non-emitting); (4) large-scale stranding of capital stock; or (5) creating additional carbon budget by net-negative-emission technologies or the conservation of natural carbon sinks (Griscom et al. 2017). Policy makers often base their policies on scenarios that are run with integrated assessment models (IAMs). Such models implicitly contain the previously described policy choices but rarely make them explicit. With the decarbonisation identity, this chapter introduces for the first time a mutually exclusive and collectively exhaustive framework that makes these choices, especially the choice to strand assets, explicit. In this context, asset stranding is said to occur when it experiences an unanticipated or premature write-down, a devaluation or even a conversion to a liability (Caldecott et al. 2013). Asset stranding can have different implications for asset owners and social planners, however (Edwards et al. 1987). For an asset owner a stranding of his investments can mean a financial loss and potentially cause him to default on his debt (Weyzig et al. 2014; Carney 2015; Battiston et al. 2017). For a policy maker, the potential scale of asset stranding has important implications in respect to the choice and feasibility of future environmental, climate and energy policies to achieve decarbonisation goals (Baldwin et al. 2016; Rozenberg et al. 2017).

The rest of this chapter is structured as follows: Section 2 introduces the theoretical framework that provides the foundation of this analysis. It contains an explanation of the importance of cumulative carbon emissions and carbon budgets for climate change (2.1), the introduction of the idea of committed cumulative emissions (2.2) and how both concepts can be combined in the decarbonisation identity (2.3). Section 3 analyzes some recent empirical findings from the power generation sector in the context of the decarbonisation identity. Section 4 discusses the framework and its implications in a wider context of policy choices (4.1), policy instruments (4.2) and a broader research agenda (4.3). Section 5 concludes the chapter.

2. A new theoretical framework

If humanity wants to stop global warming and stabilise the climate at any level, carbon emissions eventually must be reduced to near- or net-zero. The cumulative amount of LLCP emissions by the time net-zero is reached, together with the sustained rate of future emissions of short-lived climate pollutants (SLCPs), will determine the final level of climate change. Whether the world will meet its climate goals of limiting global warming to 1.5 to 2°C of warming hence depends on whether humanity stays within the carbon budgets for these climate goals. Many different reasons have been identified that could lead to an overshoot of these budgets. Some of these reasons are the lack of global cooperation (Barrett 1994), inadequate institutions (Helm 2010), the lack of a price on carbon (Carbon Pricing Leadership Coalition 2017; Klenert et al. 2017) and short-sighted voters and politicians (Levy 2014). One of the biggest obstacles in achieving these goals, however, is carbon lock-in, especially infrastructural carbon lock-in. Even if humanity stops adding assets to the polluting capital stock, the existing capital stock would probably continue to emit carbon for many years or even decades. It is possible that these committed emissions have already locked humanity in to more than 1.5 to 2°C warming and that an achievement of climate goals is only possible if either that capital stock gets retrofitted with CCS or becomes stranded or new atmospheric space, that is additional budget, is created.

This section describes the connection between carbon budgets, climate goals, SLCP emissions, committed emissions (infrastructural carbon lock-in) and negative-emission technologies. The resulting decarbonisation identity is the theoretical framework on which the analysis in this chapter is based. It describes all the distinct choices policy makers have to stay within pre-defined carbon budgets. In the following, the identity is described in general terms, applicable to all polluting capital stock, but in the remainder of this chapter it is used specifically in the context of the polluting electricity-generation capital stock and related carbon budgets. The rest of this section is structured as follows: first, the concept of a carbon budget is briefly summarised (2.1); second, the concept of committed emissions and what influences these commitments is described (2.2); and third, these two concepts are brought together in the decarbonisation identity (2.3).

2.1 Carbon budgets

In recent years CO_2 budgets have received greater attention in science, policy making and even finance. Many scientific contributions base their findings on such budgets (Rogelj et al. 2016), policy makers evaluate their policies based on whether they manage to keep cumulative emissions within these budgets (Fay et al. 2015; UNEP 2016) and financiers and investors analyse the implications of carbon budgets for their investment portfolios in fossil fuels and related infrastructure (Carney 2015).

CO_2 budgets (or carbon budgets) are inherently uncertain, however. The size of the budgets for different temperature goals, as well as the time it will take to reach or achieve them, depends on many factors that are very difficult to predict. Even staying within the 2°C (50% probability) budget of ~1,300 gigatons of carbon dioxide ($GtCO_2$) in 2005 (IPCC 2014b) will not guarantee that humanity stays below the 2°C warming it has set itself as a limit (see Table 3.1). It rather means that in scenarios that limit cumulative CO_2 emissions to this level or below there is at most a 50% probability of the global warming exceeding 2°C. That also means, however, that even if humanity stays within that budget it is as likely as not that the world's climate will warm by more than 2°C in the global average. Indeed,

Table 3.1 Remaining total carbon budgets in 2011 and 2015, in $GtCO_2$

Warming	Likelihood	IPCC		Millar et al. (2017)	
		Remaining in 2011*	*Remaining in 2015**	*Remaining in 2015 (low)**	*Remaining in 2015 (high)***
< 1.5°C	66%	400	243	747	887
	50%	550	393	817	1,110
	33%	850	693	916	n/a
< 2°C	66%	1,000	843	1,447	n/a
	50%	1,300	1,143	1,524	n/a
	33%	1,500	1,343	1,700	n/a
< 3°C	66%	2,400	2,243	n/a	n/a
	50%	2,800	2,643	n/a	n/a
	33%	3,250	3,093	n/a	n/a

* RCP8.5 simulations of CMIP5 models   ** RCP2.6 simulations of CMIP5 models

Source: Data from the IPCC, Millar et al., and the Global Carbon Budget (Hartmann, Tank and Rusticucci 2013; Le Quéré et al. 2015; Millar et al. 2017)

there is a non-negligible probability that the world would warm beyond 3°C even if humanity were to stay within its 2°C (50%) CO_2 budget.

There are several reasons for this. Whilst uncertainty in the physical climate response is a dominant source of variation, the unknown future emissions of SLCPs also play an important role. SLCP emissions stem from many different sources, such as fossil fuel extraction, transport and use, agriculture and waste and from natural emission sources (Saunois et al. 2016) and are inherently uncertain, as the future development of these sectors depends on many different factors (e.g. technological progress, demand, etc.). SLCPs are an important factor for climate change since some are much more powerful greenhouse gases (GHGs) than CO_2. Methane (CH_4), for example, has roughly 72 to 84 times the global warming potential of CO_2 over a period of 20 years (GWP20), ozone (O3) has a GWP20 of 62 to 69 and nitrous oxide (N_2O) a GWP of ~300 over a period of 100 years (GWP100; Hartmann et al. 2013). Despite staying in the atmosphere for much less time than, for example, CO_2, the greater potency of SLCPs means that they play an important role in overall anthropogenic global warming.

Total human-induced warming arises from the combination of SLCP- and LLCP-induced warming. The size of a cumulative emissions budget for LLCPs consistent with a specific target peak human-induced warming, as well as the specified probability of achieving that warming goal, hence also depends on the future sustained emissions of SLCPs (e.g. methane). It is the stock of LLCP together with the flow of SLCPs that must be limited for a successful achievement of climate targets. Table 3.1 provides the latest peer-reviewed budget estimates from the IPCC (Intergovernmental Panel on Climate Change) under the assumption that non-CO_2 forcing follows a business-as-usual scenario (RCP8.5)[4]. Non-CO_2 forcing is defined as the fraction of radiative forcing[5] that is caused by non-CO_2 climate pollutants (Myhre et al. 2013). The most recent research, however, finds a significantly higher remaining CO_2 budget. Millar et al. find that, as of 2015, humanity has a stock of approximately 747 to 887 $GtCO_2$ left for a 66% chance of limiting global warming to less than 1.5°C,[6] depending on the magnitude of the sustained flow of future SLCP emission pathways[7] (Millar et al. 2017). The upward revision has been made after it was recently discovered that most of the complex earth-system-models overestimated the warming we should see at the current level of cumulative emissions. This, however, means that they, at the same time, underestimate carbon budgets for a given future temperature goal.

2.2 Committed cumulative carbon emissions

Infrastructure carbon lock-in is typically characterised by committed cumulative carbon emissions, the cumulative amount of future carbon emissions that would be released into the atmosphere if the underlying infrastructure asset would be fully utilised under normal economic conditions until the end of its useful economic life (see Figure 3.3).

While the concept of such emission commitments was implicitly known since carbon lock-in first appeared in pertinent literature, it was first explicitly described

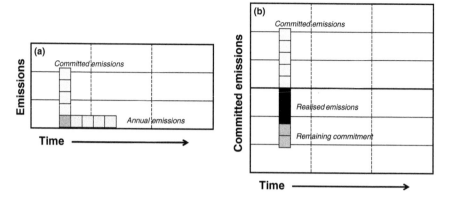

Figure 3.3 Schematic of committed emissions accounting

by Davis et al. (2010) and then in greater detail by Davis and Socolow (2014). In their paper 'Commitment Accounting of CO_2 Emissions' Davis and Socolow describe how these committed emissions develop over time, depending on assumptions regarding future utilisation, remaining lifetime and carbon efficiency (Davis and Socolow 2014). A higher utilisation of existing assets or a longer expected lifetime increases emission commitments, while investments that increase carbon efficiency (for example a switch of fuel or retrofitting of CCS), lower utilisation or an early retirement of the underlying asset reduces commitments.

2.3 The decarbonisation identity

The connection between carbon budgets and committed cumulative carbon emissions can be expressed in the following identity:

$$B_t(T) \geq E_t + N - S - A$$

where $B_t(T)$ is the remaining carbon budget for a given temperature goal T at a point in time t,[8] E_t is the committed cumulative carbon emissions from existing capital stock at that time t, N is new committed cumulative carbon emissions from future (after t) capital stock, S is the amount of existing and new capital stock that will be stranded in the future and finally A is the additional atmospheric space that can be created by negative-emission technologies (NETs) in the future, which hence increases the remaining budget.

Policy makers can choose different actions to ensure this identity is being followed. Any action that actively reduces the cumulative emissions committed from E and N can be understood as stranding S in the context of this identity, since it will likely lead to either cost or a value loss for the owner of the underlying asset as compared to a counterfactual. Additional investments in carbon efficiency–enhancing technologies or retrofit CCS, for example, would reduce the asset value as compared to a scenario in which carbon could be emitted unrestricted. Also, early retirement or underutilisation would reduce and therefore strand asset value. While stranding is expresses in cumulative emissions (i.e. MtCO2 or GtCO2) in the context of this identity, it could also be expressed in stranded capacity (GW) or even stranded capital (USD). With assumptions or knowledge regarding lifetime, utilization, carbon efficiency and capital cost, each of these measures can be converted into any of the other measures.

Carbon capture and storage (CCS) is not explicitly mentioned in this decarbonisation identity but is implicitly included in each of its components. CCS retrofitted to existing infrastructure will reduce E, while new infrastructure built with CCS will not appear in N (as it can be viewed as 'clean' capital stock). Bioenergy will also not appear in N (as its carbon balance would be largely neutral), whereas bioenergy with CCS (BECCS) would appear in A, as it would be a negative-emissions technology and hence create additional atmospheric space.

Since carbon budgets also depend on future uncertain SLCP emissions, an additional choice available to policy makers could be to protect and enhance carbon budgets by decisive action on such SLCP emissions. Millar et al. (2017), for example, find that the 2016 carbon budgets for 1.5°C amount to between 730 and 880 $GtCO_2$, depending on non-CO_2 mitigation.

Given a certain, endogenous temperature goal and the emission commitments of already-operating capital stock, policy makers therefore have five levers to influence the achievement of their climate goals: (1) protecting and enhancing carbon budgets by early and decisive action on non-CO_2 pollutants (e.g. by introducing methane emission targets); (2) retrofitting CCS to operating capital stock (e.g. by subsidising such retrofit investments); (3) making sure that additions to the capital stock do not lead to additional emission commitments (e.g. by allowing investments only in renewable energies, bioenergy or fossil fuels with CCS); (4) stranding existing or newly built capital stock (e.g. via lower utilisation rates, shorter lifetimes, or retrofit CCS); or (5) creating additional atmospheric space (e.g. by large scale BECCS, reforestation, or other NETs).

3. Recent findings from the power generation sector

In recent years, a growing body of literature has been analysing the carbon lock-in and the potential for stranded assets in the power generation sector. Power generation plays an important role in climate change, for at least three reasons. First, it is responsible for a large share of global total primary energy supply (TPES) and an even larger share of anthropogenic CO_2 emissions: today's electricity and heat generation accounts for ~15% of TPES[9] and ~13.6 $GtCO_2$ p.a., or ~42% of total annual anthropogenic CO_2 emissions from fossil fuel combustion (IEA 2016a). Second, electricity can be used as a substitute for carbon-intensive fossil fuels in many other cases: for instance, road transportation and residual housing together account for ~23% of total emissions, and industrial energy consumption is mainly used to produce heat or motion and accounts for an additional ~19% (IEA 2016a). Technologies such as electric vehicles, heat pumps and electric furnaces have the potential to replace fossil fuel-based counterparts in these sectors, thereby reducing GHG emissions. Third, recent developments show that it is feasible and probable that the global electricity generation sector will decarbonise by the second half of this century. Advances in renewable energy technologies and the rapidly decreasing cost of such technologies, most notably solar PV, have led to strong growth of renewables in recent years. 2015 was the first year in which additions to the generation capacity in the form of renewables were larger than the additions to fossil fuel capacity. A recent cross-comparison study of thousands of different possible future energy sector scenarios suggests that even under growth constraints for additional renewables and nuclear power, pessimistic assumptions for carbon capture and storage and less ambitious climate goals, a complete decarbonisation of the electricity generation sector by the second half of the century is possible in all regions of the world (Audoly et al. 2017). Other leading energy scenarios, such as for instance the International Energy Agency's (IEA) '*450 scenario*' (IEA 2016b), also imply that a decarbonisation seems possible and likely (see Figure 3.4). In addition to these characteristics, electricity-generation assets typically have a long lifetime of 35 years, for example for oil and gas generators, to almost 70 years for hydro generation (EIA 2011). Within the global polluting capital stock, therefore, electricity generators are amongst the assets with the longest lifetimes and hence are particularly suitable to study the impact of long-term commitments.

In a recent paper the '2°C capital stock' is defined as the global stock of infrastructure, which, if operated to the end of its normal economic life, implies global mean temperature increases of 2°C or more, with 50% probability (Pfeiffer et al. 2016). Using IPCC carbon budgets and the IPCC's AR5 scenario database, and assuming that future emissions from other sectors are compatible with a 2°C pathway, this paper estimates that the 2°C capital stock for power generation will be reached in 2017. In other words, even under the very optimistic assumption that other sectors reduce emissions in line with a 2°C target, no new emitting power generation infrastructure can be built after 2017 for this target to be met, unless

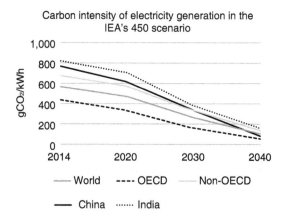

Figure 3.4 Carbon intensity of electricity generation in IEA's 450 scenario, 2014–2040

other infrastructure is retired early or retrofitted with carbon capture technologies. In the overall context of the decarbonisation identity, this paper suggests that future emissions committed by this infrastructure will likely already be as high as or even higher than the remaining budgets for the 2°C climate goal, at least under normal lifetime assumptions (40 years) (see Figure 3.5). Existing emission commitments, E, in the identity are now equal or even larger than the remaining budgets $B(2°C)$. It is no longer possible to achieve climate goals without significant amounts of stranding, S, or new atmospheric space, A. Every bit of new polluting capital stock, N, will make this situation even worse.

Other recent studies support these findings. Cost-effective transition pathways towards a decarbonised economy will probably require stranded assets, especially in the power generation sector (Bertram et al. 2015; McJeon 2015; Rozenberg et al. 2017). Such asset stranding can materialise in different ways, such as underutilisation or early retirement (Caldecott and McDaniels 2014; Caldecott et al. 2016). A recent Carbon Tracker Initiative study, for example, finds that, by mid-2016, China had ~900 GW of coal capacity that was running with a utilisation of less than 50% (CTI 2016). Also in other regions, the increasing share of renewables in the energy mix leads to low overall electricity retail prices and subsequent fossil fuel asset stranding (Caldecott et al. 2017). Bertram et al. (2015) explore how different climate policies affect capital stock additions and stranded assets. They find that weak near-term policies lead to an increased amount of asset stranding, renewable capacity additions, and the need for carbon-dioxide removal (CDR) from the atmosphere in the medium and long terms. These findings have been supported by many other studies (Johnson et al. 2015; McJeon 2015; Riahi et al. 2015; Luderer et al. 2016). They all find that weak near-term policies that would allow for the addition of fossil fuel–powered generation capacity, especially coal, would lead to an increase of stranded assets in the medium and long terms.

Based on the methodology described by Davis and Socolow (2014) and Pfeiffer et al. (2016), in two recent working papers the authors analyse the currently operating and planned power generation capital stock (Pfeiffer, Hepburn et al. 2017; Pfeiffer, Vogt-Schilb et al. 2017). They find that currently existing generators would commit to more future carbon emissions than would be compatible with remaining generation-only carbon budgets for 1.5 to 2°C. Remaining generation-only carbon budgets in this context are defined as the share of overall carbon budget for a certain temperature goal that is allocated to electricity generation. Moreover, the current pipeline of planned fossil fuel power plants would add a large amount of emission commitments to this dirty capital stock (Shearer et al. 2016, 2017). They conclude that, assuming the world will follow through with its climate goals and that negative-emissions technologies (NETs) will not play a big role, much of the currently operating or future, yet-to-be-built, generation capacity must become stranded in one way or the other.

4. Discussion

The objective of this chapter is to analyse the potential for asset stranding in the power generation sector under the framework of the decarbonisation identity and

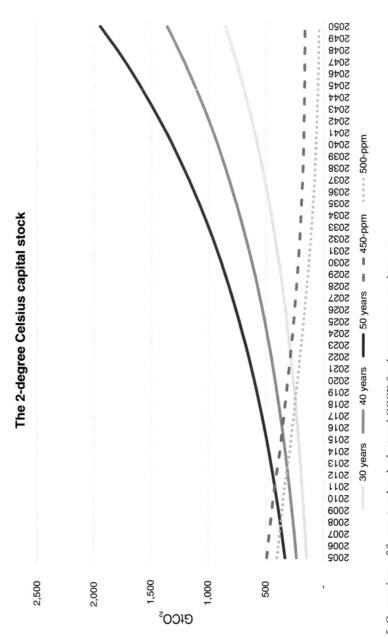

Figure 3.5 Comparison of forecast carbon budget and CCCE for the power generation sector

how this influences the choices policy makers have. Recent findings suggest that currently operating electricity generators would emit more CO_2 than is compatible with currently available generation-only carbon budgets for 1.5 to 2°C. In addition, the current pipeline of planned fossil fuel power plants would add a large amount of additional emission commitments to this capital stock. If the world is to follow through with its climate goals without NETs playing a big role, these findings suggest that much of the currently operating or future, yet-to-be-built, 'dirty' generation capacity must be retrofitted with CCS or become stranded in one way or the other. This would increase the cost of climate policy considerably and reduce the likelihood of such policies being implemented, that is the Paris goals being achieved.

4.1 Policy choices

These findings raise some immediate and significant implications for the electricity sector. As framed analytically by the decarbonisation identity, achieving the necessary transformation of the global electricity generation sector is going to require some combination of the following five options:

1   Protecting or even enhancing remaining carbon budgets.
2   Retrofitting non-zero existing generators with carbon capture and storage.
3   Reducing the carbon intensity of new generators (100% zero-carbon as soon as possible).
4   Prematurely retiring or underutilising (stranding) existing fossil assets.
5   Scaling up NETs to remove carbon from the atmosphere.

All policy choices to achieve a certain carbon budget are explicitly or implicitly a combination of these above five policy choices. The presented findings, however, suggest that for many 430 to 530 ppm pathways, that is scenarios that give humanity a good to fair chance for limiting global warming to around 1.5 to 2°C, the 'silver bullet' of stopping to invest by the time the 1.5 or 2°C capital stock is reached is not an option anymore, since the existing infrastructure already commits humanity to more emissions than would be consistent with these goals. Achieving warming of just 1.5 to 2°C will, therefore, necessarily entail some extent of asset stranding, S, and negative emissions, A. Every additional asset that adds to the polluting capital stock, N, will increase the magnitude of this trade-off. Policy makers might want to strive for the most cost-effective combination of these five options, but this will depend strongly upon achievable SLCP emission floors, the rates of decline in the costs of the relevant technologies, including nuclear, renewables (including hydro), CCS, associated grid balancing technologies (including storage) and NETs.

Many approaches that aim at identifying cost-optimal climate policies implicitly already consider this trade-off. Most notably, policy evaluation IAMs (PEMs), such as GCAM, IMAGE and MESSAGE, which look at the cost effectiveness of achieving a specific mitigation target with a given policy, for example a carbon price (Farmer et al. 2015). Such models start with an estimate of the global capital stock, much as the polluting generation capital stock in this chapter, and model the evolution of this capital stock and its emissions over time under the respective climate policy and considering the inertia of that capital stock (van Vuuren et al. 2009; Waisman et al. 2012; Bertram et al. 2015; Bauer et al. 2016). PEMs take policies and climate goals, usually defined by 2100 concentration targets, as endogenous variables and model the development of all sectors subject to these conditions. Arguably, this will include some levels of N, S and A, which will also depend on the SLCP emission pathway in each scenario.

IAMs, however, rarely make these trade-offs explicit. It is difficult to back out the implicit assumptions regarding the levels of added and stranded capacity over time. For instance, scenarios that assume a delay of climate policies until after 2030 will likely see considerable additions to the capital stock, which will then have to be stranded later in the century or balanced by NETs (Bertram et al. 2015). Yet this is often not made clear. Moreover, it is questionable whether the assumption of a consistent (optimal) global climate policy in the future is a good representation of reality. In particular, scenarios that allow for significant capacity addition in the short-term depend on stringent and decisive global policies after 2020 or 2030 to revert to a pathway that achieves the set climate targets (Bertram et al. 2015; Riahi et al. 2015). If past efforts to achieve such climate policies are any indicator for future success, it is highly questionable, at least, whether such efforts will prove successful in the future.

The decarbonisation identity explicitly shows the fundamental choices policy makers have in the absence of first-best policy instruments. The IAMs showcase the optimal policy (POMs),[10] or the cost-optimal transition pathways for a given set of policies and climate targets (PEMs). The decarbonisation identity, therefore, makes explicit the choices policy makers have if climate goals must be achieved via capital formation when other policies are not available. The findings suggest that humanity should have stopped building polluting capital stock several years ago. Policy makers now have five choices to revert to a path that achieves their climate goals. The combination of these choices will depend on the policy instruments we choose, and this work highlights how little room for manoeuvre there is. In turn these five choices are briefly considered before examining the policy interventions that could support them.

First, sustainable mitigation action on SLCP emissions can be understood as a hedge against a stronger climate response or the overshooting of the available carbon budgets (Xu and Ramanathan 2017). Carbon budgets are inherently uncertain, and thus staying within identified budgets will not guarantee that global warming stays below a certain threshold, much as it cannot be guaranteed that humanity will not overshoot its budgets despite significant mitigation efforts (Bowerman et al. 2013; Millar et al. 2017). SLCPs play a decisive role in this context. In recent years, annual methane emissions have increased strongly (Saunois et al. 2016). Reversing this trend could prove to be an important mitigation lever.

Second, significant deployment of CCS technologies, with or without carbon use, seems essential (RSC 2017). Retrofitting of CCS technologies will be needed to enable existing or future, yet-to-be-built power generators to reduce their committed emissions without being stranded. Whilst CCS technologies are currently amongst the most expensive mitigation options available today (Corsten et al. 2013), nearly all 1.5-to-2°C–consistent scenarios depend on CCS deployment to a certain extent. Such deployment typically allows for continued fossil fuel generation (mostly gas) without or with reduced carbon emissions, and provides for net–negative-emission capabilities (BECCS). Excluding CCS technologies increases the modelled cost of meeting 1.5 to 2°C by around 2.5 times (Clarke et al. 2014).

Third, given the uncertain success of future climate policies, *capital formation* should be a priority for policy makers. It is highly questionable whether climate policies that would strand or retrofit capital stock or create new atmospheric space can ever be implemented in the future. Therefore, policy makers should make every effort to avoid the addition of even more polluting capital stock. Numerous studies in recent years have showcased the rapid reductions in the cost of renewable energy technologies (Schilling and Esmundo 2009; IPCC 2011; Reichelstein and Yorston 2013), the feasibility of large-scale deployment of net– or near–zero-emissions technologies including renewables, biomass, hydro and nuclear (IPCC 2011; Hong et al. 2015; Mileva et al. 2016), the overall modest economic costs such a programme would entail (IPCC 2011; The Global Commission 2014; King et al. 2015; Stern 2015) and the significant co-benefits of zero-carbon generation (Harlan and Ruddell 2011). Important challenges remain on both cost and grid integration (Luo et al. 2015; Wagner 2015), but large-scale deployment of zero-carbon electricity appears inevitable (Audoly et al. 2017); the question is not if but how fast. Informally, one might argue that policy makers should focus on "*making the good stuff cheap*" as well as "*making the bad stuff expensive*" (Beinhocker 2017).

Fourth, some of the currently existing and yet-to-be-built fossil fuel power plants could be stranded and replaced by zero-carbon generation. This could happen either via underutilisation or early retirement of these plants. While it is unlikely that building and then stranding these assets will be economically superior to investing in zero-carbon assets in the first place, there may be some value in delay. Although the costs of zero-carbon technologies are declining rapidly, and although they have reached grid parity in some regions of the world, they currently remain more expensive than fossil fuels in others (Lazard 2016). Waiting might therefore appear to be a logical decision from a cost perspective. From an economic perspective, there is one flaw to this logic, however. Recent research shows that the decline in the cost of renewables is significantly attributable to increases in cumulative production volumes of zero-carbon technologies (Nagy et al. 2013), thus delay may slow such price declines. Earlier action to shift to investments in zero-carbon new capital stock may avoid the later stranding of assets while also accelerating the decline in costs of zero-emissions technologies. As with climate change in general, however, there is also a free-rider problem in this specific area. From the perspective of an individual investor, it makes sense to wait until others have invested enough to reduce the price sufficiently. One important task for climate and energy policy is to overcome this common problem.

Finally, given the status and current trajectory of the global polluting capital stock and the time frames required to shift all new additions to zero-carbon, the probability of overshooting the 1.5 to 2°C capital stock and hence overshooting the remaining emission budgets is significant. In fact, many scenarios consistent with 1.5 to 2°C assume such an overshoot (Krey et al. 2014; Millar et al. 2017). Increased investment in NETs could help to mitigate such overshoot and thus help avoid asset stranding (Caldecott et al. 2015). Given the current costs and technical challenges inherent in widespread CCS deployment, however (Pires et al. 2011), it would not be prudent to rely on NETs in later years as an alternative to rapid current de-carbonisation of the electricity generation system.

4.2 Policy instruments

Global warming ultimately depends on cumulative carbon emissions. Annual CO_2 emission reduction targets hence only indirectly address climate goals. If the lifetime impacts of climate policies on cumulative emissions are not taken into consideration it is possible to meet short-term flow targets while simultaneously installing new coal-fired power stations, making it economically impossible to meet cumulative emission targets. It would be preferable to target cumulative emissions directly and even better to implement policies that are a function of an index of attributable warming. Targets that are a function of time do not map directly onto cumulative emissions or to the observed climate response (Millar et al. 2017).

This distinction becomes especially relevant in the debate about the virtue of 'clean coal' or the coal-to-gas substitution that is often discussed as a policy option (Lecuyer and Vogt-Schilb 2014). Such substitution would successfully reduce near-term emission flows. A stock-based analysis, however, shows that coal-to-gas switching is only worthwhile if it reduces total cumulative emissions. This may well be achieved if the fuel switching from coal to gas involves no new construction; existing gas-fired plants are run at a higher load factors, coal-fired plants are run at lower load factors or even retired. If new capital expenditure on gas is required, however, the analysis is more complicated. For instance, a new gas plant with a lifetime of 40 years, which is constructed in 2017 to replace an existing power generator with a remaining lifetime of 10 years, might very well reduce annual emissions by half for these first 10 years of its operation. In 2027, however, how effective the original decision to substitute the new plant for the old one is will depend on the technology that is available then to mitigate climate change (see Figure 3.6).

If the coal plant could have been replaced in 2027 by zero-carbon technology, that is renewables, perhaps driven by continuing deployment and cost declines of such technologies, this substitution was not the right decision (CAT 2017). In 2027, the gas plant still has three quarters of its useful life (and emissions) remaining, while the coal plant would have emitted less than that in the meantime. In that case (and assuming the gas plant is not stranded) cumulative emissions would have increased by 50%. Furthermore, a coal-to-gas substitution is suspected to increase fugitive methane emissions from extracting, transporting and burning natural gas. As previously described, higher SLCP emissions could lead to lower available carbon budgets. Hence a replacement of coal by gas-powered generation could lead to a double-negative impact on climate mitigation – the increase of committed cumulative emissions and the reduction of carbon budgets via higher

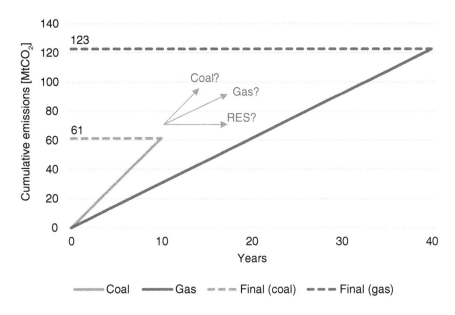

Figure 3.6 Emission profile of coal-to-gas substitution for exemplary 1GW capacity. A 1GW coal-fired power station with an emissions intensity of 1 tCO$_2$/MWh and a load factor of 70% will emit 6.1 MtCO$_2$ per annum. With a residual lifetime of 10 years, expected future cumulative CO$_2$ emissions are therefore 61MtCO$_2$. Suppose this plant were retired early and replaced by a one GW combined cycle gas turbine (CCGT) plant with emissions intensity of 0.5 tCO$_2$/MWh and a load factor of 70%, hence emitting 3.05 MtCO$_2$ per annum. With a lifetime of 40 years, expected future cumulative emissions from the CCGT would be 123 MtCO$_2$, compared to 61 MtCO$_2$ from the coal plant.

SLCP emission levels. On paper, however, this policy decision would reduce annual CO$_2$ rates in the short and even medium terms. This example illustrates that careful analysis of such decisions, and their implications, is required (Lazarus et al. 2015; Zhang et al. 2016).

In the following sections, policy instruments are discussed that are candidates for constraining cumulative emissions to meet a 1.5 to 2°C target. Each instrument incentivises one or more of the five previously discussed policy choices.

4.2.1 Carbon prices

After several drawbacks over the last decades, carbon prices have become popular again recently. Since 2016 alone, eight new pricing initiatives have been introduced in several countries (World Bank 2017), with many more countries having pledged under the Paris Agreement to implement such initiatives over the coming years.

In principle, carbon prices support action on all five options. With the right scientific approach (Allen et al. 2017) SLCP emission reductions can be converted into cumulative CO$_2$ equivalents and then be appropriately priced as an exhaustible resource (Hotelling 1931; Acemoglu et al. 2012). Carbon prices also create incentives for investors to invest in new zero-carbon assets (by making the alternatives less economically attractive), to retrofit existing assets with CCS, to retire the highest emitting stock earlier and to develop NETs. Economy-wide carbon prices have several benefits, for example being technologically neutral, and create incentives to decarbonise efficiently. They simultaneously address the demand and the supply sides by increasing the costs to consumers of fossil fuels and reducing the returns to producers.

Depending on their implementation, carbon prices could also provide an economic 'double dividend' (Goulder 1994; Parry and Bento 2000; Bento and Jacobsen 2007; Jorgenson et al. 2013). While accelerating the transition to a green economy the additional tax revenues could simultaneously be used to reform the existing tax system, which tends to tax goods, for example labour, rather than bads, such as carbon emissions or pollution. Fixing these distortionary taxes could be beneficial to the economy. A differing point of view to the 'double dividend' argues that environmental taxes typically exacerbate rather than alleviate pre-existing tax distortion (Bovenberg and de Mooij 1994). To assume that a carbon tax could provide a 'double dividend' means to assume the absence of other distortions. It should also be pointed out that carbon taxes are often more likely to be successfully implemented when the generated additional tax revenue is 'recycled' as lump-sum payments to citizens (Klenert et al. 2017). The 'double dividend' approach might be the first best solution, but other solutions might be more feasible and hence preferable.

Another often mentioned obstacle for the successful implementation of carbon prices are concerns about competitiveness and carbon leakage (Jenkins 2014). Some energy-intensive or trade-exposed industries might require government assistance in responding to a carbon price, e.g. via innovation and adaption (Aldy and Pizer 2015). This, however might weaken the price signal and create windfall profits for certain companies (Martin et al. 2014). Furthermore, reduced competitiveness and the loss of jobs in certain industries might benefit other industries, e.g. renewables (Hepburn et al. 2006).

In any case, the analysis in this chapter points out that the required scale and pace of the transformation in the energy sector is dramatic. In accordance with other literature (Acemoglu et al. 2012), it suggests that, without other instruments, the level of carbon prices required to deliver this transformation would be far higher and the implementation period much shorter than is politically feasible in most countries. This is especially true considering that current effective net carbon prices may be negative in many regions if fossil fuel subsidies are accounted for. Even meaningful carbon prices implemented immediately around the world would be unlikely to prevent the large-scale stranding of generation infrastructure in the future.

This analysis does not mean that carbon prices must be rejected; they should be implemented to the extent politically feasible (whether by a carbon tax or a quantity constraint and trading scheme). In fact, in recent years many regions have seen the introduction of a carbon price, in the form of either a carbon tax or a carbon permit trading system. Currently, more than 65 jurisdictions are pricing carbon (>25% of global emissions) and the share of CO_2 emissions covered by a carbon price has more than tripled over the past decade (World Bank 2017). The idea of pricing carbon (with lump-sum revenue recycling) finds supporters even in traditionally conservative circles, such as the Republicans in the U.S. (Worland 2017).[11] Nonetheless, additional policy instruments are required to address the carbon lock-in in the energy sector and avoid large-scale stranding of generation capacity.

4.2.2 Cumulative cap and trade

Another innovative form of carbon pricing would be an adaptive cumulative emissions cap-and-trade system (McKibbin and Wilcoxen 2002) consistent with up-to-date estimates of the remaining carbon budgets. This form of cap-and-trade carbon pricing is different to existing systems, which largely operate on a period-by-period basis. A cap on total cumulative emissions would provide early transparency in respect to the remaining carbon budget across the full lifetime of the assets. If such a system could be implemented credibly, it would create economically efficient incentives for the decarbonisation of new capital stock and the optimisation of the existing portfolio (retrofits and retirements). Such a system that sends a credible signal over a prolonged period would also create 'when' flexibility, which is crucial to make cap and trade a cost-effective instrument as it would allow emitters to minimise their compliance costs over time (Fankhauser and Hepburn 2010). Unfortunately, however, credibility over many decades is almost impossible to achieve in practice, given the nature of changing governments in democratic societies. Nevertheless, the idea of adaptive policy instruments that accommodate new findings regarding the climate response or remaining carbon budgets should be analysed and considered more closely (Allen and Frame 2007).

4.2.3 Licensing requirements

Another approach to avoid an increase in polluting capital stock and thus to prevent large-scale asset stranding is the establishment of rules to (1) require new power plants to have zero (or close to zero) emissions and (2) prevent the dirtiest of existing emitting plants from being granted life extensions. Such licensing rules have the political benefits of being simple and transparent and could potentially reduce the political economy challenges of allocating permits either within or between countries (Collier and Venables 2013). A more gradual version of this approach would be to regulate carbon intensity in $kgCO_2/kWh$, for example by introducing and implementing a clear roadmap that reduces the carbon intensity of new power plants step-wise over time. China has taken this approach in its five-year plan, as have several US states (Collier and Venables 2013). Such rules and roadmaps, however, could have the adverse effect of incentivising a rush to build high-emitting assets before the intensity target decrease ('Green Paradox') and should hence be considered and implemented carefully (van der Ploeg 2011;

Smulders, Tsur and Zemel 2012; van der Ploeg and Withagen 2012; Cairns 2014). One approach to solve this problem could be to impose carbon intensity targets on the complete power plant fleet of certain utilities, similar to certain requirements towards the fleets of carmakers in some countries.

Similar results could also be achieved with different but related instruments. *Leases* for power plants on public lands, for instance, could be phased out for existing 'dirty' plants and would not be granted for new power plants that fail to meet certain emission standards. The same could be done with phasing-out *subsidies* (e.g. tax breaks) or, conversely, by imposing a *levy* on polluting plants (as was e.g. in discussion for some lignite plants in Germany in 2014/15). All these instruments would target existing and potential new power generators that fail to meet certain emission standards to prevent the building and subsequent stranding of new infrastructure.

One important disadvantage of such approaches is the unclear effect on cumulative emissions, as showcased in the example of the coal-to-gas substitution. Given constant or growing energy demand, ending the lifetimes of some power plants might have the effect that this generation capacity must be replaced immediately by other generators. Often this replacement will come from other fossil fuel generators that just meet the emission standards at the time but add to the cumulative capital stock. Hence, in some cases, even a lifetime extension for some polluting plants might be sensible if polluting power plants cannot currently be replaced by zero-carbon technologies but could be replaced by these technologies in a few years. These policy instruments should therefore be considered carefully and decided on a case-by-case basis.

4.2.4 Technology-based deployment support

Another approach is to regulate, subsidise (or phase out subsidies) or even penalise the deployment of specific energy producing technologies. Examples include:

- A general ban on power generation from lignite.
- Requiring all new coal plants to have CCS.
- Subsidies or other regulations for accelerated renewable deployment (e.g. a feed-in-tariff or renewable portfolio standard).
- Phase-out of fossil fuel subsidies.
- A levy on all sub-critical coal plants.

Technology-based regulation has several disadvantages, however. It tends to be economically inefficient and more prone to regulatory capture, that is prone to lobbying from certain interest groups, than other broad-based economic instruments. A well-designed ramp-down to zero emissions for new electricity generation would be more effective, since it would not support one specific technology over another. For instance, renewable portfolio standards ignore potential contributions to decarbonisation from other technologies (nuclear, fossil with CCS, demand-side response, storage technologies, etc.).

Moreover, most deployment support is still being directed towards fossil fuels. A 2015 study estimates that total direct energy subsidies within the OECD amount to ~645 billion USD p.a. globally, of which the majority (~84%) benefits fossil fuels. Only ~100 bn. USD p.a. in subsidies is currently directed towards renewables (King et al. 2015). The effect of such subsidies is that, in many regions of the world, the relative competitiveness of fossil fuel generation compared with renewables generation is artificially increased. This incentivises the continued operation of otherwise unprofitable existing fossil fuel generation while reducing incentives to make new capacity additions net zero. A good enhancement of technology-based deployment support from the perspective of the decarbonisation identity would hence be a phase-out of fossil-fuel directed deployment support, that is subsidies.

4.2.5 Research and development support

An important influencer in the decarbonisation identity is the ability to add zero-carbon-generation capital stock. Policy instruments could therefore be designed to support this ability by subsidising not only deployment but also research and development (R&D) (Dechezleprêtre and Glachant 2009; Dechezleprêtre and Popp 2015). An important factor in the large-scale deployment of zero-carbon technologies is the relative cost of clean and dirty technologies. There are well-understood market failures in the research and innovation of clean technologies, and there is a clear and well-accepted role for government to support clean technology research and development (Fischer and Newell 2008; Fischer et al. 2014). It is surprising that, compared to implicit or explicit fossil fuel subsidies, currently so little funding is directed towards the development of technologies that are so crucial to solve this problem. Of ~340 billion USD p.a. government R&D expenditure within the OECD, only ~6 billion USD p.a. (~1.7%) is being spent on R&D related to renewables. In relation to the 2016 OECD GDP, this amounts to only ~0.01%. Even in the private sector, renewable energy companies spent less on R&D (~2% of revenues) than comparable companies in other sectors such as consumer electronics (5%) and pharmaceuticals (15%) (King et al. 2015). It is hence not surprising that initiatives such as the Apollo programme or the Clean Energy Fund initiative that was announced during the Paris COP and that is led by Bill Gates call for more government spending on green energy R&D. For instance, the Apollo programme asks its member countries to pledge to spend 0.02% of their GDP on renewables R&D (King et al. 2015). This would increase the size of current R&D spending by roughly 2.5 times but would still only amount to ~15 billion USD p.a. – a cost that seem acceptable given the importance of the problem this R&D sets out to solve.

It is unclear, however, into which R&D this support should be directed. This applies in a narrower technology-focussed sense, as well as in a wider solution-focussed sense. From a narrower perspective, the question would need to be answered as to which technologies promise the highest potential, for example should solar PV be given priority over concentrated solar power (CSP), or is onshore wind superior to offshore wind? In a wider solution-oriented perspective, the decision would have to be made as to which general approaches to follow. Are renewables more likely to lead to a general decarbonisation than, maybe, retrofitted CCS? How much effort should be directed towards the enablers of renewables, such as grids, storage and demand-side response? How prudent is it to direct R&D money towards NETs? The opinions about the role policy makers and regulators should play in addressing these questions differ (Mazzucato 2015). Yet the public hand has at least a questionable track record when it comes to picking 'winning' technologies (Schmidt et al. 2016), and it is unclear how policy instruments should be designed to address this.

4.3 Broader questions and directions for future research

Besides the direct implications for policy choices and instruments within the power generation sector, the findings presented in this chapter raise some broader questions within this specific area of research but also in the overall environmental context.

First, the implications for policy choices raise some immediate and urgent questions. As the decarbonisation identity illustrates, a successful achievement of the 1.5 to 2°C climate goals will always encompass a combination of the five options: (1) protect and enhance carbon budgets; (2) retrofit existing polluting capital stock with CCS; (3) avoid the addition of new polluting capital stock; (4) strand existing polluting capital stock; or (5) create new atmospheric space by scaling up NETs. It is unclear, however, what the most effective combination of these five options is. The best choice will depend on the economic cost of these options, as well as on scalability, technological availability, likelihood of success, political feasibility and their interdependencies with each other. Plenty of research exists that focusses on each individual question, be it on carbon budgets (Allen et al. 2017; Millar et al. 2017), retrofit CCS (Corsten et al. 2013), the potential of renewables (IPCC 2011), stranding (Riahi et al. 2015) or NETs (van Vuuren et al. 2013). IAMs implicitly consider these policy choices and optimise the trade-off. Yet so far, no approaches exist that tie these separate research areas together and make the policy choices explicit under the framework of the decarbonisation identity.

Second, this research and the approach it takes has implications not only for the downstream power generation sector but also for the mid- and upstream power sector (a), the energy sector in total (b) and even other CO_2-emitting sectors (c):

(a) Assessing the level of carbon lock-in in the electricity generation sector, or even more precisely *generator carbon lock-in*, encompasses only a small fraction of overall connected carbon lock-in. Closely related to the lock-in identified in this chapter is, for instance, lock-in in transmission and distribution grids, transport infrastructure (e.g. pipelines, harbours, train tracks, etc.) and even carbon lock-in in the labour market. If the generator carbon lock-in was to be broken up to be taken back on track for a 1.5 to 2°C target, for example by large-scale stranding of power generators, it would have

immediate and important impacts on connected infrastructure, local economies and even the job market. Decarbonisation efforts to achieve this must
bear those effects in mind.

(b) In addition to the immediate impacts that a breakup of generator lock-in
would have, there are some wider implications for the overall energy sector.
The demand for fossil fuels would decrease drastically if the world were to
decarbonise its power generation capital stock (Piggot et al. 2017). Across the
globe, coal mines would become unnecessary and cease operations. Sectors
along the value chain would change fundamentally – fossil fuel extraction,
processing and transport. More research should be undertaken to understand
the impacts such a decarbonisation would have.

(c) The approach taken in this chapter could be applied to other CO_2-emitting
sectors. Carbon lock-in does not only exist in the energy sector. In fact, electricity and heat production only accounts for a fraction of overall emissions
from fossil fuel combustion. Other sectors that emit CO_2 and are affected
by carbon lock-in are industry (especially iron, steel and cement), transport
(auto, aviation and shipping), buildings (mostly heating) and agriculture.
Calculating the emission commitments of currently existing capital stock in
these sectors and applying the decarbonisation identity to them could help to
identify effective decarbonisation pathways.

Finally, the approach presented in this chapter could be applied to a wider range
of environmental *stock problems*. In a well-known study from 2009, Rockström
et al. outline a safe operating space for humanity (Rockström et al. 2009). Within
this study, the authors identify 10 environmental areas that will greatly affect
humanity's ability to live on this planet and that are in turn being strongly affected
by anthropogenic activity. While some of these areas constitute *flow* problems
(e.g. rate of biodiversity loss, nitrogen cycle, phosphorus cycle or global freshwa-
ter use), most can be described as a *stock* problem (climate change, stratospheric
ozone depletion, ocean acidification, land-use change, atmospheric aerosol loading
and chemical pollution, e.g. by plastic in the oceans). Using the approach presented
in this chapter, global 'pollution commitments' arising from existing anthropogenic infrastructure could be calculated for a wider set of environmental stock
problems. This would help to identify areas in which there is still time to avoid the
worst outcomes by simply avoiding the addition of more polluting capital stock or
other areas where capital must become stranded to avoid such outcomes.

The human population has grown by almost five-fold from 1.6 billion in 1900 to
more than 7.5 billion today. Over a similar period, world average per capita output
has increased almost six-fold from 2,668 USD in 1913 to 14,717 USD in 2015.[12]
This remarkable achievement has been accompanied by significant increases in
pressure on the natural environment, and it is accordingly suggested that the current geological era be termed the *Anthropocene* (Crutzen 2006), since humans
may now be confronting planetary boundaries. The analysis in this chapter raises
a range of broader questions about the sustainability of our energy and economic
systems. Existing policies are clearly inadequate to tackle global environmental

problems, such as climate change, ocean acidification, or aerosol loading. Much greater effort is required to create economic incentives to ensure that individuals and corporations protect the natural environment.

5. Conclusion

Over the last centuries, the consumption of energy, especially from fossil fuels, has helped humanity to develop and to create the wealth of industrialised nations today. If the currently developing and least-developed nations follow the same path, however, the negative external effects of burning fossil fuels will affect the livelihoods of billions of people around the world. The international community has therefore decided to decarbonise its economy and reduce carbon emissions to net-zero to limit global warming to below 1.5 to 2°C. One important obstacle for the successful achievement of that goal is carbon lock-in. This chapter acknowledges that current power plants would emit more CO_2 in the future than the 1.5 to 2°C goal would allow. Moreover, currently planned generators and those already under construction would add a significant amount of additional emission commitments to this capital stock. Policy makers now have five choices to achieve the Paris climate goals: (1) protect and enhance carbon budgets; (2) retrofit existing power generators with CCS; (3) ensure that no new polluting capital stock is added; (4) strand a considerable amount of global electricity generation capacity; and (5) create additional atmospheric space by scaling up NETs. Over the coming years and decades, the challenge will be to identify the most effective balance of these options. Given the uncertain success of future climate policies, however, policy makers are well advised to try to avoid further lock-in by avoiding additional polluting capital stock.

Acknowledgements

I would like to thank my colleagues and collaborators at the Institute for New Economic Thinking (INET) at the Oxford Martin School (OMS), the Oxford Sustainable Finance Programme (SFP) at the Smith School for Enterprise and the Environment (SSEE), the Nature Conservatory (TNC) for financial support and especially participants of the INET's weekly researcher seminar series for their useful comments and feedback.

Notes

1 There are other LLCPs, such as, for example, nitrous oxide, N_2O, but CO_2 is by far the most important one (IPCC 2014a).
2 The carbon intensity of total primary energy supply has decreased over the last decades but is still considerably larger than zero.
3 Also known as carbon capture and sequestration.
4 RCP8.5 is one of four *representative concentration pathways* (RCPs), which are GHG concentration pathways adopted by the IPCC for its AR5.

5 Radiative forcing or climate forcing is the difference between energy (insolation) received by the earth and energy radiated back to space. Positive radiative forcing therefore causes global warming, negative forcing cooling.

6 Throughout this chapter 1.5 to 2°C scenarios refer to 430 to 480 (450) ppm scenarios that would result in warming of likely less than 2°C but more unlikely than likely less than 1.5°C (Hartmann et al. 2013).

7 RCP2.6 versus. RCP8.5 simulations.

8 For example $B_{2016}(1.5°C)$ is the remaining cumulative carbon budget in 2016 for warming less than 1.5°C. Miller et al. (2017) find that $B_{2016}(1.5°C)$ is between 747 and 887 $GtCO_2$, depending on future SLCP emissions.

9 2014 electricity generation was 23,809 TWh (~85.7 EJ), and TPES was 573.5 EJ (IEA 2016a, 2016b).

10 POMs often use a 'damage function' to calculate whether the total benefits of a policy exceed its costs and what an optimal policy looks like.

11 It should be mentioned, however, that market-based policies were innovations developed by conservatives in the Reagan, George H. W. Bush and George W. Bush administrations (Schmalensee and Stavins 2010).

12 Real GDP in international dollars (Roser 2017).

References

Acemoglu, D., Aghion, P., Bursztyn, L. and Hemous, D. 2012. The Environment and Directed Technical Change. *American Economic Review*, 102(1), 131–166.

Aldy, J. E. and Pizer, W. A. 2015. The Competitiveness Impacts of Climate Change Mitigation Policies. *Journal of the Association of Environmental and Resource Economists*, 2(4), 565–595. doi: 10.1086/683305.

Allen, M. R. and Frame, D. J. 2007. Call Off the Quest. *Science*, 318(5850), 582–583. doi: 10.1126/science.1149988.

Allen, M. R., Frame, D. J., Huntingford, C., Jones, C. D., Lowe, J. A., Meinshausen, M. and Meinshausen, N. 2009. Warming Caused by Cumulative Carbon Emissions Towards the Trillionth Tonne. *Nature*, 458(7242), 1163–1166.

Allen, M. R., Shine, K. P., Fuglestvedt, J. S., Millar, R., Cain, M., Frame, D. J. and Macey, A. H. 2018. A Solution to the Misrepresentations of CO2-Equivalent Emissions of 2 Short-Lived Climate Pollutants under Ambitious Mitigation. *Npj Climate and Atmospheric Science*.

Archer, D., Eby, M., Brovkin, V., Ridgwell, A., Cao, L., Mikolajewicz, U., Caldeira, K., Matsumoto, K., Munhoven, G., Montenegro, A. and Tokos, K. 2009. Atmospheric Lifetime of Fossil Fuel Carbon Dioxide. *Annual Review of Earth and Planetary Sciences*, 37(1), 117–134. doi: 10.1146/annurev.earth.031208.100206.

Audoly, R., Vogt-Schilb, A., Pfeiffer, A. and Guivarch, C. 2017. Pathways Toward Zero-Carbon Electricity Required for Climate Stabilization. *IDB Working Paper Series*.

Baldwin, E., Cai, Y. and Kuralbayeva, K. 2016. *Build Today, Regret Tomorrow? Infrastructure and Climate Policy*, pp. 1–2. Avalaible at: https://www.gtap.agecon.purdue.edu/resources/download/8447.pdf

Barrett, S. 1994. Self-Enforcing International Environmental Agreements. *Oxford Economic Papers*, 46, 804–878. doi: 10.1093/oep/46.Supplement_1.878.

Battiston, S., Mandel, A., Monasterolo, I., Schütze, F. and Visentin, G. 2017. A Climate Stress-Test of the Financial System. *Nature Climate Change*, 7(4). doi: 10.1038/nclimate 3255.

Bauer, N., Mouratiadou, I., Luderer, G., Baumstark, L., Brecha, R. J., Edenhofer, O. and Kriegler, E. 2016. Global Fossil Energy Markets and Climate Change Mitigation – An Analysis With REMIND. *Climatic Change*, 136(1). doi: 10.1007/s10584-013-0901-6.

Beinhocker, E. D. 2017. *The Tipping Point: How America Can Lead the Transition to a Prosperous Clean Energy Economy*. Available at: https://www.inet.ox.ac.uk/library/view/913

Bento, A. M. and Jacobsen, M. 2007. Ricardian Rents, Environmental Policy and the "Double-Dividend" Hypothesis. *Journal of Environmental Economics and Management*, 53(1), 17–31.

Bertram, C., Johnson, N., Luderer, G., Riahi, K., Isaac, M. and Eom, J. 2015. Carbon Lock-in Through Capital Stock Inertia Associated With Weak Near-Term Climate Policies. *Technological Forecasting and Social Change*, Elsevier Inc., 90(PA), 62–72. doi: 10.1016/j.techfore.2013.10.001.

Bovenberg, A. L. and de Mooij, R. A. 1994. Environmental Levies and Distortionary Taxation. *The American Economic Review*, 84(4), 1085–1089.

Bowerman, N. H. A., Frame, D. J., Huntingford, C., Lowe, J. A., Smith, S. M. and Allen, M. R. 2013. The Role of Short-Lived Climate Pollutants in Meeting Temperature Goals. *Nature Climate Change*, 3(12), 1021–1024. doi: 10.1038/nclimate2034.

Cairns, R. D. 2014. The Green Paradox of the Economics of Exhaustible Resources. *Energy Policy*, 65, 78–85. doi: 10.1016/j.enpol.2013.10.047.

Caldecott, B., Howarth, N. and McSharry, P. 2013. Stranded Assets in Agriculture: Protecting Value From Environment-Related Risks. *Smith School of Enterprise and the Environment, University of Oxford*, Oxford, UK.

Caldecott, B., Kruitwagen, L., Dericks, G., Tulloch, D. J., Kok, I. and Mitchell, J. 2016. Stranded Assets and Thermal Coal – an Analysis of Environment-Related Risk Exposure. *Smith School of Enterprise and the Environment, University of Oxford*.

Caldecott, B., Lomax, G. and Workman, M. 2015. Stranded Carbon Assets and Negative Emissions Technologies. *Smith School of Enterprise and the Environment, University of Oxford*, February.

Caldecott, B. and McDaniels, J. 2014. Stranded Generation Assets : Implications for European Capacity Mechanisms, Energy Markets and Climate Policy. *Smith School of Enterprise and the Environment, University of Oxford*, Oxford, UK (Working Paper Series).

Caldecott, B., Tilbury, J. and Carey, C. 2014. Stranded Assets and Scenarios: Discussion Paper. *Smith School of Enterprise and the Environment, University of Oxford*, January, pp. 1–22.

Caldecott, B., Tulloch, D. J., Bouveret, G., Pfeiffer, A., Kruitwagen, L., McDaniels, J. and Dericks, G. 2017. The Fate of European Coal-Fired Power Stations Planned in the Mid-2000s. *Smith School of Enterprise and the Environment, University of Oxford*.

Carbon Pricing Leadership Coalition. 2017. *Report of the High-Level Commission on Carbon Prices*, p. 68.

Carney, M. 2015. *Breaking the Tragedy of the Horizon – Climate Change and Financial Stability*. London: Bank of England.

CAT. 2017. Foot Off the Gas: Increased Reliance on Natural Gas in the Power Sector Risks an Emissions Lock-in. *CAT Decarbonisation Series*, June, pp. 1–7.

Clark, P. U., Shakun, J. D., Marcott, S. A., Mix, A. C., Eby, M., Kulp, S., Levermann, A., Milne, G. A., Pfister, P. L., Santer, B. D., Schrag, D. P., Solomon, S., Stocker, T. F., Strauss, B. H., Weaver, A. J., Winkelmann, R., Archer, D., Bard, E., Goldner, A., Lambeck, K., Pierrehumbert, R. T. and Plattner, G.-K. 2016. Consequences of Twenty-First-Century

Policy for Multi-Millennial Climate and Sea-Level Change. *Nature Climate Change*, 6(4), 360–369. doi: 10.1038/nclimate2923.

Clarke, L. E., Jiang, K., Akimoto, K., Babiker, M., Blanford, G., Fisher-Vanden, K., Hourcade, J.-C., Krey, V., Kriegler, E., Loschel, D., McCollum, S., Paltsev, S., Rose, S., Shukla, P. R., Tavoni, M., van der Zwaan, B. C. C. and van Vuuren, D. P. 2014. Assessing Transformation Pathways. In *Climate Change 2014: Mitigation of Climate Change. Contribution of Working Group III to the Fifth Assessment Report of the Intergovernmental Panel on Climate Change*. Cambridge: Cambridge University Press.

Collier, P. and Venables, A. J. 2013. *Closing Coal: Economic and Moral Incentives*. Preliminary version, September.

Corsten, M., Ramírez, A., Shen, L., Koornneef, J. and Faaij, A. 2013. Environmental Impact Assessment of CCS Chains – Lessons Learned and Limitations From LCA Literature. *International Journal of Greenhouse Gas Control*, 13. doi: 10.1016/j.ijggc.2012.12.003.

Crutzen, P. J. 2006. The Anthropocene. *Earth System Science in the Anthropocene*, 13–18. doi: 10.1007/3-540-26590-2_3.

CTI. 2016. *Chasing the Dragon? China's Coal Overcapacity Crisis and What It Means for Investors*.

Davis, S. J., Caldeira, K. and Matthews, H. D. 2010. Future CO2 Emissions and Climate Change from Existing Energy Infrastructure. *Science*, 329(5997), 1330–1333. doi: 10.1126/science.1188566.

Davis, S. J. and Socolow, R. H. 2014. Commitment Accounting of CO2 Emissions. *Environmental Research Letters*, 9(8), 84018. doi: 10.1088/1748-9326/9/8/084018.

Dechezleprêtre, A. and Glachant, M. 2009. What Drives the International Transfer of Climate Change Mitigation Technologies? Empirical Evidence From Patent Data. *Centre for Climate Change Economics and Policy*, (16), December, 1–33.

Dechezleprêtre, A. and Popp, D. 2015. *Fiscal and Regulatory Instruments for Clean Technology Development in the European Union*, July.

Edwards, J., Kay, J. and Mayer, C. 1987. *The Economic Analysis of Accounting Profitability*. Oxford: Clarendon Press.

EIA. 2011. *Age of Electric Power Generators Varies Widely, U.S. Energy Information Administration*. Available at: Age of electric power generators varies widely [Accessed September 1, 2017].

Erickson, P., Kartha, S., Lazarus, M. and Tempest, K. 2015. Assessing Carbon Lock-In. *Environmental Research Letters*, 10(8), 84023. doi: 10.1088/1748-9326/10/8/084023.

Fankhauser, S. and Hepburn, C. 2010. Designing Carbon Markets. Part I: Carbon Markets in Time. *Energy Policy*, 38(8), 4363–4370. doi: 10.1016/j.enpol.2010.03.064.

Farmer, J. D., Hepburn, C., Mealy, P. and Teytelboym, A. 2015. A Third Wave in the Economics of Climate Change. *Environmental and Resource Economics*, Springer Netherlands, 62(2), 329–357. doi: 10.1007/s10640-015-9965-2.

Fay, M., Hallegatte, S., Vogt-Schilb, A., Rozenberg, J., Narloch, U. and Kerr, T. 2015. *Decarbonizing Development: Three Steps to a Zero-Carbon Future*. Washington, DC: World Bank. doi: 10.1017/CBO9781107415324.004.

Fischer, C. and Newell, R. G. 2008. Environmental and Technology Policies for Climate Mitigation. *Journal of Environmental Economics and Management*, Elsevier, 55(2), 142–162.

Fischer, C., Newell, R. G. and Preonas, L. 2014. Environmental and Technology Policy Options in the Electricity Sector: Interactions and Outcomes. *Resources for the Future Discussion Paper*, (67).

The Global Commission. 2014. *Better Growth, Better Climate, Better Growth, Better Climate: The New Climate Economy Report*. doi: ISBN:9780990684503.

Goulder, L. H. 1994. Environmental Taxation and the Double Dividend: A Reader's Guide. *International Tax and Public Finance*, 2(2), 157–183.

Goulder, L. H., Hafstead, M. A. C. and Dworsky, M. 2010. Impacts of Alternative Emissions Allowance Allocation Methods Under a Federal Cap-and-Trade Program. *Journal of Environmental Economics and Management*, 60(3), 161–181. doi: 10.1016/j.jeem.2010.06.002.

Griscom, B. W., Adams, J., Ellis, P. W., Houghton, R. A., Lomax, G., Miteva, D. A., Schlesinger, W. H., Shoch, D., Siikamäki, J. V., Smith, P., Woodbury, P., Zganjar, C., Blackman, A., Campari, J., Conant, R. T., Delgado, C., Elias, P., Gopalakrishna, T., Hamsik, M. R., Herrero, M., Kiesecker, J., Landis, E., Laestadius, L., Leavitt, S. M., Minnemeyer, S., Polasky, S., Potapov, P., Putz, F. E., Sandermane, J., Silvius, M., Wollenberg, E. and Fargione, J. 2017. Natural Climate Solutions. *Proceedings of the National Academy of Sciences*, 114(6), 1–6. doi: 10.1073/pnas.1710465114.

Harlan, S. L. and Ruddell, D. M. 2011. Climate Change and Health in Cities: Impacts of Heat and Air Pollution and Potential Co-Benefits From Mitigation and Adaptation. *Current Opinion in Environmental Sustainability*, 3(3), 126–134. doi: 10.1016/j.cosust.2011.01.001.

Hartmann, D. L., Tank, A. M. G. K. and Rusticucci, M. 2013. IPCC Fifth Assessment Report, Climate Change 2013: The Physical Science Basis. *IPCC*, AR5, January 2014, pp. 31–39.

Helm, D. 2010. Government Failure, Rent-Seeking, and Capture: The Design of Climate Change Policy. *Oxford Review of Economic Policy*, Oxford University Press, 26(2), 182–196. doi: 10.1093/oxrep/grq006.

Hepburn, C., Neuhoff, K., Grubb, M., Matthes, F. and Tse, M. 2006. Auctioning of EU ETS Phase II Allowances: Why and How? *Climate Policy*, 6(1), 137–160.

Hong, S., Bradshaw, C. J. A. and Brook, B. W. 2015. Global Zero-Carbon Energy Pathways Using Viable Mixes of Nuclear and Renewables. *Applied Energy*, Elsevier Ltd, 143, 451–459. doi: 10.1016/j.apenergy.2015.01.006.

Hotelling, H. 1931. The Economics of Exhaustible Resources. *Journal of Political Economy*, 39(2), 137–175.

IEA. 2016a. *CO2 Emissions From Fuel Combustion*. doi: 10.1787/co2-table-2011-1-en.

IEA. 2016b. *World Energy Outlook 2016*. doi: www.iea.org/publications/freepublications/publication/WEB_WorldEnergyOutlook2015ExecutiveSummaryEnglishFinal.pdf.

IPCC. 2011. Summary for Policymakers. In Edenhofer, O., Pichs-Madruga, R., Sokona, Y., Seyboth, K., Matschoss, P., Kadner, S., Zwickel, T., Eickemeier, P., Hansen, G., Schlömer, S. and von Stechow, C. (eds.), *IPCC Special Report on Renewable Energy Sources and Climate Change Mitigation*. Cambridge: Cambridge University Press, May, pp. 5–8.

IPCC. 2014a. *Climate Change 2014: Mitigation of Climate Change, Working Group III Contribution to the Fifth Assessment Report of the Intergovernmental Panel on Climate Change*. doi: 10.1017/CBO9781107415416.

IPCC. 2014b. *Climate Change 2014 Synthesis Report*, November, pp. 1–40. doi: 10.1017/CBO9781107415324.

Iyer, G. C., Edmonds, J. A., Fawcett, A. A., Hultman, N. E., Alsalam, J., Asrar, G. R., Calvin, K. V., Clarke, L. E., Creason, J., Jeong, M., Kyle, P., McFarland, J., Mundra, A., Patel, P., Shi, W. and McJeon, H. C. 2015. The Contribution of Paris to Limit Global Warming to 2°C. *Environmental Research Letters*, IOP Publishing, 10(12), 125002. doi: 10.1088/1748-9326/10/12/125002.

Jenkins, J. D. 2014. Political Economy Constraints on Carbon Pricing Policies: What are the Implications for Economic Efficiency, Environmental Efficacy, and Climate Policy Design? *Energy Policy*, 69, 467–477. doi: 10.1016/j.enpol.2014.02.003.

Johnson, N., Krey, V., McCollum, D. L., Rao, S., Riahi, K. and Rogelj, J. 2015. Stranded on a Low-Carbon Planet: Implications of Climate Policy for the Phase-Out of Coal-Based Power Plants. *Technological Forecasting and Social Change*, Elsevier B.V., 90(PA), 89–102. doi: 10.1016/j.techfore.2014.02.028.

Jorgenson, D. W., Goettle, R. J., Ho, M. S. and Wilcoxen, P. J. 2013. *Double Dividend: Environmental Taxes and Fiscal Reform in the United States*. Cambridge, MA: MIT Press.

Kaya, Y. and Yokobori, K. 1998. *Environment, Energy and Economy: Strategies for Sustainability*. Washington, DC: Aspen Inst.

King, D., Browne, J., Layard, R., Donnell, G. O., Rees, M., Stern, N. and Turner, A. 2015. *A Global Apollo Programme to Combat Climate Change*, p. 38.

Klenert, D., Mattauch, L., Combet, E., Edenhofer, O., Hepburn, C., Rafaty, R. and Stern, N. 2017. Making Carbon Pricing Work. *MPRA Paper*.

Knutti, R., Rogelj, J., Sedláček, J. and Fischer, E. M. 2015. A Scientific Critique of the Two-Degree Climate Change Target. *Nature Geoscience*, 9(1). doi: 10.1038/ngeo2595.

Krey, V., Masera, O., Blanforde, G., Bruckner, T., Cooke, R., Fish-Vanden, K., Haberl, H., Hertwich, E., Kriegler, E., Müller, D., Paltsev, S., Price, L., Schlömer, S., Uerge-Vorsatz, D., Van Vuuren, D. and Zwickel, T. 2014. Annex II: Metrics & Methodology. In *Climate Change 2014: Mitigation of Climate Change. Contribution of Working Group III to the Fifth Assessment Report of the Intergovernmental Panel on Climate Change*, pp. 1281–1328. Cambridge: Cambridge University Press.

Lazard. 2016. *Levelized Cost of Energy Analysis*, December, pp. 1–21.

Lazarus, M., Tempest, K., Klevnäs, P. and Korsbakken, J. I. 2015. *Natural Gas: Guardrails for a Potential Climate Bridge*. The New Climate Economy- The Global Commission on the Economy and Climate, May, pp. 1–16.

Lecuyer, O. and Vogt-Schilb, A. 2014. Optimal Transition From Coal to Gas and Renewable Power Under Capacity Constraints and Adjustment Costs. *World Bank Policy Research Working Paper (6985)*, July, pp. 1–38. doi: http://papers.ssrn.com/sol3/papers.cfm?abstract_id=2475072.

Le Quéré, C., Moriarty, R., Andrew, R. M., Canadell, J. G., Sitch, S., Korsbakken, J. I., Friedlingstein, P., Peters, G. P., Andres, R. J., Boden, T. A., Houghton, R. A., House, J. I., Keeling, R. F., Tans, P., Arneth, A., Bakker, D. C. E., Barbero, L., Bopp, L., Chang, J., Chevallier, F., Chini, L. P., Ciais, P., Fader, M., Feely, R. A., Gkritzalis, T., Harris, I., Hauck, J., Ilyina, T., Jain, A. K., Kato, E., Kitidis, V., Klein Goldewijk, K., Koven, C., Landschützer, P., Lauvset, S. K., Lefèvre, N., Lenton, A., Lima, I. D., Metzl, N., Millero, F., Munro, D. R., Murata, A. S., Nabel, J. E. M., Nakaoka, S., Nojiri, Y., O'Brien, K., Olsen, A., Ono, T., Pérez, F. F., Pfeil, B., Pierrot, D., Poulter, B., Rehder, G., Rödenbeck, C., Saito, S., Schuster, U., Schwinger, J., Séférian, R., Steinhoff, T., Stocker, B. D., Sutton, A. J., Takahashi, T., Tilbrook, B., Van Der Laan-Luijkx, I. T., Van Der Werf, G. R., Van Heuven, S., Vandemark, D., Viovy, N., Wiltshire, A., Zaehle, S. and Zeng, N. 2015. Global Carbon Budget 2015. *Earth System Science Data*, 7(2). doi: 10.5194/essd-7-349-2015.

Levy, R. 2014. Soothing Politics. *Journal of Public Economics*, 120, 126–133. doi: 10.1016/j.jpubeco.2014.09.003.

Luderer, G., Bertram, C., Calvin, K., De Cian, E. and Kriegler, E. 2016. Implications of Weak Near-Term Climate Policies on Long-Term Mitigation Pathways. *Climatic Change*, 136(1). doi: 10.1007/s10584-013-0899-9.

Luo, X., Wang, J., Dooner, M. and Clarke, J. 2015. Overview of Current Development in Electrical Energy Storage Technologies and the Application Potential in Power System Operation. *Applied Energy*, Elsevier Ltd, 137, 511–536. doi: 10.1016/j.apenergy.2014.09.081.

Martin, R., Muûls, M., Laure, L. B., Wagner, U. J., Martin, B. R., Muûls, M., Preux, L. B. De and Wagner, U. J. 2014. Industry Compensation under Relocation Risk: A Firm-Level Analysis of the EU Emissions Trading Scheme. *American Economic Review*, 104(8), 2482–2508. doi: 10.1257/aer.104.8.2482.

Matthews, H. D. and Caldeira, K. 2008. Stabilizing Climate Requires Near-Zero Emissions. *Geophysical Research Letters*, 35(4). doi: 10.1029/2007GL032388.

Matthews, H. D., Gillett, N. P., Stott, P. A. and Zickfeld, K. 2009. The Proportionality of Global Warming to Cumulative Carbon Emissions. *Nature*, 459(7248), 829–832.

Mazzucato, M. 2015. *The Entrepreneurial State: Debunking Public vs. Private Sector Myths*. London: Anthem Press.

McKibbin, W. J. and Wilcoxen, P. J. 2002. The Role of Economics in Climate Change Policy. *Journal of Economic Perspectives*, 16(2), 107–129.

Meinshausen, M., Meinshausen, N., Hare, W., Raper, S. C. B., Frieler, K., Knutti, R., Frame, D. J., Allen, M. R., Frame, D. J., Huntingford, C., Jones, C. D., Lowe, J. A., Meinshausen, M. and Meinshausen, N. 2009. Greenhouse-Gas Emission Targets for Limiting Global Warming to 2-Degree Celsius. *Nature*, Nature Publishing Group, 458(7242), 1158–1162. doi: 10.1038/nature08017.

Mileva, A., Johnston, J., Nelson, J. H. and Kammen, D. M. 2016. Power System Balancing for Deep Decarbonization of the Electricity Sector. *Applied Energy*, Elsevier Ltd, 162, 1001–1009. doi: 10.1016/j.apenergy.2015.10.180.

Millar, R. J., Fuglestvedt, J. S., Friedlingstein, P., Rogelj, J., Grubb, M. J., Matthews, H. D., Skeie, R. B., Forster, P. M., Frame, D. J. and Allen, M. R. 2017. Emission Budgets and Pathways Consistent With Limiting Warming to 1.5 °C. *Nature Geoscience*, September, 1–8. doi: 10.1038/ngeo3031.

Myhre, G., Shindell, D., Bréon, F.-M., Collins, W., Fuglestvedt, J., Huang, J., Koch, D., Lamarque, J.-F., Lee, D., Mendoza, B., Nakajima, T., Robock, A., Stephens, G., Takemura, T. and Zhang, H. 2013. Anthropogenic and Natural Radiative Forcing. In *Climate Change 2013: The Physical Science Basis. Contribution of Working Group I to the Fifth Assessment Report of the Intergovernmental Panel on Climate Change*. Cambridge: Cambridge University Press, pp. 659–740. doi: 10.1017/CBO9781107415324.018.

Nagy, B., Farmer, J. D., Bui, Q. M. and Trancik, J. E. 2013. Statistical Basis for Predicting Technological Progress. *PLoS ONE*, 8(2). doi: 10.1371/journal.pone.0052669.

Parry, I. W. H. and Bento, A. M. 2000. Tax Deductions, Environmental Policy, and the "Double Dividend" Hypothesis. *Journal of Environmental Economics and Management*, 39(1), 67–96.

Pfeiffer, A., Hepburn, C. J., Vogt-Schilb, A. and Caldecott, B. 2017. *Committed Emissions From Existing and Planned Power Plants and Consequent Levels of Asset Stranding Required to Meet Global Warming Goals*. Oxford, UK (in press).

Pfeiffer, A., Millar, R., Hepburn, C. and Beinhocker, E. 2016. The 2-Degree Celsius Capital Stock for Electricity Generation: Committed Cumulative Carbon Emissions From the Electricity Generation Sector and the Transition to a Green Economy. *Applied Energy*, 179, 1395–1408. doi: 10.1016/j.apenergy.2016.02.093.

Pfeiffer, A., Vogt-Schilb, A., Tulloch, D. and Hepburn, C. J. 2017. *Dead on Arrival? Implicit Stranded Assets in Leading IAM Scenarios*. Oxford, UK (in press).

Piggot, G., Erickson, P., Lazarus, M. and Asselt, H. Van. 2017. *Addressing Fossil Fuel Production Under the UNFCCC: Paris and Beyond.*

Pires, J. C. M., Martins, F. G., Alvim-Ferraz, M. C. M. and Simoes, M. 2011. Recent Developments on Carbon Capture and Storage: An Overview. *Chemical Engineering Research and Design*, Institution of Chemical Engineers, 89(9), 1446–1460. doi: 10.1016/j.cherd.2011.01.028.

Reichelstein, S. and Yorston, M. 2013. The Prospects for Cost Competitive Solar PV Power. *Energy Policy*, Elsevier, 55, 117–127. doi: 10.1016/j.enpol.2012.11.003.

Riahi, K., Kriegler, E., Johnson, N., Bertram, C., den Elzen, M., Eom, J., Schaeffer, M., Edmonds, J., Isaac, M., Krey, V., Longden, T., Luderer, G., Méjean, A., McCollum, D. L., Mima, S., Turton, H., van Vuuren, D. P., Wada, K., Bosetti, V., Capros, P., Criqui, P., Hamdi-Cherif, M., Kainuma, M. and Edenhofer, O. 2015. Locked Into Copenhagen Pledges – Implications of Short-Term Emission Targets for the Cost and Feasibility of Long-Term Climate Goals. *Technological Forecasting and Social Change*, The Authors, 90(PA), 8–23. doi: 10.1016/j.techfore.2013.09.016.

Rockström, J., Steffen, W., Noone, K., Persson, Å., Chapin, F. S., Lambin, E. F., Lenton, T. M., Scheffer, M., Folke, C. and Schellnhuber, H. J. 2009. A Safe Operating Space for Humanity. *Nature*, Nature Publishing Group, 461(7263), 472–475.

Rogelj, J., Elzen, M. Den, Fransen, T., Fekete, H., Winkler, H., Schaeffer, R., Sha, F., Riahi, K. and Meinshausen, M. 2016. Perspective: Paris Agreement Climate Proposals Need Boost to Keep Warming Well Below 2 ° C. *Nature Climate Change*, 534, June. doi: 10.1038/nature18307.

Roser, M. 2017. *GDP Growth Over the Last Centuries, Our World in Data.* Available at: https://ourworldindata.org/economic-growth#globally-over-the-last-two-millennia-until-today [Accessed July 20, 2009].

Rozenberg, B. J., Vogt-Schilb, A. and Hallegatte, S. 2017. Instrument Choice and Stranded Assets in the Transition to Clean Capital. *IDB Working Paper Series.*

Rozenberg, J., Davis, S. J., Narloch, U. and Hallegatte, S. 2015. Climate Constraints on the Carbon Intensity of Economic Growth. *Environmental Research Letters*, IOP Publishing, 10(9), 95006. doi: 10.1088/1748-9326/10/9/095006.

RSC. 2017. The Potential and Limitations of Using Carbon Dioxide. *Policy Briefing*, The Royal Society, pp. 1–11.

Saunois, M., Bousquet, P., Poulter, B., Peregon, A., et al. 2016. The Global Methane Budget 2000–2012. *Earth System Science Data*, 8(2), 697–751. doi: 10.5194/essd-8-697-2016.

Schilling, M. A. and Esmundo, M. 2009. Technology S-Curves in Renewable Energy Alternatives: Analysis and Implications for Industry and Government. *Energy Policy*, 37(5), 1767–1781. doi: 10.1016/j.enpol.2009.01.004.

Schmalensee, R. and Stavins, R. 2010. The Power of Cap-and-Trade. *The Boston Globe.*

Schmidt, T. S., Battke, B., Grosspietsch, D. and Hoffmann, V. H. 2016. Do Deployment Policies Pick Technologies by (Not) Picking Applications? – a Simulation of Investment Decisions in Technologies With Multiple Applications. *Research Policy*, Elsevier B.V., 45(10), 1965–1983. doi: 10.1016/j.respol.2016.07.001.

Seto, K. C., Davis, S. J., Mitchell, R. B., Stokes, E. C., Unruh, G. and Ürge-Vorsatz, D. 2016. Carbon Lock-In: Types, Causes, and Policy Implications. *Annual Review of Environment and Resources*, 41(1), 425–452. doi: 10.1146/annurev-environ-110615-085934.

Shearer, C., Ghio, N., Myllyvirta, L., Yu, A. and Nace, T. 2016. *Boom and Bust 2016.* Sierra Club.

Shearer, C., Ghio, N., Myllyvirta, L., Yu, A. and Nace, T. 2017. *Boom and Bust 2017.* Sierra Club.

Smulders, S., Tsur, Y. and Zemel, A. 2012. Announcing Climate Policy: Can a Green Para-
    dox Arise Without Scarcity? *Journal of Environmental Economics and Management.*
    Elsevier, 64(3), 364–376. doi: 10.1016/j.jeem.2012.02.007.
Stern, N. 2015. *Why Are We Waiting? The Logic, Urgency, and Promise of Tackling Cli-
    mate Change.* Cambridge, MA: MIT Press.
UNEP. 2016. *The Emissions Gap Report 2016.* doi: ISBN 978-92-807-3617-5.
UNFCCC. 2015. *Adoption of the Paris Agreement.* New York: UNFCCC.
United Nations. 2017. *World Population Prospects: The 2017 Revision, Key Findings and
    Advance Tables,* p. 46. doi: 10.1017/CBO9781107415324.004.
Unruh, G. 2000. Understanding Carbon Lock-In. *Energy Policy,* 28, March, 817–830. doi:
    10.1016/S0301-4215(00)00070-7.
van der Ploeg, F. 2011. Macroeconomics of Sustainability Transitions: Second-best Cli-
    mate Policy, Green Paradox, and Renewables Subsidies. *Environmental Innovation and
    Societal Transitions,* 1(1), 130–134. doi: 10.1016/j.eist.2011.01.001.
van der Ploeg, F. and Withagen, C. 2012. Is there really a green paradox? *Journal of
    Environmental Economics and Management. Elsevier,* 64(3), 342–363. doi: 10.1016/
    j.jeem.2012.08.002.
van Vuuren, D. P., Deetman, S., van Vliet, J., van den Berg, M., van Ruijven, B. J. and
    Koelbl, B. 2013. The Role of Negative CO2 Emissions for Reaching 2* Celsius: Insights
    From Integrated Assessment Modelling. *Climatic Change,* 118(1), 1–13. doi: 10.1007/
    s10584-012-0680-5.
van Vuuren, D. P., Lowe, J., Stehfest, E., Gohar, L., Hof, A. F., Hope, C., Warren, R., Mein-
    shausen, M., Plattner, G.-K. K., Vuuren, D. P., Lowe, J., Stehfest, E., Gohar, L., Hof,
    A. F., Hope, C., Warren, R., Meinshausen, M. and Plattner, G.-K. K. 2009. How Well
    Do Integrated Assessment Models Simulate Climate Change? *Climatic Change,* 104(2),
    255–285. doi: 10.1007/s10584-009-9764-2.
Wagner, G. 2015. Push Renewables to Spur Carbon Pricing. *Nature,* 525, 27–29.
Waisman, H., Guivarch, C., Grazi, F. and Hourcade, J. C. 2012. The Imaclim-R model:
    Infrastructures, Technical Inertia and the Costs of Low Carbon Futures Under Imperfect
    Foresight. *Climatic Change,* 114(1), 101–120. doi: 10.1007/s10584-011-0387-z.
WBG. 2016. *Poverty and Shared Prosperity 2016: Taking on Inequality.* Washington, DC: WBG.
Weyzig, F., Kuepper, B., Gelder, J. W. van and Tilburg, R. 2014. *The Price of Doing: Too
    Little Too Late,* p. 11.
Worland, J. 2017. Republicans Tell Their Party It's Time to Address Climate Change. *Time,*
    February.
World Bank. 2017. *State and Trends of Carbon Pricing.* Washington, DC: World Bank.
Xu, Y. and Ramanathan, V. 2017. Well Below 2 °C: Mitigation Strategies for Avoiding
    Dangerous to Catastrophic Climate Changes. *Proceedings of the National Academy of
    Sciences,* 114(39), 201618481. doi: 10.1073/pnas.1618481114.
Zhang, X., Myhrvold, N. P., Hausfather, Z. and Caldeira, K. 2016. Climate Benefits of
    Natural Gas as a Bridge Fuel and Potential Delay of Near-Zero Energy Systems. *Applied
    Energy,* Elsevier Ltd, 167, 317–322. doi: 10.1016/j.apenergy.2015.10.016.

4 Stranded assets

An environmentally driven framework of sunk costs

Elizabeth Harnett

1. Introduction

This chapter seeks to show that investors' perceptions of stranded assets could be reframed and theorised with stranding as a version of irreversible sunk costs. This could help investors recognise the immediate and long-term investment implications of stranded assets, as investors are used to dealing with risk over varied geographical and time horizons with regards to investment costs (Blyth et al. 2007; Hallegatte et al. 2012).

Stranded assets are defined as assets which lose their value prematurely, and it is from this point that companies (and their shareholders) are therefore left with assets which are likely to be irreversible 'sunk costs' (Dixit and Pindyck 1994). Sunk costs are defined by Clark and Wrigley (1997, p. 340) in the following way: 'In contrast to fixed costs, which can be eliminated by the total cessation of production and the capital invested salvaged, sunk costs represent a non-recoverable commitment to production in an industry'. From this it is clear that stranded assets are an example of sunk costs, and it is this relationship that will be further examined in this chapter. In particular, the characteristics of sunk costs are explored in the context of stranded assets to further develop the relationship, and then a spatial-temporal framework is established to aid investors in better analysing their stranded asset risk via a sunk cost conceptualisation. While investors often suggest that they struggle to consider the risk profiles and time horizons of asset stranding (Harnett 2017a), there is a stronger history of adapting investment decisions to sunk cost calculations (Bellalah 2003; Clark and Wrigley 1997; Arkes and Blumer 1985).

Dixit and Pindyck (1994, p. 3), in their book on investment under uncertainty, assert that 'most investment decisions share three important characteristics, in varying degrees'. Firstly, they argue that all investments are partially or completely '*irreversible*'. In other words, you cannot recover all your initial investment if you change your mind – you almost always face some 'sunk costs'. Second, there is '*uncertainty*' over future rewards from the investment resulting from market, political, social and environmental factors. Third, the '*timing*' of the investment is, to a varied extent, 'fluid' – it is possible to delay a decision to get more information about future conditions and markets and about the investment itself. The risk of environmental change, and stranded assets in particular, is likely to influence each of these characteristics for a wide range of investment decisions, increasing and accelerating the irreversibility of investment decisions, increasing the uncertainty and risk associated with future conditions (including socioeconomic, political and physical environments) and ensuring that time frames of investment become more unpredictable and even more vital to reducing the likelihood of high sunk costs and stranded assets.

It is assumed in this chapter that the permanent stranding of assets necessarily results in sunk costs but that sunk costs are not necessarily stranded assets. Only if stranding is temporary, such as a drought causing the short-term cessation of activity at a hydropower station, could you argue that stranded assets do not have to result in sunk costs, as following a period of rain the electricity production can be restored. This chapter, however, will focus on permanent stranding of assets as a version of sunk costs.

This chapter offers a theoretical argument for the use of stranded assets as sunk costs frameworks in investment decision making, noting that much of the existing literature on the topic takes a more empiric approach. Further, it develops an approach to analyse investors' capacity to consider stranding risks, which has also received only scant attention to date, notably by Silver (2017), who argued that stranding risk does not fit into investors' typical risk profiles, and Caldecott and Rook (2015), who applied behavioural biases to corporate decision makers regarding stranding risk. Through the expansion and update of Clark and Wrigley's (1995) economic geography framework of sunk costs, this chapter develops a checklist of key characteristics which should aid investors in reconsidering their exposure to stranded assets and a spatial-temporal framework which could be used to identify geographic areas that could be transformed by environmental stranding risk into zones of activity or inactivity based on the prevalence of sunk costs, stranding risk and agglomeration economies.

This chapter begins by developing the relationship and comparisons between stranded assets and sunk costs, arguing that stranded assets should be viewed as a mechanism through which costs of investment will increase and become irreversible. The chapter then proposes a new spatial-temporal framework through which to view stranding risk in different geographies and time horizons, building on literatures pertaining to sunk costs, relational economic geography and behavioural finance. It concludes by offering five research propositions which sum up interactions between environmentally driven stranded assets and sunk costs and provide a baseline for future research and thought on this topic.

2. Stranded assets and sunk costs

Stranded assets are likely to increase costs for companies and investors in a range of different ways, and this chapter will outline the ways in which stranded assets share similar characteristics to sunk costs. Assets that are stranded are likely to represent sunk costs on balance sheets, and those firms with high sunk costs are also likely to lose out the most if their assets are stranded.

To establish such an association, it is important that the similarities, differences and interactions between stranded assets and sunk costs are understood. While sunk costs are traditionally seen as driven by economic factors, stranded assets are now being discussed in relation to environmental drivers (notably, physical and transition risks associated with environmental change, [Caldecott, Howarth et al. 2013; Bank of England 2015]), and this environmental stranding can be seen as an additional and separate cause of sunk costs compared to more traditional economic understandings of the drivers of investment cost decisions.

The analysis in this chapter builds upon Clark and Wrigley's (1995) economic geography framework of sunk costs, which identified the various types of sunk costs – setup, accumulated and exit costs. In drawing comparisons and similarities between stranded assets and sunk costs, it is my suggestion that stranded assets are probably most likely to be visible as accumulated and exit sunk costs rather than setup sunk costs. It is often assumed that those assets which are being stranded are ones that already physically exist and that costs associated with stranding are sunk in relation to unobtainable future revenues, whereby both fixed costs and accumulated sunk costs to date are stranded (i.e. unrecoverable sunk costs). For example, in the event of increasing extreme weather events, damage to uninsured or under-insured buildings or infrastructure could shift from being accumulated fixed and sunk costs to stranded assets and permanently sunk costs if the building is destroyed.

However, there are also some examples in which setup sunk costs could be related to stranded assets, such as sunk costs associated with exploratory drilling in the extractives and fossil fuel industries, which are then stranded due to a lack of investment or planning permissions because of environmental concerns, regulations or campaigns. Further, the growing risk of asset stranding could also raise the expected risk of entering a market if there are high setup costs that have to be sunk and might be stranded in the short, medium or long term. If a particular industry/region will be a focus of stranding, you will see fewer new entrants, potentially creating 'zones of inactivity', an idea which will be discussed in more detail later in the chapter.

Clark and Wrigley (1995) highlighted four general characteristics of sunk costs, namely recoverability, transferability, longevity and recurrent financial need. In making the link between stranded assets as sunk costs, it is clear that stranded assets can be shown to have similar characteristics and that the risk of stranding will alter the characteristics of projects' sunk costs. These four characteristics should be considered in the decision making around stranded assets as they are in the decisions of sinking costs. Sunk costs can be advantageous within a market and are often necessary (Clark and Wrigley 1995; Bellalah 2003), but their benefits depend upon these characteristics:

- *Recoverability* of sunk costs refers to the negligible likelihood of being able to sell or in some way retrieve the value of the initial investment. In this way, stranded assets are examples of sunk costs, which by their very definition are 'stranded' and therefore not recoverable – in this way, stranded assets become sunk costs on investors' and corporations' balance sheets, and environmental risks are perhaps likely to increase the proportion of unrecoverable assets in the global economy.

- *Transferability* refers to the ability of investors or a parent company to shift the burden of sunk costs onto others. This determines the extent of the cost that will be borne. Fixed costs are likely to become sunk costs if there is a significant risk of asset stranding unless there can be a transfer of the asset to a third party or a different purpose can be found for the asset. This depends on the substitutability of the assets and the willingness of others to take on the asset; infrastructure sunk costs could be repurposed away from servicing stranded assets in the fossil fuel industry, for example, and could therefore be transferable. However, if extreme weather causes asset stranding in a particular area and physical damage is done to a property, what was previously a transferable sunk cost has instead become a stranded non-transferable asset.

- *Longevity* speaks to the length of time over which a sunk cost has use-value. Under stranding scenarios, this is likely to be reduced as a result of premature write-downs and devaluations, but the longevity of assets exposed to stranding risk will vary based on a range of endogenous and exogenous factors. With both sunk costs and stranded assets, there may come a point in time where the use-value of the assets is exhausted – and investors and companies who do not adequately prepare for such times will lose out. Environmental drivers could mean that assets become stranded more suddenly, and on a larger scale, than many investors expect in coming years, reducing the longevity of existing and future projects. If projects have high sunk costs but face declining longevity, costs are likely to rise and revenues fall – awareness of stranding risk will be vital to better analyse the risks to longevity of high-sunk-cost projects.

- *Recurrent financial need* identifies that different sunk costs have different financing needs, which is the same with stranded asset projects – some will have high initial setup costs with low financing needs in the future, whereas others require ongoing funding. The split of financing needs will have a significant impact on the risk to companies and investors in scenarios of high stranding, and the appetite for the projects could therefore change as stranding becomes more visible.

A clear connection is therefore visible between stranded assets and sunk costs. This section has drawn strongly on the work of Clark and Wrigley (1995) but importantly seeks to challenge, update and extend their economic geography framework of sunk costs. This 1995 paper has been widely cited as being a seminal paper in driving a consideration of sunk costs from merely the domain of economics onto the research agenda of economic geographers (c.f. Castree et al. 2004; Dicken 2011; Hassink 2010), with several authors extending the arguments of Clark and Wrigley to examine the role of sunk costs in determining spatial variations of economic activity (Melachroinos and Spence 1999; Dicken 2011; Hudson 2001; Schoenberger 1999). Most of the criticisms of the Clark and Wrigley (1995) paper have come from those arguing that the scope of the application was too limited and that its corporate-level investigation of sunk costs missed the broader regional and institutional picture, with work such as Phelps and Fuller (2009), Hassink (2010), and Melachroinos and Spence (2001) seeking to offer intra-corporate and regional economic geography lenses.

This chapter contributes and extends further the work of others through the focus on an individual investor-lens, which has so far been neglected in the academic literature on sunk costs but is a prominent perspective for the stranded assets and responsible investment narratives. While critics have often questioned the scope of the Clark and Wrigley work, few have established a strong critique of the frameworks underpinning the paper or the propositions tendered. Although not seeking to critique this framework, it is hoped that this chapter can extend, update and expand the theoretical framework through the application to stranded asset narratives and novel understandings of economic geography and behavioural finance which have been developed in the 20 years since Clark and Wrigley wrote their papers. Furthermore, the papers written on sunk costs, from both an economic and an economic geography standpoint, focus on the economic causes and the policy/economic implications of sunk costs but fail to identify the underlying environmental factors which could contribute to increased and unexpected economic sunk costs. Given the growing awareness of the economic implications of environmental change at a range of scales, from the asset and company levels to the regional and global, it is important to address this gap in the sunk cost literatures.

Behavioural understandings of the decision-making processes of investors and individuals have advanced since the 1990s when Clark and Wrigley were writing, and it is thus possible to shift from an institutional and organisational perspective towards one which emphasises the individual agency and biases which influence stranded asset- and sunk cost–related decision making. Rational economic theory understandings at the time of Clark and Wrigley suggested that investors should not consider sunk costs in decision making but instead only consider future costs relevant to the investment decision (Arkes and Blumer 1985). However, more recent evidence from empirical behavioural finance literatures suggests that this theory does not stand up to real-world behaviour and that sunk costs do, in fact, influence investor decisions because humans are prone to loss aversion and framing effects (Kahneman 2011; Sewell 2007). This is important, as assuming that investors are not fully rational, both expected (future sunk costs) and historic sunk costs can influence decision making, and stranded assets risks can therefore be argued to have a similar influence – with expectation and experience of stranding able to affect investment decisions. This can manifest itself in a tendency to continue an endeavour once an investment in money, effort or time has been made – the 'sunk cost fallacy' (Caldecott and Rook 2015; Friedman et al. 2007; Putten and Zeelenberg 2010; Mcafee et al. 2010). Such behaviour can also be linked to other biases and heuristics, including the endowment effect, status quo bias and loss aversion (Caldecott and Rook 2015; Kahneman and Tversky 1979; Kahneman et al. 1991). Importantly, this suggests that investors who have assets in their portfolios which have required previous sunk costs are perhaps more unlikely to divest from them regardless of the risk of asset stranding. This can be seen in the continued holding of oil and gas majors (and other carbon-dependent stocks) that have already suffered some stranding in the portfolios of institutional investors.

Based on the original work of Knight (1921), it is assumed in this chapter that 'risks' refer to circumstances in which the probabilities that particular outcomes or consequences will occur in the future can be known. In contrast, 'uncertainty' reflects decisions for which probabilities cannot be known or estimated. Such definitions are an important factor in the distinctions between sunk costs and stranded assets. Generally, when investors are dealing with standard sunk cost decisions, they are dealing with risk, as they know that they will (sooner or later) face sunk costs. Stranded assets, however, could complicate such notions of sunk costs, as environmental change and the transition to a lower-carbon economy add more uncertainty into decision-making processes.

Certain environmental factors are known risks that will impact financial portfolios, such as more frequent heat waves, increased severity of storms, an increase in crop failures, and a rise in global sea levels (IPCC 2014). Although the exact timing and magnitude of these risks is not necessarily known, they can be modelled and the risks integrated into political and economic decision making. However, other potential consequences of climate change remain 'uncertain' and are as yet unknown probabilities, including the likelihood of socio-political action adaptation and the impacts of 'feedback loops' on the climate system (UKCIP 2003). While stranded asset 'risks' therefore increase the need for investors to model their exposure to increased sunk costs, they should also be aware of uncertainties in the social, environmental, political and economic systems which could result in unexpected and unprecedented sunk costs across geographies and sectors. However, it is very hard to plan for uncertain futures (Knight 1921), so it is assumed that although aware of some uncertainties involved, investors will focus on modelling and managing known risks, and it is for this purpose that the next section outlines a spatial-temporal framework of assessing stranded asset risk.

3. Towards a spatial-temporal framework of stranded assets

So far, this chapter has purported that stranded assets should be thought of as increasing sunk costs so they are seen as having both immediate and long-term investment implications. This section seeks to outline a spatial-temporal framework of stranded assets, which shows that stranded assets (and sunk costs) are more likely to have a high risk over long time periods and over wider geographic distances. Investors are not homogenous and so face a range of exposures across their different geographies and time frames (e.g. higher risk for direct capital-intensive investments than diversified listed equity portfolios, for those investors in geographies with high risk versus those with low physical climate risk). This work builds upon a strong literature of spatial-temporal frameworks used to distinguish patterns and analysis across multiple geographies and time horizons, including in economic geography (Ratcliffe 2004; Herold et al. 2003; Dietzel et al. 2005) and climate change (Eckert et al. 2010). Such a spatial-temporal framework is being proposed as a checklist of factors investors should include in their existing project and investment analysis to think through their own exposure to stranding and sunk cost risks, either at a portfolio or individual project level. Once risk exposure has been established, further methodologies could be adopted to measure the value at risk in different scenarios and portfolios and reduce exposure (TCFD 2017). Although this chapter focuses on institutional investors and asset managers, such a checklist could also be used in wider public and private investment decisions.

Before going further, it is important to briefly explore the changing dynamics of time and geography in recent years, building on the seminal works by David Harvey (1991) and Manuel Castells (1996), who have explored issues around space-time compression. Both authors focus on the importance of space and time as social phenomena constructed by economic processes and have argued that recent economic globalisation and urbanisation have shrunk space and time relations within society. Modern infrastructure and technology have facilitated such changes, including reducing the role of physical distance and speeding up processes and interactions (Knox-Hayes 2010; Tickell 2000; Dixit and Pindyck 1994). Investors are now exposed to multiple geographies, far beyond their own networks of influence and expertise, through the complex infrastructures of modern stock exchanges, investments in transnational companies and foreign direct investment.

However, this speeding up of our economic and social interaction is at loggerheads with the 'glacial time' of nature and the environment, which exists according to its own time frames and interactions (Castells 1996, p. 467). The growth of carbon markets and the integration of climate risk into decision making has meant that investors are having to reassess the speeds and distances of their economic activity to better reflect the space-times of nature (Knox-Hayes 2013, 2010), including the use of virtual finance markets to allow the incorporation of future events in decision making through instruments such as options and derivatives. It is thus becoming clear that investors must consider the environmental processes that their complex portfolios and projects are exposed to over both multiple geographies and multiple time frames, which are at one time both compressed and multifaceted. Stranding risk is one example of such a dynamic, with both the long-term and short-term risks associated with environmental change able to affect investments in a range of locations within a single portfolio. It is clear, therefore, that producing checklists, guidelines and frameworks which can help to clarify the characteristics which investors should be paying attention to can be helpful, illuminating the different spatial and temporal factors likely to be at work, although it should also be clear that these will be investor, project and context specific.

The following checklist is necessarily not exhaustive and should be used in the context of existing investment decision-making tools. I suggest that nine characterisations can be used as a checklist to help identify the level of risk of stranded assets, in the context of the earlier comparison to sunk costs, our knowledge of the causes and impacts of stranded assets and temporal and spatial understanding of economic geography and behavioural finance. These factors are:

1   Information availability – this will determine the level of risk and uncertainty surrounding an investment and is likely to be greater over shorter distances and longer time horizons.
2   Collaborative opportunities – this affects investors' ability to form investment consortia, get information and influence company and policy decisions. They are likely to be greater over shorter distances and longer time horizons due to the development of trust-based relationships.
3   Environmental risk – fundamental for determining physical exposure to environment asset stranding, environmental risks will vary from place to place and between individual assets, projects and companies and are likely to increase over time.
4   Transition risk – key to understanding the market-based, regulatory, technological and reputational risks associated with the low-carbon transition, these risks will increase over time and vary geographically.
5   Adaptation capacity – this will help determine the extent and impact of asset stranding in a region and will vary over time and space and the degree of cooperation exhibited by the public and private sectors.
6   Transferability – a key determinant of whether investors will face sunk costs as a result of stranded assets or can transform (or sell on) the asset or company to more productive future uses and is likely to be greater at shorter relational distances.
7   Recoverability – affecting the extent of asset stranding being a sunk cost, this determines the margins at which investors can recoup an investment. Likely to be higher in the short term.
8   Longevity – this will affect exposure to climate and transition stranding risk and will necessarily decline over time.
9   Financing needs of assets – the higher the financing need, the greater the risk to investors, particularly over long time frames and greater geographic distance due to the risks and uncertainties associated with such assets.

It is through such an analysis that investors can perhaps begin to understand the cost and risk implications of asset stranding within their portfolios. It is apparent that they vary over time and space, and it is therefore possible to start to develop a preliminary assessment of how different investment risk analyses might look based on investors' exposure to each characteristic, although this will necessarily vary based on individual and institutional investment factors. Such a framework is outlined in Figure 4.1. As is perhaps expected, stranding risk is likely to be greatest over long time frames and long distances if these characteristics are considered.

   Although this is a useful basic framework to highlight the different risk factors affecting likely experience of stranded assets and associated setup, accumulated or exit sunk costs, it also can demonstrate that short-term risks do exist, although

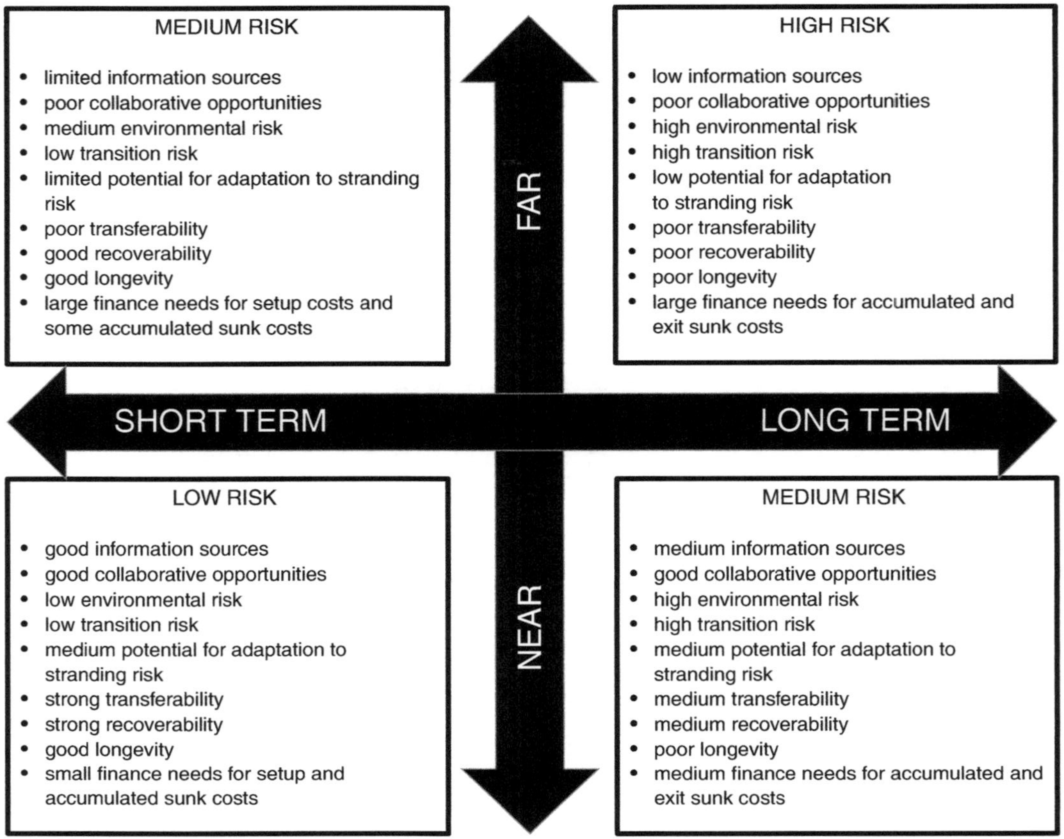

HIGH RISK

- low information sources
- poor collaborative opportunities
- high environmental risk
- high transition risk
- low potential for adaptation to stranding risk
- poor transferability
- poor recoverability
- poor longevity
- large finance needs for accumulated and exit sunk costs

MEDIUM RISK

- medium information sources
- good collaborative opportunities
- high environmental risk
- high transition risk
- medium potential for adaptation to stranding risk
- medium transferability
- medium recoverability
- poor longevity
- medium finance needs for accumulated and exit sunk costs

MEDIUM RISK

- limited information sources
- poor collaborative opportunities
- medium environmental risk
- low transition risk
- limited potential for adaptation to stranding risk
- poor transferability
- good recoverability
- good longevity
- large finance needs for setup costs and some accumulated sunk costs

LOW RISK

- good information sources
- good collaborative opportunities
- low environmental risk
- low transition risk
- medium potential for adaptation to stranding risk
- strong transferability
- strong recoverability
- good longevity
- small finance needs for setup and accumulated sunk costs

FAR

NEAR

LONG TERM

SHORT TERM

Figure 4.1 Framework for identifying stranding risk

they are likely to be smaller. However, in reality, the conceptualisations of investment are never quite this simple. Temporal aspects of investment decisions need to be properly considered and problematised. Time frames are vital to investor decision making (Dixit and Pindyck 1994) but are a potential pitfall with regards to stranded assets, as many investors focus on the long-term risk without properly assessing their short-term risk as well. As such, it is advised that an investor should assess the items on the checklist across a continuous spectrum of time to better incorporate such a spatial-temporal framework. It is assumed in this framework that information (Factor 1 in the checklist) improves over time but that environmental risk, transition risk, adaptive capacity and the transferability, longevity and recoverability of assets all deteriorate over time (Factors 3 to 8).

Time horizons affect both investors' exposure to and psychological capacity to consider stranding risks, with short-termism and the 'tragedy of the horizons' among the greatest barriers to the integration of environmental factors into investment decisions (Carney 2015; Kay 2012). This is particularly the case for large infrastructure projects, which historically have often been over budget and off schedule due to the complex decision making and realities of their design and implementation (Buehler et al. 1994; Flyvbjerg et al. 2009). However, these problems could be exacerbated by physical and transition risks and uncertainties, further undermining the time frames and increasing the sunk costs associated with such projects (Hallegatte et al. 2012). Deciding what the relevant time line to judge a particular project over is thus difficult in the context of sunk costs and stranded assets, given the fact that asset stranding could either be a long-term and slow process (e.g. gradual degradation of land/water quality affecting production), or a short-term and sudden process (e.g. flooding inundation destroying property, rapid regulatory change). As such, being aware of the different types of risks and uncertainties facing an investment from environmental factors can help investors rethink their time horizons and exposure to sunk costs and investment risk.

An important contribution of this chapter is to highlight the importance of geography in determining investors' decision-making capacity and biases. As such, it is argued that investors' relative and relational geography will influence their risk profiles – whether investors are located 'near' other investors and are close to the financial markets and agglomerated economies will determine their access to information (Factor 1) and their exposure to certain sunk cost characteristics (such as collaborative opportunities and transferability, Factors 2 and 6), as well as their exposure to environmental and transition risks (Factors 3 and 4) (Clark et al. 2000; Dixit and Pindyck 1994; Porteous 1995). Geography can be defined in a number of ways and is therefore to be interpreted within this framework as relative distance (near vs. far) compared to other investors and compared to other investment projects.

However, the international nature of modern global production networks and financial markets obfuscates these notions of a linear geography. For example, the geographies of investment in Arctic oil and gas exploration are complicated when considering the myriad stranding and environmental risks involved in any investment decision, as illustrated by the range of factors included in the checklist.

The corporations involved in such endeavours tend to be located near investment centres, with key decision makers (including regulators, policy makers, corporate executives) all in relatively close proximity to the investors themselves and therefore (comparatively) available for information, collaboration and lobbying/ engagement. However, the physical risks are typically much more remote, located in the Arctic, where oversight of the project and information about the physical environmental risks are much more unknown. Investors should thus consider both the close and far relational geographies of asset stranding. Regardless of this complexity, it is assumed that geographical distance will reduce access to information and collaborative opportunities (Factors 1 and 2), lower adaptive capacity (Factor 5), reduce transferability (Factor 6) and increase financing need (Factor 9) due to lack of scale economies and network effects. Investors should therefore be aware of the non-linear geographies involved when considering their exposure against our framework.

It is perhaps helpful to explore in more detail the different geographies at play in the framework, providing greater insight into the context of the geographies of stranded assets and sunk costs from the investor's perspective. Firstly, it is important to briefly consider the physical economic geography of stranding risk, building on the long line of economic geographers who have discussed the importance of geography in determining the location of economic activity (Dicken 2011; Clark et al. 2000; Sheppard 2002; Clark and Wrigley 1997). Physical geography can, in particular, affect an investment's exposure to both physical and transition risks associated with environmental change which directly affects exposure to stranded assets (Factors 3 and 4) (Carbon Tracker 2013b; McGlade and Ekins 2015). Investors should therefore ensure that they are not over-exposed to only a few high-risk areas, which could become 'zones of inactivity' (Clark and Wrigley 1995) as a result of concentrated asset stranding and should be aware of the climate and socio-political environments in which they are investing. This should encourage investors to adopt a more distributed model of investing, with diversification reducing the risk of 'accidents of geography or history' associated with the agglomeration of sunk costs and economic activity in a few individual locations (Clark and Wrigley 1995). However, diversified locations could perhaps face greater initial sunk costs due to poorer economies of scale, including a lack of existing infrastructure and labour pools, resulting in the need to invest in physical and educational capital as sunk firm-specific costs (Clark et al. 2000; Amin and Cohendet 2004).

Behavioural finance literatures also suggest that investors will have different capacities to consider stranding risks based on their availability heuristics linked to their investment geographies (Kahneman 2011), with investors in Australia who have seen significant water stress and extreme weather events in recent years perhaps more likely to account for environmental stranding risk (Factor 3) than those in London or New York (Harnett 2017b). Similarly, those investors and networks used to investing in markets with rapid regulatory change and technology changes (such as those in Silicon Valley, perhaps) might be more likely to consider the transition risks associated with stranded assets (Factor 4). Further, those nations and markets with stronger economic performance will perhaps also have greater capacity for both public and private adaptation to environmental catastrophe (Factors 2 and 5). As such, physical geography and the location of both investors and their investments can have a significant impact on a number of factors within the framework espoused earlier.

In addition to physical geography, it is also important to acknowledge the important influence that relational economic geography will have on stranded asset risk and its relevance to this framework. Relational approaches assume that spatial structures, including the location of economic activity in the forms of cities, assets and the like, are created by social processes, including through 'local buzz' and 'global pipelines of networking' (Bathelt and Glückler 2003; Hassink and Klaerding 2009). Stronger relational proximity within cities can improve access to information networks and knowledge sharing within and between financial centres (Bathelt and Glückler 2003; Amin and Cohendet 2004). Location and engagement within a financial centres' myriad of networks can increase an individual's relational ties, trust-based relationships, and social interactions, improving their access to information about stranded asset risk from a range of financial and nonfinancial actors. These networked knowledge spillovers, defined by Griliches (1992, p. 36) as when individuals and institutions 'are working on similar things and hence benefitting much from each other's research', could, for example, have a direct impact on analysis of stranded asset risk, the development of regulations around climate change, and the mutual sinking of costs into large-scale low-carbon technologies (affecting Factors 1 and 2). Further, this relational proximity can also affect investors' susceptibility towards availability bias (Tversky and Kahneman 1973), and it is assumed that relational proximity will increase the amount and range of information available and allowing investors to learn about their peers' experiences to influence their own decision making (Harnett 2017a).

Relational proximity can also increase investors' ability to benefit from economies of scale and increases the transferability of sunk costs and stranded assets alike due to the bigger pool of potential investment consortiums and coalitions of project partners available to share the risk (Factor 6). This is perhaps also likely to increase capacity for co-funded and collaborative adaptation and mitigation to environmental changes in these regions, so sunk costs amongst potentially stranded assets could be lowered through reduced long-term climate changes and the co-creation of economies of scale in renewable and other low-carbon technologies and infrastructure (Factors 2 and 5). This low-carbon transition can be further enabled if investors work together with policy makers, corporations and civil society. Pressure on companies to disclose and reduce their stranded asset risk is gaining traction within the market due to such collaborative efforts, with investors joining forces through shareholder resolutions, collaborative engagement initiatives such as Aiming for A[1] and through broader engagement with policy makers and regulators such as the G20 FSB Task Force on Climate Disclosures.

Whilst these arguments suggest that relational proximity can increase an investor's propensity to consider stranded assets, behaviour and responses will depend on the networks, cultures and groups that the investor belongs to and the engagement on the topic of their peer group. The danger is that this could amplify the risk of confirmation bias, which is the tendency to seek or interpret evidence in ways that are partial to existing beliefs or expectations (Kahneman 2011; Jones and Sugden 2001). This could have the effect of reducing the likelihood of changing investment practices or beliefs (Nickerson 1998). If investors are only spatially and relationally proximate to other investors who are not familiar with the term 'stranded assets', then geography could act to reinforce existing attitudes to environmental risk and ignorance of stranded assets and, by extension, reduce the information availability, collaborative opportunities for investment and adaptation, and awareness of environmental and transition risks listed in the framework (Factors 1 to 5). This can easily be linked to other behavioural biases of groupthink and herding, whereby if a group is aware and concerned (or not) by stranded assets, they are likely to act (or not; Turner and Pratkanis 1998; Bursztyn et al. 2014). However, once a network is aware of the term, action could be catalysed quickly through collaboration, with relational theories discussing the ways in which informal ideas and behaviours can transition into formal ones (including being adopted into law and regulations) through 'continuous reproduction' (Bathelt and Glückler 2003). Widening the discussion of stranded assets, perhaps through the emphasis on stranded assets as a form of sunk costs, could help facilitate a broader awareness and integration of environmental risks and uncertainties into decision making.

Financial investors are necessarily both competitive and collaborative, and such informal and interpersonal relationships within (and often between) leading financial sectors are argued to be an 'important lubricant of international finance' (Thrift 1994; Clark et al. 2000). It is these local and global relationships (Morrison et al. 2013; Bathelt et al. 2004) that can influence decision making around stranded assets as well as directly affect their exposure to stranding risk and their valuation of sunk costs.

As such, all investors must consider their exposure to sunk costs when investing, particularly in project and physical infrastructure investment (as opposed to the more flexible equity markets) and, as such, reframing stranding risk in terms of sunk costs could help provide a compass to investors who are less aware of the material risks associated with environmental changes over different time frames and complex geographies, including helping to highlight industries and regions which could become 'zones of activity or inactivity' as a result of environmental stranding.

4. Applying the spatial-temporal framework of stranded asset risk

The previous section sought to theorise the links between stranded assets and sunk costs through an outline of the basic assumptions and potential complexities of a spatial-temporal framework. To illustrate further the relevance of such a framework, this chapter will conclude with a number of examples and propositions that can be analysed on a continuous scale of time and geography to further infer that stranding risk will likely increase with time and geography. This should help demonstrate the relevance of sunk costs and highlight the notion that stranded asset risks are not exclusive to the fossil fuel sector or even high-carbon investments and emphasise that environmental change could lead to geographic and industrial 'zones of inactivity' if regions or sectors affected by stranded assets are not sufficiently diversified or resilient. Eight examples will be briefly outlined and plotted according to the framework outlined already (Figure 4.2). They further exemplify some of the complexities within the framework and demonstrate the broad range of investments to which such a framework could be applied and useful. Five propositions are then outlined to sum up interactions between environmentally driven stranded assets and sunk costs and provide a baseline for future research and thought on this topic.

> *Coca-Cola Bottling Factory, India* – As local people took to the streets in Uttar Pradesh complaining that their ground water was being depleted and polluted, corporate executives thousands of miles away faced a growing reputational concern and a potential set of stranded bottling plants as local governments took note of the growing unrest and ordered Coca-Cola to close its factories in the area (Harnett et al. 2014). This loss of social and political license to operate forced the closure of assets due to environmental damage and shows the complex geographies involved in global production networks. Geographic distance between the factory and corporate headquarters arguably enhanced the risk due to a failure of executives to comprehend the level of local unrest at the plant and fully comply with local environmental regulations, although the financial impact of the sunk costs on the corporation and investors is likely to have been small. Although water is a long-term climate risk, individual environmental (e.g. flood/drought) and social (e.g. protests, overconsumption) events can cause sudden stranding.

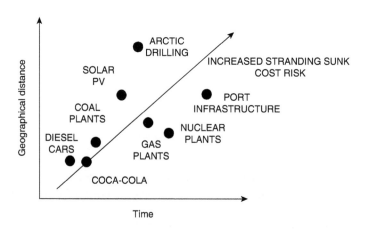

Figure 4.2 Application of framework to specific examples

Diesel Car Manufacturers, Europe – Following the (largely unpredicted) VW scandal in 2015, diesel manufacturers have faced a significant setback as a result of more stringent regulatory enforcement and social pressure (Blackwelder et al. 2016), forcing many to cut back on production and announce greater shifts in corporate investment towards electric and hybrid vehicles (Cremer 2017). Several leading manufacturers are also facing direct financial sunk costs as a result of legal liability for deceiving regulators and consumers (Tovey 2017). Furthermore, governments are now offering compensation to diesel car owners to voluntarily scrap their cars, creating a fleet of stranded cars in a bid to improve the environment in over-polluted cities. Transferability of factory technologies and infrastructures from diesel to electric production will be key to determining the extent of asset stranding and exposure to sunk costs, with asset stranding of fossil fuel–reliant transport arguably a short- to medium-term risk as the transition appears to be well underway (Simms 2015).

Gas Power Plant, Europe – Many consider that gas power will enjoy a boom in demand as a result of the low-carbon transition as the energy landscape shifts away from the most polluting power sources of coal and oil (IEA 2013). European investors have ploughed money into a new generation of high-efficiency gas power plants on the understanding that these offer a longer-term fossil fuel future. However, many did not expect that such a rapid decrease in electricity demand following the global financial crisis, changing fuel prices, the growth of renewable demand and depressed carbon prices could result in a number of stranded assets and higher sunk costs for investors (both public and private) in European gas power plants (Caldecott and McDaniels 2014). These risks have materialised over the very short term despite gas power plants being seen as relatively stable long-term investments.

Coal Power Plant, USA – Coal power plants are often associated with asset stranding, particularly since the combination of falling coal prices and a growing environmental regulatory pressure from national initiatives launched during the Obama administration have caused the premature closure of a number of power plants in the US and bankruptcy of several leading coal companies (Caldecott et al. 2015). Only a few years ago, the scale of stranding and bankruptcy would have been almost unimaginable for many investors, showing the potential for sudden shifts when a combination of forces is at play even among companies with strong investor relations and policy influence. High sunk costs and low recoverability/transferability have contributed to this, alongside strong market transitions – regardless of President Trump's campaign pledge to 'bring back coal' it is perhaps unlikely to reverse clear trends towards stranding globally (Fears 2017).

Nuclear Power Plants, Europe – Single events can cause significant asset stranding both directly and indirectly and across different geographies. This was seen following the nuclear disaster at Fukushima, Japan, with the plant immediately stranded as a result of an earthquake, but this also had wider repercussions for nuclear investments including in Germany, where the nuclear fallout from Fukushima (and previously Chernobyl) caused a significant shift in policy and public appetite for nuclear power and caused the stranding of existing facilities with significant sunk costs as a result due to the lack of transferability and recoverability (Dobbs et al. 2011; Carbon Tracker 2013b). Although nuclear power is seen as a long-term investment and is argued by some as necessary for the transition to a lower-carbon economy, sudden events such as Fukushima and longer-term regulatory changes alongside the energy transitions could have significant impacts on local, regional and global investment in nuclear power (IEA 2013).

Solar Photovoltaic (PV) Infrastructure, USA – Imagine you invested in solar PV technologies in 2005. More than a decade later, the technological innovations have been great. Those 2005 technologies are now outdated, and it is likely that it would be more efficient to simply purchase and install new technologies. Although many associate stranded asset risk with fossil fuels and other carbon-intensive industries, renewable energy and clean technologies are not immune from transition risks (IRENA 2017). The relatively new market also presents significant regulatory risks, as has been seen in changes to subsidies and tariffs (Shankleman 2015).

Port Infrastructure, Australia – Coal from the Australian outback has been fuelling the booming economies of South East Asia for a number of years, but demand has put pressure on existing infrastructure (Caldecott, Tilbury et al. 2013). Discussions are underway to develop new port infrastructure in Queensland to help deliver future coal to the Asian market. However, investments face stranding risk as a result of physical climate risk relating to sea level rise over the long term, but also face medium- (and even short-) term regulatory and market transition risks which threaten both long-term sustainability of coal export demand and supply and social and political planning licenses in ecologically important areas, most notably near the Great Barrier Reef (Carbon Tracker 2013a, 2015). This has the potential for high sunk costs due to the lack of recoverability if assets do become stranded – such large ports in Queensland rely on fossil fuel demand.

This chapter has sought to provide a preliminary spatial-temporal framework for the consideration of stranded assets through the use of a sunk cost lens. It is clear that investors should be aware of the myriad risks and opportunities presented by stranded assets but that these risks are likely to increase both over longer time horizons and over greater geographic distance (both physical and relational). Through the adoption of the lens of sunk costs, this chapter has sought to suggest a framework of characteristics that could help investors consider and analyse their stranded asset risk within their existing investment decision-making processes, thereby helping mainstream investors better incorporate environmental risks into their portfolios.

However, this has been a necessarily limited exploration of the potential for such a framework and research stream, and it is therefore perhaps useful to outline a number of propositions which sum up interactions between environmentally driven stranded assets and sunk costs and provide a baseline for future research and thought on this topic. These build upon the propositions of sunk costs in an economic geography framework espoused by Clark and Wrigley (1995) but focus on a framework for sunk costs under the influence of asset stranding.

Proposition 1: stranded assets are likely to increase sunk costs

This can be shown through a brief study of Mata's (1991) definition of sunk costs, which empirically describes the nature of sunk costs and how they can be calculated. I will briefly show how stranded assets can be shown to be a cause of and example of sunk costs:

$$SUNK = KR \, (1 - n \, ANDEP) \, (1 - RESEL)$$

where KR is the initial capital investment, n is the expected number of years that an entrant will be in the market, ANDEP is the annualised depreciated proportion of KR at the time of exit and RESEL is the recoverable portion of that investment. This equation can help demonstrate the theory behind the assumption that asset stranding will necessarily increase sunk costs. Stranded assets, by their very definition, are expected to reduce the number of years that an investment will be profitable in the market and reduce the recoverable investment whilst increasing the proportion of capital that is depreciated. The framework established in this chapter, based on behavioural finance and relational economic geography, suggests that stranding risk is likely to increase sunk costs the most over longer time frames and in more remote spaces of investment.

Proposition 2: sunk costs are not without merit – but this merit could be enhanced or undermined by stranded asset risk depending on the type of investment

Clark and Wrigley (1995, p. 213) proposed that 'sunk costs are hardly ever without merit', arguing that setup sunk costs are a necessary condition for efficient and innovative strategic shifts in competitive markets. Furthermore, they argued that sunk costs could give significant first-mover advantages and demonstrate intent in the market. Whilst not undermining this point, under the conditions of asset stranding it is clear that sinking costs in an industry likely to suffer from premature write-downs and significant asset stranding in the future are less likely to have merit, particularly in the long run and in geographies lacking the benefits of economies of scale. However, sinking costs in industries that are likely to outperform in the transition to a lower-carbon economy could, indeed, provide significant merit. It is thus clear that the potential recoverability, transferability, longevity and frequency of financial commitment needed should be explored in the context of asset stranding in analysing the likely merits of sinking costs.

Proposition 3: stranded assets could increase the sunk costs associated with market entry and act as a barrier to project setup

Although stranded assets are often associated with market incumbency and exit, increasingly investors and companies alike will need to make market entry decisions based on the risk of stranded assets given the increased risk that costs could be sunk. For most companies, there are significant setup costs involved in entering a market, many of which have limited salvage value, and the recoverable value and length of time that an entrant can be in the market could decrease as a result of asset stranding. The need to sink costs can therefore be a barrier to entry in an industry in which stranded assets are likely, potentially leaving regions as 'zones of inaction' due to their inoperable stranding risk, meaning that new industry locates elsewhere (Clark and Wrigley 1995, p. 213). However, sunk costs as entry-barrier investments also increase the risks faced by incumbents, as new entrants can learn from incumbents' mistakes and successes in terms of stranded asset experience, with new entrants able to analyse incumbents' history and geography of asset stranding and better prepare for the low-carbon economy.

Proposition 4: stranded assets are likely to increase the prevalence of sunk costs associated with exit strategies

Stranded assets are naturally associated with exit strategies much more readily than literatures on the economic geography of sunk costs, and this frame could enhance the existing paucity of research exploring the nature and characteristics of sunk costs related to the implementation of exit strategies. Clark and Wrigley (1995, p. 213) argued that the study of sunk costs is 'literally the logic of spatial persistence', purporting that the study of sunk costs in relation to exit strategies is equally as important as market entrance costs. By increasing the risk of different geographies, industries and assets facing stranding, market exit is more likely, as companies and investors will struggle to make long-term profitability in these at-risk sectors and geographies. Further, using a framework of sunk costs can help those considering the risks related to stranded assets, better facilitating a long-run investment outlook through highlighting the financial risks of stranding at the market exit, which is a time frame often negated by investors with a short time horizon.

Proposition 5: geography of stranded assets and sunk costs can contribute to zones of economic activity and zones of risk

As discussed in the previous section, geography has a strong influence over the risk of stranded assets but also the experience of sunk costs. Sunk costs will be higher in remote geographies and can therefore create zones of inaction or persistence (Clark and Wrigley 1995). This can be accentuated by agglomeration-scale economies and information availability through relational proximity to fellow investors and sector-specific knowledge and infrastructures amongst companies. The geographies of stranded assets are likely to combine further to create zones of high and low investment risk and cost, and this is likely to cause further clustering of industry but not necessarily in the same locations as at present over the long run due to the changing geographies of productivity and risk under future climate change. Although 'zones of activity and inactivity' already exist due to geographical, environmental and economic factors, stranded assets and their related sunk costs are likely to alter the geographies, creation and persistence of such zones, and this could be a productive and important area of future research.

5. Conclusions

Stranded asset risk is a growing concern among those aware of the environmental transition underway but remains an oft-intangible concept for the majority of investors given the complex uncertainties, time frames and geographies involved in calculating exposure to such risks at a portfolio or asset level. As such, this chapter has sought to highlight the comparison and association between stranded assets and sunk costs to emphasise the ways in which environmental considerations can affect investment decisions at all stages of investment cycles – from project/company establishment, toaccumulation and market exit. It has been shown that the key characteristics of sunk costs – recoverability, transferability, longevity, and financing needs – can all be associated with stranded assets. Not only are stranded assets related to sunk costs, but the environmental factors driving asset stranding are likely to increase the experience of irreversible costs over both short- and long-term investment horizons. Investors are perhaps more used to considering long-term risks involved in sunk cost decisions, so such an insight and framework is hoped to improve investors' capacity to consider asset stranding risks in their decisions.

Through the expansion and update of Clark and Wrigley's (1995) economic geography framework, including insights from relational economic geography and behavioural finance, this chapter has highlighted key characteristics that should aid investors in considering their exposure to stranded assets. It is shown that stranding-related sunk costs are impacted by and have an impact on relational and relative economic geography. Importantly, it has highlighted a spatial-temporal framework which could help identify environmental risks in portfolios over varied geographies and time frames, but also could help illuminate areas in which stranding could create zones of activity and inactivity due to the prevalence of sunk costs and agglomeration economies. Those regions with high exposure to stranded asset risk, weaker networking and co-financing opportunities, and smaller scalar economies are likely to experience higher sunk costs relating to stranded assets and could therefore face higher barriers to economic activity creating relative zones of inactivity. Awareness of the irreversibility, longevity, transferability and frequency of financial commitment needed to sustain an investment could be key to analysing investor liability and risk from stranding assets and directly relates to investors' geography and time horizons.

Note

1 The Aiming for A coalition of investors is focused on undertaking in-depth engagement with the 10 largest UK-listed extractives and utilities companies, seeking to use their combined voice and expertise to effect broad changes in practices. More information can be found at: http://investorsonclimatechange.org/portfolio/aiming-for-a/.

References

Amin, A. and Cohendet, P. 2004. *Architectures of Knowledge: Firms, Capabilities, and Communities*. Oxford: Oxford University Press.

Arkes, H. R. and Blumer, C. 1985. The Psychology of Sunk Cost. *Organizational Behavior and Human Decision Processes*, 35(1), 124–140.

Bank of England. 2015. *The Impact of Climate Change on the UK Insurance Sector A Climate Change Adaptation Report by the Prudential Regulation Authority*. London: Bank of England.

Bathelt, H. and Glückler, J. 2003. Toward a Relational Economic Geography. *Journal of Economic Geography*, 3(2), 117–144.

Bathelt, H., Malmberg, A. and Maskell, P. 2004. Clusters and Knowledge: Local Buzz, Global Pipelines and the Process of Knowledge Creation. *Progress in Human Geography*, 28(1), 31–56.

Bellalah, M. 2003. On Irreversibility, Sunk Costs and Investment Under Incomplete Information. In Paxon, D. A. (ed.), *Real R & D Options*. Burlingon, MA: Elsevier, pp. 11–29

Blackwelder, B., et al. 2016. The Volkswagen Scandal. *Robin Case Network*. Available at: http://scholarship.richmond.edu/robins-case-network/17 [Accessed October 21, 2017].

Blyth, W., et al. 2007. Investment Risks Under Uncertain Climate Change Policy. *Energy Policy*, 35(11), 5766–5773.

Buehler, R., Griffin, D. and Ross, M. 1994. Exploring the "Planning Fallacy": Why People Underestimate Their Task Completion Times. *Journal of Personality and Social Psychology*, 67(3), 366–381. http://doi.apa.org/getdoi.cfm?doi=10.1037/0022-3514.67.3.366 [Accessed May 11, 2017].

Bursztyn, L., et al. 2014. Understanding Mechanisms Underlying Peer Effects: Evidence From a Field Experiment on Financial Decisions. *Econometrica*, 82(4), 1273–1301. Available at: http://doi.wiley.com/10.3982/ECTA11991.

Caldecott, B., Dericks, G. and Mitchell, J. 2015. Stranded Assets and Subcritical Coal: The Risk to Companies and Investors. *Stranded Assets Programme, SSEE*, University of Oxford, pp. 1–78.

Caldecott, B., Howarth, N. and McSharry, P. 2013. *Stranded Assets in Agriculture: Protecting Value From Environment-Related Risks*. Oxford. Available at: www.smithschool. ox.ac.uk/research-programmes/stranded-assets/Stranded Assets Agriculture Report Final.pdf [Accessed December 2, 2015].

Caldecott, B. and McDaniels, J. 2014. *Stranded Generation Assets: Implications for European Capacity Mechanisms, Energy Markets and Climate Policy*. Available at: www.smithschool.ox.ac.uk/research-programmes/stranded-assets/Stranded Generation Assets – Working Paper – Final Version.pdf.

Caldecott, B. and Rook, D. 2015. *Cognitive Biases and Stranded Assets: Detecting Psychological Vulnerabilities Within International Oil Companies*. Oxford. Available at: www.smithschool.ox.ac.uk/research-programmes/stranded-assets/Cognitive biases and Stranded Assets – Detecting psychological vulnerabilities within International Oil Companies – 16.07.2015.pdf [Accessed March 23, 2016].

Caldecott, B., Tilbury, J. and Ma, Y. 2013. *Stranded Down Under? Environment-Related Factors Changing China's Demand for Coal and What This Means for Australian Coal Assets.* Available at: www.smithschool.ox.ac.uk/research-programmes/stranded-assets/ Stranded Down Under Report.pdf [Accessed December 2, 2015].

Carbon Tracker. 2013a. *Unburnable Carbon: Australia's Carbon Bubble.* London: Carbon Tracker Initiative.

Carbon Tracker. 2013b. *Unburnable Carbon 2013: Wasted Capital and Stranded Assets.* London: Carbon Tracker Initiative.

Carbon Tracker. 2015. *The $2 Trillion Stranded Assets Danger Zone: How Fossil Fuel Firms Risk Destroying Investor Returns.* Available at: www.carbontracker.org/wp-content/uploads/2015/11/CAR3817_Synthesis_Report_24.11.15_WEB2.pdf [Accessed July 18, 2016].

Carney, M. 2015. *Breaking the Tragedy of the Horizon – Climate Change and Financial Stability.* London. Available at: www.bankofengland.co.uk/publications/Documents/ speeches/2015/speech844.pdf [Accessed March 14, 2016].

Castells, M. 1996. *The Rise of the Network Society: Volume I*, 1st ed. London: Wiley-Blackwell.

Castree, N., et al. 2004. *Spaces of Work: Global Capitalism and the Geographies of Labour.* London: SAGE Publications.

Clark, G. L., Feldman, M. P. and Gertler, M. S. 2000. *The Oxford Handbook of Economic Geography*, 1st ed. Oxford: Oxford University Press. Available at: http:// links.jstor.org/sici?sici=0013-0095(200207)78:3%3C387:TOHOEG%3E2.0.CO; 2-A&origin=crossref.

Clark, G. L. and Wrigley, N. 1995. Sunk Costs – a Framework for Economic-Geography. *Transactions of the Institute of British Geographers*, 20(2), 204–223.

Clark, G. L. and Wrigley, N. 1997. Exit, the Firm and Sunk Costs: Reconceptualizing the Corporate Geography of Disinvestment and Plant Closure. *Progress in Human Geography*, 21(3), 338–358.

Cremer, A. 2017. Volkswagen Doubles Commitment to Electric Vehicles With €20bn Investment Pledge. *Independent.*

Dicken, P. 2011. *Global Shift: Mapping the Changing Contours of the World Economy*, 7th ed. London: SAGE Publications.

Dietzel, C., Herold, M. and Hemphill, J. 2005. Spatio-Temporal Dynamics in California's Central Valley: Empirical Links to Urban Theory. *Journal of Geographical Information Science.* Available at: www.tandfonline.com/doi/abs/10.1080/13658810410001713407 [Accessed May 31, 2017].

Dixit, A. and Pindyck, R. 1994. *Investment Under Uncertainty.* Princeton: Princeton University Press.

Dobbs, R., et al. 2011. Resource Revolution: Meeting the World's Energy, Materials, Food, and Water Needs. *McKinsey & Company*, November. www.mckinsey.com/Features/ Resource_revolution.aspx.

Eckert, N., et al. 2010. A Spatio-Temporal Modelling Framework for Assessing the Fluctuations of Avalanche Occurrence Resulting From Climate Change: Application to 60 Years of Data in the. *Climatic Change.* Available at: www.springerlink.com/index/ f4420814xgj151v8.pdf [Accessed May 31, 2017].

Fears, D. 2017. Trump Promised to Bring Back Coal Jobs. That Promise "Will Not Be Kept," Experts Say. *The Washington Post.*

Flyvbjerg, B., Garbuio, M. and Lovallo, D. 2009. Delusion and Deception in Large Infrastructure Projects: Two Models for Explaining and Preventing Executive Disaster. *California Management Review*, 51(2). Available at: http://cmr.ucpress.edu/content/51/2/170 [Accessed May 11, 2017].

Friedman, D., et al. 2007. Searching for the Sunk Cost Fallacy. *Experimental*. Available at: www.springerlink.com/index/MK2PR8T22Q81N241.pdf [Accessed May 13, 2017].

Griliches, Z. 1992. The Search for R&D Spillovers. *Scandinavian Journal of Economics*, 94: 29–47.

Hallegatte, S., et al. 2012. *Investment Decision Making Under Deep Uncertainty: Application to Climate Change*.

Harnett, E. S. 2017a. Social and Asocial Learning About Climate Change Among Institutional Investors: Lessons for Stranded Assets. *Journal of Sustainable Finance & Investment*, 7(1), 114–137. Available at: www.tandfonline.com/doi/full/10.1080/20430795.2016.1249095 [Accessed January 31, 2017].

Harnett, E. S. 2017b. *The State of Climate Change Knowledge Among UK and Australian Institutional Investors*. Oxford, UK. Available at: www.smithschool.ox.ac.uk/research-programmes/stranded-assets/State-of-climate-change-knowledge-among-UK-and-Australian-institutional-investors-SFP-Working-Paper-February-2017.pdf [Accessed March 9, 2017].

Harnett, I., Edstrom, E. and Harnett, E. S. 2014. *Stranded Assets A New Concept but a Critical Risk*. London: Absolute Strategy Research.

Harvey, D. 1991. *The Condition of Postmodernity: An Enquiry Into the Origins of Cultural Change*.

Hassink, R. 2010. Regional Resilience: A Promising Concept to Explain Differences in Regional Economic Adaptability? *Cambridge Journal of Regions, Economy and Society*, 3(1), 45–58. Available at: https://academic.oup.com/cjres/article-lookup/doi/10.1093/cjres/rsp033 [Accessed May 9, 2017].

Hassink, R. and Klaerding, C. 2009. Relational and Evolutionary Economic Geography: Competing or Complementary Paradigms? Robert. *Economic Geography*, 120–136. Available at: http://ideas.repec.org/p/egu/wpaper/0905.html.

Herold, M., Goldstein, N. and Clarke, K. 2003. The Spatiotemporal Form of Urban Growth: Measurement, Analysis and Modeling. *Remote Sensing of Environment*. Available at: www.sciencedirect.com/science/article/pii/S0034425703000750 [Accessed May 31, 2017].

Hudson, R. 2001. *Producing Places*. New York: The Guildford Press.

IEA. 2013. Redrawing the Energy Climate Map. *World Energy Outlook Special Report*, p. 134. Available at: www.worldenergyoutlook.org/media/weowebsite/2013/energyclimatemap/RedrawingEnergyClimateMap.pdf.

IPCC. 2014. *Summary for Policymakers*. In *Climate Change 2014: Impacts, Adaptation, and Vulnerability. Part A: Global and Sectoral Aspects. Contribution of Working Group II to the Fifth Assessment Report of the Intergovernmental Panel on Climate Change*. Cambridge, UK: Cambridge University Press.

IRENA. 2017. *Stranded Assets and Renewables: How the Energy Transition Affects the Value of Energy Reserves, Buildings and Capital Stock*. Available at: www.irena.org/DocumentDownloads/Publications/IRENA_REmap_Stranded_assets_and_renewables_2017.pdf [Accessed October 21, 2017].

Jones, M. and Sugden, R. 2001. Positive Confirmation Bias in the Acquisition of Information. *Theory and Decision*, 50(1), 59–99.

Kahneman, D. 2011. *Thinking, Fast and Slow*. New York: Farrar, Straus and Giroux.

Kahneman, D., Knetsch, J. L. and Thaler, R. H. 1991. Anomalies: The Endowment Effect, Loss Aversion, and Status Quo Bias. *Journal of Economic Perspectives*, 5(1), 193–206.

Kahneman, D. and Tversky, A. 1979. Prospect Theory: An Analysis of Decision Under Risk. *Econometrica: Journal of the Econometric Society*, 57(2), 263–291.

Kay, J. 2012. *The Kay Review of UK Equity Markets and Long-Term Decision Making*. London: Department for Business, Innovation and Skills.

Knight, F. H. 1921. *Risk, Uncertainty and Profit*. Boston, MA: Houghton Mifflin.

Knox-Hayes, J. 2010. Constructing Carbon Market Spacetime: Climate Change and the Onset of Neo-Modernity. *Annals of the Association of American Geographers*, 100(4), 953–962. Available at: www.tandfonline.com/doi/abs/10.1080/00045608.2010.500554.

Knox-Hayes, J. 2013. The Spatial and Temporal Dynamics of Value in Financialization: Analysis of the Infrastructure of Carbon Markets. *Geoforum*, 50, 117–128.

Mata, J. 1991. Sunk Costs and Entry by Small and Large Plants. In Geroski, P. A. and Schwalbach, J. (eds.), *Entry and Market Contestability*. Oxford: Blackwell, pp. 49–62.

Mcafee, R. P., Mialon, H. M. and Mialon, S. H. 2010. Do Sunk Costs Matter? *Economic Inquiry*, 48(2), 323–336.

McGlade, C. and Ekins, P. 2015. The Geographical Distribution of Fossil Fuels Unused When Limiting Global Warming to 2 °C. *Nature*, 517, 187–190.

Melachroinos, K. A. and Spence, N. 1999. Regional Economic Performance and Sunk Costs. *Regional Studies*, 33(9), 843–855. Available at: www.tandfonline.com/doi/abs/10.1080/00343409950075489 [Accessed May 9, 2017].

Melachroinos, K. A. and Spence, N. 2001. Conceptualizing Sunk Costs in Economic Geography: Cost Recovery and the Fluctuating Value of Fixed Capital. *Progress in Human Geography*, 25(3), 347–364. Available at: http://journals.sagepub.com/doi/10.1191/030913201680191718 [Accessed May 9, 2017].

Morrison, A., Rabellotti, R. and Zirulia, L. 2013. When Do Global Pipelines Enhance the Diffusion of Knowledge in Clusters? *Economic Geography*, 89(1), 77–96.

Nickerson, R. S. 1998. Confirmation Bias: A Ubiquitous Phenomenon in Many Guises. *Review of General Psychology*, 2(2), 175–220.

Phelps, N. A. and Fuller, C. 2009. Multinationals, Intracorporate Competition, and Regional Development. *Economic Geography*, 76(3), 224–243. Available at: http://doi.wiley.com/10.1111/j.1944-8287.2000.tb00142.x [Accessed May 9, 2017].

Porteous, D. J. 1995. *The Geography of Finance: Spatial Dimensions of Intermediary Behaviour*. Aldershot: Avebury. Available at: http://catalog.hathitrust.org/Record/002984397 [Accessed January 2, 2016].

Putten, M. van and Zeelenberg, M. 2010. Who Throws Good Money After Bad? Action vs. State Orientation Moderates the Sunk Cost Fallacy. *Judgment and Decision*. Available at: http://search.proquest.com/openview/20b67ff3fea8044d3ed5ca2f55bc58b1/1?pq-origsite=gscholar&cbl=696407 [Accessed May 13, 2017].

Ratcliffe, J. 2004. The Hotspot Matrix: A Framework for the Spatio-Temporal Targeting of Crime Reduction. *Police Practice and Research*. Available at: www.tandfonline.com/doi/abs/10.1080/1561426042000191305 [Accessed May 31, 2017].

Schoenberger, E. 1999. The Firm in the Region and the Region in the Firm. In Barnes, T. and Gertler, M. (eds.), *The New Industrial Geography: Regions, Regulations and Institutions*. Routledge, pp. 205–224. Available at: https://books.google.co.uk/books?hl=en&lr=&id=2baBAgAAQBAJ&oi=fnd&pg=PA205&ots=eSs9GtEyFC&sig=7L9X9OgQH3sgc9nYTZDIX5mKUpQ [Accessed May 9, 2017].

Sewell, M. 2007. *Behavioural Finance*. Available at: http://s3.amazonaws.com/academia.edu.documents/30766417/behavioural-finances.pdf?AWSAccessKeyId=AKIAIWOW

YYGZ2Y53UL3A&Expires=1490352204&Signature=LUd6lmFcimvDqotL6JI20p0Z3
HU%3D&response-content-disposition=inline%3Bfilename%3DBehavioural_Finance.
pdf [Accessed March 24, 2017].

Shankleman, J. 2015. Government Softens Feed-in Tariff Blow to Solar and Wind Industries. *BusinessGreen*. Available at: www.businessgreen.com/bg/news/2439587/govern
ment-softens-blow-to-solar-industry-over-feed-in-tariff-review [Accessed October 21,
2017].

Sheppard, E. 2002. The Spaces and Times of Globalization: Place, Scale, Networks, and
Positionality. *Economic Geography*, 78(3), 307–330.

Silver, N., 2017. Blindness to rRsk: Why Institutional Investors Ignore the Risk of Stranded
Sssets. *Journal of Sustainable Finance & Investment*, 7(1), 99–113.

Simms, A. 2015. Cars, Aviation, Steel: The Stranded Assets Risk Spreads Far Beyond Fossil Fuel Firms. *The Guardian*, pp. 10–12.

TCFD. 2017. *Final Report: Recommendations of the Task Force on Climate-related Financial Disclosures*. FSB Task Force on Climate-Related Disclosures.

Thrift, N. 1994. On the Social and Cultural Determinants of International Financial Centres: The Case of the City of London. In Corbridge, S. (ed.), *Money, Power and Space*.
Oxford: Blackwell, pp. 327–355.

Tickell, A. 2000. Dangerous Derivatives: Controlling and Creating Risks in International
Money. *Geoforum*, 31(1), 87–99.

Tovey, A. 2017. VW Faces "Super Claim" Over Dieselgate as UK and Netherlands Motor-
ists Join Forces. *The Telegraph*.

Turner, M. E. and Pratkanis, A. R. 1998. Twenty-Five Years of Groupthink Theory and
Research: Lessons From the Evaluation of a Theory. *Organizational Behavior and
Human Decision Processes*, 73(2–3), 105–115.

Tversky, A. and Kahneman, D. 1973. Availability: A Heuristic for Judging Frequency and
Probability. *Cognitive Psychology*, 5(2), 207–232.

UKCIP. 2003. *Climate Adaptation: Risk, Uncertainty and Decision-Making*. London.
Available at: www.ukcip.org.uk/wordpress/wp-content/PDFs/UKCIP-Risk-framework.
pdf [Accessed May 31, 2017].

5 The stranding of upstream fossil fuel assets in the context of the transition to a low-carbon economy

Jakob Thomä

1. Introduction

Fossil fuels account for around two-thirds of anthropogenic GHG emissions and four-fifths of primary energy supply (IEA 2016a). They have powered the global economy since the dawn of the industrial revolution, with the advent of coal and the subsequent rise of oil and natural gas. They are at the heart of a range of sectors key to the modern economy, including electricity, transport (automobiles, aviation, shipping), chemicals, and materials (e.g. cement, steel). This chapter focuses on upstream fossil fuel reserves and their interface with stranded assets.

Their prominent role both in powering today's economy and contributing to climate change has put fossil fuel production and the companies behind it on the front line in the debate around stranded assets in the context of the transition to a low-carbon economy. Renewables are set to be the primary driver replacing coal- and gas-fired power generation. Electric vehicles demand is growing, and potential alternatives (e.g. fuel cells) are not far behind as realistic options for the automobile sector. Efficiency measures in aviation, shipping, chemicals, and materials are gaining in prominence, as is the research around zero-carbon alternatives.

As highlighted by the Intergovernmental Panel on Climate Change (IPCC), no matter what one's belief about the level of climate change relative to pre-industrial levels at which temperatures will 'normalize', ultimately the global economy will need to balance at net zero GHG emissions. Article 4 of the Paris Agreement defining the long-term policy roadmap of the international community on climate change, phrases this in somewhat more convoluted but equally decisive terms:

> In order to achieve the long-term temperature goal set out in Article 2, Parties aim [. . .] to achieve a balance between anthropogenic emissions by sources and removals by sinks of greenhouse gases in the second half of this century, on the basis of equity, and in the context of sustainable development and efforts to eradicate poverty.

The implications for oil, gas, and coal are clear: A significant reduction of their use to zero or near-zero levels during the 21st century. The idea that peak oil could arrive before the technical peaking of oil production started to gain currency following the seminal article from (Meinshausen et al. 2009) in *Nature* arguing that to limit climate change at a maximum of 2°C, at least 66% of global fossil fuel reserves had to 'stay in the ground'. This article sparked further research from NGOs (Leaton 2011) and universities (Ansar et al. 2013; McGlade and Ekins 2015) and subsequently equity research (Robbins and Knight 2013; Spedding et al. 2013; Lewis 2014) and investment consultants (Mercer 2015).

As part of the discussion and the research done on the topic to date, it is critical to disentangle a number of different concepts. The first is that while upstream oil, gas, and coal are generally grouped under the heading 'fossil fuels' and all face fundamentally the same constraints of the incompatibility of their sustained use at current levels in the context of the decarbonization of the economy (even under optimistic carbon capture and storage assumptions), the relative mechanism through which they face those constraints and the potential implications will be different to each. Their differences make them fundamentally different products (Section 2).

The second critical aspect is that ultimately the economic risks for oil, gas, and coal will translate in some form into financial markets. However, the impact in financial markets is unlikely to reflect one to one the economic shocks (Thomä et al. 2015). Thus, it is important to distinguish the economic risks and economic stranding of assets – the stranding of the fossil fuels themselves – and the financial risks – loss in valuation and credit default driven by economic risks. For example, an oil and gas company might find that 80% of its oil reserves will be ultimately stranded. Investors, however, may already assume that that is the case and have reflected this in the share price. This then becomes, crucially, a question of timing and the extent to which different market actors – companies and investors – accurately read or forecast economic trends.

Finally, the relative materiality of the risks will be different across the investment chain. An individual coal mine, for example, may be at high risk of stranding, but the effects on a diversified mining company with only 10% of its revenues from coal production may be relatively muted (Spedding et al. 2013). These effects will be even more muted for an investor, who may have less than 1% of their portfolio invested in that company. Of course, these risks may re-aggregate to become material across an investor portfolio. These kinds of dynamics are important to disentangle for an accurate assessment not just of the likelihood of stranded assets for the oil and gas sector but also the materiality for different actors exposed to these risks. This issue will also be revisited in Section 6.

This chapter then seeks to explore the implications of this trend for the value of fossil fuel assets, notably the reserves and infrastructure built to extract these reserves, as well as the companies and stakeholders owning these reserves. Section 2 will briefly review the relative exposure of each fossil fuel to 'transition trends'; Section 3 will then explore the research around the future of fossil fuel production. Section 4 will discuss the implications for the economic stranding of assets, with Section 5 discussing the likely exposure of various companies to these risks. Section 6 will then discuss the potential implications for financial markets, with Section 7 providing some concluding remarks.

2. The relative positioning of fossil fuels

Fossil fuels are created through the anaerobic transformation of biological substances (Sato 1990). In the context of the transition to a low-carbon economy, three types of fossil fuels are of particular note – one solid (coal), one liquid (oil), one gas (natural gas). Each of these has different properties, different economic uses, different environmental footprints, and thus slightly different decarbonization stories. According to the (IEA 2016b), together, they made up 81% of total primary energy demand (TPED) in 2014 and 66% of total final energy consumption (TFC).

Oil has the largest share in both TPED (31%) and TCF (40%) (ibid.). Its use will differ significantly by region. Thus, more than one-third of Saudi Arabia's electricity generation is powered by oil, while globally – given the relative economics of oil versus other fuels – it was only around 5% in 2014. According to the US Energy Information Agency, in the United States – likely a representative country in terms of global crude oil use – around 46% of crude oil was refined into finished motor gasoline, 10% into fuel for aviation and 28% for distillate fuel oil – which can be used for road or seaways transport. The overwhelming majority of crude oil uses thus relate to transport, with a small fraction reserved for petrochemicals, electric power, and materials (e.g. asphalt). These uses are then also the most relevant in terms of being replaced. While alternatives may over time be developed for asphalt, for example (King & King 2008), it is the core use of fossil fuels that will be at the heart of the discussion in this chapter.

Coal is the second most prominent fossil fuel in terms of TPED with 29%, albeit only capturing 10% of TFC. Coal can be distinguished between thermal and metallurgical coal. Thermal coal is exclusively used to run turbines to generate electricity or heat. Metallurgical coal in turn is used for iron and steel-making and accounts for around 15% of global coal production (Aurizon 2015). The two are geologically different. From a climate perspective, it is primarily thermal coal that is of significance, given the environmental impact and the short-term opportunities for replacing thermal coal with alternatives. At the same time, metallurgical coal will also be challenged as zero-carbon alternatives to producing steel are developed. This will, however, happen over a much longer period of time. In the first half of the 21st century, it will be the question around potential demand destruction of thermal coal that will be of primary concern in the eyes of policy makers, companies, and the climate.

Natural gas is currently the third most prominent fossil fuel, albeit rapidly growing in prominence. This growth is driven primarily by a combination of climate and pollution policies targeting coal and the evolution of natural gas prices following the shale gas revolution of the past decade. Natural gas is used primarily for electricity generation and heating and thus competes directly with coal as a fuel. This is a crucial distinction between oil on the one hand and gas and coal on the other, with oil a primary fuel in transport and gas and coal more closely linked to power. Nevertheless, a small share of natural gas is also used for transport and in fertilizers, where it competes with oil.

In terms of thinking about stranded assets and fossil fuels, one critical aspect then is the question not just of the competition of fossil fuels with zero-carbon alternatives but also of fossil fuels with each other. This is particularly true for coal and gas for power. Achieving global climate objectives involves limiting the total amount of GHG that are emitted into the atmosphere. This then also implies a competition between the fuels around which one gets which slice of the 'carbon budget' associated with climate objectives.

As will be shown subsequently, this also significantly complicates the question around stranded assets, as different assumptions around the relative trajectory of each fossil fuel, not just in terms of the absolute ambition of transition roadmaps but also their relative competitiveness to each other, will lead to different results about the remaining use of these fuels. This aspect will be elaborated further in the next section.

3. The future of fossil fuel production

The first question around stranded assets is how much of the asset will still generate economic use and thus return to its owner. In terms of fossil fuels, the range of possible outcomes for fossil fuels according to different climate scenarios is extreme to say the least. For coal, the difference between the most optimistic and most pessimistic scenario on coal production until 2100 is roughly the equivalent of the total current energy joules in the economy (IEA 2016a). For gas and oil, while less volatile, the differences are also highly significant.

This diversity of outcomes across scenarios can be attributed to two key differences in the modelling assumptions used. The first is the assumption around the remaining carbon budget associated with the transition. First, there is no certainty at which point global emissions will reach net zero and how much anthropogenic GHG emissions have been emitted until then. While the well below 2°C goal constitutes a political mandate, it is unclear whether this objective will be achieved. Secondly, there is uncertainty around which economic constraint will ultimately be associated with climate change of 2°C or less. Thus, the scenarios selected here differ in the 'carbon budget' they 'allow' the economy to emit in their models (measured in gigatonnes, GT), or the ratio of carbon dioxide molecules to all other molecules in the atmosphere (measured in parts per million, ppm). Thus, the scenarios differ in part because the constraints differ.

Even when controlling for such differences, there is a second parameter that drives differences in results. This parameter involves the assumption around the extent to which GHG emissions will be captured in the use phase of coal, oil, and gas. The extent to which this is the case will then drive the extent to which coal, oil, and gas can still be used even under highly constraining carbon budgets. The key analytical question then is both an economic and a technological one. First, will carbon capture and storage be feasible at the scale at which some scenarios predict? And second, will it be economically viable in competing with low-carbon alternatives to the extent that these scenarios predict?

It should be noted that while the models around future fossil fuel production presented here are specifically climate models, not all constraints around future production are climate specific. Thus, in China, future coal production may also be lower as a function of policies to curb pollution (Jin et al. 2016). Similarly, the relative economics of battery-powered automobile motors versus internal combustion engines may also tilt as consumer preferences change and create product differentiation outside of a simple climate policy and relative prices framework.

In summary, the range of outcomes presented here demonstrates the complexity of assessing the likelihood and scale of stranded upstream fossil fuel assets. There is no one figure around the extent to which fossil fuel reserves will be economically impaired in this century. The answer depends on four key constraints: (i) the ambition and speed of economic decarbonisation, (ii) the economic viability of zero-carbon/low-carbon alternatives, (iii) the relative competitiveness of high-carbon fuels, and (iv) technical and economic viability. Parameterizing these four constraints will yield unique outcomes as to the economic impairment. The next section will explore the literature that has sought to quantify this economic impairment.

4. Carbon budgets and fossil fuel companies

Uncertainty around the ultimate scale of 'unburnable carbon' remains. Equally, assuming limited penetration of CCS and at least a 50% probability of achieving the 2°C goal is likely associated with 60 to 80% of existing fossil fuel reserves becoming 'unburnable' (Leaton 2011; McGlade and Ekins 2015).

The key question that derives from this then is what the implications are for the owners of these assets – in the first case companies and the ultimate owners of these companies, that is investors. This distinction could be thought of in a framework of the stranding of 'economic assets' related to oil, gas, and coal (i.e. the fossil fuel reserves becoming unburnable) and the stranding of 'financial assets' (i.e. the equity and credit instruments associated with these fossil fuel reserves). One critical conclusion here is that the scale of 'asset stranding' might not be the same for the two (Thomä et al. 2015).

Tackling this question requires as a first step identifying the owners of these assets. According to the International Energy Agency in the OECD roughly 82% of coal production capacity was owned by listed companies in 2012, with 10% unlisted and 9% state owned (IEA 2014). This contrasts sharply with the picture in non-OECD countries, where roughly 66% of coal production is state owned and only 20% is owned by listed companies and 14% by non-listed companies. While the IEA does not provide global aggregate figures, applying the current weights in production, this suggests that only around one-third of coal production capacity is owned by listed companies, with little more than half of coal production capacity owned by state-owned companies. This result suggests that from a stranded assets perspective, for coal, the primary 'victim' will be state-owned companies and by extension taxpayers, in particular in non-OECD markets.

For oil and gas companies in turn, the majority of assets – around 71% by IEA estimates – are also owned by national oil companies (NOCs; IEA 2014). As will be outlined further in what follows, a simple ownership analysis does not suffice for understanding the potential exposure of different actors to potential stranded assets in the upstream oil, gas, and coal. Crucially, the ownership analysis may fall short of accurately capturing who will develop and seek to earn revenues from these assets. Thus, evidence suggests international oil companies have a higher share of production than their share of reserves. This relates to the idea that state-owned reserves may ultimately be sold for development to international oil companies. Some of these trends may change, as they are driven by a capacity gap around field development that state-owned oil companies may be able to close over time. At the same time, at least some share of state-owned oil companies' reserves may be considered 'implicit' potential stranded assets for international oil companies given that their business model relies on ultimately being able to take a share of the pie of state-owned oil companies. In other words, some of today's state-owned assets may ultimately be developed by non–state-owned oil companies.

An ownership analysis of oil and gas and coal reserves may help to frame who the companies are that own these assets and thus may be exposed to the types of risks highlighted further already. At the same time, a simple ownership analysis is only a crude proxy for exposure for upstream oil and gas and coal. This applies in particular in this case given that a critical factor in understanding which assets will get developed and which ones will not is the cost of production (Leaton et al. 2013).

As outlined by Thomä et al. (2015), risk and stranded assets analysis at company level can involve three different approaches. The 'top-down, fair-share' approach allocates economic impacts related to stranded assets equitably across all companies. Under such an approach, the impact would thus be primarily felt by national oil companies and state-owned coal producers. This approach will be flawed at company level but can speak in general terms as to the extent to which companies keep or lose market share from a pure 'volume' perspective. Meaningful and material analysis of economic and financial risk then requires more sophisticated estimates around the distribution of potential stranded assets across physical assets and companies. There are two more granular approaches, notably a 'cost' approach that allocates impacts based on the cost curve of production and alternatively a 'bottom-up' assessment involving a range of parameters (ibid.).

Both of these approaches can be applied for oil and gas and coal, although in practice the current literature and analysis are limited to the cost approach. A critical advantage in this context is the relative homogeneity of upstream coal, oil, and gas products. Unlike, for example, for automobiles, where products are highly heterogeneous and thus impacts are likely to be highly idiosyncratic depending on the exact interplay between changing consumer preferences, the nature of regulatory constraints, car company responses, and other factors, in the case of oil, gas, and coal, impacts are likely to be more homogenous. This makes cost a key distinguishing feature across companies and thus a more meaningful way to distinguish the likely distribution of potential stranded assets.

The IEA reflects this dynamic in its publications, organizing the oil resource development by cost. This analysis shows that generally significant parts of the low-cost oil and gas reserves are located in countries where reserves are primarily state owned (e.g. Middle East). This implies that, from a macroeconomic perspective, listed, non–state-owned companies might be more affected than state-owned companies for oil and gas, even if they own a lower percentage of overall reserves.

This high-level assessment was evidenced by Leaton et al. (2015) using cost estimates from Rystad to identify those market actors with particularly high exposure to high-cost oil, gas, and coal reserves. The results introduced the concept of a 2°C aligned break-even price above which production would exceed the IEA 2°C carbon budget and thus would not be compatible with a 2°C transition. The ultimate break-even price then, as outlined, will depend on the assumptions around the exact nature of the 2°C transition.

It should be noted that the integration of global oil markets makes this type of assessment much more intuitive than for coal and gas, which, although perhaps even more homogenous in nature, face more fragmented markets and thus also by extension more fragmented price profiles.[1] Thus, the IEA will quote macroeconomic gas estimates by region, with generally lower gas prices in the United States relative to global gas export prices (Stern 2016).

In summary, given the homogeneity of the sector, much of the distribution of the impacts is likely to be driven by costs. A macro-analysis suggests that these costs are generally lower for established national oil companies relative to international oil companies. They are also likely to create more challenges for new market entrants that are more focused on developing unconventional oil and gas fields or offshore conventional fields that are likely to be more expensive on average (IEA 2014). While this analysis is not exactly accurate, given some market fragmentation, related to transport for gas and refining capacity for oil, and non–cost-driven drivers of demand (e.g. political considerations), it provides a comprehensive, accessible approach to tackling the question of how potential stranded assets are likely to affect different companies. The next section will then explore the potential implications for financial markets.

5. Impact of stranded assets on financial assets

This section will explore the potential implications of the previous discussion for financial markets. It is worth repeating a number of stylized facts by way of introduction. On the one hand, it appears that while the majority of upstream oil, gas, and coal reserves are owned by state-owned companies, the economic stranding of assets may be tilted towards listed companies. This conclusion is derived from the type of cost curve analysis done in the past by the Carbon Tracker Initiative (Leaton et al. 2015; McGlade and Ekins 2015, and others). This implies that financial markets, notably listed equity markets, may be more exposed to these types of risks, given the tilt of their exposure to high-cost production relative to many state-owned oil and gas companies. Of course, there are also non-economic factors that influence this equation, including potentially trade barriers and other governmental incentives.

In addition, financial institutions may also be exposed to these impacts through the issuance of bonds from state-owned companies involved in upstream oil, gas, and coal. Beyond that, there may be second- and third-order effects around exposures to banks that have lent to these sectors and may be exposed to associated financial risks.

On the other hand, as outlined in Section 1, financial institutions are as a rule diversified actors and thus – given that the concentration of these risks are limited to only a part of their portfolios – may find these potential risks less material than a company whose core business is oil and gas extraction. This then obviously depends on the ultimate exposure of the financial institution and the correlation of this risk with potential stranded assets risks in other sectors, as outlined in other chapters of this book.

The actual exposure will vary over time and will in part be dependent on the extent to which these risks are priced – a discussion that will be returned to further in what follows. In stock markets, the weight of the oil and gas and coal mining sector is a function of the market capitalisation of the listed companies, which is in turn a function of market perceptions of the company's underlying value. It also depends on idiosyncrasies around listing and historical legacies of economies.

Thus, the stock markets in France and the United Kingdom historically have had a significantly higher exposure to oil and gas companies, given the prominence of international oil companies headquartered in these countries. For example, in the United Kingdom the contribution of mining and quarrying (which includes non–oil- and gas-related activities) hovered around 3% of gross value add over the past decade, versus a share of around 10–14% in the UK stock market and 14–16% in the FTSE100, the large-cap index of FTSE Russell (Thomä et al. 2015).[2]

Equally, the source of revenues for these companies will be primarily in other countries. Germany, on the other hand, has almost no listed companies involved in oil and gas extraction, albeit some exposure to coal mining (through RWE). Investors invested in these different markets will then in most cases have different exposures to these sectors, although investors may of course choose to exclude these sectors even when they are invested in these markets through, for example, divestment (Caldecott and McDaniels 2014).

The exposure will then fluctuate with market prices. Thus, (Thomä et al. 2014) identified a relative weight of the oil and gas sector in the UK stock market of 13.2% in 2014, versus 7.4% in France and 10.8% in the United States. Following the reduction in oil prices, these shares have dropped significantly since then. They may of course rebound should oil prices rise again.

One part of the equation then is the average exposure of investors to these sectors in stock markets. The other aspect is the structure of this exposure. Coal mining is a case in point. In the United States stock market, coal reserves ownership is primarily linked to 'pure-play' coal mining companies whose primary business is coal extraction. On the other hand, ownership of reserves by European companies tends to sit with diversified mining companies (e.g. BHP Biliton, Rio Tinto) or utilities (e.g. RWE) rather than pure-play coal miners. The implication is that the decline of coal valuations in financial markets in the first part of this decade has hit pure-play coal mining companies more significantly. This has led to the de-facto elimination of coal mining from the universe of companies in the United States with large market capitalization. This effect can be seen in the fact that the S&P 500, the most prominent large-market capitalization-weighted index for the US stock market, for the first time since its expansion to 500 companies in 1957, no longer contains a coal-mining company with the elimination of Consol Energy. Thus, by extension, investors in US stock markets are less likely to own coal reserves than investors in European stock markets, given the emphasis on large-cap companies. Investors in European stock markets on the other hand are still exposed to a higher degree given the exposure to diversified miners with coal mining as one of their business segments.

This discussion so far has been focused in particular on stock markets. The discussion presents itself in similar fashion in other asset classes. Weyzig et al. (2014) found that the share of 'high-carbon loans' as a percentage of total assets was less than 2% across a sample of 20 European banks, with the percentage of corporate loans anywhere between less than 1% to around 12.5% for the largest exposure.

Interestingly, the trends may not be consistent. Thus, oil and gas companies have issued more debt in the context of falling oil prices in order to cover expenses, offset losses, and pay dividends. This implies that while the relative weight of these sectors in stock markets has increased as a result of lower valuations, the relative weight in debt markets has increased as these companies finance themselves increasingly through debt issuance (Blas 2016). Thus, investor exposure in one asset class may go up as it goes down in another. Indeed, from a potential impact on financial assets perspective, this dynamic is particularly worrying, as it may precede asset write-downs. In this sense, the oil and gas sector is undergoing the same cycle that coal mining companies in the United States began a few years ago, with an ultimate series of bankruptcies and debt defaults. While the sectors and risks are obviously different – as outlined earlier – the pattern is eerily similar. The Latin poet Ovid's words come to mind: "*Principiis obsta. Sero medicina parata, cum mala per longas convaluere moras*" (Oppose the beginnings! The medicine is prepared too late when the evil strengthens through hesitation).

Having established the relative exposure or scale of total potential risk or exposure, the natural derivative question then becomes the extent to which these risks are already integrated into financial asset pricing. Answering this question requires lifting the hood on financial market models and the assumptions therein. The market prices that ultimately 'reveal' these sentiments that these models seek to capture fluctuate continuously, and thus by extension so do the risks of potential financial asset stranding as a result of potential economic stranding. The answer to the question of the scale is thus a moving target. That is not to say that various analyses have not been done to seek to quantify the scale of these risks. Carbon

Trust and McKinsey first sought to quantify these risks in 2008 for a range of sectors, including the oil and gas exploration and production sector. Their analysis suggested a potential scale of impacts of minus 35% of asset value with a potential upside of 7% for refining companies (Carbon Trust 2008).

Robins et al. (2012, 2013) as part of their equity research at HSBC in turn found potential impacts of around 40 to 60% for different oil and gas companies. Their analysis of the coal business suggested potential impact on the coal business of -44%, albeit with more muted impacts for diversified mining companies (-7–15%). Conducted in the context of oil and gas prices well north of $100 a barrel, their analysis on oil and gas companies looked magnificently prescient as oil prices dropped to below $50 a barrel in 2015/2016, and the share prices of oil and gas companies suffered commensurately. While at a portfolio level, Mercer (2015) has also performed analysis on portfolio performance looking at sectoral effects. The key challenge of the modelling however is that the assumptions around effects for these sectors assumes that these risks are not priced in and takes a business-as-usual high-carbon trajectory as given in asset price formation.

The challenge here is to disentangle short-term and long-term effects. Are current oil and gas company valuations accurately pricing long-term risks, or are they responding to short-term changes in prices and would be even lower if such analysis also extended to more long-term risks than the current oil price? This question is somewhat esoteric or philosophical. Market prices cannot just be translated into a degree of warming, as they represent a range of diverse 'revealed' sentiments.

A brief excursion into equity valuation models and the implications for stock market valuations makes this point. Equity valuation models essentially consist of two inputs: assumptions around future earnings (e.g. dividends) and the rate at which these expected future earnings are discounted to the present. This discount rate in traditional financial market theory consists of the 'risk-free' interest rate and a 'risk premium'. This discount rate is then what complicates the linking of financial market prices to stranded assets and investor sentiments.

Revenues could of course be calculated based on simple alternative assumptions around decarbonization pathways. Thus, it is possible to compare expected future cash flows under a high-carbon scenario (e.g. 6°C warming) to a low-carbon scenario (e.g. 2°C scenario). This type of analysis has been done by Kepler-Cheuvreux, showing a difference in total revenues of around $28 trillion (Lewis 2014). The calculations combine the International Energy Agency estimates around commodity prices and production volumes. Thus, according to the IEA (2015, 2016a), the total volume difference between 6°C and 2°C in terms of oil & gas production between 2015 and 2040 is ~10 to 15%. This suggests that the impact of difference in production on total revenues over a 25-year time window is around that. By 2040, the sector will be significantly smaller (as measured by production volume), namely around 35 to 40% relative to what the production volume is estimated to be under a 6°C scenario.

This growth scenario, however, does not appear to be a good benchmark given that even within the industry it is not used for estimations.[3] Relative to a NPS/NPS+ (i.e. middle between the New Policy [4°C] and Current Policy [6°C] scenario), the difference shrinks to ~25 to 30%. In absolute production terms in turn, the difference between current production and production in 2040 shrinks by only around ~18%. Obviously, these trends then accelerate over time. Depending on how you slice it, however, the total impact of production volume on revenues over the next 25 years is likely to be limited (~10–15%). The actual revenues in the year 2040 will be smaller but also not much more significantly (~18%). The IEA does rely significantly on CCS in their scenarios and relatively pessimistic assumptions around renewables. But oil doesn't directly compete with renewables, and their automobile transport roadmap actually is relatively ambitious. Moreover, CCS even for the IEA isn't a fundamental game changer in the next 25 years, with most of these impacts expected post-2040 to 2050.

The second input into revenues then is prices. Estimating prices is notoriously difficult and even more difficult across scenarios. The IEA World Energy Outlook 2015 estimates that oil prices will be around 66% lower in the 450 Scenario than the CP Scenario in 2040 and ~80% lower in the 450 Low Oil Price Scenario. In absolute terms, however, even the Low Oil Price Scenario sees prices increase by around 60% relative to current levels. While revenues may stay flat, costs may rise.

This implies two things. First, changes in production volume may hit them harder than other producers, where these producers will see an increased reduction in their production as they are priced out of the market. Second, to the extent that these producers preserve production, they are facing an increasing squeeze on their profits as costs and revenues match. The wild card in all of this is of course technological innovation and changes in relative input prices that can alter this equation. Shale oil and gas production, for example, has already seen significant drops in costs of extraction in the past 1 to 2 years in response to the oil and gas price squeeze. Ultimately, there is large uncertainty around this factor and, indeed, the distribution of this impact across different oil and gas producers.

It should be noted however that given that revenues are estimated to oscillate around current levels under a 2°C transition, which few actors see as likely, these impacts are unlikely to shock the current large oil and gas majors. This is particularly true given that in relative terms these oil and gas majors tend to still be better positioned than smaller independent oil and gas producers in terms of the cost curve.

Overall then, back-of-the-envelope estimates suggest oil and gas total revenues over the next 25 years are around 30% to 40% lower in relative terms between 6°C and 2°C. As shown here, this type of back-of-the-envelope analysis, as briefly reviewed here and done in the past by Kepler-Cheuvreux, can be linked to decarbonization pathways. The key challenge is how these are discounted. Thus, the difference in net present value of applying these two scenarios in a simple valuation model is the equivalent of a roughly 1.5% increase in the discount rate, where the net present value of a 6°C revenue assumption is the equivalent of a 2°C revenue assumption when increasing the discount rate by 1.5% relative to the 2°C discount rate.

While financial analysts will use these discount rates, it is unclear what the actual discount rate is when looking at market prices. This makes the ultimate question of impact on asset prices essentially unsolvable at a macroeconomic level. It is, however, possible of course for individual investors to identify their own results based on their discount rates. This challenge was reflected in analysis by Grant et al. (2016) looking at the net present value of a business-as-usual oil and gas portfolio versus a 2°C portfolio, which provided two different discount rates. One challenge is that comparing a 6°C and 2°C scenario is likely a false simplification as the truth around asset valuation, company's business plans, and asset development at this stage is much more likely to be somewhere in the middle.

There is one final aspect worth exploring in this context, namely the extent to which companies will respond to these risks. At this stage, the options are generally viewed as (i) structured decline and wind-down of the company involving increasing dividends and cutting capital expenditure; (ii) diversification of the company into other business sectors; and (iii) 'chaotic decline' with significant write-offs and unmanaged bankruptcies (see for example Leaton et al. 2015).

The first and third options assume essentially an inability of oil and gas companies to adapt. At the same time, total primary energy demand is estimated to stay more or less flat under a decarbonization pathway according to the IEA ETP. This suggests that oil and gas companies can hypothetically keep their share in TPED by switching to renewables or other zero-carbon technologies – thus the second option avoids decline. Here, oil and gas companies face some competitive disadvantages given the different profile, with much of this evolution potentially favouring smaller and national/local players catering to distributed electricity generation, national and regional grid management technologies; and utility scale power generation. Whatever the ultimate 'adaptive capacity', it remains a wild card in thinking about stranded assets risks for financial assets and will require further research.

6. Conclusion

This chapter provided a tour of the questions around potential upstream oil and gas and coal stranded assets, both in the economy and in financial markets. The results suggest a lot of uncertainty around the ultimate stranding of oil, gas, and coal reserves, given the uncertainty around both the scale and speed of the economic transition to a low-carbon economy, as well as the nature of this transition and the technologies underlying it. Estimates around stranded assets can thus differ widely but can go as high as 80% of remaining reserves. These estimates then will also be fossil fuel specific, with the future of oil, gas, and coal respectively potentially fundamentally different. For example, the shift to electric vehicles for the automobile sector may favour more sustained coal production for electricity generation at the expense of oil production.

From a financial markets perspective, there are some stylized facts that can be derived from this discussion. There is little evidence that the managed decline feared for oil and gas companies is likely to be that dramatic over a 25-year time window, even under a 2°C transition roadmap. In addition, it is unclear whether this decline is already priced in to current expectations. Moreover, if and when it does get priced, market actors may 'over-react' to certain long-term signals and deliver a more chaotic decline even if in the short term market fundamentals don't see a radical shift. In the long run, oil and gas companies – as companies whose primary business is the sale of oil and natural gas – will eventually for all intents and purposes disappear, but this process is likely to be much more long term than can be gleaned from some of the current discourse (e.g. 40–60 years rather than 5).

This still leaves the question of the evolution of the business model. As outlined, upstream oil, gas, and coal companies will do a lot better if CCS technologies materialize given the fact that the technical sophistication of CCS will likely require the geological, engineering, and capital management skills of large companies, with oil and gas companies at a distinct competitive advantage over newer, smaller players (this assumes CCS will indeed be a large-scale technology (in terms of size of projects), which appears this way so far). It also implies a 'stretching' of the amount of fossil fuels that can be burnt under a specific carbon budget. If oil and gas extraction becomes more and more difficult from an engineering perspective, it will favour large companies that can deploy large-scale capital. So instead of a managed decline, it seems likely that the next decades will see an era of managed consolidation coupled with some degree of value stagnation or loss.

Acknowledgments

The author would like to acknowledge Johannes Honneth and Marco Duran (2° Investing Initiative), as well as Christopher Weber (WWF) for their research support in drafting this chapter.

Notes

1 This is largely a function of gaps and cost challenges to transporting gas and trade flows around coal, with some trade barriers for example to coal imports in China.
2 The percentage figures can fluctuate significantly dependent on oil and gas prices, with analysis taken here from 2017 index factsheets and prior analysis by 2Dii 2015.
3 See research from CTI on this.

References

Ansar, A., Caldecott, B. and Tilbury, J. 2013. *Stranded Assets and the Fossil Fuel Divestment Campaign: What Does Divestment Mean for the Valuation of Fossil Fuel Assets?* Oxford: University of Oxford.
Aurizon. 2015. *Future of Coal – Sustainability Report.*
Blas, J. 2016. *Crude Slump Sees Oil Majors' Debt Burden Double to $138 Billion.* [Online] Available at: www.bloomberg.com/news/articles/2016-08-04/oil-slump-sees-majors-debt-double-to-138-billion [Accessed June 2017].
Caldecott, B. and McDaniels, J. 2014. *Financial Dynamics of the Environment: Risks, Impacts, and Barriers to Resilience.* Oxford: University of Oxford.

Carbon Trust. 2008. *Climate Change – a Business Revolution? How Tracking Climate Change Could Create or Destroy Company Value*. London: The Carbon Trust.

Grant, A., Leaton, J., Spedding, P. and Fulton, M. 2016. *Sense & Sensitivity: Maximising Value With a 2D Portfolio*. London: Carbon Tracker.

IEA. 2014. *World Energy Outlook*. Paris: International Energy Agency.

IEA. 2015. *World Energy Outlook*. Paris: International Energy Agency.

IEA. 2016a. *Energy Technology Perspectives*. Paris: International Energy Agency.

IEA. 2016b. *World Energy Outlook*. Paris: International Energy Agency.

Jin, Y., Andersson, H. and Zhang, S. 2016. Air Pollution Control Policies in China: A Retrospective and Prospects. *International Journal of Environmental Research and Public Health*, 13, 1219.

King, G. and King, H. 2008. *Asphalt Alternatives*. Lanham: NAPA.

Leaton, J. 2011. *Unburnable Carbon – Are the World's Financial Markets Carrying a Carbon Bubble?* London: Carbon Tracke Initiative.

Leaton, J., et al. 2013. *Unburnable Carbon 2013: Wasted Capital and Stranded Assets*. London: Carbon Tracker Initiative.

Leaton, J., Grant, A., Gray, M. and Sussam, L. 2015. *Carbon Supply Cost Curves: Evaluating Financial Risk to Gas Capital Expenditures*. London: Carbon Tracker Initiative.

Lewis, M. C. 2014. *Stranded Assets, Fossilised Revenues*. Paris: Kepler Cheuvreux.

McGlade, C. and Ekins, P. 2015. The Geographical Distribution of Fossil Fuels Unused When Limiting Global Warming to 2C. *Letter Research*, 517, 187.

Meinshausen, M., et al. 2009. Greenhouse-Gas Emission Targets for Limiting Global Warming to 2 °C. *Nature*, 458, 1158–1162.

Mercer. 2015. *Investing in a Time of Climate Change*. Paris: Mercer.

Robbins, N. and Knight, Z. 2012. *Coal and Carbon – Stranded Assets: Assessing the Risk*. London: HSBC Global Research.

Robbins, N. and Knight, Z. 2013. *Scoring Climate Change Risk G20 Vulnerability Increases*. London: HSBC Global Research.

Sato, M. 1990. *Thermochemistry of the Formation of Fossil Fuels*. Washington, DC: The Geochemical Society.

Spedding, P., Mehta, K. and Robins, N. 2013. *Oil & Carbon Revisited: Value at Risk From 'Unburnable' Reserves*. London: HSBC Global Research.

Stern, J. 2016. *Natural Gas Pricing: Future Perspectives and Competitiveness With Coal*. Oxford: The Oxford Institute for Energy Studies.

Thomä, J., et al. 2014. *Optimal Diversification and The Energy Transition: Impact of Equity Benchmarks on Portfolio Diversification and Climate Change*. Paris: 2 Degrees Investing Initiative.

Thomä, J., et al. 2015. *Assessing the Alignment of Portfolios With Climate Goals: Climate Scenarios Translated Into a 2C Benchmark*. Paris: 2 Degrees Investing Initiative.

Weyzig, F., Kuepper, B., van Gelder, J. W. and van Tilburg, R. 2014. *The Price of Doing Too Little Too Late. The Impact of the Carbon Bubble on the EU Financial System*. Brussels: Green European Foundation.

6 Examining stranded assets in power generation

Coal, gas and nuclear

Daniel J. Tulloch

1. Introduction

The purpose of this chapter is to examine stranded assets in the electricity industry, with a focus on coal, gas and nuclear generation technologies. The electricity industry is typically comprised of four major components, though variations do exist at the national level. First, the industry begins with *generators*, which generate electricity using a range of technologies, including renewable energy sources (RES), biomass, nuclear, coal, gas and oil. Second, the *transmission* network transports electricity over long distances to centres of consumption using high-voltage transmission lines. Large industrial consumers may take electricity directly from the transmission line for use. However, and third, most electricity is stepped down via transformers for transport over a *distribution* network. The local distribution network transports the lower-voltage electricity through utility poles for consumption by households and domestic consumers. Finally, *retailers* are responsible for soliciting customers and collecting rents for consumption of electricity. This chapter's primary focus will be the *generation* component of the supply chain, as generating assets are most sensitive to stranded asset risks.

Traditionally, global electricity sectors were based on regional markets in which vertically integrated companies could generate, transmit, distribute and retail electricity to nearby consumers. Utilities were assumed to have natural, regional monopolies which prevented competition. Internationally, a wave of deregulation determined that the generation and retail components of the electricity supply chain had the potential to be competitive. Retailers could compete to attract a greater market share of consumers, while generators could compete on price to supply a greater proportion of electricity to the wholesale market. Introducing competition was expected to result in higher economic welfare (Helm and Jenkinson 1997). Competition was expected to increase overall efficiency of electricity generation, as inefficient generators would slowly be phased out of the system. End consumers would be provided with a greater range of choice regarding the underlying generating technology and would also benefit from lower electricity prices through more efficient dispatch.

In addition to the wave of deregulation, electric utilities were also subjected to a second legislative theme: decarbonisation. While decarbonisation has been on the international agenda for the past few decades, the most significant decarbonisation legislation is the Paris Agreement. At the Paris climate conference (COP21) in December 2015, 195 countries adopted the first-ever universal, legally binding global climate deal. The agreement aims to limit global warming levels to below 2°C, pursuing efforts to achieve 1.5°C. To meet the 2°C target, countries must achieve net-zero global greenhouse gas (GHG) emissions by the second half of the 21st century. The electricity industry is expected to make major contributions to emission reduction efforts.

The combination of deregulation and decarbonisation has significantly contributed to the stranding of generation assets in the industry. The issue of stranded generation assets is of major concern for utility companies, considering the enormous amounts of capital at stake and the lengthy life of the assets, which can be decades at a time. The lengthy time horizons make generation assets particularly vulnerable to changes in regulation or market conditions, which can impact the profitability and financial performance of electric utilities. Empirical evidence has shown that investors are now beginning to incorporate the materiality of these long-term changes in market conditions into the valuation of utility companies (Tulloch et al. 2017a).

The aim of this chapter is to provide an overview of the various environment-related risk factors which can strand generation assets and some responses to stranded asset risks. There is no standardised method through which stranded assets can be examined, as the risks and impacts are idiosyncratic by nature. Each electricity industry, technology and stakeholder will contain its own opportunities, risks and challenges. This chapter aims to assist a researcher in accurately identifying stranded asset risks for a specific asset. The researcher must implement a bottom-up analysis, with vernacular knowledge of their system of interest, to understand and analyse the risks. This chapter provides a flexible framework which can be applied to a variety of global electricity industries, which, themselves, differ in structure, regulation and operating environments.

This chapter proceeds as follows. Section 2 provides both a definition of stranded generation assets and an overview of the various environment-related risk factors which can strand generation assets. Section 3 provides an up-to-date assessment of the stranded asset risk materiality. The section provides three case studies on various regions and gas, coal and nuclear generating technologies. Section 4 presents tools and strategies of how to manage these stranded asset risks. Finally, Section 5 concludes the chapter.

2. Stranded assets in the power generation industry

Stranded generation assets are one of the major risks faced by merchant power plants.[1] As part of a project life cycle, typical investments must accommodate a wide range of risks. These risks include (1) cost overrun during construction, (2) volatility in operating costs and profitability (including commodity price risk), (3) end-of-life remediation or decommission costs and (4) reduced economic life of the asset. In this section, we discuss the definition of a stranded generation asset, some of the environment-related risks factors which strand generation assets and the system-level impacts of stranded generation assets.

The concept of a stranded generation asset has existed in the academic literature under various nomenclatures. Terms which closely describe stranded assets include *strandable investments, stranded investments, stranded costs, stranded commitments* and/or *transition costs* (Garcia-Martin 2001). The Smith School of Enterprise and the Environment (Smith School), University of Oxford, formalised the definition of stranded assets in 2013 to understand the contemporary environment-related challenges various industries face in their modern environment. The general definition given to any stranded assets is any assets that have suffered from an unanticipated or premature write-down, devaluation, or conversion to liability (Caldecott et al. 2013). The definition for stranded generation assets is tailored further for the electricity industry.

2.1 Defining a stranded generation asset

Generation assets become uneconomic to operate when the marginal cost of generation exceeds the price for electricity over an extended period. Two major factors contribute to stranding generation assets, which are not mutually exclusive. First, generation assets can become *uncompetitive* when the market price of electricity is below the marginal cost of generation, making operations unprofitable. Second, generation assets can become *underutilised* when market mechanisms or regulation reduce the volume of turnover. Put simply, stranded generation assets arise when merchant electricity generation does not generate enough profits or turnover to warrant keeping the asset operational in the long term. The long-term aspect of this definition is critical, as we will see that utilities can sometimes operate at a loss in the short term.

The impact of a stranded generation is primarily borne by the utility and the utility's investors. If plants are forced to close or idled (mothballed) due to poor profitability or underutilisation before capital costs have been significantly depreciated, then owners may be left with sunk costs which are rendered unrecoverable in competitive markets.

2.2 Risk factors which can strand generation assets

Risk factors which strand generation assets in the electricity industry can broadly be grouped into the six themes, illustrated in Figure 6.1. These themes represent six broad lenses through which the major environment-related risks can be identified. These six risk factors are non-exhaustive, and a researcher can adapt their risk factors for local conditions. For example, stranded asset research conducted by the Smith School identify both national risk factors which affect entire countries and local risk hypotheses which only affect some generation assets or specific regions (Caldecott et al. 2017; Caldecott, Dericks et al. 2016; Caldecott, Kruitwagen et al. 2016; Caldecott and McDaniels 2014). These risk factors not only represent downside risks, but some can also represent significant opportunities which

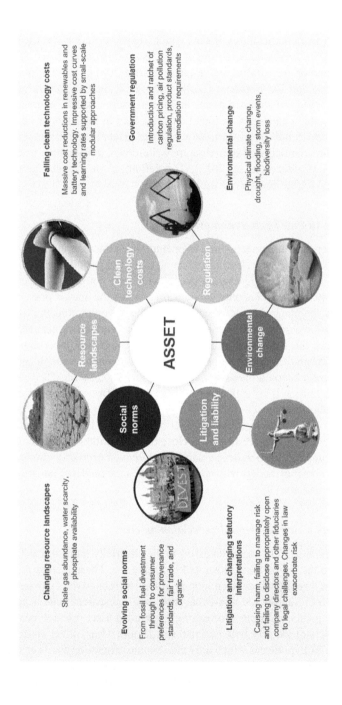

Changing resource landscapes

Shale gas abundance, water scarcity, phosphate availability

Evolving social norms

From fossil fuel divestment through to consumer preferences for provenance standards, fair trade, and organic

Litigation and changing statutory interpretations

Causing harm, failing to manage risk and failing to disclose appropriately open company directors and other fiduciaries to legal challenges. Changes in law exacerbate risk

Falling clean technology costs

Massive cost reductions in renewables and battery technology. Impressive cost curves and learning rates supported by small-scale modular approaches

Government regulation

Introduction and ratchet of carbon pricing, air pollution regulation, product standards, remediation requirements

Environmental change

Physical climate change, drought, flooding, storm events, biodiversity loss

Figure 6.1 Typology of environment-related risk factors

Source: Caldecott et al. (2013)

utilities can exploit for economic gain. In the following subsections, we briefly discuss each of the risk factors and the impacts they have on utilities' assets. Each type of generating technology (solar, wind, coal, gas etc.) can have different characteristics and magnitudes of sensitivity to each risk factor.

2.2.1 Changing resource landscape

Resource landscape refers to both direct and indirect resources required to generate electricity. For thermal generators, direct resources typically refer to fuels such as coal, natural gas or oil. For RES generators, this can also include wind, sun and water availability. Given the abundance of all hydrocarbon reserves and the ability for thermal generators to switch fuel (Söderholm 1998), the physical availability of resources is of less concern than the cost of obtaining the resource. The cost of obtaining generating fuels can affect the competitiveness of different generating technologies.

This event occurred in the EU, where a dramatic drop in global coal prices increased the cost competitiveness of coal-fired generation compared to natural gas-fired generation. Between 2011 and 2015, the price of thermal coal fell from more than US$120/t to less than US$60/t in Europe and Asia (IEA 2015a). The dramatic drop in coal price was driven by increasing supplies from countries such as Australia and Indonesia, in conjunction with decreasing demand from major coal users such as China and the United States. The abundance of cheap coal meant that coal-fired generators could often undercut the relatively expensive gas-fired generators. As such, an increasing number of gas-fired turbines were being temporarily mothballed or shut down until market conditions improved (Caldecott and McDaniels 2014).

In addition to direct resources, there are also secondary resources which are critical to facilitate electricity generation. A key indirect resource is the availability of water to cool generating equipment. These indirect resources are often not a major cost but have major impacts on operating hours. For example, in March 2016, a dip in water levels at the Farakka Feeder Canal in Murshidabad district of West Bengal forced some thermal generators to temporarily idle. The National Thermal Power Corporation was forced to shut down five of its six generating units. Overnight, the plant's generating capacity fell from 2,100 MW to only 500 MW (The Times of India 2016). Such a large drop in capacity is a major threat to the region's security of energy supply. Further, it also has a major impact on the profitability of the generating plant.

China has also faced similar water scarcity and quality-control challenges, which potentially hinder the operations of its coal-fired utility operations. China's attempt to limit air pollution in Eastern China pushed coal-fired generators towards western provinces. Unfortunately, these regions were subject to extreme water scarcity issues (Caldecott et al. 2017). To limit the impact of water scarcity, China had three responses. First, in 2010, China attempted to overcome water scarcity issue through policy. China sought to establish 'three red lines' regarding water use, including (1) standards for water use efficiency, (2) minimum water quality and (3) total aggregate use (Moore 2013). Second, China encouraged the adoption of dry-cooling coal-fired technology at the expense of plant operating efficiency. By the end of 2012, 14 per cent of the country's thermal generating capacity was dry-cooled (Zhang et al. 2014). Third, in 2014 the Ministry of Water Resources issued guidance for water reforms which would value water through market mechanisms and issued plans which prevent the development of large coal bases which threaten water resource availability.

2.2.2 Falling clean technology costs

There are multiple reasons to explain why RES and low-carbon technologies have begun to dominate the generation landscape. First, renewable energy technologies have been able to establish a foothold in the global electricity industry due to government subsidies during the early years. This facilitated investment when the underlying cost of installing the solar photovoltaics (PV) made the technology economically unattractive or unattainable. Second, RES possesses great economies of scale. Swanson's law, the learning curve for PV, shows that the price of solar PV modules drops approximately 20 per cent for every doubling of cumulative volume. That is, the cost approximately halves every 10 years (Swanson 2006).

RES and low-carbon technologies are also gaining market share, as the technologies face a dramatically different cost structure to conventional thermal generating technology. Conventional thermal generators are operating expenditure (OPEX) technologies. While the installation cost can vary, OPEX technologies must procure fuel (such as coal and gas) throughout their life cycle, which is a significant operating cost. In contrast, renewable generation is a capital expenditure (CAPEX) technology, thus the bulk of the lifecycle cost lies in installation. As such, there are no fuel costs to renewable technologies. As their technological efficiency improves over successive installations, their associated costs decrease. Despite the cost of both thermal coal and natural gas falling since 2008, which makes the two commodities relatively inexpensive fuels for electricity generation, the near-zero marginal cost of RES (such as wind and sun) means the renewable generators can always undercut thermal generators in wholesale markets to guarantee sale of electricity.

Another consideration is the role of negative-emissions technologies such as carbon capture and storage (CCS). To limit global warming to 2°C, the electricity system will have to most likely phase out all thermal (particularly coal-fired) electricity generation in the absence of CCS (Eom et al. 2015; Johnson et al. 2015). At present, CCS is not developing at a pace consistent with the 2°C policy scenarios of IEA and IPCC. IEA's estimate of deployed CCS must store 4,000 $MtCO_2$ per annum by 2040. To achieve this goal requires a compounded growth rate of CCS at 22 per cent per annum relative to 2015 operating levels of 28.4 $MtCO_2$ per annum (Caldecott, Kruitwagen et al. 2016). Without policy support, rapid CCS deployment is unrealistic. Even assuming high CCS deployment, with high availability of geological space to store the carbon, the economic viability of storage remains an issue. Further, issues of potential leakage and long-term stability of carbon act as barriers to acceptance. Finally, other mitigation options are becoming cost competitive much more quickly than CCS.

2.2.3 New government regulations

Understanding market structure is a powerful tool through which to analyse generators as, in the long run, the generator's profitability is determined by the regulatory environment in which it operates. Rather than focus on any one country, this section outlines a general framework for understanding the importance of various market structures of the electricity industry globally. The section continues with a discussion of the challenges faced by inducing competition in the electricity industry.

Market structure can typically be separated into four categories: monopoly, oligopoly, monopolistic competition and perfect competition. Many developing countries are characterised as monopolies or oligopolies. In these market structures, competitive forces have a limited role in stranding generation assets, whereas firm behaviour and regulation have greater roles. In monopolies, there is a single electricity utility in the market which can operate without constraint and exercises control over prices and output decisions. In the electricity industry, few monopolies exist at the country level but can exist at the local or industry level. Oligopolies exists when a relatively small number of electricity utilities supply the market. Each utility must consider retaliatory and reactionary strategies of other utilities in the same market when prices of quantities supplied change, such as their ability to rapidly ramp up production.

Most developed electricity industries conform to some form of competitive market structure. The market is characterised by many buyers and sellers, who trade a homogenous product, and no single producer is large enough to influence market prices alone. When competing on price, the low-cost generator often dispatches electricity first. In most cases, the near-zero marginal cost of RES generators ensures their full dispatch ahead of all other generating technologies. The electricity industry more closely conforms to the definition of monopolistic competition rather than perfect competition, as generators can create monopoly-like conditions through product differentiation. The generator can exercise some degree of pricing power if the market believes their product is different. For example, despite each unit of electricity (a kilowatt-hour, kWh) being a homogenous product, renewable generators can differentiate their electricity from thermal generators due to the fuel source or, alternatively, lower carbon emissions. In monopolistic competition, some generators thrive, as they are better suited to current market conditions. For example, they meet specific emission standards, or social norms dictate a preference for RES technologies as opposed to thermal generation. In this market arrangement, asset stranding typically occurs between different generating technologies.

Since the mid-20th century, global electricity utilities in developed countries have been impacted by a myriad of policy interventions which aim to deregulate the industry. Many of these interventions sought to transform the electricity industry from one dominated by state-owned, vertically integrated utilities with regional monopolies to unbundled, competitive, privately owned utilities.

The challenge of deregulating the electricity industry is that it exposes utilities to competition from new entrants. The new entrants are likely to be newer and flexible and to have more efficient technologies. Research from the US showed that major liberalisation policies have exposed public utilities to the profit effects of cost and demand shocks, leading to greater earnings variability and higher systematic risk (Nwaeze 2000). The inability to pass through incurred costs through the value chain results in shareholders bearing a larger share of market risk (Henderson and Hughes II 2010). Using a sample of European utilities, Tulloch et al. (2017a, 2017b) empirically show that liberalisation and environmental policies have increased systematic risk exposure of utility companies and also had a negative impact on the value of energy utilities, reducing financial returns between -1.32 and -6.25 per cent. Competition from such entrants makes it difficult to recover both historical and future capital expenditure for incumbent utilities. High-cost and inefficient utilities are forced to write down the value of assets and equipment which are rendered obsolete in a competitive environment.

2.2.4 Environmental change and extreme weather events

Environmental change as a risk factor involves understanding a two-way impact between operations in the electricity industry and the environment. The most pressing concern for the electricity industry is the threat of anthropogenic climate change. The Earth's climate is very complex and is naturally variable. The consensus from the scientific community is that increased emissions from fossil fuel combustion increases CO_2 emissions; CO_2 emissions are among the family of greenhouse gases which contribute to climate change; climate change increases the severity and frequency of extreme weather events.

Since the industrial revolution, global annual CO_2 emissions from fuel combustion has increased from nearly zero to more than 32 $GtCO_2$ in 2014. Of this, electricity and heat production represented the largest emitting sector, responsible for 42 per cent of total CO_2 emissions (IEA 2016a). This is due in part to the global reliance on coal in power generation, the most carbon-intensive fossil fuel. Coal provides approximately 41 per cent of the world's electricity needs and around 32 per cent of primary energy consumption globally (IEA 2015b; ITRE Committee and Parliament 2014). The Paris Agreement established a global action plan to limit global warming levels to less than 2°C, and pursue efforts to achieve 1.5°C. To achieve these goals, the concentration of greenhouse gases needs to be limited to < 430 parts per million (ppm) by 2100, with an emission reduction milestone of 70 per cent to 95 per cent by 2050. This target is broadly consistent with the IEA's World Energy Outlook, which suggests limiting greenhouse gases to 450 ppm (IEA 2016a). Reducing carbon emissions from the electricity industry is fundamental to reducing the impact of anthropogenic climate change.

A rise in the average climate temperature can increase the frequency and severity of extreme weather events. Extreme and volatile weather have already impacted energy utilities in several ways. First, extreme weather events can cause damage to equipment and reduce operating hours. This has a significant economic cost on assets and operations and forces some assets to be temporarily idled. Second, short- and medium-term weather forecasts can be a vital source of operational information for electric utilities. To minimise costs, many utilities may base their electricity demand forecasts on estimates of supply from different generating sources. RES generators are heavily dependent on weather conditions, making supply sensitive to volatile weather conditions and inducing considerable uncertainty to operations. Third, large hydroelectric generators are heavily reliant on precipitation and ample supply in their reservoirs to operate. Extreme drought events can result in significant stranding of hydroelectric generation.

2.2.5 Litigation and changing statutory interpretations

As mentioned previously, the regulatory environment in which utilities operate is key to their long-term financial performance and profitability. Utilities have been subject to a range of environmental policies, including carbon pricing, emissions performance standards or other similar measures designed to reduce carbon emissions. Investors are beginning to recognise the economic impact of such policies on the fundamental risk-return trade-off for EU utilities (Tulloch et al. 2017a). Among the primary legislative concerns for electricity generators is their emerging liabilities due to their actions, their inactions and changing statutory interpretations.

The first legal challenge relates to electricity generators' contribution to climate change. Utilities have always been liable for any specific activities which cause grievous environmental harm (for example, heavy metals or radioactive waste water leakages). In the last decade, the introduction of carbon prices has become an additional liability for high-emission generators. Carbon prices from either carbon taxes or quotas now cover almost 25 per cent of global emissions and are present in more than 40 national and 25 subnational jurisdictions (World Bank and Ecofys 2017). Research has shown that extremely high-emitting EU utilities have a significantly higher risk premium for carbon, which results in a higher cost of capital and a loss of equity value (Koch and Bassen 2013; Oberndorfer 2009)

Utilities are also increasingly becoming liable for their environmental damages through changing statutory interpretations. Liability risks can also raise the compensation of damages which may have occurred because of a failure to appropriately respond to climate change. This can also include practices which are considered negligent or at fault. Perhaps the most prominent example is the 2015 Urgenda Climate Case. The landmark case included a coalition of 900 Dutch citizens who took their government to court for insufficient action to combat climate change. The case argued a wrongful act by the state, as the Dutch government acknowledged its actions were insufficient to prevent dangerous climate change. The District Court of The Hague[2] ruled that the Dutch government is required to meet its emission reduction of at least 25 per cent (relative to 1990 levels) by the end of 2020. The ruling, in effect, forces the government to take more effective action on climate change. This ruling opens the pathway for companies to be held liable for climate pledges of the past and potentially for inaction to combat climate change when a range of mitigation or alternative generating technologies are available. Moreover, developments in the climate science, which underpins the apportioning of legal responsibility, is making it more viable to attribute climate damage to companies or technologies. This means that more cases against utilities may become possible in the future.

2.2.6 Evolving social norms

Evolving social norms are among the most difficult to identify and analyse, as social norms are the rules or behaviours which are considered acceptable to a group or society. These social norms can differ from the legal and regulatory environment. A direct impact from social norms may be the ostracism of companies who break social norms. An example of such behaviour would be protests, vilification of companies or divestment campaigns. Alternatively, there can be some indirect consequences of social norms. These indirect impacts typically manifest as decisions regarding how a consumer uses electricity. Most developed countries have seen overall energy consumption plateau or begin to decline. This contrasts with the historical consumption growth observed over many decades. By changing their energy consumption for endogenous reasons, consumers are reducing operating times for various generating utilities. The following paragraphs discuss several factors which have contributed to the ways consumers interact with electricity.

First, consumers are becoming more vocal and decisive about their electricity choices. Advancements in technologies and business models are providing consumers with greater choice and changing how they interact with electricity. Innovative and new retail tariffs, such as time-of-use or spot-price tariffs, are allowing consumers to adapt their own consumption as the price of electricity varies throughout the day. Effectively, consumers have greater control over their consumption and are economically incentivised to reduce consumption during peak hours. Consumers are also increasingly making choices with regards to the source of their electricity generation, choosing to buy RES electricity over thermal generators.

Second, consumers are increasingly aware of the impact of their overall energy consumption. Some legislation, particularly in the EU, is encouraging energy efficiency through product labelling and certification schemes. The labelling scheme implemented produces a standardised measure of an appliance's energy efficiency, rating overall energy consumption. The incentive for purchasing more energy-efficient appliances is an overall reduction in energy consumption, further reducing annual fuel bills over time.

Third, the falling cost of distributed generating technologies (such as solar PV), batteries and smart appliances is making these technologies more accessible at the household level. An uptake of distributed generation reduces a household's reliance on the centralised energy system. Consumers are increasingly generating their own electricity and becoming producers and consumers, or 'prosumers', of electricity. Furthermore, in some countries consumers have the option to sell excess electricity to the electricity grid. Consumers can compete their distributed generation against large generators, which can reduce overall operating hours.

3. Case studies in stranded assets: the materiality of environment-related risk factors

Understanding how environment-related factors interact and affect companies, countries or investors requires a detailed examination of the company's specific asset base. This section provides an up-to-date assessment of the materiality of environment-related risk factors on generation assets. This section provides an overview of research conducted by the University of Oxford's Smith School of Enterprise and the Environment. The research analyses the attributes of various electricity-generating assets, integrating this data with indicators of environment-related risk, to develop asset-specific analyses of risk exposure. The analysis adopts a bottom-up approach from asset-level data, which is aggregated at the investment portfolio, company or country level.

The section is divided into three subparts to provide an overview of stranded asset risks across technologies, countries and risk factors. The first case study is an overview of Caldecott and McDaniels (2014), which examined stranded gas-fired generation assets in the EU. The second case is an overview of Caldecott et al. (2017), which examined the impact of market reform on coal-fired generators in China. Finally, the third case study extends Caldecott, Dericks et al. (2016), examining the impact of catastrophic events and social norms on nuclear power in Japan.

3.1 Stranded gas-fired assets in the EU: examining changing resource landscapes and regulatory responses

In the 1990s, gas held a relatively small role in the EUs generating fuel-mix, representing only 4.0 per cent of installed generating capacity and 8.6 per cent of total electricity supply. In 1996, a newly liberalised electricity sector introduced privatisation and competition into the industry. Many EU utilities sought to expand across borders to gain economies of scale and increase their market share. Concurrently, domestic utilities had to defend against predatory foreign competitors.

Over the past decades, and simultaneous to liberalisation, the EU has sought to reduce its overall CO_2 emissions from the electricity sector. This was achieved through various energy efficiency and renewable energy legislation (Tulloch 2016). In the absence of significant contributions from nuclear energy or CCS technology, combined-cycle gas turbine (CCGT) power plants were placed as the cleanest and most flexible thermal base-load technology (Hromadko 2013; Patel 2013; Platts 2013). The natural gas–fired technology also possesses the advantageous combination of short start-up time and high ramping rates, which allowed rapid response to variability in the system (Riesz and Milligan 2015). Some utilities experienced a period of rapid growth in gas-fired generation assets, driven by the fast build times for gas-fired units and the relatively cheap wholesale price of gas.

The utilities continued to build additional generating capacity, as the industry held bullish market beliefs. The market expected economic growth to grow by 1.6 per cent annum (The Economist 2005), while expected total demand in the EU would increase by 1.5 per cent per annum as it had done linearly over the previous decades (see Figure 6.2). By 2008, gas-fired generation had grown to represent 12.8 per cent of installed capacity and 24.4 per cent of total electricity demand.

The 2007–2008 global financial crisis (GFC) dramatically changed the operating environment of all EU generating assets and rapidly pushed gas-fired generation out of favour. First, the GFC resulted in slow economic growth and a significant reduction in electricity demand. Electricity demand in the OECD fell, on a year-on-year basis, by 2.5 per cent in the fourth quarter of 2008 and a further 4.9 per cent in the first quarter of 2009 (IEA 2009). Second, the EU Emissions Trading Scheme failed to deliver a high and durable carbon price. An oversupply of carbon allowances, strict emissions standards and lower overall energy demand pushed the price of allowances from nearly €29 in 2008 to only €10 in 2009. Between 2013 and 2017, allowances fell further to around €4. The low-carbon price reduced the penalty for high-emission generating technologies, increasing competitiveness of coal-fired generation. Third, a glut of coal from the United States, Australia and Indonesia saturated the global market and decreased coal prices from US$150 per ton in 2010 to only US$44 in 2015, further increasing coal's competitiveness. More recent estimates suggest that coal prices would need to increase to at least US$163 per ton for gas to be a competitive option for major European utilities (Gloystein 2013).

In response to deteriorating market conditions for gas-fired generation, between 2012 and 2013, 10 major utilities announced and implemented mothballing and closure actions for 20 GW of CCGT capacity 8.8 GW of which was built or acquired in the past 10 years (Caldecott and McDaniels 2014). Recent estimates suggest that 51 GW of the EU's generating capacity is currently mothballed, and one-third of the EU's 330 GW of thermal capacity in operation could be retired or mothballed within a few years – where the situation is particularly severe for CCGT (CERA 2013; CEZ 2013; Linklaters 2014). The decision to mothball gas-fired generators has led to increasing carbon emissions in some countries, as coal-fired generation has met excess demand and maintained system security.

The mothballed CCGT assets represent a considerable loss on investment, and many utilities have been faced with significant write-downs in asset values. Caldecott and McDaniels (2014) estimate that six major EU utilities[3] suffered €6bn of impairment charges on their gas-fired assets in 2013. Beyond balance sheet impacts, stranded assets also affect the ability and willingness of firms to invest in new plants. This impact has mostly been observed in equity markets, where the market capitalisation of the MSCI EU Utilities index fell from €1 trillion to €500bn between 2008 and 2013 (The Economist 2013), while the market capitalisation of the top 26 EU utilities has fallen more than €230bn. The impact was also

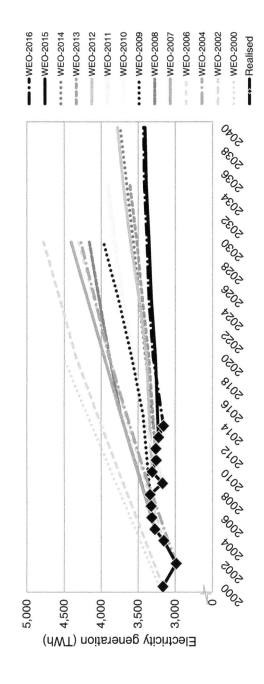

Figure 6.2 Electricity generation in the EU

Source: IEA *World Energy Outlook* reports (2000 to 2016)

felt in debt markets. Since the EU industry was deregulated, EU utility investment was primarily driven by debt finance. As the economic downturn unfolded in 2008, the growth expected by energy utilities did not materialise, and energy utilities found themselves burdened with relatively high levels of debt.

EU Member States, particularly the UK and Germany, have implemented regulatory responses to stranded generation assets by introducing capacity remuneration mechanisms (CRMs). The UK has implemented an auction-based CRM, while Germany has implemented a targeted 'strategic reserve' CRM to maintain system security. The underlying principle of all CRMs involves making out-of-market payments to ensure generating capacity is available when needed rather than paying for electricity delivered (European Commission 2015).

In the UK, the auctions take place years in advance of expected delivery, allowing generators to build the capacity required in advance. The 2014 and 2015 auctions produced electricity prices 60 per cent below expectations, at £19.40 and £18.00 kW/year, respectively (National Grid 2014, 2015). Moreover, the 2015 auction saw fossil fuel generators win 71.5 per cent of the 46.4 GW of capacity available (National Grid 2015). Consequently, there are already concerns that CRMs contradict the objective of phasing out environmentally harmful subsidies (European Commission 2015). Moreover, Fiddler's Ferry, a coal-fired winner of the 2015 auction, decided to pay the UK government £33m in lieu of the capacity agreement, raising issues regarding how robust these capacity contracts are (SSE 2015). In response, there are already calls to change auction rules.

Germany's 'strategic reserve' CRM adopted a different approach to the UK. To reduce CO_2 emissions from power generation, Germany identified 2.7 GW of inefficient lignite plants as temporary 'security standby', which were immediately mothballed for four years (to be decommissioned entirely thereafter). The plants are reimbursed while on standby, which is expected to cost €230m but will support security of supply when all market-based options are exhausted. Germany's Strategic Reserve CRM has been criticised for being inefficient and distorting market prices (Caldecott and McDaniels 2014), as the reserve plants are remunerated for fixed costs and will depress wholesale prices when ramped up, as they must only recover variable (fuel and operation) costs.

There are also criticisms around providing payments to existing generators. Why provide payments to plants that would otherwise (i) be stranded assets or (ii) remain without such payments? The simplest answer is that an ideal energy-only market would also pay existing generators (Cramton et al. 2013). Both the energy-only and capacity markets rely on regulator and government to determine appropriate level of reliability, and both desires are argued to utilize high spot prices to incentivise capacity investment (Cramton et al. 2013; Cramton and Ockenfels 2012). Further, CRMs that only reward long-term adequacy, such as the German strategic reserve, do not incentivise flexibility of storage. Both flexibility and long-term adequacy will be valuable in the future electricity system.

The difficulty arises from the fact that Member States are unlikely to agree on the same CRM. The variety of CRMs in the EU may also affect national system security as well as profitability of domestic generators that are displaced by more modern and efficient investments from foreign companies. Further, as policy support across Member States varies in absolute terms and per MWh, 'subsidy shopping' becomes a material risk which affects upgrading and replacing existing generation capacity (European Commission 2014; Megaw 2015). For example, in 2015 the UK cut RES subsidies, which collapsed a number of small RES companies (Brown et al. 2015). Larger companies such as RWE Innogy transferred 1GW (worth £250m) of allocated UK RES investment capital to projects in the Netherlands and Germany which offered more attractive subsidy support.

The EU is being forced to address the complex harmonisation of climate and energy policies across multiple Member States. Evidence of stranded gas-fired assets and the conflicts arising over the regulatory response are illustrating that national governments are realising unintended consequences of regulatory intervention and are not fully prepared to deal with the market impacts of stranded generation assets. Ensuring that gas generation plays an appropriate role as a transitional thermal technology towards a low-carbon economy, avoiding potential lock-in emissions, remains a challenge for EU energy policy.

3.2 Stranded coal-fired assets in China: the impact of market reform

China's gross domestic product (GDP) has expanded by an average of 10 per cent per annum over three decades. Ordinarily, greater economic growth is linked to increased energy demand as wealth effects and increased business activity result in greater electricity consumption (Narayan and Prasad 2008; Narayan and Smyth 2009; Shiu and Lam 2004). To meet burgeoning electricity demand, China is rapidly expanding its generating fleet. China's electricity market is now the world's largest, having produced 6,015 terawatt-hours (TWh) of electricity in 2016 (Enerdata 2017). Non-residential (i.e. industrial) users consume approximately 86 per cent of this power (Department of Energy Statistics and National Bureau of Statistics 2014). China's current electric generation capacity is also the world's largest, totalling 1,525 GW, where coal (978 GW, 64 per cent) and hydro-power (259 GW, 17 per cent) are the two largest generating sources.

China has the world's third-largest reserves of coal, behind Russia and the United States, making coal a preferable fuel in domestic electricity supply. Due to ample domestic supply, some state-owned coal companies are obliged to provide coal at below-market prices to the state-owned power and steel sectors, making coal a relatively cheap generating fuel (Wright 2012). Consequently, coal accounts for about 73 per cent of China's total energy production, 70 per cent of electric power and 93 per cent of all thermal generation (Chen et al. 2013; National Bureau of Statistics 2014).

Since 1978, China has undergone rapid reforms within its internal markets, transitioning from a planned, state-owned economy towards a more market-based economy. The transition can be divided into three periods: the socialist period (1949 to 1978), the reform period (late 1970s to mid-1990s) and the capitalist period (mid-1990s to present). In 2002, the modern structure of the Chinese power system was reformed even further. The State Council authorised three major liberalisation events, which unbundled the vertical integration of the Chinese power supply. The stages included the separation of (1) power transmission and generation, (2) distribution from transmission and construction of wholesale power markets and (3) retail sales from distribution and construction of retail power markets (Shaofeng and Wenyin 2006). These changes were expected to further promote competition in and efficient operation of the Chinese electricity industry.

Beyond market reform, China is also facing major macroeconomic challenges. The historic economic growth that China has experienced over the past decades has begun to slow down, with its slowest growth rate in 25 years. Further, there has been a shift away from energy-intensive sectors, such as cement and steel, towards more domestic- and service-orientated industries. These latter sectors create a less energy-intensive growth economy configuration. As such, China's electricity demand growth in 2015 was its lowest since 1980, at only 0.5 per cent (Wildau, 2016).

China also faces significant regulatory and structural challenges. Regulatory challenges include more stringent carbon emission and air pollution targets, which are threatening the viability of coal-fired assets. Further, the industry is also facing structural challenges with existing coal installations. As opposed to the United States or other energy markets, where electricity is dispatched based on lowest marginal cost, China assigns approximately the same number of operating hours for each power plant. This method of dispatch was designed to ensure that each power plant investment generated sufficient revenue to cover the capital costs of installation. This also means that older, inefficient plants are given the same number of operating hours as more efficient generating technologies – reducing competitive pressures on inefficient generators. The state is now struggling to contain excess capacity arising from legacy investments combined with the rapid expansion of renewable capacity (Myllyvirta 2016). Beyond the 978 GW of operating coal-fired capacity, at end-2016 China had an additional 256 GW of capacity already under construction and a further 608 GW at various stages of planning. By mid-2016, the utilisation of thermal generation units fell to 44.8 per cent (Stanway 2016), which represents the lowest utilisation rate since 1969 (Greenpeace 2016).

International investors have begun to recognise the deteriorating market conditions in China. Between 1995 and 2015, total assets in the Chinese electricity industry grew from approximately CNY41.8 billion to more than CNY1,180 billion; a compounded average growth rate of 18 per cent per annum.[4] This growth in assets was primarily funded by foreign-capital investment. Like most economies globally, the value of the Chinese power industry declined rapidly from late 2007 during the global financial crisis (GFC). From November 2007, the market capitalisation of a 54-strong sample of Chinese utilities fell 73 per cent, from a peak of CNY4.8 trillion to CNY1.3 trillion.

China has begun to respond to the challenges the sector faces. The global average age of retirement for coal-fired generation assets is approximately 35 years, yet many coal-fired assets operate beyond their useful life. In China, most coal-fired retirements occur within 16 to 34 years. Consequently, China has one of the world's youngest and most modern coal fleets, where many of its plants operate at supercritical efficiencies or better. Second, China is addressing low utilisation rates by cancelling 372 GW of new coal-fired generation construction (Carbon Tracker Initiative 2016) and postponing (until the 2020s) a further 30 coal-fired projects, with a combined capacity of 17 GW, which had already been financed and broken ground (Johnson 2016). In 2016, a further 114 GW of planned coal-fired capacity was also cancelled, representing the single largest drop in its coal pipeline history (Doyle 2016). However, with these cutbacks, there is still 256 GW of coal-fired capacity currently under construction and plans to expand the renewable energy fleet, particularly wind and solar, which would displace coal in competitive markets. Therefore, the future of coal remains highly dependent on continued growth in power demand. Third, and through regulation, China is forcing the industry to become more efficient. China is rolling out a nationwide emissions trading scheme, which will penalise high-emission coal-fired generators. Many non-GHG emission policies are also forcing the closure of coal-fired power generation in the heavily polluted eastern provinces (Caldecott et al. 2015). In 2007, China also forced the closure of small and inefficient plants. A total of 77 GW of small generating units were replaced by large supercritical (600 MW) and ultra-supercritical (1,000 MW) units (Wu and Huo 2014).

Despite these efforts, there are still concerns that the aggregate size of China's coal-fired generating fleet will result in China exceeding its 2°C carbon budget by 2040 (Carbon Tracker Initiative 2016). To remain within the budget, China will require either significant asset stranding or the adoption of (yet unproven) carbon capture and storage technology. It is estimated that, unless a nationwide CCS policy is implemented by early 2020, it will not be possible to retrofit enough coal-fired generators in time to remain within the carbon budget (Carbon Tracker Initiative 2016). Further, retrofitting CCS to China's coal-fired units would add $34 to $129 to the levelised cost of electricity for each MWh generated, more than doubling the cost of power (IEA 2015c, 2016b). By contrast, China's solar PV projects were being developed for as little as $78 per MWh, which would displace coal-fired generation in a competitive market.

3.3 Stranded nuclear in Japan: catastrophe and changing public opinion

For more than six decades, nuclear power was the preferred technology for the provision of low-carbon energy in Japan. In 1954, Japan allocated ¥230 million to begin its nuclear energy programme. Japan's first commercial nuclear power reactor began operating in 1966, and nuclear energy has been a national strategic priority since 1973. The 1980 to 2000 period saw the most marked increase in nuclear generation, increasing from little under 100 TWh per annum to around 300 TWhs.

Since the 1980s, public confidence in nuclear power has been fragile due to many nuclear-related incidents. Incidences ranged from fires and natural disasters, such as earthquakes, to serious malpractice events, the latter resulting in death, uncontrolled nuclear reactions and accidental criticalities. Table 6.1 provides a non-exhaustive list of nuclear incidents in Japan. Beyond these incidences, Tokyo Electric Power Company (TEPCO) has been accused of falsifying numerous inspection reports between 1989 and 2002. Subsequently, support for nuclear power has weakened, resulting in protests and opposition to the construction of more nuclear power.

By 2011, Japan had 54 nuclear reactors, which provided 30 per cent of its total electricity demand. This share of electricity supply was expected to increase to at least 40 per cent by 2017, 50 per cent by 2030, and 60 per cent by 2100. The reliance of nuclear power would also make significant contributions to reducing carbon emissions. With nuclear being the preferred energy source, Japan's Ministry of Economy, Trade and Industry (METI) and the Japanese Atomic Energy Agency (JAEA) projected, relative to 2000 levels, a 54 per cent reduction in carbon emission by 2050, increasing to 90 per cent by 2100.

On 11 March 2011, an undersea earthquake struck off the Oshika Peninsula of Tōhoku. The magnitude 9.1 earthquake was the largest earthquake ever recorded in Japan. The earthquake triggered enormous tsunami waves, which devastated the Northeast coast of the main island. The disaster caused meltdowns in three reactors of the Fukushima Daiichi Nuclear Power Plant complex. Hundreds of thousands of residents within a 20 km radius of Fukushima Daiichi Nuclear Power Plant and 10 km of the Fukushima Daini Nuclear Power Plant were evacuated amidst safety

Table 6.1 Examples of nuclear incidents in Japan

This table provides a non-exhaustive list of major nuclear-related incidences in Japan between 1979 and 2008.

1979	Mihama, Japan	Fuel rods unexpectedly bowed and damaged the fuel supply system.	11
1981	Tsuruga, Japan	Fuel rod ruptured, exposing 278 workers to excessive radiation levels.	3
1999	Shika, Ishikawa, Japan	Uncontrolled nuclear reaction due to control rod malfunction.	34
1999	Ibaraki Prefecture, Japan	Malpractice. Workers at Tokaimura uranium processing facility mixed uranium in buckets to save time. Two workers died and 1,200 were injured.	54
2004	Fukui Prefecture, Japan	Steam explosion at Mihama Nuclear Power Plant killed five workers and injured dozens more.	9
2007	Kashiwazaki, Japan	A 6.8-magnitude earthquake caused Tokyo Electric Power Company's Kariwa nuclear plant to leak 1,192 litres of radioactive water into the Sea of Japan.	2
2008	Fukushima Province, Japan	A 7.2-magnitude earthquake damaged reactor cooling towers and spent fuel storage facilities. More than 19 litres of radioactive waste water spilled, and Tokyo Electric Power Company's No. 2 Kurihara Power Plant was damaged.	45

Source: Sovacool (2010)

concerns. The World Bank estimates the event caused up to $235 billion in damages, placing it among the world's worst disasters.

The disaster caused a dramatic shift in energy policy and rapidly degraded public sentiment towards nuclear power. Citizens accused both the government and TEPCO of failing to prepare anti-tsunami measures. Numerous reports in the years preceding the disaster stated that the plant had a 20 per cent risk of a tsunami striking in the next 30 years (RT 2017). The reports also warned that various measures, such as installing diesel generators on higher ground, could prevent a nuclear disaster. The government shut down all 54 nuclear power reactors, comprising approximately 49 GW, pending significant safety reviews (World Nuclear Association 2016). Figure 6.3 shows that nuclear generating fell from 288 GWh in 2010 to only 16 GWh in 2012.

For the most part, thermal generation (gas, coal and oil) compensated for the drop in total electricity supply. Due to its flexibility, gas initially took the largest residual share of generation, quickly followed by coal. While the proportion of electricity from RES has also increased since the disaster, RES remains a minority in Japanese electricity supply. The increased uptake of thermal generation has undoubtedly threatened Japan's carbon emission goals. During the UN climate talks in Warsaw, Japan faced strong international criticism for abandoning its 2020 emission targets and revising targets from 25 per cent to only 3.8 per cent relative to 1990 levels (Vidal and Macalister 2013). A second consequence of the disaster is that Japan is now more reliant on imported energy, which has hindered the economic growth–boosting programmes and resulted in higher electricity prices. The latter has negatively impacted thousands of smaller manufacturers.

The future of Japanese electricity supply is now substantially uncertain, with fundamental drivers like climate change policies and renewables subsidies, commodity prices, the prospect of nuclear restarts and macroeconomic factors (population and GDP growth) all likely to affect demand for power and its supply. It is almost certain that Japan's nuclear fleet will continue to be returned to service, and numerous attempts have been made to date. The Oi nuclear power plant had initially been restarted in 2012 but was taken offline for a second time due to political opposition. The Sendai nuclear power plant was restarted in 2015 (Simms 2015). As of late 2016, 3 reactors (totalling 2.5 GW) are now operating, 12 reactors (7.2 GW) have been permanently closed, 20 reactors (19.5 GW) have pending restart applications and one new reactor (1.4 GW) is under construction. The remaining 17 reactors (16 GW) are yet to submit restart applications (EIA 2016).

A major factor preventing rapid restarts is the implementation cost. The costs for restarting Japan's idle reactors range from US$700 million to US$1 billion per unit, regardless of reactor size or age, and face lengthy restart times. Japan also faces a shortage in both the level of expertise required and the number of staff the Nuclear Regulation Authority (NRA) is able to deploy to conduct complex and time-consuming safety reviews and approvals (Forbes 2015). An optimistic estimate is that around 10 reactors could be added to the generation fleet every year, and a total of 35 reactors can be online within five years (World Nuclear Association 2016). It is uncertain whether those restarts will fall short of, meet or

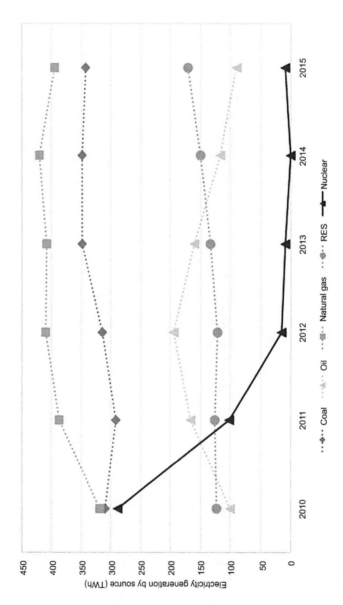

Figure 6.3 Japan's electricity generation by source, 2010–2015

Source: IEA (2016c)

exceed the government's targets, although given the challenges articulated here, a shortfall seems more likely.

4. Methods of managing stranded asset risk: tools and strategies for stakeholders

4.1 Government responses

The best strategy that national governments can implement is regulatory consistency. The useful life of a generating asset can vary from decades (for distributed generating assets) to more than a century (in the case of large-scale hydro). Naturally, many of these assets will outlive multiple election periods and particular politicians or governments. Perhaps the greatest risk for any utility asset is that the regulatory environment will change during the asset's lifetime. When proposing legislative changes, government should think clearly about how different amendments to market design may affect the competitive advantages of various generating technologies. Regulatory changes can immediately shift the advantages and disadvantages for various generating technologies. As observed in the stranded nuclear case study, the decision to idle all nuclear assets created both major challenges (for nuclear) and opportunities (for thermal generating technologies).

Governments should also be mindful of how regulatory intervention can affect an investor's confidence in the electricity industry. This is particularly pertinent, as private or foreign capital is a major source of funding for utility projects. As a corollary to the latter point, government should understand that investors prefer regulatory certainty. Investors are only likely to commit capital to a utility project if it is reasonably expected that they will recover *at least* the cost of the investment. Thus, frequent regulatory interventions can either deter investors from committing capital to capacity investment projects or significantly raise the investor's required rate of return to compensate for additional (regulatory) risk borne.

As illustrated in the stranded gas case study, governments also have a range of out-of-market payment options to remunerate prematurely stranded assets or maintain system adequacy. Yet there are still many questions regarding the effectiveness and efficiency of out-of-market payments. The broader question with such mechanisms concerns whether these transition arrangements should be established to provide a reasonable opportunity for utilities to recover stranded assets. Can these discretionary policy mechanisms increase the ability of firms to manipulate decisions around stranded assets for private benefit? Moreover, is a discretionary payment the most cost-efficient way to maintain security of supply? As observed in Japan, a range of technologies were ready and willing to maintain system security. Governments with short-term security of supply issues should ensure plants targeted for short-term service through discretionary payments are not awarded undue subsidies (Caldecott and McDaniels 2014). However, calculating the appropriate level of compensation is a difficult task. Stranded assets are measured at the plant level, and there is no way to calculate the magnitude of stranded assets in advance with certainty.

4.2 Company responses

The primary tools available to electricity utilities are reactive; that is, they can only prepare and respond to the challenge of stranded assets. The three most useful tools for a firm are transparency, stress testing assets and contingency plans. A major hurdle for investors is the lack of transparency. Investors use all available information to determine what risk factors may affect their investment portfolio and the materiality of such risks. Therefore, the first tool available to a firm is voluntarily disclosure of information which could materially affect an investor's portfolio. This can include asset-level disclosure, such as the generating assets (and fuels) used, and being open about the range of environment-related risk factors both the generating assets and firm are facing. This can be achieved using the clear and comparable framework identified in Figure 6.1.

The second tool includes stress testing assets. Stress testing existing (or planned) assets provides a clearer view of the firm's attitude towards current and future potential for stranded assets across the generation portfolio. Not only does this establish a baseline level of environment-related risk, but it also examines how a change in one or more of the environment-related risk factors is likely to impact the generating portfolio. While it is likely that stress testing of assets already occurs in house, the results are rarely shared with investors. This is most likely due to the commercial nature of the information contained within the reports. Firms should use these stress testing reports to convert a challenge into an opportunity, identifying a potential remedy or a contingency plan for the issue. Not only will this benefit investors, but it also benefits the entire electricity system, as it provides a clearer picture of the market participants and conditions both now and in the future. The latter leads to better system planning and a net benefit for the economy.

Finally, firms should make contingency plans public when faced with stranded assets. If stranded assets are unavoidable, firms should develop contingency plans which recoup (as much as possible) the sunk costs of the generating assets. Firms can also develop a range of options to either improve, diversify or convert the range of cash-generating activities that an individual generating asset may have. This should be accompanied by a clear cost–benefit analysis to scale the potential avenues and outcomes. In some cases, it is not economical to remedy a stranded asset (for example, an asset near the end of its useful life). In these cases, the firm should be open about its decision. Firms can use the contingency plans to expand upon recent efforts to diversify their generating portfolio to adapt to the needs of a rapidly decarbonising energy system.

4.3 Investor responses

What is clear from recent developments is that the dynamics of asset stranding in the electricity industry are changing, and utility investments are becoming increasingly exposed to stranded asset risks. Being external to the firm and separate from day-to-day operations, investors are faced with the difficult challenge of assessing the range of risk factors faced by each type of generating asset in their investment portfolio.

Investor have a range of tools to respond to such challenges. First, investors can encourage companies to sign up to voluntary reporting frameworks which are designed to increase transparency in the industry. Power generators may be willing to disclose asset-specific characteristics which would enable investors, researchers and analysts to undertake their own research on the risks, challenges and opportunities facing the company's portfolio of assets (Caldecott, Kruitwagen et al. 2016). Investors may face resistance with this approach, as companies in the natural resource industry, such as thermal generators, are reluctant to disclose any asset-specific information, instead suggesting that stakeholders should trust the company's judgement (Rook and Caldecott 2015).

An investor can also take steps to alter their endogenous risk profile through a range of hedging instruments in financial markets. In theory, a well-developed market with a range of derivatives can be used to hedge many of the risks faced by competition. An investor can diversify their investment portfolio and invest in an instrument or asset which offsets the risk faced.

Finally, a divestment campaign from a company or generating technology is also a final tool available to investors. Divestment involves the withholding of capital from firms which are seen to be engaged in reprehensible activities (Ansar et al. 2013). The aim of a divestment campaign is threefold. First, divestment can 'force the hand' of companies engaging in a variety of undesirable acts, including those which are seen a socially irresponsible. Second, divestment encourages the industry to undergo transformative change, which can reduce the frequency or severity of the reprehensible act. Third, providing there is significant pressure from an interest group, divestment can pressure lawmakers to enact legislation which is more restrictive.

5. Conclusions

Stranded generation assets are a major challenge facing generating technologies around the world. This chapter has presented a broad framework to understand what stranded generation assets are, what risk factors can strand generation assets and some methods to manage stranded generation assets. Due to the evolving nature of the electricity industry and environment-related risk factors, we have provided a flexible framework through which a range of environment-related risk factors can be defined and understood. To assist in this endeavour, we also provided three major case studies which will be of great importance in the coming decades. The studies focused on empirical evidence of stranded coal, gas and nuclear generating technologies. The studies showed that there is no 'one-size-fits-all' tool to understanding stranded generation assets.

In the first case study, changes in global commodity prices increased the competitiveness of coal-fired generation relative to gas. The EU saw reduced utilisation of recently built and high-efficiency gas-fired generators. The EU's regulatory response brought existing gas and coal back online, however this was at the expense of RES capacity, prevented new capacity being built and depressed wholesale prices. In the second case study, regulatory changes initiated many of the challenges. The study focused on stranded coal in China. China's transition from a regulated market to an increasingly competitive market attracted massive foreign investment to meet burgeoning electricity demand. As demand began to plateau and the economy moved towards less energy-intensive industries, China was faced with overcapacity challenges and reduced utilisation rates. As such, China has begun to cancel future capacity plans – even for projects which have been financed and broken ground. The third case study focused on stranded nuclear assets in Japan. The catastrophic 2011 Fukushima Daiichi disaster diminished the public's already fragile confidence in nuclear power. In response, the government ordered the closure of all nuclear generators, and thermal generation met much of Japan's excess energy demand. These thermal generators have increased Japan's emission levels and have threatened Japan's viability to meet its global emission reduction pledge.

This chapter presented some potential tools and strategies to combat the threat of stranded generation assets. The purpose is to translate these challenges into decision-relevant action for government, companies and investors. The key message conveyed in this chapter is that every electricity industry is continually evolving, and stranded generation assets is a multi-disciplinary, multi-faceted and holistic analysis. An individual must draw on multiple areas of expertise: economics, engineering, sociology, politics and finance to name a few. They must apply their vernacular knowledge of the industry to truly understand their market structure, their generating technologies and how technologies may respond to the threat of environment-related risk factors. But more importantly, they must understand that the threat of stranded generation assets will be persistent. In competitive market structures, the more efficient technologies out-compete inefficient technologies, and low-cost generators out-compete expensive generators.

Notes

1 Merchant power plants are independent power plants competing to sell power.
2 *Climate case – Urgenda – Samen Sneller*. Available at: www.urgenda.nl/en/climate-case/
3 Statkraft, GDF Suez, SSE, Verbund, Vattenfall, and RWE.
4 Data extracted from S&P Capital IQ.

References

Ansar, A., Caldecott, B. and Tibury, J. 2013. Stranded Assets and the Fossil Fuel Divestment Campaign: What Does Divestment Mean for the Valuation of Fossil Fuel Assets? *Stranded Assets Programme, SSEE, University of Oxford*, October, pp. 1–81.

Brown, J. M., Adams, C. and Noble, J. 2015. UK Energy Policy Slammed as Solar Company Collapses. *The Financial Times*. Available at: www.ft.com/cms/s/0/f3ff7db4-6d9e-11e5-8171-ba1968cf791a.html#axzz3oYWUxJBj.

Caldecott, B., Dericks, G. and Mitchell, J. 2015. Stranded Assets and Subcritical Coal: The Risk to Companies and Investors. *Stranded Assets Programme, SSEE, University of Oxford*, pp. 1–78.

Caldecott, B., Dericks, G., Tulloch, D. J., Kruitwagen, L. and Kok, I. 2016. Stranded Assets and Thermal Coal in Japan: An Analysis of Environment-Related Risk Exposure. *Stranded Assets Programme, SSEE, University of Oxford, 2016*, pp. 1–106.

Caldecott, B., Dericks, G., Tulloch, D. J., Liao, X., Kruitwagen, L., Bouveret, G. and Mitchell, J. 2017. Stranded Assets and Thermal Coal in China: An Analysis of Environment-Related Risk Exposure. *Sustainable Finance Programme, SSEE, University of Oxford, Working Paper*, Oxford, pp. 1–116.

Caldecott, B., Howarth, N. and McSharry, P. 2013. Stranded Assets in Agriculture: Protecting Value from Environment-Related Risks. *Stranded Assets Programme, SSEE, University of Oxford*. Available at: www.smithschool.ox.ac.uk/research-programmes/stranded-assets/Stranded Assets Agriculture Report Final.pdf.

Caldecott, B., Kruitwagen, L., Dericks, G., Tulloch, D. J., Kok, I. and Mitchell, J. 2016. Stranded Assets and Thermal Coal: An Analysis of Environment-Related Risk Exposure. *Stranded Assets Programme, SSEE, University of Oxford*, pp. 1–188.

Caldecott, B. and McDaniels, J. 2014. Stranded Generation Assets: Implications for European Capacity Mechanisms, Energy Markets and Climate Policy. *Stranded Assets Programme, SSEE, University of Oxford*, pp. 1–62.

Carbon Tracker Initiative. 2016. *Chasing the Dragon? China's Coal Overcapacity Crisis and What It Means for Investors*. London: Carbon Tracker Initiative.

CEZ. 2013. Heads of 10 Leading European Energy Companies Propose Concrete Measures to Rebuild Europe's Energy Policy. *Press Release*. Available at: www.cez.cz/edee/content/file/pro-media-2013/10-rijen/leaflet_ceos_08-10-2013.pdf.

Chen, Z., Wang, J.-N., Ma, G.-X. and Zhang, Y.-S. 2013. China Tackles the Health Effects of Air Pollution. *Lancet*, 382(9909), 1959–1960.

Cramton, P. and Ockenfels, A. 2012. Economics and Design of Capacity Markets for the Power Sector. *Zeitschrift Für Energiewirtschaft*, 36(2), 113–134.

Cramton, P., Ockenfels, A. and Stoft, S. 2013. Capacity Market Fundamentals. *Economics of Energy & Environmental Policy*, 2(2), 27–46.

Department of Energy Statistics and National Bureau of Statistics. 2014. *China Energy Statistical Yearbook 2014*. Beijing: China Statistics Press.

Doyle, A. 2016. Global Coal Power Plans Fall in 2016, Led by China, India: Study. *Reuters*, September 6. Available at: www.reuters.com/article/us-global-coal-idUSKCN11C2N4.

The Economist. 2005. Europe's Coming Merger Boom. *The Economist*.

The Economist. 2013. How to Lose Half a Trillion Euros. *The Economist*, pp. 27–29.

EIA. 2016. *Five and a Half Years After Fukushima, 3 of Japan's 54 Nuclear Reactors Are Operating*. Available at: www.eia.gov/todayinenergy/detail.php?id=27912.

Enerdata. 2017. *Global Energy Statistical Yearbook 2016*. Available at: https://yearbook.enerdata.net/electricity/world-electricity-production-statistics.html

Eom, J., Edmonds, J., Krey, V., Johnson, N., Longden, T., Luderer, G., Riahi, K., et al. 2015. The Impact of Near-Term Climate Policy Choices on Technology and Emission Transition Pathways. *Technological Forecasting and Social Change*, 90(PA), 73–88.

European Commission. 2014. Competition Policy Brief: Improving State Aid for Energy and the Environment. *Press Release*.

European Commission. 2015. *Launching the Public Consultation Process on a New Energy Market Design*, Vol. COM(2015).

Forbes, A. 2015. Back to a Nuclear Future: The Abe Government Restarts Japan's Energy Policy. *Energy Post*. Available at: www.energypost.eu/back-nuclear-future-abe-government-restarts-japans-energy-policy/.

Garcia-Martin, J. A. 2001. Stranded Costs: An Overview. *Working Paper No. 108*, Madrid.

Gloystein, H. 2013. European Coal Prices Need $80 Rise for Gas to Become Competitive. *Reuters*. Available at: www.reuters.com/article/energy-europe-gas-coal-idUSL5E 9C85US20130108.

Greenpeace. 2016. *Study on Economics of Coal-Fired Power Generation Projects in China*. Available at: www.greenpeace.org/eastasia/Global/eastasia/publications/reports/climate-energy/2016/Study on Economics of Coal-fired Power Generation Projects in China Report.pdf.

Helm, D. and Jenkinson, T. 1997. The Assessment Introducing Competition Into Regulated Industries. *Oxford Review of Economic Policy*, Oxford University Press, 13(1), 1–14.

Henderson, B. C. and Hughes II, K. E. 2010. Valuation Implications of Regulatory Climate for Utilities Facing Future Environmental Costs. *Advances in Accounting*, 26(1), 13–24.

HIS CERA. 2013. *Keeping the Lights On: Design and Impact of Capacity Mechanisms*. Cambridge: IHS CERA.

Hromadko, J. 2013. Shale Boom Is a Bust for Europe's Gas Plants. *The Wall Street Journal*, 8, May, 2013.

IEA. 2009. *The Impact of the Financial and Economic Crisis on Global Energy Investment*. Paris: IEA/OECD. Available at: www.iea.org/publications/freepublications/pub lication/impact.pdf.

IEA. 2015a. *Medium-Term Coal Market Report 2015: Market Analysis and Forecasts to 2020*. Paris, France: IEA.

IEA. 2015b. *Coal*. Available at: www.iea.org/aboutus/faqs/coal/.

IEA. 2015c. *Projected Costs of Generating Electricity*. Paris, France: IEA.

IEA. 2016a. *World Energy Outlook*. Paris, France: IEA.

IEA. 2016b. *Ready for CCS Retrofit*. Paris, France: IEA.

IEA. 2016c. Japan 2016 Review. In *Energy Policies of IEA Countries*. Paris, France: IEA, pp. 1–183.

ITRE Committee and European Parliament. 2014. *The Impact of the Oil Price on EU Energy Prices*. Brussels: European Parliament. Available at: http://doi.org/10.2861/53107.

Johnson, N., Krey, V., McCollum, D. L., Rao, S., Riahi, K. and Rogelj, J. 2015. Stranded on a Low-Carbon Planet: Implications of Climate Policy for the Phase-Out of Coal-Based Power Plants. *Technological Forecasting and Social Change*, 90(Part A), 89–102.

Johnson, S. 2016. China Axes Part-Built Coal Power Plants. *The Financial Times*, October 22. Available at: www.ft.com/content/78db1ca6-96ab-11e6-a80e-bcd69f323a8b.

Koch, N. and Bassen, A. 2013. Valuing the Carbon Exposure of European Utilities. The Role of Fuel Mix, Permit Allocation and Replacement Investments. *Energy Economics*, 36, 431–443.

Linklaters. 2014. *Capacity Mechanisms. Reigniting Europe's Energy Markets*. London: Linklaters. Available at: linklaters.com/capacitymechanisms.

Megaw, N. 2015. UK Energy Groups Warn Subsidy Cuts Threaten Old Wind Farms. *The Financial Times*. Available at: http://on.ft.com/1P5WiQT.

Moore, S. 2013. *Issue Brief: Water Resource Issues, Policy and Politics in China*. Washington, DC: The Brookings Institution. Available at: http://www. Brookings.edu/research/papers/2013/02/water-Politics-China-Moore#_edn1

Myllyvirta, A. 2016. China Keeps Building Coal Plants Despite New Overcapacity Policy. *Greenpeace Energy Desk*.

Narayan, P. K. and Prasad, A. 2008. Electricity Consumption – Real GDP Causality Nexus: Evidence From a Bootstrapped Causality Test for 30 OECD Countries. *Energy Policy*, 36(2), 910–918.

Narayan, P. K. and Smyth, R. 2009. Multivariate Granger Causality Between Electricity Consumption, Exports and GDP: Evidence From a Panel of Middle Eastern Countries. *Energy Policy*, 37(1), 229–236.

National Bureau of Statistics. 2014. *China Statistical Yearbook*. Available at: http://www.stats.gov.cn/tjsj/ndsj/2014/indexeh.htm

National Grid. 2014. *Provisional Auction Results: T-4 Capacity Market Auction 2014.* Available at: https://www.gov.uk/government/uploads/system/uploads/attachment_data/file/389832/Provisional_Results_Report-Ammendment.pdf

National Grid. 2015. *Provisional Auction Results: T-4 Capacity Market Auction for 2019/20*. Available at: https://www.emrdeliverybody.com/Capacity%20Markets%20Document%20Library/2015%20T-4%20Capacity%20Market%20Provisional%20Results.pdf

Nwaeze, E. T. 2000. Deregulation of the Electric Power Industry: The Earnings, Risk, and Return Effects. *Journal of Regulatory Economics*, Kluwer Academic Publishers, 17(1), 49–67.

Oberndorfer, U. 2009. EU Emission Allowances and the Stock Market: Evidence From the Electricity Industry. *Ecological Economics*, 68(4), 1116–1126.

Patel, T. 2013. GDF Suez CEO Decries 'Crisis' in Europe's Gas-Fired Power Plants. *Bloomberg*. Available at: www.bloomberg.com/news/articles/2013-05-02/gdf-suez-ceo-decries-crisis-in-europe-s-gas-fired-power-plants.

Platts. 2013. *German Coal-Fired Power Rises Above 50% in First-Half 2013 Genera-tion Mix*. Available at: www.platts.com/latest-news/electric-power/london/german-coal-fired-power-rises-above-50-in-first-26089429.

Riesz, J. and Milligan, M. 2015. Designing Electricity Markets for a High Penetration of Variable Renewables. *Wiley Interdisciplinary Reviews: Energy and Environment*, 4(3), 279–289.

Rook, D. and Caldecott, B. 2015. Evaluating Capex Risk: New Metrics to Assess Extrac-tive Industry Project Portfolios. *Working Paper*.

RT. 2017. Japan Govt & Tokyo Power Firm Liable for 'Preventable' Fukushima Melt-down – Court. *R*, March 17. Available at: https://on.rt.com/863m.

Shaofeng, X. and Wenyin, C. 2006. The Reform of Electricity Power Sector in the PR of China. *Energy Policy*, 34, 2455–2465.

Shiu, A. and Lam, P.-L. 2004. Electricity Consumption and Economic Growth in China. *Energy Policy*, 32(1), 47–54.

Simms, J. 2015. Outlook Cloudy for Japan's Renewable Energy Drive. *The Financial Times*. Available at: www.ft.com/cms/s/0/dae47c8c-d927-11e4-b907-00144feab7de.html#axzz459PztpkK.

Söderholm, P. 1998. Fuel Choice in West European Power Generation Since the 1960s. *OPEC Review*, Blackwell Publishers Ltd, 22(3), 201–231.

Sovacool, B. K. 2010. A Critical Evaluation of Nuclear Power and Renewable Electricity in Asia. *Journal of Contemporary Asia*, Taylor & Francis, 40(3), 369–400.

SSE. 2015. *SSE Statement of Capacity Market Auction Provisional Results – Fidder's Ferry Power Station*. Available at: http://sse.com/newsandviews/allarticles/2015/12/sse-statement-on-capacity-market-auction-provisional-results-fiddlers-ferry-power-station/ [Accessed April 25, 2016].

Stanway, D. 2016. China Building 200 GW of Coal-Fired Power Despite Capacity Glut: Greenpeace. *Reuters*.

Swanson, R. M. 2006. A Vision for Crystalline Silicon Photovoltaics. *Progress in Photo-voltaics: Research and Applications*, Wiley Online Library, 14(5), 443–453.

The Times of India. 2016. Farakka Shutdown Triggers Power Crisis. *The Times of India*, March 14. Available at: http://timesofindia.indiatimes.com/city/bhubaneswar/Farakka-shutdown-triggers-power-crisis/articleshow/51389075.cms?from=mdr.

Tulloch, D. J. 2016. *The Impact of Risk Factors and Regulatory Change in the Returns of European Energy Utilities*. New Zealand: University of Otago.

Tulloch, D. J., Diaz-Rainey, I. and Premachandra, I. M. 2017a. The Impact of Liberalization and Environmental Policy on the Financial Returns of European Energy Utilities. *The Energy Journal*, 38(2), 77–106.

Tulloch, D. J., Diaz-Rainey, I. and Premachandra, I. M. 2017b. The Impact of Regulatory Change on EU Energy Utility Returns: The Three Liberalization Packages. *Applied Economics*, Taylor & Francis, 1–16.

Vidal, J. and Macalister, T. 2013. Japan Under Fire for Scaling Back Plans to Cut Greenhouse Gases. *The Guardian*. Available at: www.theguardian.com/global-development/2013/nov/15/japan-scaling-back-cut-greenhouse-gases.

Wildau, G. 2016. China's: The State-Owned Zombie Economy. *The Financial Times*, February 29. Available at: www.ft.com/content/253d7eb0-ca6c-11e5-84df-70594b99fc47.

World Bank and Ecofys. 2017. *Carbon Pricing Watch 2017*. Washington, DC. Available at: https://openknowledge.worldbank.org/handle/10986/26565.

World Nuclear Association. 2016. *Nuclear Power in Japan*. Available at: www.world-nuclear.org/information-library/country-profiles/countries-g-n/japan-nuclear-power.aspx.

Wright, T. 2012. *The Political Economy of the Chinese Coal Industry: Black Gold and Blood-Stained Coal, Vol. 45*. London: Routledge.

Wu, L. and Huo, H. 2014. Energy Efficiency Achievements in China's Industrial and Transport Sectors: How Do They Rate? *Energy Policy*, 73, 38–46.

Zhang, C., Diaz Anadon, L., Mo, H., Zhao, Z. and Liu, Z. 2014. Water-Carbon Trade-Off in China's Coal Power Industry. *Environmental Science and Technology*, 48(9), 11082–11089.

7 Understanding climate-related stranded assets in the global real estate sector

Kevin Muldoon-Smith and Paul Greenhalgh

1. Introduction

The aim of this chapter is to introduce the fertile topic of climate-related 'stranded assets' (Caldecott et al. 2017) into the heterogeneous global real estate asset class. Real estate is taken to mean, broadly, all residential, commercial, and operational property. The chapter focuses on the issue of climate-related risk and opportunity, primarily the idea that climate change policy and associated environmental risk factors could induce the stranding of some conventional real estate assets. Principally, the focus for study is the UK; however, comparisons are made internationally, and key distinctions are made between developed and developing countries. The chapter observes that stranded assets are not new in real estate, as the changing consumer demand of occupiers has regularly rendered property assets redundant or obsolete – exhibiting the creative destruction outlined by Joseph Schumpeter (1950). However, what is new is the influence and systemic reach of climate change and associated environmental policy on some property assets and related capital markets.

At the same time, the global real estate sector is going through its own set of structural growing pains in response to dynamic changes in residential and business practices – potentially coalescing with and exacerbating the climate-related stranded asset issue. For example, the appetite for smaller commercial floorplans in the office sector, the impact of the internet on the retail sector, and the disruptive influence of new property technology on conventional real estate living and working conditions have all increased uncertainty in the global real estate market. Reflecting on this dynamic and potentially volatile situation, this chapter sets out a methodology for understanding climate-related stranded asset exposure in the global real estate sector using building energy performance labelling. At the same time, it reflects on the requirements, challenges, and opportunities associated with a reallocation of global capital towards investments aligned with global environmental sustainability. Necessarily, the chapter is broad in nature, providing a commentary on stranded assets in the global real estate market, with the intention of acting as a staging post for new research into how environmental related risk might transpire and strand real estate assets. The chapter concludes by outlining a research agenda for stranded assets in global real estate and some opportunities relating to climate-related stranded assets.

2. Climate change and nature of real estate markets

In response to climate-based threats and associated environment policy, there is now pre-emptive need for new arrangements of land, unconventional forms of buildings, and creative adaptations to the existing property stock to combat the threat of devaluation (Wilkinson et al. 2014; Eames et al. 2017). However, at the same time, there are several opposing forces that make pre-emptive action involving energy-efficient retrofit measures (or new sustainable construction) difficult in the developed world. Grabher's (1993) treatment of path dependence and 'lock-in' is a suitable analytical framework to understand this situation. Setting aside the sheer cost involved in adapting real estate assets in the face of climate change (Eames et al. 2017), path dependence and lock-in is concerned with the persistent behaviour of people, society, business, and locations as they maintain and reinforce *historical behaviour in contexts that are significantly different to the original historical circumstances* (Henning et al. 2013). Grabher (1993), researching in the field of regional economics, describes three interrelated types of 'lock-in': political, functional, and cognitive lock-in. These same constructs can also be used to help explain the existence and silence of stranded assets in global real estate debate and practice.

Political lock-in explains circumstances in which traditional courses of development are retained and reinforced by pre-existing stakeholders and institutions, inhibiting adjustment to new considerations and policy directives. Bishop and Williams (2012) and Henneberry (2017, pp. 1–2) illustrate this situation when they argue that cities in the developed world have gradually become more 'formalised and permanent'. Proliferating layers and intensities of legislation '(some with a long history but most introduced in the 20th Century) covering building construction, fire prevention, public health, building conservation and land use planning have solidified the urban built environment'. This intransigent situation makes it more difficult for the existing built environment to change. This is subsequently compounded by the slow turnover of real estate stock, which typically only accounts for 2% of total property supply each year (IRENA 2017).

Cognitive lock-in relates to collective ideas and beliefs that inhibit the acceptance of new ideas – overlaying physical rigidity in the built environment is a climate of institutional inertia. Muldavin (2010) argues that although important steps have been taken, the real estate sector is struggling to confirm the value of sustainability in property investment. Despite amendments to the RICS Red Book in 2014 and the publication of the RICS Guidance note on Sustainability and Commercial Property Valuation in 2013,[1] it has been difficult for the traditionally sluggish real estate sector to take on board sustainability objectives, as there has been no demonstrable enhancement to return (Dixon 2014). This is because the imperfect implications of stranded assets – implicit in sustainable development – are very awkward for mainstream real estate research to digest. Traditional paradigms in real estate economics and related practice, for example the valuation of property, and modern portfolio theory are anchored in the maximising presumptions of the rational investor. It is not straightforward to capture the cost or potential premium afforded by sustainability, as valuation is typically backward looking (Diaz and Hansz 2001), resulting in a lack of scrutiny by valuation professionals (Lützkendorf and Lorenz 2005; Lorenz and Lützkendorf 2011; Michl et al. 2016). Similarly, real estate investors make decisions and monitor progress against retrospective performance benchmarks and indices provided by the Investment Property Databank (IPD) and CB Richard Ellis.

Functional lock-in, in this case, relates to the too-close connection between historical building functions and worth, which inhibits consideration of external change. Illustrating this situation in the real estate sector, the common treatment has been to situate the analysis of stranded assets in the depreciation and obsolescence literature. There is a variety of informative applied depreciation studies by Baum (1991), Baum and McElhinney (1997), Dixon et al. (1999), Dunse and Jones (2002), Andrew and Pitt (2006), Crosby and Devaney (2006), Mansfield (2009), and Crosby et al. (2011). However, broadly speaking, in this perspective functional real estate assets grow old, become less productive, and must then be improved or replaced. Through this process, loss of value occurs gradually in a typically linear fashion related to the original function of the building rather than under external conditions of sudden market disruption (Christensen 1997).

On one hand, the potential stranded asset threat, initially associated with value of unburnable carbon stocks (Krause et al. 1990; Carbon Tracker Initiative 2013) and more recently following the Paris Agreement (Covington 2016), has the potential to blow this market lethargy wide open. This is because, until now, sustainability has mostly been seen as an altruistic choice or government concern associated with environmental objectives rather than business necessity. On the other hand, traditional real estate valuation methods are still based on the most recent comparable transaction advice rather than any forecast of sustainability value or fossil fuel liability, resulting in a stranded asset knowledge deficit. Illustrating the consequences of this situation, Warren-Myers (2012) argues that without confirmation of environmental value, sustainable investment (or fossil fuel disinvestment) will be constrained in the real estate sector. This chapter, in part, aims to fill this gap in knowledge by setting out a framework for understanding climate-related stranded asset exposure and value in the real estate asset market.

3. Stranded assets and the global real estate market

In recent years, climate-related stranded assets have received international attention from the UN (McGrath 2014), the North American government (Friedman 2014), the OECD (Gurria 2013), the Inter-American Development Bank (Caldecott et al. 2016), the G20 Financial Stability Board, and the Bank of England (Carney 2015). However, the same issue has received very little attention in the real estate sector (IRENA 2017 is a notable exception), even though the real estate sector shares and potentially intensifies many of these same risks downstream. Given that real assets make up a large part of total global investment worth and are a significant store of national, corporate, and individual wealth, the omission of real estate from the stranded assets discourse is a significant omission.

Traditionally, real estate assets share many of the same imperfect investment characteristics as fossil fuel assets in relation to liquidity, fungibility, and transmission of potential risk. For example, both assets classes are heterogeneous, typically, no two assets are the same and they take considerable initial investment to exploit, there are few buyers and sellers in the market place (due to cost and location), market entry and exit is difficult (due to ownership monopolies, the illiquid nature of assets, and government legislation), and both types of asset are typically fixed in location (either under it or built on top of it).

The respective asset classes are also interrelated. Traditionally, residential and commercial property assets have been powered by fossil fuel–dependent heating and ventilation systems. Furthermore, the urban sprawl associated with suburban residential property, out-of-town office parks, and retail centres, has evolved in tandem with the fossil fuel-based automobile. There is also a distinct and highly expensive set of operational property assets that has been constructed to directly serve the fossil fuel sector, for example, coal-fired power stations, which are typically highly leveraged and have no obvious alternative use (IRENA 2017).

This volatile but largely hidden situation frames the underlying theme in this chapter: to what extent is the global real estate market exposed to the stranded asset threat, and how can it take steps to mitigate the potential risk? The global value of already-developed real estate is $217 trillion, roughly 2.7 times global GDP, making up roughly 60% of all mainstream investment assets (Savills 2016). Furthermore, the value of the new construction market will be $10.3 trillion in 2030, an $8 trillion increase on present-day values (Global Construction Perspectives and Oxford Economics 2015). In large part, the volume of real estate assets in global investment portfolios and the circulation of the same assets in international capital markets is down to increasing levels of financialisation (Weber 2010).

Hitherto, stationary physical real estate assets have been increasingly repackaged into a rash of financial products and funds, including derivatives, real estate investment trusts, and debt vehicles. This has expanded the tentacles of property asset value throughout global finance networks. The implication is that stranded real estate assets provide a vehicle for intensifying the threat of climate-related stranded assets because they reach further into and have broader exposure in capital markets than fossil fuels assets. Look no further than the 2008 global financial crash for an illustration of the sudden impact and systemic influence of real estate–based financial products. Despite sustainable intervention, including enhanced insulation, better glazing, and utilising solar power and bio-mass, global property stock is still reliant on fossil fuel for heating and ventilation.

The remainder of this chapter considers this situation. It utilises the outputs of international building energy performance legislation to develop a model for understanding climate-related stranded asset exposure and sets out a framework for further research into the real estate asset sector. Such an evaluation should provide a sound basis for policy makers when they evaluate ideas for climate change adaptation in the real estate sector. For those property professionals involved in the day-to-day management of real estate assets in the developed world, the chapter provides an approach to understanding the wider significance of climate-related threats which we hope will contribute to more knowledgeable and effective practice in relation to real estate–based stranded assets. Expanding knowledge in this area will help investment portfolio and asset managers in mature urban areas deal with the challenges of adapting an ageing property stock. However, it is also hoped that this approach will help property professionals dealing with the demands of accelerating urbanisation in the developing world, which requires an understanding of urban development processes and the potential impact of stranded assets. Encouragingly, developing countries have the potential opportunity to leapfrog climate-related stranded asset risk in real estate, bypassing intermediary stages of urban development, avoiding the costs of adaptation, and potentially becoming leaders in sustainable property through new urbanisation and smart city development.

4. Climate-based real estate legislation

Global real estate is essential for urban development. However, it expends physical resources and is the origin of considerable emissions. A conservative estimate is that global real estate consumes 40% of global energy annually and accounts for more than 20% of international carbon emissions (World Economic Forum 2016). As part of international efforts to reduce carbon emissions, real estate and its associated built environment has been identified as a major contributor toward planetary warming (IPCC 2014). For example, the UK government aims to reduce UK real estate CO_2 emissions to close to zero by 2050 to attain its energy-efficiency targets. This aim has been repeated around the world.

Consequently, in recent decades, the real estate sector has been at the forefront of climate change legislation, designed to reduce its impact on the global environment. Environmental labelling, endorsement based and comparative (Reed et al. 2009), has been a central tool in reducing the environmental impact of building stock. Typically, environmental labelling has adopted either a multi-criteria sustainability approach or a narrower focus on energy (Sayce et al. 2010). In the 1990s, the BREEAM[2] tool led the way in the UK (multi-criteria), soon to be followed in France by the HQE[3] model (multi-criteria), the Swiss Minergie[4], and the North American Energy Star[5] (both energy). In the 2000s these models were joined by further multi-criteria schemes, LEED[6] (North America), CASBEE[7] (Japan), Green Globe[8] (Canada), and Green Star[9] (Australia).

Latterly, the most comprehensive approach can be seen in the European Union (EU). Following the 2010 EU Energy Performance of Building Directive, it is mandatory for all European properties to hold an Energy Performance Certificate and monitor their heating and air conditioning (all 28 Member States signed up to this directive). Energy Performance Certificates (EPCs) have a significant relationship with climate-related stranded assets in real estate. They are a key enabler of building improvement, as they influence decision making in real estate transactions and provide cost-optimal recommendations for energy performance improvement (BPIE 2014). They provide the opportunity for governments to enforce minimum energy performance standards, and they are an important information tool for building owners, occupiers, and real estate stakeholders. These latter two themes form the basis for the remainder of this section. Firstly, the potential for climate-related legislation to strand real estate assets will be considered, before, secondly, the information by-products of energy performance labels will be assessed for their potential in measuring stranded asset exposure.

4.1 Climate-related obsolescence

The England and Wales government has used EPCs as the basis for legally enforceable Minimum Energy Efficiency Standards (MEES), legislated through the Energy Efficiency (Private Rented Property) (England and Wales) Regulation Act 2015. These regulations have fixed a minimum standard for both domestic and non-domestic privately rented property. Commencing in April 2018, any domestic or non-domestic property that is available to let with an energy performance rating below E (those properties with F and G ratings) will be deemed illegal to let – in 2020 the same rule will apply to residential property. In England and Wales, it is estimated that 10% of residential property stock (£570bn) and 18% (£157bn) of commercial stock are under this threshold. In addition, the Government in England and Wales is also considering the merits of committing to a forward plan for MEES. This would mean that the minimum energy performance regulatory standard is increased over time in order to provide medium- to long-term certainty regarding when the progressive standards will apply and when any necessary physical improvements will need to be made (DECC 2014).

From 1 April 2023, these regulations will apply to all non-domestic property, not only those agreeing a new let, lease renewal if an EPC is already in place, or tenants wishing to sublet (Green Construction Board 2014; The Non-Domestic Minimum Building Energy Performance Standards Working Group 2014). Failure to meet these new rules, for example, the illegal letting of a sub-standard property, will result in a minimum fine of £150,000. There are several potential exemptions to MEES, primarily:

- Any building improvement that would alter the character or appearance of an historical (in a conservation area) or listed building,
- Where energy efficient improvements would reduce market value by more than 5%,
- The improvements do not pay for themselves through energy cost saving within a seven-year time frame,
- If the landlord cannot get consent from planning authority or incumbent tenant,
- Temporary buildings and detached buildings under 50 sqm.

To protect against MEES avoidance techniques, all exemptions must be held on the Private Rented Sector Exemption Register. The implication is that any substandard building will still be publicly named and shamed and may suffer yield and value depreciation. The MEES in England and Wales indicates a potential future trajectory for international property legislation, in which governments tighten up on building emissions in order to achieve climate change targets. Using the minimum energy exposure figures in England and Wales as a proxy for international energy policy and combining them with the recent estimate of global real estate value provided by Savills (2016), it is possible to gauge global real estate exposure to climate-related stranded assets. If all international governments followed the same strategy, the risk value for global residential property assets would be $16 trillion and $10 trillion for global commercial assets.

However, the introduction of MEES has not been without difficulty. Potentially 70% of EPC ratings in England and Wales could be incorrect (either too low or too high) due to the inconsistent quality of assessments (Hobbs 2013; Hosgood 2017) and the evolving nature of the underlying method of calculation (the Simplified Building Energy Model – SBEM). Furthermore, the flagship finance mechanism that accompanied MEES in the residential sector, the Green Deal Finance Model, has been abandoned by the government, and it was never introduced for commercial property. The consequence is that the England and Wales Government has sent out a very strong policy signal in favour of building improvement but has removed the primary financial means of doing so.

4.2 Exploiting climate change legislation to create an information baseline for real estate stranded assets

The first stage in tackling climate-related stranded assets in the real estate sector must be identifying their existence. IRENA (2017) have proposed an ambitious methodology for assessing the global real estate stranding asset exposure. The method utilises estimates of existing floor space, forecasted new building space, and natural demolition rates to quantify for the first time climate-related stranded assets in building stock, the impact of delayed policy action, and the cost of retrofitting sub-standard properties in response to climate-related policy action. The method lays important foundations for studying the impact of fossil fuel–related stranded assets in the real estate sector, for the first time linking the upstream fossil fuel sector into downstream real estate assets. However, due to the lack of information transparency in the real estate sector (Fuerst et al. 2011), IRENEA (2017) concede that the method rests on a number of necessary estimates and presumptions and utilises a broad econometric methodology. There is considerable scope to build on this method with more detailed data sets and information resources.

The granularity and scope of the IRENA model could be significantly enhanced by using already-existing energy labelling information. For example, the mandatory EPC information held in the EU Building Stock Observatory and English and Wales EPC registry could be used to provide accurate accounts of energy use, floor space, building retrofit advice (and cost), type of property, and location. This could then be augmented with additional information from the Building Performance Data Base in North America and the National Australian Built

Environment Rating System. In principle energy performance labelling provides an opportunity to accurately measure climate-related stranded asset exposure in the developed world. Information is less readily available in the developing world; however, those areas of the world with less transparent property markets, for example China (the Three Star Rating Building System) and South America (for example the RTQ-C and RTQ-R methodologies in Brazil), are increasingly adopting building energy performance standards, which reveal the opportunity for comprehensive international energy performance data bases in the future.

Information generated from mandatory EPC assessments could be taken further. Issues of consistency and accuracy (a problem shared with the wider real estate market) significantly hamper meaningful assessment of stranded assets and energy performance in real estate stock. Increasingly, contemporary real estate data sets include Unique Property Reference Numbers (UPRN). UPRNs enable the linking of disparate data sets to provide more powerful, multi-criteria data sets and provide a consistent identifier throughout the building life cycle – from initial planning consent to final demolition. However, EPCs do not carry a requirement for a UPRN; this is a missed opportunity. For example, in England and Wales, the presence of a consistent UPRN would enable the linking of EPC information to National Valuation data sets. Each property in England and Wales is valued every five years for taxation purposes; linking both data sets would facilitate accurate measurement of energy use, floor space, and value and would assist, in part, the measurement of real estate–related stranded assets exposure to government revenues. Most developed countries typically derive some of their taxation from property, indicating the international potential for this coupling. This would potentially lead to an energy performance baseline which could be used to benchmark and monitor the risk of climate-related stranded assets and more generally the value of sustainability. This would be an important innovation, as it would increase the overall quality of property valuation by integrating carbon into statutory methods of property valuation.

5. Developing a stranded asset research agenda in global real estate

The previous section dealt, in the main, with climate-related stranded asset exposure in the developed world, initially addressing this situation through the use of informational by-products from building energy labelling. In contrast, the proceeding section focuses on the developing world and the development of a stranded asset research agenda for global real estate. The burgeoning climate-related stranded asset literature has begun to tackle the issue in lower-income and emerging countries (Caldecott et al. 2016, 2017). However, there is very little direct analysis of climate-related stranded assets, as they specifically relate to real estate, in these locations.

Physical real estate development and supporting professional practice is fairly well established in the developed world, anchored in rigid functionality and institutions. However, real estate, as it relates to energy use, in the developing world, particularly in rural locations, is more diverse – influenced by variation in population size, economic activity, resource levels, and energy profile. Due to the rapid nature of development in these locations, there is also a congested policy landscape which makes focusing on climate-related stranded assets problematic – not least the thorny subject of whether such locations should face the same stringent climate standards as the developed world when they have not had the opportunity to exploit the economic growth associated with fossil fuel use. Nevertheless, such regions can have key geographical features which aid fossil fuel divestment in real estate. For example, generous space and excellent access to sunlight has the potential to aid the exploitation of wind and solar energy (in contrast, energy use retrofitting in the western world is exacerbated by less proximity to natural resources). This resource landscape is particularly advantageous in those locations – for example rural India – where it is difficult or unduly expensive to develop fossil fuel infrastructure or to interface with a national energy grid. This awkward situation is primarily related to the sheer logistical challenges associated with expansive and unforgiving locations and/or the paucity of capital finance.

The stranded asset situation in the developing world also needs to be understood in the context of vastly differing circumstances. For every exemplar self-contained smart city, for example Masdar City (in the United Arab Emirates) or the Songdo International Business District (in South Korea) – exhibiting high-tech digital infrastructure, carbon-neutral buildings, green urban planning, and abundant capital finance – there are many more largely rural locations, for example Xinjiang Province in China and Bihar State in India, exhibiting marginal and fragmented locational attributes. They are quite literally operating off the conventional energy grid and outside conventional fossil fuel infrastructure routes. However, all of these locations are united by rapidly increasing levels of population and concurrent energy demand, which has put these locations on a rapid energy provision trajectory. Understanding this trajectory provides an opportunity to minimise climate-related stranded assets before they happen whilst achieving the decarbonisation agenda (IRENA 2017).

6. Opportunities for further research

The first challenge for global real estate stakeholders and their professional bodies is in connection to the recognition of climate-related stranded assets. This involves creating the informational baselines that reflect the existence and cost of stranding – a methodology has been outlined in this chapter. An initial informational baseline only provides a broad measurement of climate-related stranded asset exposure. This must be supplemented with an appraisal of timing, probability, and the scale of risk with regard to climate-related stranded assets. This reveals the potential for a transferable framework that can be used to stress-test investment portfolios and locations against the various risks associated with building characteristics, practice, and location. In order to create the conditions for such a framework, systematic research should take place in the following six areas if the stranding problem is going to be solved and potentially exploited:

1   What physical strategies are available for mitigating and reversing stranded assets, such as adaptive re-use and sustainable urban retrofit? The global real estate sector is hugely disparate – how might climate-related stranded assets be more or less important for different types of property assets and geographies.
2   What is the relationship between the normal refurbishment cycle and the problem of stranding? Although the building replacement cycle is notoriously sluggish, the occupation of buildings, particularly in the commercial sector, is increasingly dynamic and short lived. Could the new era of short leases and increased opportunity for landlord/tenant negotiation at lease renewal help ameliorate the problem of climate-related stranding?
3   What can the evolution of physical locations tell us about the trajectory and potential amelioration of stranded assets? Could new understanding in this area help inform intervention and so-called leapfrog development before fossil fuel dependency is ingrained?
4   How can considerations of sustainability, in particular its pricing, be aligned with the problem of stranded assets? Could the expansion of valuation exercises and the publication of practical guidelines and recommendations (to include the stranding problem) help to influence behaviour in global real estate sectors, supply chains, and companies?
5   What other factors (besides environmental legislation) cause stranding in global real estate markets, and how do such factors interact with location and geography? Do certain types of property, markets, and locations have systemic risk because of their underlying characteristics?
6   Is the presumption of stranding itself overplayed in global real estate markets? For example, do new economic factors and market movements (such as permitted development right rule changes for office to residential conversion in England) have the capacity to ameliorate the stranding problem?

7. Conclusion

Adapting and then echoing the recent arguments of Silver (2016), there are two not necessarily mutually exclusive explanations for the silence of climate-related stranded assets in global real estate markets. First is that the real estate market has digested the stranded asset threat and decided that environmental legislation will be sufficiently diluted that climate-related stranding will not impact global real estate assets. In other words, real estate stakeholders believe that the lobbying power of private and public capital held in global real estate and the force of the fossil fuel sector will win out against the climate change consensus. Under this position, significant policy related change 'just won't happen.' Second, the institutions and traditional 'ways of working' in the real estate market are largely blind to the stranded asset threat – they simply don't account for it. Both positions are untenable, as they leave real estate assets prone to an uncertain future. Adopting the principles of Pascal's Wager, it is rational to plan for potent climate-related policy enforcement. Adapting existing buildings and constructing new developments that are not reliant on fossil fuels, although potentially costlier in the short term, can create a more resilient (and therefore valuable) asset. Ignoring climate change exposes physical real estate assets to the risk of permanent disruption as clean technology becomes more affordable, as social norms and consumer behaviour increasingly accept principles of environmental sustainability, and as investment managers and financiers increasingly demand that companies disclose business model exposure to climate change.

Attitudes could change very quickly following the impending 2018 minimum energy performance legislation in England and Wales (and similar minimum energy performance initiatives elsewhere in the world). It can be speculated that rapid devaluation in certain property assets could ensue if the legislation is robustly enforced. If revaluation is significant in size and speed this could impact values and behaviour in other international markets, in particular, those areas with similar property stock characteristics in terms of vintage, heating, ventilation and air-conditioning, and construction type. However, in order to begin to understand climate-related stranded assets in global real estate, it is necessary to qualify the research in this chapter. The wide urban context of the international perspective reveals the need for some cautionary words in relation to the context and content of the findings and conclusions in this chapter.

The empirical approach has necessarily been one of broad review rather than detailed analysis – consequently, we must be careful of over-generalisation and simplification. Each international property market contains a variety of comparable but highly specific contexts which are contingent and socially produced in each context. Moreover, there are a multitude of factors involved in real estate obsolescence; only one of these is the climate-related stranded assets. Energy policy is only one part of a complex web of actors, interests, and relations, particularly developers but also investors, occupiers, and members of the community who are either directly or indirectly involved in the production and reproduction of global real estate assets. A great deal more research will be needed to fully understand the specific and variegated nature of climate-related stranded assets in the international context.

Yet despite these caveats, we consider that the material within provides a perspective through which a picture of climate-related stranded assets in global real estate begins to emerge. In the energy sector the aim of legislation is to reduce fossil fuel consumption by leaving existing assets in the ground and halting the development of new ones. However, the impact of energy policy on global real estate assets is different. The aim of legislation is to improve the quality of property and reduce its negative impact upon the environment. For example, in the UK there is a chronic housing stock shortage with new property drip-fed into supply to maintain high values or simply prohibited through land supply and policy issues. The implication is that those existing properties reliant on fossil fuels will need to be improved in order to meet the needs of continued urbanisation – such properties can't just be written off as a loss. Illustrating the magnitude of this ret-rofit challenge, at the turn of the millennium, Kincaid (2002), referring to the UK, argued that the vast majority of 2050 property stock had already been built (some of it centuries ago in mature urban locations). Reinforcing this argument, Kelly (2008) indicates that 87% of current stock will still be standing in 2050. In other words, developed nations must go back to the future to solve the climate-related stranded asset problem through adaptation and retrofit. Conversely, developing nations have the opportunity to skip real estate asset fossil fuel dependency in order to define their own future.

Notes

1 The Royal Institution of Chartered Surveyors (RICS) publish and regularly update the RICS Valuation – Professional Standards (the 'Red Book'), and accompanying addi-tional supplementary guidance. These publications detail mandatory rules, best practice guidance, and related commentary for valuers undertaking asset valuations.
2 BREEAM (Building Research Establishment Environmental Assessment Method), first published by the Building Research Establishment (BRE) in 1990, is the world's longest-established method of assessing, rating, and certifying the sustainability of buildings.
3 The *Haute Qualité Environnementale* or HQE (high-quality environmental standard) is a standard for green building in France, based on the principles of sustainable development.
4 Minergie is a registered quality label for new and refurbished low-energy-consumption buildings. This label is mutually supported by the Swiss Confederation, the Swiss Can-tons, and the Principality of Liechtenstein along with Trade and Industry.
5 Energy Star (trademarked *ENERGY STAR*), originating in North America, is an interna-tional standard for energy-efficient consumer products that can be applied to residential and commercial properties.
6 Leadership in Energy and Environmental Design (LEED) is one of the most popular green building certification programs used worldwide. Developed by the non-profit U.S. Green Building Council (USGBC), it includes a set of rating systems for the design, con-struction, operation, and maintenance of green buildings, homes, and neighbourhoods.
7 Comprehensive Assessment System for Built Environment Efficiency (CASBEE) is a method for evaluating and rating the environmental performance of buildings and the built environment.
8 Green Globes is an online green building rating and certification tool that is used primar-ily in Canada and the United States. Green Globes was developed by ECD Energy and Environment Canada, an arms-length division of JLL. Green Globes is licensed for use by BOMA Canada (Existing Buildings) and the Green Building Initiative in the United States (New and Existing Buildings).
9 Green Star is a voluntary sustainability rating system for buildings in Australia. The Green Star rating system assesses the sustainability of projects at all stages of the built-environment life cycle. Ratings can be achieved at the planning phase for communi-ties, during the design, construction, or fit-out phase of buildings, or during the ongoing operational phase.

References

Andrew, A. and Pitt, M. 2006. Property Depreciation in Government. *Journal of Property Investment & Finance*, 24(3), 259–263.

Baum, A. 1991. *Property Investment Depreciation and Obsolescence*. Editore: Cengage Learning: EMEA.

Baum, A. and McElhinney, A. 1997. *The Causes and Effects of Depreciation in Office Buildings: A Ten-Year Update*. London: RICS – Royal Institution of Chartered Surveyors.

Bishop, P. and Williams, L. 2012. *The Temporary City*. London: Routledge.

BPIE. 2014. *Energy Performance Certificates Across the EU: A Mapping of National Approaches*. Brussels: BPIE.

Caldecott, B., Harnett, E., Cojoianu, T., Kok, I. and Pfieffer, A. 2016. *Stranded Assets: A Climate Risk Challenge*. Washington, DC: Inter-American Development Banks.

Caldecott, B., Dericks, G., Tulloch, D. J., Liao, X., Kruitwagen, L., Bouveret, G. and Mitchell, J. 2017. Stranded Assets and Thermal Coal in China: An Analysis of Environmental-Related Risk Exposure. *Working Paper*, Smith School of Enterprise and the Environment, February, Oxford.

Carbon Tracker Initiative. 2011. *Unburnable Carbon: Are the World's Financial Markets Carrying a Carbon Bubble*. London: Carbon Tracker Initiative.

Carbon Tracker Initiative. 2013. *Unburnable Carbon 2013: Wasted Capital Stranded Assets*. London: Carbon Tracker Initiative.

Carney, M. 2015. *Breaking the Tragedy of the Horizon – Climate Change and Financial Stability*. Speech given at Lloyd's of London by the Governor of Bank of England.

Christensen, C. 1997. *The Innovators Dilemma*. Cambridge, MA: Harvard Business Review Press.

Covington, H. 2016. Investment Consequences of the Paris Climate Agreement. *Journal of Sustainable Finance and Investment*, 7(1), 54–63.

Crosby, N. and Devaney, S. 2006. Depreciation and Its Impact on the Total Return of UK Commercial Real Estate 1994–2003. *University of Reading Working Papers in Real Estate and Planning*.

Crosby, N., Devaney, S. and Law, V. 2011. Benchmarking and Valuation Issues in Measuring Depreciation for European Office Markets. *Journal of European Real Estate Research*, 4(1), 7–28.

Department of Energy and Climate Change. 2014. *Private Rented Sector Minimum Energy Efficiency Standard Regulations (Non-Domestic) England and Wales*. London: DECC.

Diaz, H. and Hansz, J. 2001. Valuation Bias in Commercial Appraisal: A Transaction Price Feedback Experiment. *Real Estate Economics*, 29(4), 553–565.

Dixon, T. 2014. What Does "Retrofit" Mean, and How Can We Scale Up Action in the UK Sector? *Journal of Property Investment and Finance*, 32(4), 443–452.

Dixon, T. and Eames, M. 2013. Scaling Up: The Challenges of Urban Retrofit. *Building Research and Information*, 41, 499–503.

Dixon, T., Law, V. and Cooper, J. 1999. *The Dynamics and Measurement of Commercial Property Depreciation in the UK*. Project Report, CEM Reading.

Dunse, N. and Jones, C. A. 2002. Rental Depreciation, Obsolescence and Location: The Case of Industrial Properties. Paper presented at *Proceedings of the 2002 European Real Estate Conference*, Glasgow.

Eames, M., Dixon, T., Hunt, M. and Lannon, S. (eds.). 2017. *Retrofitting Cities for Tomorrow's World*. Oxford: Wiley-Blackwell.

Friedman, T. L. 2014. Obama on Obama on Climate. *The New York Times* [Accessed June 7, 2014].

Fuerst, F., McAllister, P., van de Wetering, J. and Wyatt, P. 2011. Measuring the Financial Performance of Green Buildings in the UK Commercial Property Market: Addressing the Data Issues. *Journal of Financial Management of Property and Construction*, 16, 163–185.

Global Construction Perspectives and Oxford Economics. 2015. *Global Construction 2030*, November.

Grabher, G. 1993. The Weakness of Strong Ties: The Lock-In of Regional Development in the Ruhr Area. In Grabher, G. (ed.), *The Embedded Firm: On the Socioeconomics of Industrial Networks*. London: Routledge, pp. 255–277.

Green Construction Board. 2014. *Mapping the Impacts of Minimum Energy Efficiency Standards for Commercial Real Estate*. Project GCB630, Valuation and Demand Working Group.

Gurría, A. 2013. *The Climate Challenge: Achieving Zero Emissions*. Lecture by OECD Secretary-General. Available at: http://www.oecd.org/env/the-climate-challenge-achieving-zero-emissions.htm.

Henneberry, J. 2017. *Urban Transience*. London: Wiley.

Henning, M., Stam, E. and Wenting, R. 2013. Path Dependence Research in Regional Economic Development: Cacophony or Knowledge Accumulation? *Regional Studies*, 47(8), 1348–1362.

Hobbs, D. 2013. *So You Thought the Accuracy of EPCs Was Improving?* Available at: www.building.co.uk/so-you-thought-the-accuracy-of-epcs-was-improving?/5063502. article [Accessed August 16, 2017]

Hosgood, G. 2017. Understanding the New Minimum Energy Efficiency Standards. *Allspp*.

IPCC. 2014. *Intergovernmental Panel on Climate Change*. Fifth Assessment Report (AR5).

IRENA. 2017. Stranded Assets and Renewables: How the Energy Transition Affects the Value of Energy Reserves, Buildings and Capital Stock. *Working Paper*.

Kelly, M. J. 2008. *Britain's Building Stock – a Carbon Challenge*. London: DCLG.

Kincaid, D. 2002. *Adapting Buildings for Changing Uses: Guidelines for Change of Use and Refurbishment*. London: Spon Press.

Krause, F., Bach, W. and Koomey, J. 1990. *Energy Policy in the Greenhouse*. London: Earthscan Books.

Lorenz, D. and Lützkendorf, T. 2011. Sustainability and Property Valuation: Systematisation of Existing Approaches and Recommendations for Future Action. *Journal of Property Investment and Finance*, 29(6), 644–676.

Lützkendorf, T. and Lorenz, D. 2005. Sustainable Property Investment: Valuing Sustainable Buildings Through Property Performance Assessment. *Building Research & Information*, 33(3), 212–234.

Mansfield, J. 2009. Sustainable Refurbishment: Policy Direction and Support in the UK. *Structural Survey*, 27(2), 148–161.

McGrath, P. 2014. *Ban Ki-Moon Urges Pension Funds to Dump Fossil Fuel Investments*. New York: ABC.

Michl, P., Lorenz, D., Lützkendorf, T. and Sayce, S. 2016. Reflecting Sustainability in Property Valuation – a Progress Report. *Journal of Property Investment & Finance*, 34(6), 552–577.

Muldavin, G. 2010. *Value Beyond Cost Savings: How to Underwrite Sustainable Properties*. San Rafael: Green Building Finance Consortium.

The Non-Domestic Minimum Building Energy Performance Standards Working Group. 2014. *Report to Government*.

Reed, R., Bilos, A., Wilkinson, S. and Schulte, K. W. 2009. International Comparison of Sustainable Rating Tools. *The Journal of Sustainable Real Estate*, 1(1), 1–22.

RICS. 2013. *Sustainability and Commercial Property Valuation*, 2nd ed. London: Guidance Note.

RICS. 2014. *RICS Valuation – Professional Standards (the 'Red Book')* January 2014 published in November 2013. London: RICS.

Savills. 2016. *Around the World in Dollars and Cents*, January.

Sayce, S., Sundberg, A. and Clements, W. 2010. *Is Sustainability Reflected in Commercial Property Prices: A Review of the Evidence Base*. London: RICS Research.

Schumpeter, J. 1950. *Capitalism, Socialism and Democracy*, 3rd ed. New York: Harper.

Silver, N. 2016. Blindness to Risk: Why Institutional Investors Ignore the Risk of Stranded Assets. *Journal of Sustainable Finance and Investment*, 7(1), 99–113.

Warren-Myers, G. 2012. The Value of Sustainability in Real Estate: A Review From a Valuation Perspective. *Journal of Property Investment and Finance*, 30(2), 115–144.

Weber, R. 2010. Selling City Futures: The Financialisation of Urban Redevelopment Policy. *Economic Geography*, 86(3), 251–274.

Wilkinson, S. J., Remøy, H. and Langston, C. 2014. *Sustainable Building Adaptations*. Oxford: Wiley-Blackwell.

World Economic Forum. 2016. *Environmental Sustainability Principles for the Real Estate Industry: Industry Agenda*. World Economic Forum Industry Agenda Council on the Future of Real Estate and Urbanisation, January.

8 Knowing the risks

How stranded assets relate to credit risk assessment and the debt markets

Michael Wilkins

1. Why stranded assets are of vital significance to the debt capital markets

1.1 Effects on credit quality and debt issuance in the energy markets

The valuation of publicly traded oil, gas, and extractive companies is based on the projected cash flow from projects and reserves – the majority of which are expected to be monetised (converted into revenue streams) in the short to medium term; any inability to monetise these reserves could have a significant impact on investors' confidence in extractive companies' debt issues. As a confluence of political and economic trends makes fossil fuels increasingly unprofitable, the threat of "unburnable reserves" – the term used to describe fossil fuel reserves that effectively might not be monetised – grows (Sussams et al. 2014, p. 2). This could pose a serious risk to companies' creditworthiness – the crucial measure of their ability to meet financial obligations, service debt, or make the necessary investments to manage or respond to risks.

Another threat to creditworthiness could be the need to recover costs, as fossil fuel companies look to preserve their cash flow in the face of further asset devaluation. Firms under cash-flow stress for protracted periods may take on additional debt to maintain or adapt their strategies – raising leverage, increasing the risk of default, and impairing prospects of recovery should default occur. As carbon emission-restricting regulation grows, the threat of cash-flow attrition due to unmitigated environmental risks becomes more significant.

But the impact of asset stranding extends far beyond the upstream sector of the energy industry: it also affects capital stock investments in wider infrastructure in the midstream and downstream sectors – such as refining and transport infrastructure – which contribute to a firm's overall valuation.

1.1.1 What types of credit are most at risk?

The risk of stranding is perceived to be of most concern to the coal, oil, and gas sectors. Greater awareness of, and steps to mitigate, climate change could expose some companies to significant operational risks. Tougher regulatory and tax changes designed to enforce reductions in carbon dioxide emissions and investments in energy efficiency could trigger a sharp deterioration in corporate credit quality, potentially reducing investor confidence in debt issues.

OIL AND GAS

The oil and gas sectors have faced significant credit quality constraints. Given unpredictability and tumbling commodity prices, many companies face losses, with even major global players forced to economise. A collapse in oil prices can lead to lower revenues across the supply chain: the emphasis on cutting capital expenditure and downsizing investment can lead to the decommissioning of oil rigs and a sharp decline in investment dedicated to exploration and production.

Operational costs rise as finding and exploiting new reserves becomes more difficult and companies' exposure to unconventional technology – which may be able to better withstand regulatory restrictions – grows. In hostile consumer and regulatory environments, weaker oil demand could see persistent price declines. With weaker operating cash flows and credit measures, along with less-certain returns on investment and less-robust reserve replacement, meaningful pressure could build on companies' credit ratings – and, hence, on the attractiveness of their debt issues (Leaton 2013, in Redmond and Wilkins, p. 4).

Yet, as investors look to understand the possible effects of future carbon constraints in the oil and gas sector, the financial models that depend on past performance and creditworthiness may be insufficient. To better integrate climate change risk and credit analysis, S&P Global Ratings (where the author of this chapter is affiliated) undertook a study with the Carbon Tracker Initiative to assess the risk implications for both major oil and gas producers – large, geographically diversified companies with both upstream and downstream assets – and smaller, independent, less-diversified firms. The results showed that while the effect on the major producers would be more muted, there is a likely deterioration in the financial risk profiles of the smaller companies to a degree that would potentially lead to negative outlook revisions and then downgrades in the medium term (Redmond and Wilkins 2013, p. 2).

COAL

The coal industry is suffering tighter margins and increasingly poor creditworthiness. As coal-fired power plants and their environmental impact continue to be subjected to closer public scrutiny, many assets face devaluation.

In the United States, depressed prices and long-term uncertainty have led to coal miners writing off assets from their balance sheets. Numerous companies – notably Patriot Coal, Walter Energy, Alpha Natural Resources, Arch Coal, and Peabody Energy – have filed for bankruptcy protection (Silverberg and Vitta 2016, p. 1). The shale gas boom has also threatened credit in the coal industry, having provided an alternative and cheaper energy source.

In Europe, there could be additional credit constraints on companies dependent on fossil fuel assets. Ageing coal-fired power plants have faced closure in the UK, where, under the capacity market – an auction mechanism introduced in 2015 to support security of electricity supply – fossil fuel-based power plants have struggled to compete for tenders in a regulatory environment designed to prioritise efficiency (Ferguson 2015, pp. 8–9).

Coal companies' creditworthiness could be constrained on an even greater scale in China. The world's greatest coal consumer – responsible for some 45% of global demand – has made increasing regulatory attempts to curb pollution by placing caps on emissions, closing mines, halting new coal-fired power plant construction, and connecting new renewable generation to its power grids. The country has effectively been able to "decouple" greenhouse gas emissions from economic growth. Should China's coal demand peak before 2030, up to 437 GW of its coal-fired power generation capacity could be at risk of stranding (Sussams et al. 2014, pp. 5–7).

1.2 Pressures and problems that might result from underestimating environment-related risk in the financial sector

Stranded assets could generate ripple effects on credit quality in the financial markets well beyond their immediate owners. The impact on the financial services sector of carbon risk exposure is likely to be significant over the long term; yet greater threats are likely to be found on the macroeconomic level, with the indirect costs expected to be far higher than the direct costs (Petkov, Birry and Plesser 2016, pp. 2–3). As regulatory environments grow more constrictive, measures of creditworthiness may also have to take the costs of litigation (see Chapter 9) and adverse reputational risk into greater account.

1.2.1 Effects on banks

As environmental regulation grows, banks will have to deal with the challenge of stranded assets on their balance sheets. If restrictions on carbon dioxide emissions mean that the reserves currently allowed for in the valuations of fossil-fuel companies are unlikely to be realised, those banks heavily exposed to carbon-intensive sectors could see a material deterioration in the value of collateral in their loan portfolios, with their capital ratios likely affected (Petkov, Birry and Wilkins 2016, p. 10). If a bank is anticipated to suffer losses on its investments and loan books, the assessment of its credit risk position may be revised down and its credit rating put under pressure.

Future political decisions may also determine the rate and ways in which financial service providers are affected and which investments will be more vulnerable. If measures to reduce carbon dioxide are introduced later rather than sooner, the effect on those companies exposed to stranded assets will be delayed and reduced in the short term. However, unchecked carbon dioxide emissions may lead to more extreme weather patterns, which could hurt revenues in other industries – such as agriculture – meaning that financial service providers with material exposure to such industries may in turn suffer (Petkov, Birry and Wilkins 2016, p. 8). Indeed, even if a bank reduces its exposure to carbon-intensive sectors, the pressure on its business position may not ease until it finds an adequate replacement for lost revenues.

1.2.2 Wider macroeconomic effects

Were regulatory or tax measures to be imposed suddenly, there could be a material deterioration in asset values. Effects could accumulate, triggering a deterioration in the overall macroeconomic and financial environment. As companies face significant losses, banks could witness an increase in bad loans, borrowers' ability to repay loans may deteriorate significantly, and weaker economic prospects could constrict revenues. Insurance companies could also find themselves dealing with higher – and more frequent – claims (Petkov, Birry and Plesser 2016, p. 6).

The impact would be heightened should a lack of transparency regarding each bank's exposure to the devalued assets cause a lack of confidence in the financial system. For instance, without adequate risk analysis, investors and issuers might underestimate environment-related risk premia for loans and bonds. Such a scenario would be similar to events during the subprime mortgage crisis, and the risks may be highest in countries with carbon-intensive economies – especially those that do not have a clear policy on transitioning toward low-carbon alternatives (Petkov, Birry and Plesser 2016, p. 6).

Some authorities have suggested carrying out stress tests for banks that focus on exposure to climate risks and impaired carbon assets, and it is possible that regulators could one day introduce higher capital requirements for exposure to polluting industries or companies that emit high levels of carbon dioxide. Although the idea is likely to meet some resistance, particularly given the number of regulatory reforms already under way, climate risk exposure could eventually become a feature of regulatory requirements for some banks (see Chapter 10).

1.2.3 Additional pressure from litigation and reputational risk

The need to mitigate climate change could also expose financial services companies with fossil-fuel assets on their balance sheets to additional reputational and operational risks; all types of financial service providers could potentially be considered complicit in failing to mitigate climate change-related risk.

Social advocacy against fossil fuels and a greater emphasis on sustainability as a result of increased awareness of climate change may also have a significant impact on banks, institutional investors, and other financial services companies. If not perceived to be doing enough to "divest" from fossil fuel assets – that is, to sell off their stakes in carbon-intensive companies, subsidiaries, real estate, or energy projects – they could become the target of activist groups.

With climate change litigation rapidly expanding its profile in certain jurisdictions – and within international law – companies could also potentially be held accountable for adverse drivers of climate change. Should financial service providers fail to adequately account for stranded assets and climate change when managing their customers' investment funds, for instance, they might become the target of legal actions. If a bank's operating position is exposed to significant legal risks, its credit risk assessment may weaken. Years of litigation and settlements could become a risk of non-compliance; in some countries, dealing with litigation has become familiar to financial service providers (Petkov, Birry and Plesser 2016, p. 5). Higher-than-expected costs of litigation could, in turn, affect insurers as they are faced with increasing claims. Indeed, the threat of litigation could force companies to offer greater disclosure of risks, such as their exposure to stranded assets, to their investors.

The complex nature of climate change means that a long list of potential risks to financial services companies can easily be created. While it is unclear how quickly these risks may emerge, it is likely that there will be additional, unanticipated effects.

2. Accounting for the risks of stranded assets in credit risk assessment

2.1 Addressing the risk in the financial sector

Debt issuers, capital market investors, and analysts are increasingly focusing on companies' carbon exposure – fundamentally rethinking their approach to align corporate credit analysis with climate change risk.

Financial institutions can represent companies' biggest investors – so they could have a considerable impact when demanding improved assessment of environmental and sustainability risks and accountability for the carbon assets on their balance sheets. In particular, they could prompt a shift in attitudes in those sectors that make the biggest contribution to carbon dioxide emissions, such as energy industries and some agricultural sectors (Petkov, Birry and Wilkins 2016, p. 4).

Wider reputational, regulatory, fiscal, and legal risks may also provide a greater incentive to better address climate change-related risks in the financial sector – given that they may present the greatest threats in the short-to-medium term (Petkov, Birry and Plesser 2016, p. 4).

2.2 A ratings agency's work on carbon asset exposure

S&P Global Ratings and other credit ratings agencies have been identifying new ways of better factoring carbon exposure into their analysis.

2.2.1 Existing corporate carbon risk assessments

As environmental, social, and governance (ESG) concerns become more important to ratings agencies' assessments, carbon price risk management strategies that companies have adopted are helpful in evaluating the net impact on corporate creditworthiness. There is a large amount of information on carbon risk available in the market from resources such as emissions data or corporate responsibility reports.

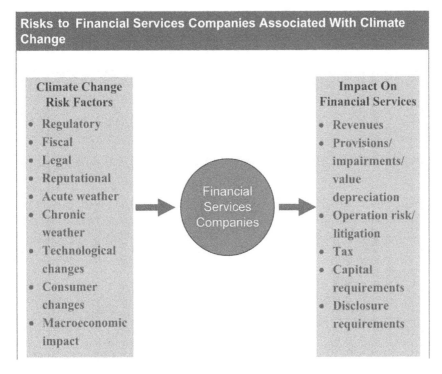

Figure 8.1 Risks to financial services companies associated with climate change

Source: Petkov, M., Birry, A., Plesser, S. and Wilkins, M. 2016. *Climate Change–Related Legal And Regulatory Threats Should Spur Financial Service Providers To Action.* S&P Global Ratings. 3.

Investors' focus has, to date, largely been on regulated liabilities that reflect direct risks from regulations such as emissions trading schemes and other carbon pricing mechanisms (see Figure 8.1). Focusing solely on a company's direct liability to emissions regulation may not fully reflect its true carbon exposure because it ignores the *indirect* carbon price risks that affect almost all companies to some degree.

For instance, while the energy, materials, and utilities sectors may have the highest direct carbon intensity, the property and financial services sectors also entail significant carbon price risk exposure towards the downstream end of the supply chain in terms of investments and leased assets.

Conventional financial impact analysis of carbon price risk focuses on a regulated liability – such as a coal-fired power station. It thus overlooks the unregulated liability (known as the "shadow liability") which is caused by potential carbon price obligations resulting from indirect exposures in the upstream and downstream process (see Figures 8.2 and 8.3) – that is, a coal-fired power station will rely both on coal mines and on power distribution networks (Bhatia et al. 2013, p. 11).

Exposure	Profitability Impacts	Asset Valuation Impacts	Cash Flow Impacts
Direct Exposure			
Carbon permit trading	Sale of excess permits may increase income	Excess carbon permit inventory can add value; however, the valuation may be subject to market price volatility	Operating cash flow can be affected depending on the holding position of the company and market price of carbon permits
	Purchase of carbon permits may increase the cost of production and reduce profit	Expected obligation to purchase carbon permits can be off balance sheet	
	Carbon permits trading and hedging affects profit in either direction		
Risk management	Actions to abate emissions may increase expenses	Investment to protect assets may have a positive effect on asset valuations	While companies spend additional operating cash outflow to manage risk, the cash inflow from such management may not incur at the same period, causing a short-term cash balance reduction
	The pass-through of compliance costs to downstream customers may mitigate impact on profitability		
Indirect Exposure			
Supply-chain cost	Supply-chain cost increases could raise the cost of production, leading to gross margin decline	The costs flowing through the supply chain could increase inventory costs, which may be higher than market price, and such over-valuation can lead to inventory impairment	Cash net flow may fall if higher supply chain cost cannot be passed through suppliers and customers
	Fixed and overhead costs (transport cost, for instance) could increase and reduce net profit	The "shadow liability" is off balance sheet	

Figure 8.2 Financial effects of carbon costs

Source: Wilkins, M. 2014. *Corporate Carbon Risks Go Well Beyond Regulated Liabilities*. S&P Global Ratings. 12.

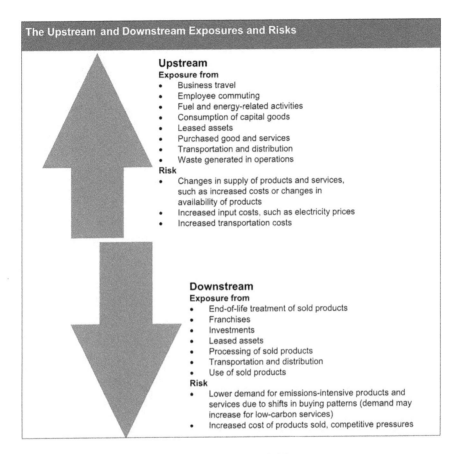

Figure 8.3 Upstream and downstream exposures and risks

Source: Wilkins, M. 2014. *Corporate Carbon Risks Go Well Beyond Regulated Liabilities.* S&P Global Ratings. 7.

This shadow liability is difficult to observe due to the limited availability – and quality – of emissions data. The full obligation is also hard to accurately quantify because applicable carbon prices are not clearly defined. There are no widely adopted guidelines to standardise liability valuation across sectors, nor are companies mandated to disclose their indirect exposure and resultant liabilities (Wilkins 2014, p. 11).

2.2.2 Factoring carbon risks into corporate creditworthiness

Credit rating agencies are able to provide a more complete analysis of carbon price risk exposure that offers greater insight into the effects on corporate credit quality across all of a company's operations.

For example, S&P Global Ratings considers both the direct and indirect financial effects of carbon exposure on corporate credit quality, accounting for the cost of a carbon liability being passed down an entire supply chain (see Figure 8.4). These range from regulatory controls on emissions to potential increases in input costs due to fluctuating market prices for raw materials supply, and from upstream emissions in supply chains to levels of downstream emissions as a result of changes in end demand for products and services (Wilkins 2014, p. 1).

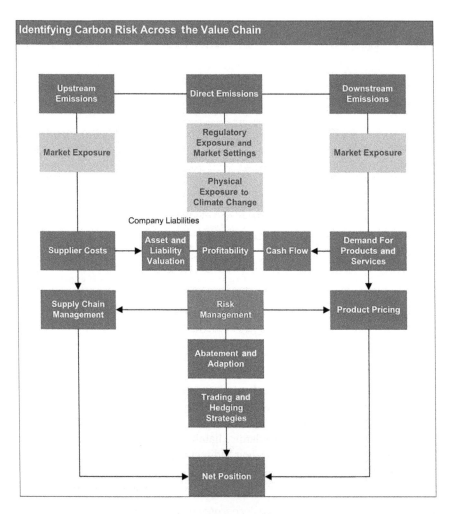

Figure 8.4 Identifying carbon risk across the value chain

Source: Wilkins, M. 2014. *Corporate Carbon Risks Go Well Beyond Regulated Liabilities*. S&P Global Ratings. 3.

As Figure 8.5 shows, S&P's methodology is based on four risk aspects:

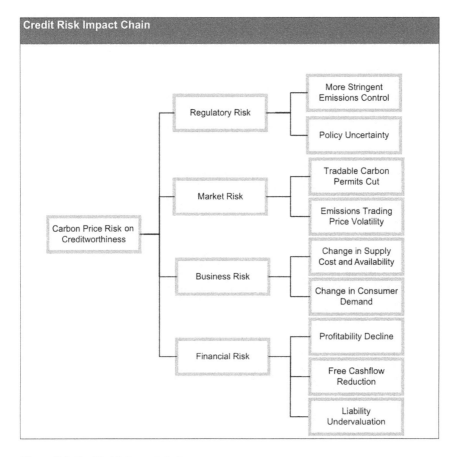

Figure 8.5 Credit risk impact chain

Source: Wilkins, M. 2014. *Corporate Carbon Risks Go Well Beyond Regulated Liabilities.* S&P Global Ratings. 13.

First is regulatory risk, which is becoming inevitable because of the trend for governments to impose more stringent emissions controls and the uncertainty of environmental policy over the long term.

Second is market risk, which accounts for emissions market pricing. Although different from conventional commodity markets, emissions markets create carbon price risk because the market price fluctuates and governments control the total supply of carbon permits; the availability of these permits can decrease in the future – particularly in free-floating emissions markets.

Third is business risk, which is analysed across a company's value chain. Increases in supply costs and changes in customer demand may raise levels of business risk, especially for companies that have weak supplier and customer bargaining power.

Fourth is financial risk, which takes into account profitability, cash flow, and asset and liability valuation. Financial risk results mainly from lower profitability and free cash flow and the limited visibility into "shadow liabilities".

2.2.3 Comparing national exposure to carbon risk

In addition to companies, national economies at large are also exposed to stranded asset risk. To this end, comparison of the biggest financial markets – those of the G20 countries – can offer a useful indicator of relative carbon exposure (Petkov, Birry and Wilkins 2016, p. 2). S&P Global Ratings has ranked the G20 financial systems by four factors: (1) the extent of a national economy's reliance on fossil fuels; (2) the level of commitment to decarbonisation in government policy; (3) the attractiveness of low-carbon investment options; and (4) the vulnerability of the country and its infrastructure to climate risk. Higher degrees of risk generated higher scores. To judge an economy's reliance on fossil fuels, S&P Global Ratings used Climate Transparency's assessments published in its report "Brown to Green" (Burck et al., September 2016, p. 7). To assess the attractiveness of low-carbon investments, S&P Global Ratings used Allianz Climate Solutions' investment attractiveness assessment, published in its Energy and Climate Monitor (Allianz, May 2016). To measure a country's exposure to climate risk, S&P Global Ratings used the University of Notre Dame's Global Adaptation Index (ND-GAIN), which captures both climate risk and the level of vulnerabilities. (University of Notre Dame 2015).

The financial systems of Saudi Arabia, Turkey, South Africa, and Russia emerged with the greatest exposure to the risk of macroeconomic shock caused by climate change. These economies are all highly carbon intensive, and their governments do not have strong climate policies. Although Australia, Japan, and Korea share these weaknesses, their overall risk is somewhat mitigated by more favourable green investment environments. The strength of China's climate policy has similarly reduced its exposure. Revealing favourable scores across almost all the elements used in S&P's ranking, the financial systems with the lowest risks are those of the UK, Germany, France, and the US (Petkov, Birry and Wilkins 2016, p. 4).

3. Future evolution of the response

3.1 Factoring the environment into investment decisions

With awareness of climate change growing and investors seeking to divest from carbon-intensive assets, the capital markets are playing a major part – both providing networks of institutions committed to decarbonisation of investment portfolios and identifying new areas of green finance (Hazell and Dreyer 2015, p. 2). A number of sustainable finance initiatives have emerged, including:

	Carbon Intensity	*Climate Policy*	*Green Investment Attractiveness*	*Climate Risk Exposure*	*Overall Score*
France	2.7	2.5	2.0	3.0	2.6
Germany	3.3	2.5	2.0	2.0	2.6
UK	3.3	2.5	2.0	2.0	2.6
US	3.8	2.5	3.0	2.0	2.9
Brazil	2.0	3.0	4.0	4.0	3.0
Italy	2.7	3.5	3.0	3.0	3.1
Mexico	2.8	2.5	4.0	4.0	3.1
Canada	3.2	4.0	3.0	2.0	3.2
India	3.2	2.5	3.0	5.0	3.2
Indonesia	2.7	3.5	4.0	4.0	3.4
China	4.2	2.5	3.0	4.0	3.4
Argentina	3.0	4.0	4.0	4.0	3.7
Korea	4.2	4.0	3.0	3.0	3.7
Japan	3.8	4.5	3.0	3.0	3.8
Australia	4.5	4.5	3.0	2.0	3.8
Russia	4.0	3.5	5.0	3.0	3.8
South Africa	4.3	3.5	4.0	4.0	3.9
Turkey	3.2	4.5	5.0	4.0	4.1
Saudi Arabia	4.0	4.5	5.0	4.0	4.3

Figure 8.6 G20 financial systems' exposure to climate change risk

Source: Petkov, M., Birry, A. and Wilkins, M. 2016. *Policymakers Play a Role in Preparing Financial Systems For Climate Change Risk*. S&P Global Ratings. 4.

- The Portfolio Decarbonization Coalition (PDC). This initiative is supported by the United Nations Environment Programme (UNEP). All PDC members commit to quantifying their carbon footprint and to meeting concrete decarbonisation targets – for example, by reallocating capital from carbon-intensive to carbon-efficient companies, projects, and technologies (Sullivan and Petrovic 2016).
- The Principles for Responsible Investment (PRI). Sponsored by the UN, the leading global investor network promotes the incorporation of ESG factors into investment decisions to better manage risk and generate sustainable, long-term returns (UN 2016).
- The Carbon Disclosure Project (CDP). This initiative serves as a global collection of self-reported environmental data, allowing its network of investors and purchasers – together representing more than US$100 trillion – to make better-informed investment decisions.
- The Montreal Carbon Pledge. By signing this pledge, supported by the PRI, investors commit to measure and publicly disclose the annual carbon footprint (the total greenhouse gas emissions caused, directly and indirectly) of their investment portfolios.
- The Banking Environment Initiative. Created to encourage the banking industry to act collectively, this seeks to channel capital toward environmentally and socially sustainable economic development.

- The UNEP Finance Initiative Principles for Sustainable Insurance. These principles serve as a global framework for the insurance industry to address ESG risks and opportunities.
- The Geneva Association's Climate Risk Statement. This recognises the substantial role insurance can play in global efforts to tackle climate-related risks and aims to coordinate efforts to research and mitigate the effects (Petkov, Birry and Plesser 2016, p. 7).
- Global Investor Coalition on Climate Change. This is a joint initiative of four regional groups that represent and provide networking for investors on climate change and the transition to a low-carbon economy: AIGCC (Asia), Ceres (North America), IGCC (Australia/NZ), and IIGCC (Europe).
- Global Sustainable Investment Alliance. This is a collaboration of membership associations for sustainable and responsible investment and financial services. UKSIF (UK), USSIF (USA), FIR (France), Middle East SIF, EUROSIF (Europe), LatinSIF (South America), RIA (Canada), RIAA (Australia/NZ), ASriA (Asia).
- Low Carbon Registry. A voluntary, partial, global public online database of low-carbon and clean-energy investments and investments to reduce GHG exposure. The project is an initiative of the Global Investor Coalition on Climate Change.
- Aiming for A. This is an investor coalition currently undertaking in-depth engagement with the 10 largest UK-listed extractive and utility companies, and is expanding to become pan-European. Established by CCLA and other leading asset owners, the coalition works closely with the PRI and the Carbon Asset Risk initiative.
- City of London Green Finance Initiative. Launched by the City of London Corporation in 2016, this aims to improve the financing options for sustainable infrastructure projects and support the sector's development.
- ERIN (European Responsible Investor Network). Launched by ShareAction, this network brings together organisations across Europe that are committed to a sustainable investment system. Network members work together to engage with large institutional investors and corporations to encourage more responsible practices.
- A4S CFO Leadership Network. Brings together a group of leading CFOs from large businesses seeking to embed the management of environmental and social issues into business processes and strategy. Develops practical guides for business aimed at addressing key sustainability challenges, including how companies disclose to and engage with their shareholders.
- ICGN (International Corporate Governance Network). Aims to influence policy by providing a reliable source of investor opinion on governance and stewardship. The network also connects peers at global events to enhance dialogue between companies and investors around long-term value creation and informs dialogue through knowledge and education to enhance the professionalism of governance and stewardship practices.
- Green Bond Principles. Voluntary process guidelines developed by the International Capital Market Association (ICMA) and updated as of June 2016.

They recommend transparency and disclosure and promote integrity in the development of the Green Bond market by clarifying the approach for issuance of a green bond.

3.2 Properly accounting for the environment in credit risk assessment

Credit analysis that can account for ESG risk and offer adequate transparency on environmental data will help capital market investors to make environmentally sound decisions.

As Figure 8.7 shows, the availability of such data has made significant progress over the last two decades. Reporting platforms like the CDP and GRI have attracted voluntary sustainability reporting from a large number of companies, while mandatory disclosure regimes have been of significant value to both investors and S&P Global Ratings in their credit risk research. More than 11,700 companies around the world now practise some kind of ESG reporting, while about 20 global stock exchanges publish guidance on ESG disclosure (Wilkins 2017, p. 5).

The scope of the available data, however, inherently constrains credit analysis of debt issuers. Climate-related disclosure has often been limited to corporate greenhouse gas emissions at the level of a parent company – with information out of date and reporting procedures slow. It is critical that analysts have access to more holistic and real-time ranges of data in order to better understand how a variety of risks might converge to strand once-valuable assets.

3.2.1 Climate risk disclosure regimes

Information on carbon exposure and climate-related and ESG risk is currently obtained through disclosure and reporting regimes. Both mandatory and voluntary, these are making progress beyond dedicated sustainability reporting by demonstrating how improvements in environmental risk management are core to company performance. Environmental disclosure provides a basis for dialogue between investors and disclosing companies – providing valuable insights into how companies operating or investing in carbon-intensive areas are dealing with

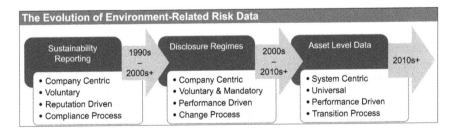

Figure 8.7 Evolution of environment-related risk data

Source: Caldecott, B. and Kruitwagen, L. 2016. *How Asset Level Data Can Improve the Assessment of Environmental Risk In Credit Analysis.* S&P Global Ratings. 4.

climate change. Disclosure has already made great progress in establishing the profile and understanding of environmental risks among debt issuers.

Three persistent problems remain, however: (1) a lack of coherent financial reporting frameworks; (2) that investors, creditors, and underwriters face difficulties in using existing disclosures in their financial decisions; and (3) that regulators meet obstacles when using existing financial disclosures to determine whether financial systems might be vulnerable to climate-related risks.

HOW TO IMPROVE DISCLOSURE

Improved disclosure will help investors to identify environmental risks and spur more allocation of capital to sustainable areas, and some in the markets are taking up the challenge. For instance, in December 2016, following the UN's COP22 Marrakesh climate change conference, the Task Force on Climate-related Financial Disclosures (TCFD) – set up by the Fiscal Stability Board – announced recommendations for improved quantitative and qualitative climate-related disclosures. Finalised in June 2017, these recommendations seek to develop voluntary, consistent climate-related financial risk disclosures for use by companies in providing information to investors, lenders, insurers, and other stakeholders (Bloomberg 2017).

Not only have the recommendations added a degree of momentum to the reporting trend, but they have also – and more importantly – started to provide a basic level of market standardisation. This will aid comparability, which in turn should improve the usability of disclosure for investors.

According to the TCFD, the recommendations aim to address three areas of the market where challenges currently exist:

- Issuers who generally have an obligation under existing law to disclose material information but lack a coherent framework to do so for climate-related information;
- Investors, lenders, and insurers who need climate-related information to make informed capital allocation and financial decisions; and
- Regulators who need to understand risks that may be building up in the financial system.

The recommendations describe information that both financial and non-financial companies should disclose to help investors, lenders, and insurance underwriters better understand how they oversee and manage climate-related risks and opportunities, as well as the material climate-related risks and opportunities to which they are exposed.

The TCFD's recommendations fall into four main categories: (1) governance; (2) strategy; (3) risk management; and (4) metric and targets, and will apply to all sectors equally. However, there is supplemental guidance available for the financial sector, including banks, insurance companies, asset owners, and asset managers, and for a number of non-financial sectors (energy, transportation, materials and buildings and agriculture, and food and forest products) (Wilkins and Williams 2016, pp. 2–3).

The recommendations have elevated the importance of climate-related risks and opportunities for corporations and investors alike. This is pertinent because climate-related risk is a non-diversifiable risk that affects nearly all industries. Climate-related and environmental risk is also often misconstrued as being only a longer-term risk and not relevant to financial plans and other decisions made today. All organisations with public debt or equity are covered by the recommendations, including asset managers, asset owners, public- and private-sector pension plans, endowments, and foundations.

The TCFD's recommendations could go further still. For example, specific metrics and key performance indicators are prescribed in only a few instances, such as the recommendation that asset owners should provide the weighted-average carbon intensity for each fund or investment strategy. The recommendations do not pre-set the parameters of the scenario analysis either. They purely suggest that users prepare a scenario showing the impact of a 2° Celsius increase in average global temperatures; however, a wide margin for variation in the assumptions that underpin any given two-degree scenario exists. This flexibility is important for businesses to acclimatise to these recommendations and should enable wider uptake of the voluntary recommendations, as well as provide opportunity for companies to tailor the disclosures to information most relevant to them. Nevertheless, it is likely to lead to inconsistencies and gaps in disclosure which will make it harder to use the information for peer analysis. Over time, this could be an area for further development.

Climate-related disclosures will likely evolve significantly assuming wide-scale adoption and implementation of the TCFD's recommendations over the next decade. Improved disclosure may spur more financial and investment activity, such as green bond issuance, related to environmental and climate issues, including modal shifts to clean energy.

3.2.2 Asset-level data

Building on disclosure regimes, Caldecott and Kruitwagen (2016) argue that "asset-level data" can be used to assess environmental risks to companies' creditworthiness in a standardised and more detailed manner. These high-resolution data allow the direct measurement of the exposure of company assets to environmental risk and offer key insights into its business and financial risk positions. This information is then extrapolated to the level of the issuing company itself in order to reveal competitive differences, strengths, and weaknesses in creditworthiness for investors (Caldecott and Kruitwagen 2016, p. 3).

PROVIDING GREATER TRANSPARENCY ON ENVIRONMENTAL RISKS

By offering bottom-up and forward-looking outlooks on the financial and business performance of a company, asset-level data provide investors with transparent information on carbon-exposed assets. Forming the key link between the real and financial economies, asset-level data allow investors to make informed, long-term decisions in the capital markets and be better placed to channel their capital to those debt issuers more likely to weather the transition to a sustainable economy.

With asset-level data on a company with considerable fixed-asset investments – such as a utility – potential investors can understand which assets might represent a drag on cash flow in the future. Insights into the size and lifespan of that utility's coal-fired power plant, for instance, mean investors are better-placed to understand implications for that utility's creditworthiness before committing capital.

OFFERING NEW OPPORTUNITIES

Asset-level data can be made available in a more efficient and timely manner than disclosure obtained from traditional reporting regimes. This enables investors to assess their long-term exposure to environment-related risks – a key consideration when assessing the threat of impaired fossil-fuel assets (Caldecott and Kruitwagen 2016, p. 5).

Asset-level data can be found in local or national registries and public records, existing proprietary and non-proprietary databases, and company reporting to financial markets and regulators. If brought together and effectively matched, they can be relied upon to offer universal coverage of credit risk analysis even in jurisdictions without effective disclosure regimes.

Existing data can also be augmented by new sources of asset-level data and the inclusion of more sophisticated forms of analysis, such as remote sensing and big data. Due to the continual rather than periodic availability of asset-level data, accurate changes in environmental risk exposure can be used to inform analysts at low costs and close to real time rather than on annual reporting cycles. Coverage of multiple industries could also enable analysts to consider industry-level cross-effects, such as competition for a limited carbon budget between oil and gas and coal extractive companies. Such an approach marks a considerable step forward in the evaluation of environmental risk – and hence, the risk of stranded assets – in the capital markets.

3.2.3   Credit ratings agencies' work in ESG risk assessment

The United Nations Principles for Responsible Investment (PRI) has offered an overview of how global, regional, and specialist credit ratings agencies are incorporating ESG factors into their credit analysis. The PRI's report, *Shifting Perceptions: ESG, Credit Risk and Ratings*, explores credit ratings agencies' reasons for increasingly integrating ESG issues into their analysis, identifies the focus of their research, assesses their internal capacity to perform such research, evaluates the transparency of their methodologies, and looks at the challenges that persist (Chavagnon et al. 2017, pp. 16–24).

S&P Global Ratings, for its part, is increasingly reviewing the following areas to look for evidence of a higher level of preparedness to deal with the impact of climate change:

- Investments in green energy;
- Green credentials, based on ESG statements and climate commitments;
- History of supporting sustainability votes at annual general meetings; and
- Availability of disclosures supporting low risk exposure.

S&P Global Ratings also considers new information and metrics as and when they emerge in order to assess how climate change and asset impairment may affect companies in the future.

Examining ESG risks will continue to form an essential element of S&P Global Ratings' credit analysis (Hazell and Dreyer 2015, pp. 2–3). As fundamental drivers of business and financial risk exposure, these have the potential to transform exposed sectors, whether by constraining demand for carbon-intensive products or by reducing the pollution intensity of industrial operations. Indeed, the competitive landscape may shift – potentially favouring entities that have lowered their exposure to stranded asset risk at the expense of those that have not.

ESG RISK ASSESSMENT AS PART OF A CREDIT RATINGS METHODOLOGY

Assessment of ESG risks forms part of S&P Global Ratings' analysis of a company's "management and governance" (M&G) criteria, which account for the view of its directors' oversight of environmental and social factors. S&P Global Ratings' M&G criteria include the likely impact – and the company's mitigation – of risks such as climate change, pollution, and resource depletion and its adherence to legal and regulatory requirements when dealing with environmental and social risks (Hazell and Dreyer 2015, p. 2). Since these factors act as modifiers in S&P Global Ratings' corporate rating methodology, an issuing company's commitment to ESG issues and concerns can directly influence its credit rating over time. S&P Global Ratings expects environmental and social factors to receive greater prominence in the future, with emerging risks potentially leading to further rating changes (Wilkins et al. 2015, p. 7).

Under such a framework, a credit assessment could therefore be affected by management's decisions regarding exposure to fossil-fuel assets. A company's operating efficiency is a significant driver of its credit quality, and one that is increasingly affected by environmental regulation; decreases in cash flow brought about by carbon pricing may disproportionally affect those highly exposed to fossil fuels, such as energy generating companies, which are characterised by high fixed costs and exposed to coal assets at risk of impairment. Increased spending on environmental retrofitting could lead to higher operating leverage – constraining credit quality. If this transition is costly enough, therefore, a company's credit measures could worsen to a point that its rating is lowered.

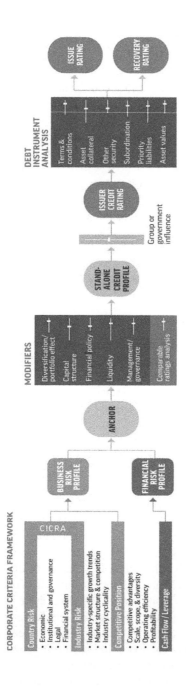

Figure 8.8 Corporate criteria framework

Source: S&P Global Ratings, *Corporate Ratings Methodology.* 2014. 2.

Firms that are better positioned to adapt to and benefit from these changing risks, however – such as those that have reduced their exposure to carbon – may enjoy a competitive advantage relative to their peers. Either voluntarily or in response to regulatory requirements or a legal challenge, a company may decide to try a new production method to lower or eliminate climate-changing or toxic emissions, for instance. If a bank develops expertise and becomes an industry leader in a climate change-related niche, it could reinforce its business profile, to some extent, by strengthening revenue stability and increasing market share. S&P Global Ratings' analysts would thus consider the potential advantages of an issuer being an "early adopter" of new technologies or positioning itself as a "clean" supplier of energy or products. The skills of corporate management in terms of how they used equity and debt to achieve such a transformation would be key elements in terms of making S&P Global Ratings' credit assessment.

CREDIT RISK INDICATORS

Certain indicators can help determine companies' relative exposure to, and level of preparedness for, the emerging direct, indirect, and macroeconomic risks of climate change, of which stranded assets are a key concern. Figure 8.9 illustrates the key risk indicators that S&P Global Ratings considers have the potential to most materially affect corporate credit profiles: these indicators cover those metrics for which there exist the best data available, either internally or externally.

These data may not be fully consistent and accurate, and such simple indicators may fail to capture the range and complexity of the ways in which climate risk may affect various institutions. It also remains difficult to quantify the potential impact. In general, disclosure about climate-related exposures remains insufficient for an accurate determination. Even where this is enough data, persistent uncertainty and the complex nature of the risks themselves create significant difficulties in estimating the potential impact. Uncertainties include how exactly global warming will affect the climate, future legal and regulatory changes, and technological developments that may be introduced to combat the consequences of climate change.

The data can, however, provide useful insights into the potential longer-term impact of climate change on the credit risk of specific companies. Disclosure and quantification methods are also expected to improve over time, along with advances in science and modelling, providing new analysis of risks such as stranded assets in the financial markets (Petkov, Birry and Wilkins 2016, p. 7).

4. Drivers of a greener economy

4.1 The role of regulators

Transnational organisations, sovereign governments, and local authorities have been playing a key role in the move towards a greener economy. By intensifying regulation on carbon emissions, and applying ever more stringent tax and legal measures to enforce reductions in pollutants, limit coal and oil exploration projects,

Metric	Proxy for Climate Change Risk	Risk Type	Level of Exposure
Fossil fuel companies assets as a proportion of total assets	Exposure to stranded assets	Transition risk	Company exposure
Average vulnerability to climate change of the countries in which the company operates	Exposure to acute and chronic weather	Physical exposure	Country exposure
Revenue arising from agriculture exposures as a proportion of total revenue	Exposure to chronic weather	Physical exposure	Company exposure
Capital requirements for insurance exposure to weather-related catastrophic events as a percentage of total available capital (for insurers only)	Insurance exposure to acute weather	Physical exposure	Company exposure
Property assets in coastal areas as a proportion of total assets	Value of properties exposed to increase in the risk of coastal flooding due to the rise in sea levels	Physical exposure	Company exposure
Average target for reducing carbon dioxide emissions in the countries where the company operates	Risk of adverse of green tax/regulations	Regulatory/ legal	Country exposure
Carbon footprint of the company, including that of lending/investments	Risk of adverse of green tax/regulations	Regulatory/ legal	Company exposure
Litigation culture of countries where the company operates	Litigation risk	Regulatory/ legal	Country exposure
Material noncompliance with major industry decarbonisation/ sustainability initiatives	Reputational damage	Reputational risk	Company exposure
History of bad "green" publicity	Reputational damage	Reputational risk	Company exposure
Size (by assets)	Reputational damage (we consider that the bigger the company, the more likely it is that it could be targeted by activists)	Reputational risk	Company exposure
Quality of disclosure	Transparency of climate change exposure	All risks	Company exposure

Figure 8.9 Indicators to help assess a company's risk exposure to climate change

Source: Petkov, M., Birry, A., Plesser, S. and Wilkins, M. 2016. *Climate Change–Related Legal and Regulatory Threats Should Spur Financial Service Providers to Action.* S&P Global Ratings. 7–8.

and improve energy efficiency, they have been contributing to the direction of investment away from fossil fuel sectors (Petkov, Birry and Plesser 2016, p. 4).

4.1.1 Moving away from fossil fuels

Use by governments of policy tools at their disposal may incentivise the financial markets to decarbonise, and incentivise financial service companies to manage down their exposure to stranded assets. Some regulators have been monetising the transition from hydrocarbons – ensuring that carbon must be priced by establishing predictable and transparent carbon trading mechanisms or by levying more direct carbon taxes (Ferguson 2015, p. 4).

Under carbon-trading frameworks, for example – the most widespread form of carbon regulation worldwide – companies must operate under caps on the volume of their emissions and source permits to cover their output. Companies can acquire these permits via free allocations from regulators, by purchasing them at auction, or by accessing secondary markets. In the case of a breach of these allowances, companies face fines. Since the world's most established carbon market, the European Emissions Trading Scheme (ETS), launched in 2005, ETS emissions trading regulation has spread worldwide. Since 2017, China's Green Dispatch system has also been in place to give regulatory preference to lower-carbon energy sources in the country's electricity markets (Wilkins 2014, p. 4).

4.1.2 Supporting new investment opportunities

Regulatory authorities may play a key role in influencing long-term investments in the clean, low-carbon energy technologies that will replace impaired hydrocarbon assets in national infrastructure, balance sheets, and investment portfolios. Such authorities may create more favourable environments for stakeholders to invest in green debt and for corporations issuing debt to finance green projects.

For instance, governments have been helping to provide impetus to the expansion of renewable and low-carbon energy infrastructure. The UN's 2015 COP21 meetings in Paris facilitated the establishment of the International Solar Alliance, spearheaded by the Indian and French governments and backed by 120 others, which aims to provide US$1 trillion of global investment in solar power – representing 1 terawatt (1,000 GW) of capacity – by 2030. China and India's public commitments to develop their renewable energy sectors in the Paris meetings – given the size of their economies and demand for power – could double the world's wind and solar capacity within 15 years (Wilkins et al. 2015, pp. 7–8).

4.1.3 Supporting credit quality and building investor confidence

Regulatory support – through tariff schemes and subsidy mechanisms – has been helpful to the capital market investors that finance clean energy commitments.

In the UK, for example, the Contracts for Difference (CfD) scheme has attracted billions of pounds of investment in wind farms by allowing low-carbon projects to better compete with more conventional, fossil fuel-based energy in the market. Usually in effect for around 15 years, CfDs shield electricity generators from exposure to volatile wholesale electricity prices. Signed by a power generator and the dedicated government subsidiary, the Low Carbon Contracts Company (LCCC), these contracts guarantee returns to investors in new low-carbon projects, such as offshore wind farms and solar plants. Under a CfD's terms, both parties agree a benchmark for the price of electricity per megawatt hour (MWh), which is known as a strike price. Should electricity prices fall below this fixed price, the LCCC guarantees the difference to the generator; when prices rise above the benchmark, the generator returns the difference to the LCCC (Wilkins 2016, p. 3).

Government subsidy schemes have also attracted investment to Germany's and Denmark's flourishing offshore wind sectors, enabling them to bring online thousands of megawatts (MW) of offshore wind capacity. As an example, development of the 288 MW Meerwind wind farm off the coast of Germany in 2015 benefitted from a lucrative "feed-in tariff" scheme. Offered by a government keen to support development of the country's renewable sector, a long-term contract (in this case lasting for 13 years) guarantees that the generator receives revenues significantly higher than the market rates for power. It allows the project to compete with fossil fuel-based generators. The tariff helped secure the project bond an S&P Global Ratings investment-grade rating of "BBB-". (Ferguson et al. 2016, p. 2).

4.2 Increasing demand for new resilient types of credit

As increasing environment-related regulatory policy facilitates a shift towards a greener economy, investors are looking for investments outside of the coal, oil, and gas sectors that can offer sustained returns on debt. As hydrocarbon assets become impaired, debt investors who may once have leaned towards issues from coal and oil-based power generators may seek to divest from fossil fuels and increasingly move toward more sustainable sectors that can better weather the energy transition. These could include areas of infrastructure more resilient to the adverse effects of climate change, low-carbon or renewable energy, energy storage, and those companies that can prove – through their corporate disclosure regimes – that they are well prepared to meet increasingly stringent regulatory demands.

Institutional asset managers are, in turn, likely to continue to develop new strategies to suit new investor preferences and allocate money to "climate-friendly" funds. With climate change and stranded asset risk potentially weighing most heavily on the creditworthiness of these firms, offerings from those that develop a recognised expertise in the low-carbon and renewable sectors may appeal to a growing segment of the investor community. "Greener" asset managers could thus differentiate themselves from their peers – expanding their asset bases faster than those that have been less interested or successful in attracting green assets (Wilkins and Williams 2016, pp. 7–8).

AN ECONOMIC CASE FOR RENEWABLE ALTERNATIVES AND DIVESTMENT
FROM FOSSIL-FUEL DEBT

Although the drivers for divestment from fossil fuels relate largely to the ethics of mitigating climate change – along with the increasing political and social pressure – with fossil fuel-based assets no longer offering as strong returns as before, the economic value of divestment is also becoming a driver for change.

Alternative sectors are witnessing rapid expansion, and investment is starting to make sense based on economics alone. This may further erode the long-term value of investments in fossil fuels – putting the creditworthiness of companies in traditional energy industries made less profitable under yet greater pressure.

New technologies – in particular onshore wind and solar photovoltaic – are increasingly less dependent on regulatory support. This helps to alleviate regulatory risk barriers to investment and improve payback periods for renewable projects. The costs of renewable energy technologies have also plunged, outstripping most predictions. Solar photovoltaic costs have fallen by over a quarter since 1976; given further potential cost reductions in materials and processing, this decline is not expected to end soon. Due in large part to improvements in turbine size and efficiency, wind power costs have also declined sharply – falling by almost a third between 2007 and 2016 alone (Wilkins and Williams 2016, p. 8). Such developments have been key to helping boost investor confidence in renewables' ability to compete in the markets with fossil fuels.

ADVANCEMENTS IN ENERGY STORAGE TECHNOLOGY

Energy storage technology is playing a significant role in unlocking the full potential of renewables – and hence is a key component in the transition from fossil-fuel debt. Through the use of advanced battery infrastructure, this allows the energy generated by renewable resources to be banked in order to balance the crucial intermittency in supply and offer potential investors more reliable streams of revenue.

Interest and investment in energy storage is growing worldwide, with a number of local and national governments having introduced policy initiatives designed to encourage investor appetite. Puerto Rico, for instance, was one of the first jurisdictions to require that renewable energy projects include storage as a means of short-term load balancing, while the states of California and Ontario have mandated the consideration or installation of energy storage as part of system-wide power grid solutions.

The costs of lithium ion battery storage have also declined significantly, by 65% from 2010 to 2015 alone; further falls in cost are possible (Wilkins and Williams 2016, p. 8). As a result, large energy companies like Total have made takeover bids for increasingly valuable storage providers and battery producers.

4.2.1 Growing demand for green bonds to move capital away from assets at risk of stranding

Investment of some US$90 trillion is needed in the next 15 years to achieve global sustainable development and climate objectives (G20 2017, p. 2).

With green bonds, the debt capital markets can help meet the demand for this capital. Unlike mainstream corporate debt issuance, green bonds are specifically designed to fund sustainable developments, with their proceeds ring-fenced and allotted to finance or refinance projects addressing environmental issues (Tanguy and Roquai 2016, pp. 2–3). The credit instrument will assist in remaining both environmentally sustainable and financially resilient as coal, oil, and gas assets become ever more at risk of stranding.

INVESTORS ARE WELL PLACED TO TAP THE POTENTIAL OF GREEN BONDS

For investors keen to allocate more capital to socially responsible projects, green bonds have proven an attractive method of diversifying and decarbonising port-folios in order to reduce exposure to regulatory and climate change risk. This is because investors view green issuers as better attuned to the risks of climate change, better able to adapt and tackle them, and hence more likely to weather an environment of impaired or stranded coal, oil, and gas assets (Tanguy and Roquai 2016, pp. 2–3).

Institutional and sovereign investment funds, for example, have been increas-ingly scrutinising the presence of carbon assets in their portfolios. Most notably, the Portfolio Decarbonization Coalition of institutional investors (including pension funds and insurance companies) has committed to decarbonising US$600 billion worth of global assets, transferring capital to low-carbon, more energy-efficient alternatives. As well as helping to reduce its members' exposure to stranded fossil-fuel intensive assets and the risks of climate change, green bonds should help provide the Coalition with the means to meet its target (Wilkins et al. 2016, p. 9).

MARKET GROWTH OF GREEN BONDS

Green bonds are only a relatively recent phenomenon, regarded as an "emerging" asset class, yet the size of the global green bond market has consistently grown – doubling between 2015 and 2016 alone (Wilkins 2017, p. 2). Investor demand has outweighed supply, with issuances often oversubscribed.

Investors in the large emerging economies of Brazil, India, and China have been providing a further boost to the market. In India, for example, investor demand for "green masala bonds" – rupee-denominated offshore bonds used for funding renewable projects – is growing, while green bonds issued in the country's power sector are likely to pave the way for further corporate issuance (Dangra and Suk-kuawala 2016, p. 1).

From the issuer's perspective, a green bond allows companies to source the capital they need to invest in low-carbon projects, thus offering alternatives to fuel-intensive investments and assets at risk of impairment. As Mark Carney sug-gested to the UN General Assembly on the Sustainable Development Goals in April 2016, they "have the potential to align the interests of issuers and investors" (Tanguy and Roquai 2016, p. 3).

MULTILATERAL ISSUANCE

Development banks, central banks, municipalities, and multilateral institutions, such as the International Finance Corporation and World Bank, have traditionally

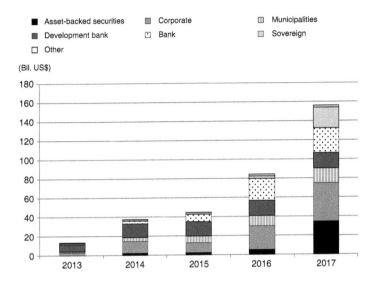

Figure 8.10 Total annual green bond issuance by issuer type

been the main issuers of green bonds (Wilkins et al. 2014, p. 8). Through its green bond issuances, for instance, the World Bank is able to raise funds for projects that seek to reduce emissions – including energy-efficiency improvements to rail networks – or help developing countries deal with the risks of climate change – such as by building roads and bridges more resilient to natural disasters.

CORPORATE ISSUANCE

Corporate green bonds enable those companies keen to develop environmentally friendly practices to diversify their pool of investors. With the proceeds, firms across a wide range of industries – from consumer goods brands and car makers to construction companies and paper producers – can invest in more sustainable supply chains and energy-efficiency measures (Wilkins et al. 2014, p. 7).

Progress has been driven by high-profile issuances from well-known companies such as Apple, Toyota, Électricité de France (EDF), and Unilever. Apple issued its first-ever green bond in February 2016, worth US$1.5 billion, the proceeds of which finance energy storage and renewable energy projects, along with energy-efficient buildings, across the company's supply chains. EDF's issuances have supported its investment in wind, solar, and hydropower facilities across Europe (Wilkins et al. 2016, p. 2).

The credit risk of a corporate green bond remains on the issuer's balance sheet: given risk generally correlates with yield, this means that, unlike with multilateral bank issuance, investors do not have to sacrifice yield to gain access to green assets or significantly increase their risk profile in order to invest in environmental efforts. Creditworthiness has typically been investment grade, with credit ratings at the A+ or A mark (Wilkins et al. 2014, pp. 3–4).

ISSUANCE IN THE INFRASTRUCTURE SECTOR

Green bonds are also being used by the infrastructure sector to reduce its carbon exposure: municipalities can use the instruments to meet public demand for projects that serve sustainable long-term environmental objectives with adequate private finance. In the United States alone, funds have been raised for a variety of uses, from energy-efficient buildings in Texas and waste management in Minnesota to water systems in California and transport infrastructure in New York (Forsgren and Buswick 2016, pp. 7–8).

One particular industry with a major presence in the debt capital markets, the US power sector, is witnessing more green issuances. While green bonds can enable power utilities to invest in carbon capture technology, some power suppliers, such as the Georgia Power Company, have issued green bonds to fund investments in solar-powered electric generation facilities and electric vehicle-charging stations. American utilities' green bonds have also been attracting greater interest from non-US investors (Wilkins et al. 2016, p. 4).

ISSUANCE IN REAL ESTATE

The real estate sector, too, has been taking advantage of green bonds. Buildings use about 40% of global energy, 25% of global water, and 40% of global resources and emit approximately one-third of greenhouse gas emissions (Tanguy and Roquai 2016, p. 6). But corporate tenants increasingly want high-performance, sustainable buildings that are energy efficient and carbon neutral. These not only help them reduce their energy bill but also offer an extra benefit to their corporate image. Real estate companies are using green bonds to source the funds they need to develop or acquire these new assets – enabling them, and by extension their tenants, to reduce exposure to fossil fuels.

FINANCIAL SERVICES POISED TO TAKE ADVANTAGE

In Europe, large financial institutions such as Barclays, Credit Agricole, HSBC, KfW, and Zurich have all committed to invest billions in the green bond market in recent years (Wilkins et al. 2016, pp. 2–3). Indeed, when low interest rates and restrained credit demand are widespread – dampening financial providers' earnings prospects – financing the low-carbon transition through green bonds could offer the sector a much-needed sustainable growth prospect. Underwriting these new types of asset classes will require insurers and banks to develop new modelling and structuring approaches, but acquiring the necessary experience and expertise could offer first movers a key competitive advantage, with banks best positioned to arrange or underwrite green finance and green investment funds potentially outpacing their peers (Petkov, Birry and Plesser 2016, p. 6).

THE NEED TO EVALUATE A GREEN BOND

While continued issuance and investor uptake of green bonds could spur the global divestment from carbon assets at risk of stranding, sustained development of this emerging asset class would be facilitated by better transparency on the bonds themselves. The Climate Bond Initiative (CBI) has determined that much global issuance is, in fact, not "green" according to its definition but rather only according to Chinese definitions, which include investments in projects such as clean coal – and hence do not fully address the stranded asset risk (Wilkins 2017, p. 9). These discrepancies carry reputational and litigation risks for issuers, deterring them from green labelling and, in effect, subduing supply below its potential. New, closer analysis of the environmental impact of green bonds should help to address this.

4.2.2 BEYOND GREEN BONDS: GROWTH OF SUSTAINABLE FINANCE

In addition to green bonds, broader forms of sustainable finance – including green loans, other types of debt such as green securitisations, and sustainable equity portfolios – could also contribute to decarbonising the global economy and mitigating the risk of asset impairment.

GREEN LOANS

Green loans draw on similar governance principles as labelled green bonds, with ring-fencing of proceeds and certification against Green Bond Principles. As an example, in February 2016 Spanish utility Iberdrola secured a six-year US\$533 million green labelled loan from banking group BBVA, then the largest green loan issued to date (Wilkins 2017, pp. 3–4).

GREEN SECURITISATIONS

A green securitisation allows smaller-scale assets to be pooled to reach large capital-market investors. For example, green loans or mortgages for green buildings could be pooled so that banks can take them off their balance sheets.

Despite constraints to widespread market use – such as an insufficient volume of identifiable green loans to bundle, the absence of standardised green loan contracts, and a lack of standards to ensure the environmental quality of these products – new asset-backed financings in the green space have started to emerge. In March 2017, French bank Crédit Agricole freed up capital by transferring the risk of a US\$3 billion portfolio of infrastructure loans to US hedge fund Mariner Investment Group. The loans remained on the bank's balance sheet; the risk transfer meant that Mariner shared some of the liability in the event of any default. Crucially, this risk transfer allowed the bank to hold less regulatory capital (the levels of capital banks must carry as reserves, which are higher following the global financial crisis). The use of the resulting US\$2 billion of freed-up capital is what made this synthetic deal so innovative: Crédit Agricole committed it in full to new green lending (Foley 2017).

THE ROLE OF ANALYTICS IN SUSTAINABLE FINANCE

Historically, there have been few market standards that allow investors to benchmark pricing of financial instruments based on their level of greenness, in the same way that credit ratings facilitate the pricing of credit risk through a risk premium or spread over the risk-free rate (Wilkins 2017, p. 5). This lack of widely recognised benchmarks available in the green-label finance market has inhibited market growth and transparency on pricing.

Similarly, a historical lack of analytical capacity to quantify the benefits of a green financing project can result in investment decisions based on incomplete information – leading to a higher cost of financing for developers in comparison to that which could be achieved if the environmental benefits of the project were properly priced in. Indeed, where environmental impact analysis does happen, the lack of a standard analytical approach can hinder decision making.

Comprehensive, more standardised green analytics, however, can lead to consistent, clear price premia in the market and help drive and meet demand for sustainable finance of all kinds. This is because the ability to compare investments based on the environmental benefits they deliver to a wider stakeholder base will enable investors to rank – and therefore price – green securities according to their environmental quality.

The debt capital markets will need to be prepared for the energy transition and the potential stranding of assets in the years and decades to come. All investors and stakeholders will benefit from transparency on carbon-related risk, awareness of market developments, and the means to assess credit and environmental quality.

References

Allianz. 2016. *Climate and Energy Monitor: Assessing the Needs and Attractiveness of Low-Carbon Investments in G20 Countries.*

Barclays. 2016. COP Till You Drop: Paris Keeps 2°C Door Ajar 2015. In Wilkins, M., Georges, P., Redmond, S., Gerrish, R., Ferguson, M. and Baggaley, P. (eds.), *The Paris Agreement: A New Dawn for Tackling Climate Change, or More of the Same?* London: S&P Global Ratings, December.

Bhatia, P., Cummis, C., Brown, A., Rich, D., Draucker, L. and Lahd, H. 2013. *Corporate Value Chain (Scope 3) Accounting and Reporting Standard.* Greenhouse Gas Protocol.

Bloomberg, M. 2017. *Recommendations of the Task Force on Climate-Related Financial Disclosures.* Fiscal Stability Board Task Force on Climate-Related Financial Disclosures.

Burck, J., Höhne, N., Hagemann, N., Gonzales-Zuñiga, S., Leipold, G., Marten, F., Schindler, H., Barnard, S. and Nakhooda, S. 2016. *Brown to Green: Assessing the G20 Transition to a Low-Carbon Economy.* Climate Transparency.

Caldecott, B. and Kruitwagen, L. 2016. *How Asset Level Data Can Improve the Assessment of Environmental Risk in Credit Analysis.* London: S&P Global Ratings.

Chavagnon, E., Beeching, A. and Nuzzo, C. 2017. *Shifting Perceptions: ESG, Credit Risk and Ratings.* Principles for Responsible Investment.

Dangra, A. and Sukkuawala. 2016. *As 'Masala' Bonds Find Favour With Investors, More 'Green Bonds' Could Sprout.* London: S&P Global Ratings.

Ferguson, M., Wilkins, M., Berberian, L. and D'Olier-Lees, T. 2016. *With Offshore Wind Projects Set to Take Flight, What Factors Will Move Ratings?* London: S&P Global Ratings.

Ferguson, T. 2015. *How National Commitments to Lower Carbon Emissions Will Alter Global Power Generation.* London: S&P Global Ratings.

Foley, S. 2017. A Synthetic Path to Green Lending That Might Just Work. *Financial Times*, March 6.

Forsgren, K. E. and Buswick, G. E. 2016. *What's Next for U.S. Municipal Green Bonds?* London: S&P Global Ratings.

G20. 2016, 2017. Green Finance Synthesis Report. In Wilkins, M. (ed.), *Beyond Green Bonds: Sustainable Finance Comes of Age.* London: S&P Global Ratings, September.

Hazell, L. and Dreyer, S. 2015. *ESG Risks in Corporate Credit Ratings – an Overview.* London: S&P Global Ratings.

Leaton, J. 2013. Carbon Tracker. In Redmond, S. and Wilkins, M. (eds.), *What a Carbon-Constrained Future Could Mean for Oil Companies' Creditworthiness.* London: S&P Global Ratings, March.

Petkov, M., Birry, A., Plesser, S. and Wilkins, M. 2016. *Climate Change–Related Legal and Regulatory Threats Should Spur Financial Service Providers to Action.* London: S&P Global Ratings.

Petkov, M., Birry, A. and Wilkins, M. 2016. *Policymakers Play a Role in Preparing Financial Systems for Climate Change Risk.* London: S&P Global Ratings.

Redmond, S. and Wilkins, M. 2013. *What a Carbon-Constrained Future Could Mean for Oil Companies' Creditworthiness.* London: S&P Global Ratings.

S&P Global Ratings. 2014. *Corporate Ratings Methodology.* London: S&P Global Ratings.

S&P Global Ratings. 2017. *Green Evaluation: Time to Turn Over a New Leaf?* London: S&P Global Ratings.

Silverberg, M. and Vitta, C. 2016. *Projecting Valuations and Recoveries for Creditors of U.S. Coal Producers – a Box as Black as Coal?* London: S&P Global Ratings.

Sullivan, R. and Petrovic, L. 2016. *Investment Portfolios in a Carbon Constrained World.* The Portfolio Decarbonization Coalition.

Sussams, L., Robinson, J. and Zadek, S. 2014. *The Great Coal Cap.* London: Carbon Tracker Initiative.

Tanguy, E. and Roquai, M. C. 2016. *New Shoots Emerging in Green Bond Market for Real Estate.* London: S&P Global Ratings.

United Nations. 2016. *Principles for Responsible Investment.* Washington, DC: United Nations.

University of Notre Dame. 2015. *Global Adaptation Index.* Notre Dame: University of Notre Dame.

Wilkins, M. 2014. *Corporate Carbon Risks Go Well Beyond Regulated Liabilities.* London: S&P Global Ratings.

Wilkins, M. 2016. *Assessing the Credit Risks of U.K. Power Projects Backed by Contracts for Difference.* London: S&P Global Ratings.

Wilkins, M. 2017. *Beyond Green Bonds: Sustainable Finance Comes of Age.* London: S&P Global Ratings.

Wilkins, M., Elliot, T. and Zhuang, M. 2014. *The Greening of the Corporate Bond Market.* London: S&P Global Ratings.

Wilkins, M., Petkov, M. and D'Olier-Lees, T. 2015. *How Environmental and Climate Risks Factor Into Global Corporate Ratings.* London: S&P Global Ratings.

Wilkins, M., Petkov, M., Williams, J. and Martin, N. D. 2017. *Green Evaluation Analytical Approach*. London: S&P Global Ratings.

Wilkins, M., Shipman, T. A. and Wade, T. 2016. *The Corporate Green Bond Market Fizzes as the Global Economy Decarbonizes*. London: S&P Global Ratings.

Wilkins, M. and Williams, J. 2016. *New Recommendations for Climate Risk Disclosure Follow a Positive Outcome at Marrakech*. London: S&P Global Ratings.

9　An introduction to directors' duties in relation to stranded asset risks

Sarah Barker

1. Introduction

This chapter explores the emerging points of liability exposure for the directors of listed, for-profit corporations who fail to adequately assess and/or disclose the impacts of climate change-related issues on corporate risk and strategy. The analysis focuses, in particular, on directors' statutory and fiduciary duties to govern with regard to 'stranded asset risk' exposures: that is, the potential for policy changes, technological advancements, developments in market dynamics and reputational factors to prematurely devalue corporate assets (or increase liability exposures, provisions or contingencies). It seeks to answer the question: what forms of governance action (or inaction) in relation to stranded asset risk exposures are likely to breach the duties of company directors? Whilst the chapter largely employs a 'first principles' approach to the analysis of corporate governance regimes around the world, the laws of the United States (Delaware), UK and Australia are used to illustrate key points. Similarly, whilst the principles discussed may apply to 'stranded asset' risk across industry sectors, the analysis in this chapter focuses on energy and resources as an area in which the issue is likely to have particular significance.

This chapter is structured as follows. Part 2 provides a brief overview of the evolution of climate risk from an 'ethical externality' to material financial issue. Part 3 examines directors' liability exposure under their core statutory and fiduciary duties. It first offers general observations about fiduciary regimes around the world, followed by specific discussion of the legal frameworks prevailing in the United States (primarily focusing on the law applicable to Delaware corporations),[1] the United Kingdom and Australia. It then considers circumstances in which a failure to govern for stranded asset risks may raise particular duties liability exposure issues. Part 4 briefly raises another area of liability exposure closely related to fiduciary duties: that for a failure to adequately disclose climate-related risks under securities fraud (misleading disclosure) laws. Part 5 concludes.

This chapter is not intended to provide a definitive analysis of corporate governance and commercial laws in their application to stranded asset risks. Rather, it contains a high-level, introductory exploration of the application of directors' duties laws and proposes general principles that may act as the starting point for further detailed application to particular factual scenarios in individual jurisdictions.

2. The evolution of climate change from an 'ethical externality' to material financial issue

2.1 Climate change as a material financial issue

There is little doubt that climate change has evolved rapidly in recent years to become an issue that presents a foreseeable – and often material – risk of harm to corporations in many industries, sectors and markets, within mainstream planning and investment horizons (Hutley and Hartford-Davis 2016, p. 2). Indeed, with a solidification of the relevant science, the attention of capital markets has increasingly turned to the material financial issues associated with both the physical impacts of climate change and the market risks associated with the economic transition to a low-carbon economy. These issues are further particularised in an extract from the Final Recommendations of the G20 Financial Stability Board's Taskforce on Climate-related Financial Disclosures (TCFD) (see Figure 9.1). They include:

(a) Physical impact risks: both acute (extreme/catastrophic weather events) and chronic (gradual onset, such as rising sea levels, ocean acidification, sustained average higher temperatures), which can cause extreme precipitation in some areas, more intense droughts in others, fresh water scarcity, an increase in bush/wildfires, changes in crop yields, coral bleaching and other marine ecosystem loss and biodiversity loss. In turn, these impacts can give rise to commercial issues including (for example) population dislocation, reduced workforce productivity, business interruption (from plant and infrastructure outages, upstream changes in the availability and price of key inputs and downstream distribution interruption), insurance restrictions, energy price volatility, increases in adaptation capex and increased risk of customer default; and

(b) Transition risks: these include:

   • policy responses that attempt either to constrain the actions that contribute to adverse climate change (such as emissions restrictions or carbon pricing mechanisms) or to promote adaptation to its impacts that may result in rapid re-pricing of assets. This includes the strong market signal conveyed by 196 nation signatories to the Paris Agreement (settled at the 21st Conference of the Parties to the United Nations Framework Convention on Climate Change [COP21] on 12 December 2015), which entered into force on 5 November 2016. The Paris Agreement commits its parties to collective goals (amongst other measures):

      • limiting the 'increase in the global average temperature to well below 2°C above pre-industrial levels' and to pursue 'efforts to limit the

Type	Climate-Related Risks[a]	Potential Financial Impacts	Type	Climate-Related Opportunities[a]	Potential Financial Impacts
Transition Risks — Policy and Legal	– Increased pricing of GHG emissions – Enhanced emissions-reporting obligations – Mandates on and regulation of existing products and services – Exposure to litigation	– Increased operating costs (e.g., higher compliance costs, increased insurance premiums) – Write-offs, asset impairment, and early retirement of existing assets due to policy changes – Increased costs and/or reduced demand for products and services resulting from fines and judgments	**Resource Efficiency**	– Use of more efficient modes of transport – Use of more efficient production and distribution processes – Use of recycling – Move to more efficient buildings – Reduced water usage and consumption	– Reduced operating costs (e.g., through efficiency gains and cost reductions) – Increased production capacity, resulting in increased revenues – Increased value of fixed assets (e.g., highly rated energy-efficient buildings) – Benefits to workforce management and planning (e.g., improved health and safety, employee satisfaction) resulting in lower costs
Technology	– Substitution of existing products and services with lower emissions options – Unsuccessful investment in new technologies – Costs to transition to lower emissions technology	– Write-offs and early retirement of existing assets – Reduced demand for products and services – Research and development (R&D) expenditures in new and alternative technologies – Capital investments in technology development – Costs to adopt/deploy new practices and processes	**Energy Source**	– Use of lower-emission sources of energy – Use of supportive policy incentives – Use of new technologies – Participation in carbon market – Shift toward decentralized energy generation	– Reduced operational costs (e.g., through use of lowest cost abatement) – Reduced exposure to future fossil fuel price increases – Reduced exposure to GHG emissions and therefore less sensitivity to changes in cost of carbon – Returns on investment in low-emission technology – Increased capital availability (e.g., as more investors favor lower-emissions producers) – Reputational benefits resulting in increased demand for goods/services
Market	– Changing customer behavior – Uncertainty in market signals – Increased cost of raw materials	– Reduced demand for goods and services due to shift in consumer preferences – Increased production costs due to changing input prices (e.g., energy, water) and output requirements (e.g., waste treatment) – Abrupt and unexpected shifts in energy costs – Change in revenue mix and sources, resulting in decreased revenues – Re-pricing of assets (e.g., fossil fuel reserves, land valuations, securities valuations)	**Products and Services**	– Development and/or expansion of low emission goods and services – Development of climate adaptation and insurance risk solutions – Development of new products or services through R&D and innovation – Ability to diversify business activities – Shift in consumer preferences	– Increased revenue through demand for lower emissions products and services – Increased revenue through new solutions to adaptation needs (e.g., insurance risk transfer products and services) – Better competitive position to reflect shifting consumer preferences, resulting in increased revenues
Reputation	– Shifts in consumer preferences – Stigmatization of sector – Increased stakeholder concern or negative stakeholder feedback	– Reduced revenue from decreased demand for goods/services – Reduced revenue from decreased production capacity (e.g., delayed planning approvals, supply chain interruptions) – Reduced revenue from negative impacts on workforce management and planning (e.g., employee attraction and retention) – Reduction in capital availability	**Markets**	– Access to new markets – Use of public-sector incentives – Access to new assets and locations needing insurance coverage	– Increased revenues through access to new and emerging markets (e.g., partnerships with governments, development banks) – Increased diversification of financial assets (e.g., green bonds and infrastructure)
Physical Risks — Acute	– Increased severity of extreme weather events such as cyclones and floods	– Reduced revenue from decreased production capacity (e.g., transport difficulties, supply chain interruptions) – Reduced revenue and higher costs from negative impacts on workforce (e.g., health, safety, absenteeism) – Write-offs and early retirement of existing assets (e.g., damage to property and assets in "high-risk" locations) – Increased operating costs (e.g., inadequate water supply for hydroelectric plants or to cool nuclear and fossil fuel plants) – Increased capital costs (e.g., damage to facilities) – Reduced revenues from lower sales/output – Increased insurance premiums and potential for reduced availability of insurance on assets in "high-risk" locations	**Resilience**	– Participation in renewable energy programs and adoption of energy-efficiency measures – Resource substitutes/diversification	– Increased market valuation through resilience planning (e.g., infrastructure, land, buildings) – Increased reliability of supply chain and ability to operate under various conditions – Increased revenue through new products and services related to ensuring resiliency
Chronic	– Changes in precipitation patterns and extreme variability in weather patterns – Rising mean temperatures – Rising sea levels				

Figure 9.1 TCFD examples of climate-related risks and potential financial impacts

Source: TCFD (2017) *Final Recommendations of the Taskforce on Climate-related Financial Disclosures*

temperature increase to 1.5°C above pre-industrial levels' (Article 2(1)(a)). This goal is to be achieved by each signatory implementing emissions reduction (and other policy) commitments pledged under Nationally Determined Contributions (or NDCs), which are subject to a 'five- year review and ratchet' mechanism (Article 4(3) and (9)); and

- 'net zero' global emissions (that is, where the anthropogenic emission of greenhouse gases is equally offset by their removal by sinks) in the second half of the century (Article 4(1)).

The achievement of these policy goals will require a significant reduction to 'business-as-usual' emissions (which the IPCC estimates would result in warming of up to 4.8°C by 2100) (IPCC 2014, p. 10). The reductions will need to exceed even the post-2020 emissions-mitigation NDC pledges made to date (which, if implemented, have been estimated to hold global warming to approximately 2.7°C; IEA 2015, p. 4). Those reductions will, in turn, necessitate a significant transformation in the global economy to a low-carbon norm;

- technology risks, that is, 'creative destruction' of 'old' technologies, developments in renewable energy generation, battery storage (for both the stationary energy and transport sectors), energy efficiency and carbon capture and storage;
- market risks, that is impacts on supply and demand dynamics; and
- reputation risks associated with evolving stakeholder perceptions and expectations; and, consequently

(c) Legal/litigation risks: legal claims arising from either (or both) the physical impacts or economic transition risks associated with climate change. Such claims may arise in a number of broad categories, including a failure to mitigate emissions, a failure to adapt to the foreseeable impacts associated with climate change, a failure to disclose the risks associated with climate change where an obligation exists to do so (including, for example, under corporate reporting and securities laws) and a failure to comply with climate-specific regulatory obligations (such as emissions intensity standards) (2Dii and MinterEllison 2017; BoEPRA 2015; TCFD 2017; UNEP and Sabin Center 2017).

This chapter refers, and defers, to the warnings of leading market stakeholders that both these physical and economic transition factors may present financial risks (and opportunities) that are not only foreseeable but often material – if not unparalleled – and are increasingly relevant over mainstream investment horizons.[2] Although these risks are pervasive and ubiquitous (SASB 2016, p. 2) across the economy, their impacts are differentiated across sectors. The analysis in this chapter specifically focuses on one aspect of the financial risks associated with climate change – 'stranded asset' risks – and considers the potential liability exposure of directors of corporations exposed to those risks in the energy and resources sector.

2.2 'Stranded asset' risks and susceptible sectors

'Stranded asset' exposures refer to the risk(s) that an asset cannot viably be exploited at a value or for the life for which it was expected to be utilised, which negatively impacts its current value. In a climate change context, stranded asset risks most commonly arise as a function of transition risks – *viz* changes in policy/ regulation (including emissions pricing or controls), technological developments (particularly in renewable energy sources and battery storage technologies, which drives substitution of legacy plant and infrastructure with lower-emissions assets) and market and reputational risks as the economy shifts to a low-carbon norm. Not only can such market developments provoke rapid re-pricing of exposed assets, but they can also increasingly impact the cost and availability of capital funding, as financiers begin to price this risk into their lending criteria (SASB 2016, pp. 16–17; TCFD 2017).

Climate-related stranded asset risks are particularly acute in industries whose operations and/or outputs have high energy or emissions intensities, are dependent on water availability, have relatively long planning and break-even horizons and/or require the deployment of capital-intensive, long-lived physical plant and infrastructure (TCFD 2017a, pp. 52–55). For the purposes of illustration the analysis in this chapter is confined to a sector that, in general, exhibits all these susceptibilities and where stranded asset risks have been subject of significant recent investor concern: that of energy and resources (including, in particular, coal, oil, gas and conventional electrical utilities) (SASB 2016, p. 10; TCFD 2017a, p. 50; APRA 2017, pp. 4–5). The potential risks in this sector are brought into sharp focus by studies that conclude a significant proportion (in some cases 60–80 percent) of the coal, oil, and gas reserves of listed firms will need to remain unexploited in order to avoid a rise in global average temperature of more than 2°C above pre-industrial levels (ASRIA and Chubb 2015, pp. 20–29; Boston Common Asset Management 2015; Carbon Tracker 2013; SASB 2016, p. 10; Stathers and Zavos 2015, p. 4). Similarly, a recent report by the International Energy Agency estimated that a step-change in energy markets towards renewable energy consistent with the Paris Agreement goals would strand US$1 trillion of oil assets, US$300 billion of coal-fired power plants and US$300m of natural gas assets by 2050 (IEA 2017).

Despite the focus of this chapter on the energy and resources sector, it is acknowledged that stranded asset risks cut across many sectors of the economy – notably including transport and automotive, agriculture and forestry, real estate and infrastructure sectors (Guyatt 2015; SASB 2016, pp. 16–17; TCFD 2017a) and financial market participants who may have debt or equity exposures to companies in those sectors (banks, insurance companies, asset owners and asset managers) (*ibid.*; French Treasury 2017, p. 9).

Investor concerns about the materiality of stranded asset risks for corporations in these highly exposed industries has been reinforced in the sharp increase in shareholder resolutions seeking disclosure on this point. Indeed, such resolutions are increasingly being filed not only by 'activist shareholders' seeking to advance their external agendas but by mainstream, institutional investors with a genuine demand for decision-useful information on what they consider to be a material financial risk issue.[3]

This chapter does not purport to engage in an analysis of the extent to which climate change impacts the risk and strategy of any given corporation. However, it proceeds on the basis that stranded assets are demonstrably a material financial issue for corporations in the energy and resources sector, requiring particular consideration in their financial planning, strategy, asset valuation, risk assessment and disclosure.

3. Directors' duties

3.1 Directors' duties: general observations and first principles

3.1.1 Corporations and the role of the board

A significant proportion of commerce within and between jurisdictions is conducted via 'corporations'. Corporations are 'legal constructs' incorporated to 'manage the generation of wealth' (Anam 2012, p. 9). They are 'owned' by shareholders, who have a residual claim over assets and profits (Easterbrook and Fishel 1991; Hargovan and Harris 2013, p. 436; Magnier 2017) but are managed by or under the direction of a board of directors.[4] In practice, boards delegate operational matters to executive management. However, they remain responsible for the oversight of corporate performance, for the monitoring and supervision of its compliance (or 'conformance'), the approval of significant transactions and external reporting (Amado and Adams 2012, p. 11; Bainbridge 2012, p. 43).

The directorial role to supervise corporate performance inherently requires the oversight of corporate risk management and strategy. In the corporate context, 'risk' is simply 'the effect of uncertainty on objectives' (Standards Australia 2009, p. 1). It is clear that risk management and strategy are interrelated and that board governance and oversight of both is critical to the creation of corporate value (ASXCGC 2010, p. 33).

3.1.2 Directors as 'fiduciaries' of the corporation

As early as the 18th century, common law courts have recognised that directors are 'fiduciaries' of their corporation (Jacobs 2015, p. 145).[5] A 'fiduciary' relationship exists where one party (the fiduciary) exercises power and/or holds property on behalf of and for the benefit of another (the principal).[6] The term 'fiduciary' derives from the Latin *fiducia*, meaning trust, confidence and reliance (Edelman 2014, p. 23; Morwood 2001).

The particular wording with which modern directors' duties are expressed in statute, regulatory instruments and case law and the extent to which such duties are characterised as being 'fiduciary' *per se* differs by jurisdiction (Bruner 2013; Collins 2014; Teele-Langford 2013; Waitzer and Sarro 2014).[7] However, corporate governance laws commonly reflect fiduciary *precepts* – that a fiduciary must act to prioritise the interests of their principal and so set out obligations relating to:

(a) Trust and loyalty (including, for example, duties relating to acting in the best interests of the corporation, avoidance of conflicts, honesty and good faith and proper purposes); and

(b) Competence or attentiveness (including duties to act with prudence and/or due care, skill and diligence) (Gerner-Beuerle Paech and Schuster 2013 [EU law]; Hill and McDonnell 2012 [US law]; Kay 2012, p. 66 [UK law]; Magnier 2017; Richardson 2012).[8]

Historically, debates around the extent to which directors must, and indeed *whether* they may, have regard to issues associated with climate change was centred on the first sub-set of duties – those relating to trust and loyalty. This debate largely took place within the context of broader discussions of 'corporate social responsibility' (or 'CSR') (Barker et al. 2016; Magnier 2017). The CSR debate focuses on the *scope* of directors' duties and *to whom* they are owed; specifically, whether the 'best interests of the corporation' for which a director must govern are limited to profit and shareholder wealth maximisation (to which social or environmental concerns are peripheral; 'shareholder primacy' theory) (Freidman 1962; Magnier 2017; Marshall and Ramsay 2012), or, at the other end of the spectrum, whether directors' duties are owed not only to shareholders but to other stakeholders whose interests are impacted by corporate activities (such as employees, the community and the natural environment; 'stakeholder theory') (Freeman 1984, pp. 31–42; Freeman 2010, p. 235; Jensen 2001, p. 9; Magnier 2017; Marshall and Ramsay 2012). Historically, the CSR literature largely framed climate change (and, by implication, risks associated with it) as an 'ethical' or 'environmental' issue, whose impact on financial risk/return was either negative or immaterial. In contrast, this chapter takes a somewhat antithetical perspective on the intersection between risks associated with climate change and wealth-based objectives. In particular, (as set out in Part 2), it accepts that climate change risk has evolved to become an issue of squarely *financial* import for many corporations: not only consistent with but commonly *prerequisite to* the maximisation of wealth. Accordingly, as with any other material financial issue or foreseeable financial risk, it will be incumbent on directors of affected corporations to have regard to associated risks in pursuit of corporate best interests under any theory of CSR. This applies *a fortiori* to the stranded asset risks faced by corporations with long-lived assets in carbon-intensive sectors.

On that basis, the relevant issues for interrogation in this chapter become:

(a) Trust and loyalty: whether a conscious disregard of or wilful blindness to stranded asset risks may contravene directors' obligations to act in good faith, for a proper purpose and/or in the best (financial) interests of their corporation; and

(b) Competence: the degree of due care and diligence is required in considering this issue in order to satisfy directors' obligations of competence.

The content of directors' duties of trust and loyalty is considered in Part 3.2 and its application to the governance of stranded asset risks in Part 3.3. The content and application of the duties of competence are considered in Parts 3.4 and 3.5.

In considering the content of these duties, it is important to note that whether a particular claim may be successfully pursued in respect of the breach will also turn on procedural and evidentiary requirements, which vary depending on the relevant jurisdiction, plaintiff, cause of action and remedies sought. These include, for example, including standing prerequisites (such as the permission of the court required to bring a shareholders' derivative action under section 261 of the Companies Act 2006 (UK) or the threshold of 'demand futility' under Delaware law), other barriers to claim such as laches (statutes of limitation) and evidentiary requisites in relation to causation and loss (see for example discussion in Gelter 2017).[9] These issues are beyond the scope of this chapter, which is limited in its consideration of the content of the duties themselves with regard to stranded asset risks.

3.2 *Duties of loyalty in Australia, the UK and US (Delaware)*

In general, obligations in relation to trust and loyalty under corporate governance laws commonly turn on (interrelated) themes including:

(a) consciousness of impropriety: whether the director acted honestly and, if so, whether that is sufficient to satisfy their duties;
(b) proper purposes: whether the director's conduct was solely directed towards the pursuit of the best interests of the corporation rather than their own or those of a third party; and
(c) conflicts of interest.

The content of the relevant duties under US (Delaware), United Kingdom and Australian law is summarised in what follows.

3.2.1 *Australia*

Duties of loyalty owed by Australian company directors are primarily codified under the Corporations Act 2001 (Cth) ('Corporations Act'):

AUSTRALIA – GOOD FAITH AND BEST INTERESTS

Section 181(1)(a) of the Corporations Act provides that a director must exercise their powers and discharge their duties in 'good faith in the best interests of the corporation' and for a 'proper purpose'. Under section 184, the failure may be a criminal offence if the director acts recklessly, or with intentional dishonesty. However, a consciousness of impropriety (i.e. subjective bad faith or dishonesty) is not otherwise a precondition to breach.

AUSTRALIA – CONFLICTS OF INTEREST

Directors must also avoid (or adequately manage) material 'conflicts of interest' – both as an inherent requirement of their duty to act in good faith in the best interests of the corporation and under the common law. An actionable conflict will arise where there is a 'real or sensible possibility' that the duality of interest would compromise the director's ability to exercise their independent judgment in the best interests of the corporation'.[10] Such interests may be financial or personal (non-financial) in nature.[11]

AUSTRALIA – NOTABLE FRAMEWORK FEATURES

The Australian duties enforcement regime has an important feature that distinguishes it from the frameworks in Delaware and the UK. In addition to the rights of shareholders to bring derivative (i.e. on behalf of the corporation) claims against the directors, the statutory regulator, the Australian Securities & Investments Commission (ASIC) has the power to investigate and prosecute directorial breaches of duty. This regulatory enforcement overlay adds a significant level of litigation risk for Australian directors. Although its means are not unlimited, ASIC is a well-resourced litigant, with a history of proactive investigation supported by statutory powers to compel information disclosure and production. In addition, its enforcement activities are not constrained by the derivative action standing requirements faced by shareholders seeking to bring a breach-of-duty claim on behalf of the corporation, nor the need to prove causation, reliance and loss – factors commonly cited as significant barriers for private litigants.

3.2.2 United Kingdom

The general duties of UK company directors are codified in Part 2, Chapter 10 of the Companies Act 2006 ('Companies Act'). The relevant duties of loyalty include:

UK – GOOD FAITH AND BEST INTERESTS

Under section 172(1) of the Companies Act directors must act in the way that they consider, 'in good faith', would be most likely to 'promote the success of the company' for the benefit of its members as a whole and in doing so have regard (amongst other matters) to the:

(a) likely consequences of the decision in the long term;
(b) interests of the company's employees;
(c) need to foster the company's business relationships with suppliers, customers and others;
(d) impact of the company's operations on the community and the environment;
(e) desirability of the company maintaining a reputation for high standards of business conduct;
(f) need to act fairly as between members of the company (see generally Shepherd and Ridley 2015, 10.2.2).[12]

The duty to act in the best interests of the company set out in section 172 (and its common law predecessor) has historically been regarded as subjective in nature – that is, turning on whether the director was acting in good faith, with a subjective belief that their actions were directed towards the best interests of the company.[13] This is consistent with the principle that the court will not latterly substitute its own view of corporate best interests for the director's commercial judgment. More recently, however, the Courts have added a gloss to the subjective nature of this test – including in circumstances in which there is no evidence that the director *actually* considered the best interests of the company. In such cases, an objective 'credibility' overlay is applied – that is, 'whether an intelligent and honest man in the position of [the director] could, in the circumstances, have reasonably believed that the transaction was for the benefit of the company'. Moreover, a claim that a director has failed to exercise their powers for a proper purpose does not require proof of dishonesty or knowledge that the purpose was a collateral one (i.e. proof of mala fides or bad faith). To that end, the test may also be regarded as objective.[14]

UK – CONFLICTS OF INTEREST

Under section 175(1) of the Companies Act directors have a duty to 'avoid conflicts of interest' (other than those arising due to a transaction with the company – see section 175(3)). Specifically they must 'avoid a situation in which [they have], or can have, a direct or indirect interest that conflicts, or possibly may conflict, with the interests of the company'. Sub-section (4) provides that this duty is not infringed – (a) if the situation cannot reasonably be regarded as likely to give rise to a conflict of interest or (b) if the matter has been authorised by the directors (with section 180 providing further exculpation where the matter has been authorised by the shareholders or under the company's articles of association). Similarly to the Australian law, in the UK a conflict will only be material if a reasonable person would consider that there was a real possibility of conflict in the circumstances.[15]

A breach of the duty of due care and diligence under section 174 of the Companies Act (discussed in Parts 3.4 and 3.5) may also breach a director's duty to promote the success of the company under section 172 where no intelligent and honest person could have reasonably believed the relevant decision was for its benefit.[16]

UK – NOTABLE FRAMEWORK FEATURES

There is no regulatory authority in the UK that is empowered to enforce breaches of directorial duties: the only right of enforcement lies with the company (through the board itself or by the shareholders acting derivatively or by the liquidator or administrator in the event of insolvency). A member of a company who brings a derivative claim regarding an actual or proposed breach of the directors' duties must apply to the court for consent to continue it pursuant to section 261 of the Companies Act. Where the plaintiffs have leave to proceed, they can seek remedies including declaratory relief, injunctions, compensatory damages (payable to the company) or restoration.

3.2.3 US (Delaware corporations)

Directors' duties under Delaware law are founded in equity.[17] Those duties are owed to and enforceable by the company or by the shareholders in a derivative action on the company's behalf.

The Delaware duty of loyalty encompasses a number of (often overlapping) obligations, including:

DELAWARE – GOOD FAITH AND BEST INTERESTS

The duty of 'good faith', which requires Delaware directors to act 'honestly, in the best interest of the corporation' and in a manner that is not knowingly unlawful or contrary to public policy. The court will infer the directors' subjective motivations from the objective facts. Only fairly egregious conduct (such as a knowing and deliberate indifference to a potential risk of harm to the corporation) will rise to the level of 'bad faith'.[18]

DELAWARE – CONFLICTS OF INTEREST

The duty to avoid (or handle with propriety) material 'conflicts of interest'.[19] A material conflict may manifest where the director's decision is not 'based entirely on the corporate merits of the transaction but . . . influenced by personal or extraneous considerations'.[20] Such conflicts can include, for example, decisions that were influenced by 'non-stockholder–related influences'.[21] Proof that the director 'consciously disregarded' their duty to pursue the best financial outcome for shareholders is not required to establish self-interest, only that the decision aligns with the receipt of a 'substantial benefit' by the director (such as common change-of-control incentives).[22] The point at which director self-interest is of such materiality to translate into disloyalty is a question of fact in each case.[23]

DELAWARE – DUTY TO MONITOR

Whilst the directors' role in the supervision and oversight of executive management (the 'duty to monitor') is generally litigated as a requirement of the duty of care in Australia and the UK, following the decision in *Stone v. Ritter*[24] the Delaware courts have now squarely positioned a claim for such conduct as a subset of the duties of loyalty and good faith. The leading case on point is *Caremark*,[25] in which the court held that directors must assure themselves that a corporation's reporting systems will enable the board to reach informed business judgments 'concerning both the corporation's compliance with law and its business performance.'[26]

In short, there are two scenarios in which a director may breach duties of oversight under *Caremark* principles:

(a) where the directors utterly failed to implement any reporting or information system or controls; or

(b) having implemented such a system or controls, consciously failed to monitor or oversee its operations thus disabling themselves from being informed of risks or problems requiring their attention'.[27] As observed by the Delaware Supreme Court in *In re General Motors Derivative Action*, this second limb requires the plaintiff to demonstrate 'red flags' that put (or should have put) the directors on notice that there were problems with their systems, which the directors then consciously disregarded.[28]

Despite the express reference to 'business performance' in the *Caremark* judgment, in *Citigroup* the court expressed the view that a director could *not* in fact be held liable for a failure to monitor business risk. In that case, the plaintiffs unsuccessfully argued that the directors were liable under *Caremark* principles for their failure to adequately oversee and manage the corporation's loan portfolio risk exposure and ignorance of several red flags that warned of the deteriorating subprime mortgage market.[29]

DELAWARE – NOTABLE FRAMEWORK FEATURES

Delaware plaintiffs face a number of significant hurdles in establishing a breach of any of the duties of loyalty. First, Delaware law applies a 'business judgment rule', under which defendant directors enjoy the presumption that their duties of loyalty are satisfied: *viz* 'in making a business decision the directors of a corporation acted on an informed basis, in good faith and in the honest belief that the action taken was in the best interests of the company'.[30] Whilst this presumption can be rebutted where the plaintiff provides evidence to the contrary, it has been described as placing 'a thumb on the scale in favour of the directors' (Yeager 2015, p. 1389). Secondly, even if the business judgment rule presumption is rebutted, this does not amount to a *per se* or automatic finding of directorial liability. Rather, the burden then shifts to the defendant directors to establish whether, objectively,[31] the outcome of the relevant transaction or conduct was 'entirely fair'.[32]

Having laid out the duties of loyalty in Australia, the UK and Delaware, we can now consider what directorial acts or omissions in relation to stranded asset risks may be likely to breach their terms.

3.3 Application of the duty of loyalty to governance failures with regard to stranded asset risks

It is conceivable that a failure to have regard to or inadequate consideration of stranded assets risks in the energy and resources sector may raise issues under the duties of good faith and loyalty in the following contexts:

3.3.1 Bad faith/best interests – Australia, UK and US

Directors who consciously disregard or are wilfully blind to stranded asset risks in their governance of risk and strategy may fail to act in good faith in the best (financial) interests of their company under the terms of the duties in each of the three subject jurisdictions.[33] For example, where such governance conduct is motivated by an extraneous interest, such as (for example) 'default denialism' consistent with the position promulgated by a partisan political or industry-based association with which the director is affiliated, a claim may potentially be raised that the director failed to discharge their duty to prioritise the best interests of the company or, in the words of the court in *In re Disney*, as 'a deliberate indifference of the potential risk of harm to the corporation'.[34]

Where a director's external position or affiliation may materially compromise their ability to exercise independent judgment on the governance of stranded asset risks, this may also give risk to an actionable conflict of interest (see what follows). Whilst judicious disclosure and management of competing interests are often determinative of whether a conflict of interest comprises a breach of duty, such conflict may in fact be intractable where the director's membership of the extraneous organisation requires them to subscribe to (or promote) a particular position on climate change.

3.3.2 Conflicts of interest – Australia, UK and US

In general terms, the potential for conflicts of interest to arise from the discretionary or contingent components of a director's financial incentivisation is well recognised under fiduciary law principles. For example, there is a significant body of jurisprudence in Delaware (in particular) on director conflicts in merger transactions in which directors are financially incentivised to favour the change of control. The courts are yet to consider this issue in the specific context of remuneration linked to stranded assets (or management of climate-related risks in general). This is not to suggest that directors who obtain pecuniary benefit due to their shareholding in their company will be in breach of duty merely because this arises as an incident of their conduct in promoting corporate best interests.[35] In theory, however, a potential conflict may emerge between the financial interests of a company operating in the fossil fuel extractives sectors and the personal financial interests of its directors, where (for example) contingent or discretionary components of remuneration are tied (in whole or in part) to reserve replacement ratios. This may financially incentivise directors to pursue a strategy of maximising fossil fuel reserve exploration and expansion or to build 'conventional' power stations with no economically credible plans for carbon capture and storage, without regard to whether such a 'business as usual' approach to strategy is in the best financial interests of the company.

3.3.3 Duty to monitor – US

As outlined earlier, Delaware law is unique in its approach to directors' obligations of supervision and oversight (or the 'duty to monitor') amongst the three subject jurisdictions, as an element of their duties of loyalty rather than competence/due care.

A 'duty to monitor' (or '*Caremark*') claim typically arises after a corporation suffers a major trauma which results in significant expense, loss or harm. In the *Botox Derivative Case*, the court held that:

> The list of corporate traumas for which stockholders theoretically could seek to hold directors accountable is long and ever expanding: regulatory sanctions, criminal or civil fines, environmental disasters, accounting restatements, misconduct by officers or employees, massive business losses, and innumerable other potential calamities.[36]

The first limb of the *Caremark* test is particularly difficult for a plaintiff to satisfy. Even relatively scant efforts to oversee a corporation's climate change risk management are likely to preclude a claim that the board 'utterly failed' to oversee the implementation of controls. However, it is at least theoretically possible that a claim under the second (or 'red flags') limb of the *Caremark* test may arise for consideration in a stranded assets risk context. In particular, such a claim may be constructed where a corporation suffers significant harm (such as legal costs, damages awards or loss in stock value) due to a failure to comply with:

- emissions regulations: for example, due to the technical inability of a company in an emissions-intensive industry to adapt to more stringent emissions controls (as starkly illustrated in the recent 'Dieselgate' scandal involving automotive giant VW); or
- securities law obligations: regarding the disclosure of climate-related risks. This could include, for example, the 2015 settlement between the New York Attorney General (NYAG) and Peabody Coal relating to the selective disclosure of forward-looking demand scenarios, and inconsistency between Peabody's stated position on the potential climate risks and its internal analysis; or the current Securities & Exchange Commission (SEC) and NYAG investigations into ExxonMobil's climate risk disclosures and failure to revalue its proven reserves despite a collapse in the price of oil (see generally Poon 2017).

In order to raise a credible '*Caremark* claim' under the second ('red flag') limb, the plaintiff would likely need to establish, first, that the directors had actual or constructive knowledge that the corporation was at risk of harm due to a potential breach of the law or 'serious misconduct' and, second, that their failure to take steps to investigate, prevent or remedy the situation was causative of that harm.[37] To the first element, it is likely that a board of directors would have direct and actual notice of a regulatory investigation into its company's conduct or practices under even the most basic of risk management and escalation frameworks – particularly where that regulator is one as powerful as the Department of Justice, the SEC or the NYAG. Even in the unlikely event that the board had not been directly and specifically apprised of the relevant investigation, there is authority to suggest that media reports of the investigations may comprise 'red flags', at least where those reports occur extensively within the mainstream press.[38] What is less clear is whether the high-profile media reports of such regulatory investigations into *other companies* in that same sector would comprise a relevant 'red flag' to the directors of their own corporation's exposure, such that a review of the sufficiency of their internal compliance structures would be necessary to avoid a similar investigation or claim. It certainly would not take a leap of judicial logic to conclude that the extensive media coverage of the plethora of regulatory investigations and private claims against VW in relation to the Dieselgate scandal would be sufficient to comprise a red flag to directors of other automotive companies of the necessity to investigate their own fleet's emissions management software to ensure it did not contain a similar 'defeat device'. Similarly, it would not be unreasonable to argue that the SEC and NYAG investigations into ExxonMobil and NYAG's settlement with Peabody Coal would be a red flag to the directors of other coal, oil and gas companies that regulators no longer consider 'disclosure as usual' to be compliant with their securities law obligations.

If the relevant red flags are held to be sufficient to provide actual or constructive notice of the illegality to the board, a breach of the duty will turn on whether the directors then took action to investigate the company's exposure to the risk and the adequacy of its internal controls in relation to stranded asset risk assessment and disclosure. This will, of course, be a question of fact in the particular case.

There is no doubt that a *Caremark* claim would be extremely difficult to establish in a stranded asset risk context. However, at least as a matter of legal theory, it is not impossible.[39] The cause of action continues to be deployed by plaintiffs, including in a recent series of derivative claims against the directors of corporations that have suffered loss due to cyber-attack, which have alleged (amongst other claims) that the directors breached their duty of loyalty by failing to implement internal controls to prevent and detect data breaches.[40] Whilst no '*Caremark* cyber-claim' has yet survived a motion to dismiss, additional claims continue to be filed,[41] and leading commentators continue to suggest that there remains a credible prospect of a successful claim in the right factual circumstances (LaCroix 2016).

3.3.4 Conclusion: when is a failure to govern for stranded asset risks a potential breach of directors' duties of loyalty?

It is conceivable that a failure to have regard to or inadequate consideration of stranded assets risks in the energy and resources sector may raise issues under the duties of good faith and loyalty in three contexts:

- Breach of loyalty/good faith: strategic inaction on stranded asset risks due to conscious disregard or wilful blindness of climate change–related risks (including that motivated by an extraneous association or interest, rather than a genuine pursuit of corporate success or best interests). The latter may also give risk to a potential conflict of interest, *viz:*
- Conflicts of interest: where the director has extraneous obligations that require them to maintain a position of climate change denial or obfuscation or

financial incentives aligned with 'business-as-usual' carbon-intensive business strategies (such as remuneration in the fossil fuel extractives sector tied to reserve replacement ratios) that are of such significance as to compromise the director's ability to make an independent judgment in the best interests of the corporation; and

- Duty to monitor: a failure of oversight that causes the corporation to breach the law (Delaware only): a failure by directors to adequately monitor compliance mechanisms, which facilitates the corporation's breach of emissions regulations or securities law disclosure obligations. Under *Caremark* principles (second limb), this would require proof of the directors' actual knowledge that their corporation's misconduct was being legally challenged or investigated (the red flag – for example, regulatory investigations into its compliance with emissions regulations or securities fraud allegations over a failure to restate the booked value of stranded assets) and that they then failed to ensure that the corporation had adequate systems and processes in place to mitigate that risk (which failure caused the harm to the company). There is no current precedent that supports a contention that high-profile claims against the corporation's *competitors* may constitute a constructive red flag to which directors would be obliged to respond, although this may be reasonably arguable where such reports are mainstream and extensive. Such a claim would be difficult to make out but is not inconceivable on the basis of prevailing case law.

In relation to the first two contexts, as a general observation the Australian duties regime may present the greatest liability exposure for directors. This is primarily due to the duality of prosecution avenues – by the company (derivatively via its shareholders) and the securities regulator, ASIC. This exposure is compounded by the fact that the Australian economy is heavily skewed towards companies in the high-risk stranded assets, with nearly two-thirds of the Australian Stock Exchange (by value) in the extractives, energy or financial services sectors. This exposure was reinforced by a recent study by S&P Dow Jones in May 2017, Barometer of Financial Markets' Carbon Efficiency, that rated the ASX50 as having the greatest exposure to climate change–related stranded asset risks of *any* major international share index.

3.4 Duties of competence – the standard of review in the US, UK and Australia

In general, directors' duties of 'competence' are given force in obligations that require the exercise of due care, skill and diligence in the discharge of their position. The standard against which conduct is tested varies between jurisdictions (for example, as against that of the 'ordinary prudent person' under Delaware law versus that of a 'reasonable director' in Australia), as does the degree of failure or culpability required in order to establish liability ('gross negligence' in Delaware, more akin to 'mere' negligence in Australia). Despite these variations, there are a number of common components of the obligation to exercise due care and diligence across each of the three subject jurisdictions, including:

(a) a requirement to remain adequately informed via a proactive and deliberative inquisitive process;
(b) obligations to apply independent judgment and critical evaluation (and, conversely, the limits of delegation and reliance); and
(c) proactive supervision and oversight of executive management.

The content of each of these duties under the laws of Australia, the UK and Delaware and the circumstances in which failures or omissions in the governance of stranded asset risks may breach their terms is considered in what follows. To avoid overlap with the duties relating to trust and loyalty discussed in Parts 3.2 and 3.3, the application of the relevant duties of due care and diligence proceeds on the assumption that the director (although potentially under-informed or ill advised) is independent and disinterested, acting honestly and with subjective good faith.

3.4.1 Australia

The Australian duties regime is widely recognised as imposing particularly stringent standards of proactivity and professionalism on corporate directors. That jurisdiction's duty of due care and diligence is the closest to 'mere' negligence of the three regimes subject to analysis in this chapter. Significantly, proof of dishonesty and/or bad faith are not necessary to establish breach.

The general duty of due care and diligence of Australian company directors is set out in section 180(1) of the Corporations Act. It requires directors to 'exercise their powers and discharge their duties with the degree of due care and diligence that a reasonable person would exercise' in the relevant circumstances.

In assessing the reasonableness (or otherwise) of a director's conduct, Australian courts apply the *subjective* characteristics of the director and their corporation (including the type of company involved, the size and nature of its business or businesses, its constitution, the composition of the board and its reserved powers and whether the company is public or private)[42] to an *objective* assessment of whether the director has taken 'all reasonable steps to be in a position to guide and manage the company'.[43] This, in turn, requires a balancing of the magnitude of the relevant risk (its gravity, frequency and imminence) and the probability that it will crystallise, as against the expense, difficulty and inconvenience of any countermeasures, and the defendant's conflicting responsibilities.[44]

The courts have emphasised that, regardless of the circumstances at hand, directors must discharge certain *minimum* standards to satisfy their duty of due care and diligence.[45] This includes the proactive acquisition and maintenance of relevant knowledge (including making enquiries of management and/or independent experts where this is warranted), active monitoring of the corporation's affairs and an independent and critical evaluation of the matters for which they are responsible.[46] In this regard, the director's duty of care 'is not . . . limited by the director's knowledge and experience or ignorance and inaction'.[47]

AUSTRALIA – REQUIREMENT TO INFORM

As an element of their duty of due care and diligence, Australian directors must acquire and maintain an 'irreducible core' of knowledge and understanding of the fundamentals of their corporation, including in relation to its activities, its financial position and the regulatory environment. This requires proactive inquiry, obliging directors to 'take a diligent and intelligent interest in the information available to them or which they might appropriately demand from the executives or other employees and agents of the company'.[48] Directors may be obliged to make (or procure the making of) further inquiries where a 'dearth of material' on a relevant issue[49] or a conflicting body of material,[50] is otherwise placed before them, and/or to seek 'professional or expert advice' from persons that are expert, reliable and competent where faced with complex issues.

AUSTRALIA – REQUIREMENTS TO CRITICALLY EVALUATE

The information proactively obtained and advice received must then be brought to bear in a process of active, 'careful', 'real and genuine consideration':[51] an independent and critical evaluation of the matters for which the directors are responsible.[52]

AUSTRALIA – SUPERVISION/OVERSIGHT

Delegation and reliance on delegates' advice is specifically contemplated under sections 198D ('Delegation'), 189 ('Reliance on information or advice provided by others'), and 190 ('Responsibility for Actions of Delegate') of the Corporations Act. However, the director's delegation and reliance must itself be reasonable to avoid a potential breach of their duty of due care and diligence. A director's reliance on the advice of an employee or expert may *not* be reasonable where the director did not believe, on reasonable grounds,[53] that the delegate or advisor was reliable and competent in the relevant matters, or the reliance was not made in good faith, or the director did not make an independent assessment of the information or advice.

Notable circumstances in which a plaintiff has been able to establish that reliance on the professional advice was unreasonable include where the delegate themselves has a conflict of interest,[54] where the advisers had no technical qualifications or experience which justified reliance upon them,[55] where the directors failed to interrogate superficial or inadequate answers by the delegate which indicated further investigation was warranted[56] and where the directors completely or solely relied on the conclusions of relevant experts without their own independent review or consideration.[57]

The obligation to exercise due care and diligence is tempered by a 'business judgment rule' defence under section 180(2). The defence applies where the directors make a conscious judgment that relates to the performance, risk or strategy of the business and that judgment is made:

- in good faith for a proper purpose;
- free from material personal interest;
- upon the basis of information about the subject matter that the director reasonably believes to be appropriate; and
- with a rational belief that the judgment is in the best interests of the corporation.

The Australian business judgment rule is routinely raised by defendant directors. However, it is *unsuccessful* in providing a defence in nearly all cases. Defendants (having been found liable for a breach of their duty of due care and diligence) are usually unable to discharge either the threshold issue that they made a conscious judgement (as opposed to a course of action resultant of a failure to consider a matter) and/or that that judgment was based upon a robust informational basis in satisfaction of the last two limbs of the test.

3.4.2 United Kingdom

Section 174 of the UK's Companies Act requires directors to exercise reasonable care, skill and diligence. The test has both objective and subjective elements.[58] The standard of care to which a director is held is that which would be exercised by a reasonably diligent person with 'the general knowledge, skill and experience that may reasonably be expected of a person carrying out the functions carried out by the director in relation to the company' and 'the general knowledge, skill and experience that the director has'. This includes knowledge of facts which, given reasonable diligence and an appropriate level of general knowledge, skill and experience, were ascertainable by the director.[59] To the extent that the subjective knowledge, skill or experience of the director is taken into account, it can only be relied upon to enhance the standard to which they are held rather than to justify a lowering of the standard for less experienced directors.[60]

There is (by comparison to US and Australian jurisprudence) relatively little case law on the UK duty of due care and diligence – either in relation to the section 174 duty specifically or to the common law and equitable principles on which the statutory provision is based (Loughrey 2013, p. 16). Historically, it has not been clear whether it is necessary to establish *gross negligence* in order to prove a breach of this duty. However, leading commentators suggest that, following the codification of the common law duty into the Companies Act into a test that incorporates *objective* considerations, it is likely that a standard of 'mere' negligence is likely to apply (although *cf. Optaglio Ltd v. Tethal* [2015] EWCA Civ 1002, [23], where the Court of Appeal unanimously held that 'the test to be applied is a high one. It must be shown that the decision complained of [was] . . . one which no reasonable director could have reached'; Loughrey 2013, p. 17).

'Soft law' instruments such as the Financial Reporting Council's Corporate Governance Code provide persuasive guidance on the expectations of a 'reasonable director' in particular circumstances. For example, Principle C2 of that Code provides that boards are responsible for determining significant risks to the business and A4 that non-executive directors are expected to challenge management constructively. Moreover, the issues in relation to which directors must exercise due care and diligence are likely to be informed by the list of interests to be taken into account in 'promoting the success' of the company set out in section 172 of the Companies Act. That list (relevantly) includes the likely consequences of the decision in the long term and the impact of the company's operations on the community and the environment.

Similarly to the Australian duty of care, a breach of the UK law is likely to turn on whether the process applied to arrive at the relevant decision was robust: whether the director was informed of pertinent information, critically evaluated it and oversaw or monitored the relevant activities of their delegates:

UK – REQUIREMENT TO INFORM, SUPERVISE AND OVERSEE

The leading UK case establishing that a breach of the duty of due care and diligence may arise from either lack of information or inadequate supervision/oversight is the disqualification case of *Secretary of State for Trade and Industry v. Baker (No 5) (Re Barings) (No 5)*.[61] In that case, the court held:

(i) Directors have, both collectively and individually, a continuing duty to acquire and maintain a sufficient knowledge and understanding of the company's business to enable them properly to discharge their duties as directors. (ii) Whilst directors are entitled (subject to the articles of association of the company) to delegate particular functions to those below them in the management chain, and to trust their competence and integrity to a reasonable extent, the exercise of the power of delegation does not absolve a director from the duty to supervise the discharge of the delegated functions. (iii) No rule of universal application can be formulated as to the duty referred to in (ii) above. The extent of the duty, and the question whether it has been discharged, must depend on the facts of each particular case, including the director's role in the management of the company.

UK – REQUIREMENT TO CRITICALLY EVALUATE

UK directors can breach their duty of care when they fail to appropriately interrogate information provided to them by another.[62] This does not mean that they have to bring specialist expertise to bear on every question but to consider, probe, test and independently evaluate the information that is provided by the experts in the context of their role as governors of the company. Unquestioning reliance on advice may comprise a breach of the duty of due care and diligence[63] (and/or an additional, specific duty to exercise independent judgment under section 173(1) of the Companies Act).

Whilst there is no express 'business judgment rule' under the Companies Act, the UK courts are reluctant to intervene in honest business misjudgements or failures when these have been arrived upon honestly and in good faith in the pursuit of corporate objectives and by the application of a robust process.

3.4.3 US – Delaware

Bruner describes Delaware's legal framework for the analysis of the duty of care as 'hardly a picture of clarity', with complexity compounded by doctrinal 'growth by accretion' (Bruner 2013, pp. 1029 and 1031).

The height of the plaintiff's burden in establishing a breach of the duty of care (without more) before the Delaware courts is difficult to overstate (Velasco 2015, pp. 648–649). This is due to both the operation of the business judgment rule and the near-universal application of a 'directors' damages immunity'.

Under the Delaware business judgment rule, defendant directors enjoy the presumption that 'in making a business decision the directors of a corporation acted on an informed basis, in good faith and in the honest belief that the action taken was in the best interests of the company'.[64] This operates to shield directors from liability for a breach of the duty of care 'in all but the most extreme cases' (Velasco 2015, p. 649. See also Lafferty et al. 2012, p. 841: 'The business judgment rule is a deferential standard of review; Delaware courts will generally refrain from unreasonably imposing themselves upon the business and affairs of a corporation when the board's decision can be attributed to some rational corporate purpose').[65]

The prescription that directors 'act on an informed basis' is applied as the primary exposition of the 'duty of care' element of the business judgment rule presumption. The lack of care is adjudged against the standard of gross negligence (Jacobs 2015, p. 145):[66] *viz* whether the directors exhibited a 'reckless indifference to or a deliberate disregard of the whole body of stockholders or actions which are without the bounds of reason'.[67]

This duty of care contemplates 'informed reasonable deliberation'[68] by the defendant directors. That concept in turn incorporates three elements (any of which the plaintiff may attempt to disprove in order to rebut the presumption) – that the directors failed to either/or (1) make a conscious decision in relation to the matter in question,[69] (2) act on an informed basis based on material information available to them and (3) having become so informed, failed to act with appropriate care in arriving at their decision.[70] The practical steps that may be required to satisfy these elements are neatly described by Egan (2016, p. 54):

> Compliance with the duty of care requires active diligence. Accordingly, directors should attend board meetings regularly; they should take time to review, digest, and evaluate all materials and other information provided to

them; they should take reasonable steps to assure that all material information bearing on a decision has been considered by the directors or by those upon whom the directors will rely; they should actively participate in board deliberations, ask appropriate questions, and discuss each proposal's strengths and weaknesses; they should seek out the advice of legal counsel, financial advisors, and other professionals, as needed; they should, where appropriate, reasonably rely upon information, reports, and opinions provided by officers, experts or board committees; and they should take sufficient time (as may be dictated by the circumstances) to reflect on decisions before making them.

Whether the plaintiff can rebut the presumption for want of care (and whether, if the defendant directors obtained advice on the issue in question, the directors reasonably believed the advisor had appropriate competence and had been selected by the corporation with reasonable care pursuant to section 141(e)) will be a fact-specific inquiry in each case. However, the business judgment rule clearly demands that the directors exercise a degree of *attentiveness* to relevant information and its evaluation, in a similar manner to the duties of care in Australia and the UK.

DELAWARE – REQUIREMENT TO INFORM

Plaintiffs may rebut the business judgment rule's presumption of due care by demonstrating that the defendant directors were not adequately informed.[71] This requires directors to 'inform themselves of all material information reasonably available' before voting on a transaction.[72] The informational process cannot be passive but must be undertaken in a full and 'deliberate manner'.[73] Seeking the advice of appropriate experts may be a relevant factor.[74]

DELAWARE – REQUIREMENT TO CRITICALLY EVALUATE

Alternatively, plaintiffs may rebut the business judgment rule's presumption of due care by demonstrating that the defendant directors, whilst adequately informed, then failed to act with appropriate care in arriving at their decision.[75] Cases such as *Graham v. Allis-Chalmers* and *Walt Disney* have held that directors must apply 'that amount of care which ordinarily careful and prudent men would use in similar circumstances'.[76] Where the decision was arrived at with the benefit of advice (from management or external experts), the directors may be entitled to the benefit of section 141(e) of the Delaware General Corporation Law, which provides:

> A [director] shall . . . be fully protected in relying in good faith upon . . . such information, opinions, reports or statements presented to the corporation by any of the corporation's officers or employees, or committees of the board of directors, or by any other person as to matters the member reasonably believes are within such other person's professional or expert competence and who has been selected with reasonable care by or on behalf of the corporation.

However, the 'full protection' offered under section 141(e) is not absolute. Directorial reliance on the relevant report(s) must be both based on a reasonable belief in the professional or expert competence of the advisor, with that advisor having been selected upon the application of reasonable care by the corporation or its agents. In addition, reliance 'in good faith' does not equate to 'blind reliance'[77] or exempt a director from undertaking their own evaluation of and reasonable inquiry into the information presented. It may also be material to the rebuttal of the business judgment rule presumption that a 'prudent search for alternatives' has not been conducted.[78]

DELAWARE – A NOTE RE THE 'ENTIRE FAIRNESS' TEST

As discussed in relation to the Delaware duties of good faith and loyalty in Part 3.2, an 'entire fairness' test is ordinarily applicable to decisions in which the business judgement rule is rebutted. However, unlike in relation to the duty of loyalty (where the central concern relates to the director's propriety in favouring their own interests over those of the company), this test does not sit easily in the assessment of a breach of the duty of care – where the directors have not sought to subsume the company interests to those of another but demonstrated gross negligence in the discharge of their duties. Accordingly, whilst *Cede v. Technicolor* stands as authority that the 'entire fairness' test *should* be applied where the business judgment rule presumption is rebutted on duty-of-care grounds,[79] later commentary has queried whether its application is germane to decisions made by disinterested directors (Allen et al. 2001, pp. 1302–1303; Bainbridge 2012, p. 585; Bruner 2013, pp. 1042–1043; Velasco 2015, p. 682).

DELAWARE – NOTABLE FRAMEWORK FEATURES: THE CONSTITUTIONAL
DAMAGES IMMUNITY

Even where the plaintiff can discharge the high burden to rebut the business judgment rule by establishing the defendant directors(s) have failed to exercise due care, the Delaware General Corporation Law allows the certificate or articles of incorporation (i.e. the corporate constitution) to provide a corporate exculpation of directors from personal liability for a breach of their duty of care (i.e. for *damages* flowing from such breach).[80] This relevant section of the law was inserted as a direct legislative response to the Delaware Supreme Court's finding that directors were personally liable for gross negligence in *Smith v. Van Gorkom*.[81]

The immunity has since been subject to near universal adoption in the charters of Delaware corporations (Brown and Gopalan 2009, pp. 309–310; Hamermesh 2000, p. 490; Miller 2010, p. 322, Velasco 2015, p. 652). Plaintiffs who plead a claim for monetary damages that is exculpated by the immunity will not survive a motion to dismiss.[82]

With the legal principles in each of the three subject jurisdictions set out, we can now consider the circumstances in which directors' failure to consider or inadequate consideration of stranded asset risk may breach their duty of due care and diligence.

3.5 *Application of the duty of due care and diligence to governance failures with regard to stranded asset risks*

It is important to note at the outset of this analysis that the duty of care and diligence – in any of the subject jurisdictions – does not impose liability for incorrect commercial judgments *per se*. The courts are extremely reluctant to engage in a judicial re-assessment of the commercial wisdom of a particular decision. The fact that a company underperforms – or even suffers a loss in value – is not in and of itself a breach of duty.[83] Rather, as outlined earlier, compliance with the duty of due care and diligence is assessed by reference to the robustness of the *process* of information gathering and deliberation rather than a retrospective assessment of whether an optimum financial outcome was achieved (Collins 2014, p. 634; Thornton 2008, p. 410).[84] The relevant inquiry is whether the *procedural effort* applied to the consideration and governance of stranded asset risks is so inadequate as to risk breach of the minimum standards of due care and diligence expected of directors in the circumstances.

The answer to that question will, of course, turn on both the facts of each case and the particularities of the standard of review under the governing law. The material risks and opportunities associated with climate change (and stranded assets in particular) and appropriate risk management treatments vary across geographies, industries and corporations and will need to be weighed against conflicting corporate obligations and expenses. It is therefore difficult to set out a universal governance strategy that will satisfy the duty in directors' governance of stranded asset risks (or, conversely, that are unlikely to do so) (Waitzer and Sarro 2014, pp. 1090–1091). However, the scope, scale and probability of the relevant risks will be relevant in considering the standard of governance conduct required. The significant materiality of the stranded asset risks in the energy and resources sector (as discussed in Part 2) suggests that the minimum benchmark of care and diligence that should be applied in the circumstances is proportionately high.[85] With that general proposition in place, we can assess whether the nature of governance of stranded asset risks by directors in that sector is likely to be sufficient to satisfy their duty of due care and diligence in two broad categories, *viz*:

(a) A total failure to consider and govern for stranded asset risks in strategic planning and risk management: either in general or in relation to material projects or acquisitions that require board oversight or approval, due to honest ignorance, or blind or unquestioning reliance on the advice of delegates or advisors on point; or
(b) Inadequate or deficient consideration and governance for stranded asset risk exposures, due to lack of critical analysis, unreasonable reliance, lack of oversight or inadequate information.

Whilst difficult, on the face of the prevailing law a claim that a director has breached their duty of due care and diligence is not impossible in either of these categories, in particular governance scenarios, under the laws of each of the three jurisdictions considered.

3.5.1 Total failure

It is clear that an issue of such high profile and potential economic significance as stranded asset risks (as set out in Part 2) would put a reasonable director in the energy and resources sector on notice that consideration is warranted about the impact of this issue on their corporation's risk assessment and management, strategy, asset valuation and liability contingencies or provisions, financial planning and capex and disclosures (Hutley and Hartford-Davis 2016). Accordingly, a failure to consider the risks and/or opportunities presented by stranded asset risks for want of the relevant knowledge – either in general or in relation to material projects or acquisitions – appears to present grounds for review for breach of the duty of care in all three of the subject jurisdictions. This holds whether the director's ignorance is as a result of presumptive climate change denial or scepticism (Liddell 2015; Loechel et al. 2013, p. 473), or a simple absence of consideration due to lack of knowledge.[86]

Importantly, in each of the three subject jurisdictions it is no defence that the director was not *provided* with information on stranded asset risks by their corporation by management. In all three, the law imposes expectations of proactive inquiry: the responsibility to seek adequate advice on material issues where it is not otherwise provided lies squarely with the directors themselves.[87] The obligation to seek appropriate advice is further considered under the category of 'Inadequate Consideration' in what follows.

Given the profile and magnitude of the issue of stranded assets for the energy and resources sector, it may seem intuitively unlikely that a director in the industry would *not* have knowledge of the stranded asset risks associated with climate change. However, analysis of current corporate disclosures suggests otherwise. For example, a recent study by EY reported that of the 36 listed corporations in the ASX200 operating in the energy, mining and/or metals sectors, nearly one-third (11) had *no* public disclosure or discussion of climate change–related issues (let alone decision-useful information regarding the relevance/impact of associated issues such as stranded asset risks in the context of governance, risk, strategy and/ or metrics/targets) (EY 2017, pp. 11–13). Whilst a failure to report is an imperfect proxy indicator for the diligence of board deliberations, it may be instructive in relation to an issue of such profile and economic significance for the energy and resources sector. More particularly, such non-disclosure may indicate that *either* (a) climate change–related risks *have* been robustly considered and interrogated and assessed as having an immaterial impact on the corporation (a conclusion that does not seem to be likely for such a high proportion of corporations in the sector, given the significance of the relevant risk issues) or (b) that the issue has been considered and interrogated with an appropriate degree of due care and diligence and assessed as material in the circumstances of the corporation but not disclosed (which raises the question of misleading disclosure; see what follows) or (c) the non-disclosure is a product of a failure to consider (or perhaps adequately consider, as discussed in what follows).

The position in Australia (for example) is aptly summarised in the recent opinion on the application of the Australian duty of due care and diligence to the governance of risks associated with climate change of senior commercial barrister Mr Noel Hutley SC (Hutley and Hartford-Davis 2016, [34]):

> It would be difficult for a director to escape liability for a foreseeable risk of harm to the company on the basis that he or she did not believe in the reality of climate change, or indeed that climate change is human-induced. The Court will ask whether the director *should have known* of the danger. This would involve an assessment [of] the conduct of the individual director against the standard of a reasonable person, by reference to the prevailing state of knowledge as publicized at the time. The law has often had to deal with liability for negligence in the context of rapidly developing science. At one time, for example, knowledge was such that an employee could be exposed to asbestos without negligence, or a patient could be infected with HIV through an unsafe intravenous blood transfusion. At a certain point, however, ignorant defendants became liable for these risks on the basis that a reasonable person would have known [of] them. When it comes to climate change, the science has been ventilated with sufficient publicity to deduce that this point has already passed . . .

Moreover, the business judgment rule, whilst varied in its formulation and application across the subject jurisdictions, is not designed to protect directors who are uninformed, who make no conscious decision or who exercise no judgment.[88]

Accordingly, it is relatively uncontroversial that an abject failure to consider an issue with as significant an economic profile as climate change (and stranded asset risks in particular) may comprise a breach of the duty of due care and diligence of directors in the energy and resources sector in the three subject jurisdictions.

3.5.2 Inadequate consideration

A far more complicated question as to whether a director may have breached their duty of competence arises when a director *has* in fact considered stranded asset risks, but that process was inadequate or deficient. However, there are three circumstances in which it may be possible to raise a credible claim of breach in all three jurisdictions (although the *extent* of the failure required to breach the law may be higher under the 'gross negligence' standard prevailing under the Delaware law):

- whilst having turned their minds to the issue and having some information at their disposal, the directors have failed to become adequately informed of relevant material information; the related

- failure to appoint and/or obtain advice from an appropriately qualified advisor; and a
- failure to evaluate critically the advice received.

In addition, in Australia and the UK an additional claim for breach of the duty of due care and diligence may be raised for a failure to duly monitor, supervise or oversee delegates. As outlined, such failure-of-oversight claims are generally litigated as an incident of the duty(s) to act in good faith in the best interests of the company in the United States under *Caremark* principles.

FAILURE TO BECOME (AND REMAIN) ADEQUATELY INFORMED

The inquiry into whether directors have sufficient information in order to duly consider stranded asset risks (and subsequently applied critical assessment to their independent evaluation thereof) is necessarily a question of fact in each particular case. Whilst a board must be reasonably informed, it is not required to be informed of every fact. Whether the board has sufficient understanding of the relevant issue (under Delaware law, 'all material information') is a question that depends on the nature of the issue, the quality of the information, the advice considered and whether the board had adequate 'opportunity to acquire knowledge concerning the problem before acting'.[89] However, given the significance of climate-related risks for corporations in the energy and resources sector (as set out in Part 2), the courts are likely to require a proportionately high standard of evaluation of the relevant issues in order to discharge the directors' duty of care.

The proliferation of 'soft law' instruments that provide guidance to corporations about their disclosure of climate-related risks (and stranded asset risks in particular) are likely to be increasingly persuasive indicators of those kinds of information that directors must inform themselves of and then critically evaluate in order to discharge their duty of care. Stranded asset risk exposures have been raised by various regulators in all three of the jurisdictions subject of this chapter – including the SEC in the United States, the Bank of England Prudential Regulation Authority in the UK and the Australian Prudential Regulation Authority in Australia. Additional guidance has been promulgated by respected bodies such as the Climate Standards Disclosure Board and the Sustainability Accounting Standards Board and, notably, in the Recommendations of the TCFD. The connection between disclosure standards and boardroom conduct has been well made by the CEO of the UK FRC, Stephen Haddrill (FRC 2016):

> In considering what to report it is worth remembering that reporting serves two purposes. It puts information into the capital markets that enables shareholders and lenders to judge performance and so determine how investment should be directed. But it also shapes the debate in the boardroom. That which is reported is discussed.

Consideration by this author of the guidance frameworks described earlier illustrates the scope of information (and, in its absence, inquiry) that may be required to effectively discharge directors' governance obligations in relation to stranded asset risks (from the review and guidance of corporate strategy and risk tolerances, risk management policies, approval/oversight of major capex/acquisitions/divestitures, supervision of management, financial planning, reporting and disclosure). Such information may include (although may not be limited to):

- What is our company's position on the physical, economic transition and liability risks (and opportunities) associated with climate change? This may include (for example) potential physical impacts (such as water stress, increases in the frequency and/or severity of extreme weather events and gradual-onset impacts such as sea-level rise and changes in temperature and precipitation patterns), along with economic transition risks (policy/regulatory responses, technological developments and shifts in stakeholder preferences) and more 'unconventional' risks such as litigation). What are our central beliefs on point?
- What are 'stranded asset risks'? How do stranded asset risks manifest in the industries we operate in?
- What is our particular exposure to stranded asset risks – under various future scenarios and time horizons (short, medium and long term)? On what basis have we formed these views? What do we define 'short', 'medium' and 'long term' to be in the context of our business(es)? How do we identify and assess materiality (absolute and relative significance) in relation to those risks? How should these risks be prioritised and why? How should relevant stranded asset risks (and opportunities) be factored into our strategy and financial planning?
- How has our company's exposure to stranded asset risks been assessed? By whom, and how are they appropriately qualified to conduct this assessment? What is the appropriate unit(s) of measure for this exposure? How often does the analysis occur? On what critical input parameters, assumptions and analytical choices on critical climate risk variables (physical/ecological impacts, trajectory of regulatory reform and relevant technological development, e.g. trends in renewable energy generation and battery storage for the stationary energy sector; penetration forecasts for electric/hydrogen-powered and autonomous vehicles for the oil sector), shadow price(s) on carbon, relevant time horizons etc.) does this analysis employ, over what time frames? On what basis/by whom have these parameters been proposed as reasonable and appropriate? What resources and tools (such as third-party data) have been utilised in this process? Has forward-looking scenario analysis/stress testing been conducted under a plausible range of climate futures (including adverse scenarios with major disruptions) – including with a scenario consistent with the Paris Agreement commitments of $< 2°C$ and net-zero emissions in the second half of the century? On what basis do we believe those scenarios represent an adequate range of credible future policy, technological and other developments that could reasonably be expected to impact our business performance or prospects?
- What is the potential financial impact under each plausible scenario – including under the confluence of a number of adverse factors? Does that analysis consider potential impacts such as increased costs of compliance, costs and

availability of factors of production (energy water, other key inputs), cost of outputs (e.g. waste and emissions), costs and interruptions to distribution and operation, asset impairments, increases in insurance premiums, reduced demand for our products/services, any requirement for increased R&D capital/expenditure on new/alternative technologies, shifts in stakeholder preferences (investor and customer), shifts in revenue/sales streams, human capital planning and management and so forth? How do these scenarios factor in the negative macro-economic implications associated with climate change – especially above 2°C?

- Which scenario do we use as our 'central case' internally? Why has that scenario been chosen? What average temperature rise would that central case equate to, with what probability?
- How do we assess 'materiality' in relation to these risks – for both corporate performance and risk management purposes? Over what time frames?
- What are our company's strategic options for managing these risks (including any corporate emissions reductions targets) and taking advantage of associated opportunities? How does this impact and factor into our strategy formulation, business planning and capex more broadly? Over what time frames? Do these options and/or our preferred strategy differ depending on which forward-looking scenario is applied? How do we integrate the identification, assessment, management, monitoring and reporting of these risks into our risk management processes?
- How do we determine the relative significance and priority given to these risks in relation to other risks?
- Do we need to adjust the recognition or booked value of our assets (and/or impairments, liability provisions) to account for our assessment of stranded asset risks? Why/why not?
- What signposts do we monitor to gauge whether our central (and other) case assumptions require revision? What are the trigger points for our re-assessment of these issues?
- How do we engage with, or otherwise seek to influence, stakeholders in relation to these risks and our management of them – beyond business fencelines? for example government, suppliers, customers and so on?
- How are these risks, the processes by which we assess them and their materiality and our response to them, disclosed in our annual reports and other disclosure documents (including mandatory financial statements (and the notes thereto) and directors'/strategic report filings, continuous disclosure obligations and fund raising disclosure documents)? What scenarios do we publish? If these differ from the range of scenarios applied for internal risk management and planning purposes, why have these scenarios been selected for disclosure?
- Does our reporting align with any mandatory requirements that apply, as well as leading voluntary guidance such as (for example) the Final Recommendations of the G20 FSB TCFD? Why/why not?
- Are our mandatory filing disclosures consistent with voluntary disclosures that our company has made (e.g. in response to CDP [formerly the

Carbon Disclosure Project] and AODP [Asset Owners Disclosure Project] questionnaires)?

- Has a review been done of our remuneration policies and structures at board and executive level to ensure that there are no perverse incentives that may favour capex/investment in assets that are at risk of being stranded? Conversely, have we considered opportunities to link consideration of climate change risks and opportunities to remuneration policies?
- What governance structures are appropriate to enable us to discharge our strategic and oversight duties in relation to this category of financial risk? How do we monitor and oversee compliance with climate-related laws, goals and targets – and those in relation to stranded asset risks (and opportunities) in particular? What reports do and should we receive?
- What processes are in place to ensure that we as a board and executive management maintain current awareness of this issue?

It must be emphasised that whether a board's governance of the stranded assets issue is duly diligent will necessarily be unique to the circumstances of each case – and so inherently ill suited to prescription via 'checklist'. Accordingly, it is not suggested that a failure to be appropriately informed of (and consider) any one (or more) of the listed points of information would necessarily be determinative of a breach of duty in any particular case. However, this list illustrates the breadth and depth of information that may be required for directors of companies in the energy and resources sector to obtain assurance that a robust interrogation of stranded asset risk exposures has been undertaken by their company and themselves as a governing board.

FAILURE TO OBTAIN INDEPENDENT ADVICE

In complex situations requiring specialised knowledge directors are not only permitted but can be required to seek out expert or professional advice from within or outside their company in order to satisfy their duty of due care and diligence (see generally Hutley and Hartford-Davis 2016). This applies both in their consideration of the *strategic* response to stranded asset risks and as an input into significant capex or acquisition decisions.

For example, in *Smith v. Van Gorkom* (at 878) the court held that the fact that the directors lacked expert advice prior to their consideration of a merger proposal contributed to the conclusion that it 'lacked valuation information adequate to reach an informed business judgment as to the fairness [of the price]' and the finding that the Delaware directors were grossly negligent. This was despite the fact that (at 876) 'fairness opinions by independent investment bankers are [not] required as a matter of law' – although were customary as a matter of practice. By analogy, in a stranded assets context, this case suggests that a board may be liable for gross negligence (and, by extrapolation, breach the lower standard of 'mere' negligence that applies in jurisdictions such as Australia and, potentially, the UK) where they fail to seek an independent assessment of the stranded asset risks in respect of an asset prior to purchase or in relation to significant capital expenditure.

In particular, in informing themselves of (and critically evaluating) the issues listed, directors would be likely to require the input of independent, expert advice on this dynamic and specialised area – including in relation to issues such as relevant technological trends and costs of substitute lower-emissions products, carbon pricing regimes, emissions reduction scenarios, the likelihood of each scenario crystallising and the impacts of each on price and demand, asset valuation, strategy and financial planning.

Where advice has been sought, an issue will still arise as to whether the directors' process of delegation and evaluation of the advice received will be sufficient to satisfy the duty of care. Relevant concerns may include where the 'expert' advisor was not appropriately qualified or independent or their advice was coloured by a set of biased or inadequate assumptions. These issues are considered under a failure to 'critically evaluate' in what follows.

FAILURE TO CRITICALLY EVALUATE

In all three jurisdictions, directors are entitled to rely on the advice provided by management and experts. However, the entitlement is not absolute. In each case, the duty of care requires more than passive acceptance of information provided by management or independent experts. Rather, the law requires directors to assess such information with a 'critical eye' in their pursuit of the best interests of the corporation.[90] 'Blind reliance' (Delaware),[91] 'unquestioning reliance' (UK)[92] or 'complete and sole reliance' (Australia)[93] on the conclusions of appointed experts are unlikely to satisfy the directors' duty of care. The obligation may conceivably extend to interrogation of the scope of the advisor's instructions or related limitations/assumptions where those parameters indicate that the brief may have been engineered to produce a conclusion that is consistent with a pre-determined outcome or course of action.[94]

A failure of critical evaluation may also arise where directors fail to assure themselves that the delegate or advisor was reasonably competent to provide the relevant advice (by reference to either their qualifications or independence). In particular, it is conceivable that directors may not discharge their duty of care where they obtain advice *only* from advisors who, by their mission or articulated policies, may have interests skewed towards a particular outcome (such as the American Petroleum Institute or Minerals Council of Australia on the one hand or the World Wildlife Fund on the other).[95]

Further analogies may be drawn to other cases in which directors have breached their duty of due care, such as when:

- directors failed to make inquiries and were satisfied with superficial or inadequate answers in relation to issues critical to the risks of a proposed transaction.[96] In a stranded assets context, this may arise when (for example) the advice to directors is based on outdated demand data/projections or renewable energy power cost/penetration rates or by applying an unrealistically low shadow price on carbon in capex and financial planning decisions or when

- directors deferred, without independent review, to the conclusions of management and external auditors in relation to whether financial statements presented a true and fair view of company performance and prospects.[97] In a stranded assets context, this may include a failure to ensure that stranded asset risks have been considered in the preparation of financial statements (to avoid any material overstatement of assets of under-provisioning of liabilities) and/or adequately disclosed in the accompanying management reports.

To the latter point, scenario analysis and stress testing (including against the sub-2°C scenario contemplated under the Paris Agreement) are rapidly emerging as benchmark tools to aid the formulation of a corporation's strategic response to climate-related risks, their management and disclosure. The disclosure of this information (with the implicit presumption that it would reflect underlying strategy and risk management) has in fact been the primary focus of shareholder resolutions seeking disclosure by fossil fuel companies (and the financial services companies that finance their operations) in recent years. It is increasingly the subject of 'soft-law' guidance by regulators such as the Australian Prudential Regulation Authority and influential, industry-led frameworks such as that promulgated by the TCFD. It is also a central requirement of mandatory disclosure regimes emerging in Europe and in US states such as California. Accordingly, the courts may, increasingly, be persuaded such analysis is essential to the discharge of directorial due care and diligence in the energy and resources sector. Liability risks may be particularly acute in Australia (of the three jurisdictions considered), for reasons including: (i) the courts have been particularly progressive in holding directors to high standards of proactivity and professionalism, (ii) a significant proportion of the economy is tied to sectors with high stranded asset risks, with more than half of the value of the Australian Stock Exchange comprised of corporations in the resources and financial services sectors, (iii) corporate leadership on the application and disclosure of climate risk stress testing already being undertaken by listed companies including BHP Billiton and AGL and (iv) an explicit expectation expressed by the Australian Prudential Regulation Authority that 'sophisticated scenario-based analysis of climate risks at the firm level' is the 'new standard' for risk management (APRA 2017, pp. 4–5).

FAILURE TO MONITOR/DULY OVERSEE/SUPERVISE (UK AND AUSTRALIA)

In the UK and Australia,[98] directors may also breach their obligations of due care and diligence where the process of deliberation on stranded asset risks is compromised by a failure to monitor – that is, to assure themselves that management has implemented a compliance, risk and reporting system that effectively identifies and manages stranded asset–related risks. This may be a product of 'negligent oversight' of corporate systems or in the supervision of management. The relevant oversight omission may also include a failure to ensure that management has considered the resilience of business plans against a sub-2°C scenario, as outlined.

3.5.3 Conclusion – duty of due care and diligence

In all three jurisdictions, it is likely that a director who is uninformed as to the risks relating to stranded assets or who makes no conscious decision or judgment on this issue in their consideration of corporate strategy, planning and risk management or in their consideration of transactions coming before them for approval would fail to discharge their duty of due care and diligence. In all three jurisdictions, the board is required to inquire where information is not presented to them and to seek advice on specialist and complicated issues.

It is also likely that inadequate consideration of stranded asset risks will breach their duty – although the point at which a failing will manifest as breach will vary under the laws of each jurisdiction and on the facts of each particular case. In Australia (in particular), courts tend to hold directors to particularly high standards of proactivity, professionalism and robust process. When considered in concert with the magnitude of stranded asset risks for companies in the energy and resources sector (which make up a significant portion of the value listed on the Australian Stock Exchange), the courts in that jurisdiction are likely to hold directors to higher standards of proactive inquiry, expert advice (from management or independent specialists) and board evaluation of relevant issues. Moreover, Australian courts have shown a specific propensity to hold directors liable for deficiencies in the parameters or assumptions in which the advice or reports of delegates are based.

At the other extreme, it must be acknowledged that the constraints imposed by the business judgment rule presumption and ubiquitous damages immunity operate to significantly limit the window of credible claims against directors under Delaware law. However, at least as a matter of legal theory, it does not shut that window completely. In particular, an 'independent and disinterested' director, acting honestly and in good faith, is likely to remain exposed to a claim for a breach of their duty of care where they exhibit a total or manifestly inadequate failure to consider the risks associated with climate change in their consideration of a particular transaction or acquisition *and* where the claim is not barred under the company's articles of incorporation. That is a narrow window, potentially only open where:

- the business judgment rule can be rebutted due to gross negligence – that is, where: (a) the directors fail to consider *all material information reasonably available* – in circumstances where there is an enormous, high-profile – and ever-increasing – volume of commercial information on stranded asset risks and/or (b) they fail to seek expert advice on point where that is clearly warranted and/or (c) they 'blindly accept' advice from delegates or experts without their own critical evaluation; and
- the claim does not *solely* seek monetary damages.[99] This is because the permitted directorial exculpation does not extend to actions seeking injunctive

relief or rescission (Lubben and Darnell 2006). Accordingly, it is unlikely to bar a derivative claim for breach of the duty of care when the plaintiff shareholders are seeking to injunct a particular transaction from proceeding (for example, a large acquisition of coal, oil or gas reserves, or infrastructure investments when stranded asset or other physical or economic transition risks associated with climate change have not been considered in the corporation's commercial assessments).

Moreover, a determination that a claim for a failure of due care is exculpated by the constitutional immunity does not preclude claims for all breaches of fiduciary duty – particularly when the conduct contravenes not only the duty of due care but those of loyalty and good faith (as considered in Part 3.2). Indeed, as noted by Velasco, the limitations on personal liability for a breach of a director's duty of care have led both plaintiffs and the courts to emphasise those elements of the claims that overlap with the duty of loyalty (Velasco 2015, p. 653).

Finally, the duty of disclosure/candour or a claim under securities laws for misleading or fraudulent disclosures may be strategically deployed as an alternative cause of action to prosecute inadequate consideration or analysis by Delaware company directors (and those of other jurisdictions). This may provide an avenue of potential claim in which the governance conduct, albeit deficient, is not so egregious as to trigger the court's review under the duty of care. Directors' liability for misleading disclosure is raised, in brief, in Part 4.

4. Other actions: misleading disclosure/securities fraud

The focus of this chapter lies squarely on directors' potential liability for inadequate climate risk governance under their core duties. However, it is also worth noting another significant and often related claim that may be raised against directors of listed corporations under prevailing corporations and securities laws, *viz*, liability for misleading disclosure or securities fraud. The Bank of England Prudential Regulation Authority has explicitly warned that claims alleging misleading disclosure are likely to be amongst the 'quickest to evolve' in relation to climate risk (BoEPRA 2015, p. 59).

In fact, with the focus of this chapter on directors' duties, it bears note that in some jurisdictions directors have a *duty*, as an incident of their other core duties, to ensure that the corporation does not issue misleading disclosures to the market. For example, Delaware law recognises that directors have a 'duty to disclose' as a sub-set of their duties of loyalty and care. In Australia, recent case law has recognised that misleading corporate disclosures can be a 'stepping stone' to establishing liability for a breach of the directors' duty of care under section 180(1) of the *Corporations Act* (see generally Teele-Langford 2016).[100]

The limited scope of this chapter does not permit detailed discussion of misleading disclosure and/or securities fraud in a climate risk context – *viz* the circumstances in which a disclosure (or omission) of climate risk–related issue does not present a true and fair view of the corporation's performance, risks management or prospects. Such analysis itself warrants an entire chapter. However, the potential for directors to be exposed to liability – both primary and accessorial – for such corporate misstatements must be duly noted in any commentary or analysis of this area.

5. Conclusion

This chapter has sought to interrogate the question of what forms of governance action (or inaction) in relation to stranded asset risk exposures are likely to breach the duties of company directors in the energy and resources sector. The precise answer to that question will, of course, turn on the minutiae of the corporate governance laws in each jurisdiction, along with the particularities of the particular company's exposures and risk management systems. However, a number of general principles may be derived from the foregoing analysis, which are suggestive of areas that warrant specific consideration in given circumstances.

5.1 Duty of loyalty

Directors of energy and resources companies who fail to proactively govern for stranded asset risks may breach their duty(s) of loyalty, specifically the duties to:

- act in good faith, in the best interests of the company and/or to promote its success. This risk is particularly acute where the failure emanates from a personal view of climate change scepticism or denialism, which is in turn a product of the director loyalty to extraneous political interests or associations; and
- avoid (or appropriately manage) material conflicts of interest. This risk primarily accrues where there is a material conflict between the directors' financial remuneration (esp. where the discretionary or contingent components are tied to 'business-as-usual' strategies, such as fossil fuel reserve replacement ratios) and the best financial interests of the company.

Directors of Delaware corporations may also breach a particular sub-set of their duties of good faith and loyalty, the duty to monitor, when their failure to adequately monitor compliance mechanisms facilitates the corporation's breach of emissions regulations or securities law disclosure obligations. Under the relevant *Caremark* principles, this would require proof of the directors' actual knowledge that their corporation's misconduct was being legally challenged or investigated (the red flag – for example, regulatory investigations into its compliance with emissions regulations or securities fraud allegations over a failure to restate the booked value of stranded assets) and that they then failed to ensure that the corporation had adequate systems and processes in place to mitigate that risk (which failure caused the harm to the company). Such a claim would be difficult to make out but is not inconceivable (at least in theory) on the basis of prevailing case law.

5.2 Duty of due care and diligence

Directors' duties of 'competence' are given force in obligations that require they exercise due care, skill and diligence in the discharge of their position. The standard against which conduct is tested varies between jurisdictions (for example, as against that of the 'ordinary prudent person' under Delaware law to that of a 'reasonable director' in Australia), as does the degree of failure or culpability required in order to establish liability ('gross negligence' in Delaware, more akin to 'mere' negligence in Australia).

Whilst courts are reluctant to reconsider the commercial merits of substantive judgments, they will hold directors to account for a failure breach their duty of due care and diligence if they fail to consider material stranded asset risks – at all or where that consideration was arrived upon under an inadequate process of deliberation. Whether the decision-making process satisfies the standards of due care and diligence required in a particular jurisdiction will turn on factors that include whether:

- material information has been proactively obtained and considered;
- advice of appropriately qualified delegates/independent experts has been obtained where warranted; and
- the decision has been arrived at under a process of critical evaluation.

Particular circumstances that may be suggestive of a failure to apply due care and diligence to stranded asset risk issues include:

- lack of awareness of the material physical and economic transition risks to the corporation arising from climate change (whether due to climate change denial or honest ignorance);
- a failure to ascertain whether advisors are appropriately qualified, competent and independent;
- blind or unquestioning reliance on the recommendations of advisors;
- a failure to scenario plan/stress test business plans and transactional outcomes against a range of potential climate futures (including 'adverse' scenarios, such as the < 2°C warming ceiling agreed to by the parties to the Paris Agreement); and, particularly in Australia,
- a failure to interrogate the parameters, assumptions and methodologies on which advice is based.

5.3 Observations on particular jurisdictions

As a general statement, the Australian corporate governance framework presents as imposing the most stringent expectations of directorial conduct – in relation to both duties and misleading disclosure. Litigation exposures in that jurisdiction are compounded by the strong prosecutorial presence of the independent regulator, ASIC.

By comparison, there is little case law in the UK, and duties are only enforceable at the petition of the company itself (or its shareholders, acting derivatively).

Plaintiffs also face significant enforcement hurdles under Delaware law due to the 'business judgment rule' presumption, the secondary 'entire fairness' test (most relevantly for duties of loyalty) and the ubiquitous directors' damages immunity provided under corporate articles of incorporation (damages claims for breach of the duty of due care and diligence). However, there remain circumstances in which a failure to govern for stranded asset risks may be actionable even under the constraints of the Delaware regime. These include:

- a breach of the duties of good faith, best interests and/or conflicts of interest (as mentioned), to which the damages immunity does not apply; and
- claims for breach of the duty of due care and diligence (as discussed) where the relief sought extends beyond that for damages (injunctive relief, rescission etc.), to which the damages immunity, again, does not apply.

Moreover, Delaware corporations (and their directors) may face significant litigation exposures for misleading disclosure/securities fraud under state-based 'blue sky' securities laws. Those laws (such as the New York Martin Act, enforced by the New York Attorney-General) impose obligations akin to those under the Australian misleading disclosure regime – a threshold for illegality that, unlike the securities fraud provisions of the federal Securities Exchange Act 1934, does not require proof of knowledge or intent.

Whilst enforcement challenges may prevail, the analysis in this chapter demonstrates that the prospect of board liability exposure for a failure to govern for the risks associated with climate change cannot be dismissed. The potential for such an action is credible, the stakes mean that incentives for directors and their insurers to settle is high, and the capacity of determined litigants – whether driven by economic loss or environmental belief – should not be underestimated.

To conclude with the words of Noel Hutley SC (Hutley and Hartford-Davis 2016, p. 51):

> It is likely to be only a matter of time before we see litigation against a director who has failed to perceive, disclose or take steps in relation to a foreseeable climate-related risk that can be demonstrated to have cause harm to a company (including, perhaps, reputational harm).[101]

Directors in sectors with acute stranded asset risks would be well advised to heed this as a signal to fortify their approach to governance on point.

Acknowledgements

Author association: Special Counsel, MinterEllison; PhD candidate, School of Law, University of Melbourne; Academic Visitor, Oxford Sustainable Finance Programme, Smith School of Enterprise and the Environment, University of Oxford.

This chapter was partly written with funding provided by the Australian Federal Government under an Australian Government Research Training Program Scholarship.

Notes

1 The law of the state of Delaware is being applied as proxy for the 'US corporate law' for the purposes of this chapter. Despite the diminutive size of that State's area and populous, it is this State in which the majority of public companies in the US are incorporated.

2 Such stakeholders include, for example, the 195 government signatories to the Paris Agreement in December 2015 (UNFCCC 2015); regulators such as APRA 2016, the Bank of England 2015 and SEC 2010; the world's largest asset owners and managers from AXA Group 2017 to BlackRock 2016, Norges Bank Investment Management 2017, Schroders 2017 to Vanguard 2017 and the UN Principles of Responsible Investment (representing USD59 trillion in assets under management, or close to half the total global institutional asset base) (see Sullivan et al. 2015); and credit ratings agencies such as Standard & Poors 2015 and Moody's 2017 – to name but a few.

3 For example, in May 2017 special shareholder resolutions seeking analysis and disclosure of stranded asset risks under Paris Agreement climate targets were passed by a majority of shareholders, against the recommendation of management, at the AGMs of ExxonMobil (62.3% in favour) and Occidental Petroleum (67%). Similar resolutions were filed in the 2017 US reporting season at companies including Dominion Resources (48%) and Duke Energy (46%) and Southern Co. (46%), although the resolutions narrowly failed to attract majority shareholder support. This followed the passage of special shareholder resolutions at the 2015 AGMs of European oil giants Shell, BP and Statoil requiring them to stress test their forward strategies against potential climate change futures endorsed by the International Energy Agency (including one consistent with limiting global warming to < 2°C above pre-industrial averages). These resolutions were both supported by the board and passed with resounding majorities of 98.3, 99.8 and 99.9% of the shareholder votes, respectively. Similar resolutions were passed, again by significant majorities, at the 2016 AGMs of multi-national resource companies such as Anglo American, Rio Tinto and Glencore. See also BlackRock. *Engagement Priorities 2017–18.* Available at: www.blackrock.com/corporate/en-us/about-us/investment-stewardship/engagement-priorities; Proxy Preview. *Proxy Preview 2017.* Available at: www.proxypreview.org/proxy-preview-2017/

4 See for example under the Delaware General Corporation Law §141(a): '*The business and affairs of every corporation organized under this chapter shall be managed by or under the direction of a board of directors . . .*'.; section 198A of the *Corporations Act 2001.*

5 *Charitable Corp. v. Sutton*, 2 Atk. 400, 406, 26 Eng. Rep. 642, 645 (Ch. 1742).

6 See for example under Australian law Murphy JA (with whom McLure P and Buss JA agreed on this point) in *Streeter v. Western Areas Exploration Pty Ltd [No.2]* (2011) 29 ACLC ¶11–012, at 364–365: 'The critical feature of a fiduciary relationship is that the fiduciary undertakes or agrees to act for or in the interest of another person. The fiduciary acts in a representative character', applying *Hospital Products Ltd v. United States Surgical Corporation* [1984] HCA 64; (1984) 156 CLR 41, 96–97; *Pilmer v. The Duke Group Ltd (in liq)* [2001] HCA 31; (2001) 207 CLR 165, 196–197 [71]; *John Alexander Tennis Club v. White City Tennis Club* (2010) 241 CLR 1, [87] (French CJ, Gummow, Hayne, Heydon, and Kiefel JJ). Under United States law, see REST 3d TRUSTS § 2, comment b: '[A] person in a fiduciary relationship to another is under a duty to act for the benefit of the other as to matters within the scope of the relationship.' Under UK law, see for example *Bristol and West Building Society v. Mothew* [1998]

Ch 1, 18: a fiduciary is 'someone who has undertaken to act for or on behalf of another in a particular matter in circumstances which give rise to a relationship of trust and confidence'.

7 For judicial authority that the duty to exercise reasonable care is *not* 'fiduciary' in character under UK law, see *Madoff Securities International Ltd (in liquidation) v. Raven* [2013] WL 5338134 at para. 209 and *Maidment v. Attwood & Ors* [2012] EWCA Civ 998, ara 22; and in Australia: *Breen v. Williams* (1996) 186 CLR 1 and *Australian Securities and Investments Commission (ASIC) v. Rich* (at 7190).

8 See also *Invensys Australia Superannuation Fund Pty Ltd v. Austrac Investments* (2006) 198 FLR 302 at 324.

9 For a discussion of the causal connection required between a director's omission or failure to act and the plaintiff's loss, see for example under UK law *Lexi Holdings (in administration) v. Luqman* [2009] EWCA Civ 117, [2009] 2 BCLC 1, [2009] BCC 716; *Bishopsgate Investment Management Ltd (in liquidation) v. Maxwell (No 2)* [1994] 1 All ER 261 at 264, [1993] BCLC 1282 at 1285, per Hoffmann LJ.

10 See for example *McGellin v. Mount King Mining NL* (1998) 144 FLR 288; *Chan v. Zacharia* (1984) 154 CLR 178 at 199 ("significant possibility" of conflict); *Hospital Products Ltd v. United States Surgical Corp* (1984) 156 CLR 41 at 103 ("a real or substantial possibility of a conflict") and *Bell Group Ltd (in liq) v. Westpac Banking Corporation (No 9)* (2008) 70 ACSR 1 at [4506] and [4508] (in which Owen J used the terms "a real sensible possibility of conflict" and "a real or substantial possibility of conflict.").

11 See for example *Bell Group Ltd (in liq) v. Westpac Banking Corporation (No 9)* (2008) 70 ACSR 1 at [4509].

12 This duty is based on the equitable principle that directors must act bona fide in what they consider to be the best interests of the company as a whole*: Re Smith & Fawcett Ltd* (1942) Ch 304, 306*; Item Software (UK) Ltd v. Fassihi* (2004). It turns on the director's subjective state of mind: *Birdi v. Specsavers Optical Group Ltd* [2015] EWHC 2870 (Ch) at [61], [2015] All ER (D) 144 (Oct)).

13 *Re Smith & Fawcett Ltd* [1942] Ch 304, 306.

14 See for example *Extrasure Travel Insurances Ltd v. Scattergood* [2002] EWHC 3093 (Ch) at [92], [2003] 1 BCLC 598 at [92].

15 *Boardman v. Phipps* [1967] 2 AC 46 at 124, [1966] 3 All ER 721 at 756, per Lord Upjohn; *Bhullar v. Bhullar* [2003] EWCA Civ 424, [2003] 2 BCLC 241.

16 *Simtel Communications Ltd v. Rebak* [2006] EWHC 572; [2006] 2 BCLC 571.

17 *Aronson*, 473 A.2d at 811 (citing *Guth v. Loft, Inc.*, 5 A.2d 503 (Del. 1939)).

18 *Disney, 906 A.2d at 63*; see generally Egan 2016.

19 *Solash v. Telex Corp.*, No. 9518, 9528, 9525, 1988 WL 3587, at *7 (Del. Ch. 1988).

20 *Cede & Co. v. Technicolor, Inc.*, 634 A.2d 345, 362 (Del. 1993).

21 *Chen v. Howard-Anderson*, 87 A.3d 648 (Del. Ch. 2014).

22 *Chen v. Howard-Anderson*, 87 A.3d 648 (Del. Ch. 2014).

23 *Cede & Co. v. Technicolor, Inc.*, 634 A.2d 345, 364 (Del. 1993).

24 *Stone v. Ritter*, 911 A.2d 362, 370 (Del. 2006).

25 *In re Caremark Int'l Inc. Deriv. Litig.*, 698 A.2d 959 (Del. Ch. 1996)

26 *Caremark*, 698 A.2d at 970. See also *In re Citigroup Inc. S'holder Derivative Litig.*, 964 A.2d 106, 123 (Del. Ch. 2009); *In re Massey Energy Co.*, C.A. No. 5430-VCS, 2011 BL 14964 (Del. Ch. May 31, 2011); *Rich v. Chong*, C.A. No. 7616-VCG, 2013 BL 177416 (Del. Ch. July 2, 2013). Justice Jacobs (speaking extra-curially) in fact recognised the doctrinal problems created by the *Caremark* decision in its failure to clearly articulate what category of fiduciary duty the oversight duty belonged to – care, loyalty, or 'good faith'. Justice Jacobs clarifies (Jacobs 2015, 151) that it was ten years later that *Stone v. Ritter* 'enabled that court to confirm Caremark as settled Delaware law and bad faith as the standard of liability for an oversight violation'.

27 *Stone v. Ritter*, 911 A.2d 362, 370 (Del. 2006).
28 *In re General Motors Company Derivative Litigation Consolidated* C.A. No. 9627-VCG at 39–40.
29 *In Re Citigroup Inc. Shareholder Derivative Litigation* 964 A.2d at 114–15, 126–27. In rejecting the plaintiff's claim (at 129–131), the court found that: (a) directors may only be liable under *Caremark* principles for failing to prevent or halt misconduct or breaches of the law and (b) the court will not hold directors liable for business decisions that later prove to have been unwise. The narrow interpretation of the *Caremark* principles by the court in *Citigroup* has been subject to some criticism by commentators – see for example Pan 2010, 2. See also *In re Goldman Sachs Grp., Inc. S'holder Litig.*, C.A. No. 5215-VCG (Del. Ch. Oct. 12, 2011).
30 *Aronson v. Lewis*, 473 A.2d 805, 812 (Del.1984) ((citing *Kaplan v. Centex Corp.*, 284 A.2d 119, 124 (Del. Ch. 1971)), overruled on other grounds by *Brehm v. Eisner*, 746 A.2d 244 (Del.2000), *Espinoza v. Dimon* 797 F.3d 229 (2015).
31 *Gesoff v. IIC Indus., Inc.*, 902 A.2d 1130, 1145 (Del. Ch. 2006) stands for the proposition that the entire fairness test is an objective one: in other words, the transaction must be *objectively* fair, rather than dependent on the honest belief of the directors.
32 *Cede & Co. v. Technicolor, Inc.*, 634 A.2d 345, 361 (Del. 1993). The entire fairness review requires the court to 'consider carefully how the board of directors discharged all if its fiduciary duties with respect to each aspect of the non-bifurcated components of entire fairness: fair dealing and fair price' – see *Emerald Partners v. Berlin* 787 A.2d 85, 97 (Del. 2001). The assessment of fair dealing involves consideration of the transaction's timing, how it was initiated, structured and negotiated, and the manner in which the requisite approvals were obtained. Fair price involves an assessment of the economic and financial issues underlying the transaction: see for example *Weinberger v. UOP Inc.*, 457 A.2d 701 (Del. 1983).
33 Or under the terms of section 172(1) of the UK *Companies Act*, failed, in good faith, to 'promote the success of the company for the benefit of its members as a whole'.
34 *In re Disney*, 906 A.2d at 63.
35 See for example *Hirsche v. Sims* [1894] AC 654, 660.
36 *Louisiana Municipal Police Retirement System et al v. Pyott et al* C.A. No. 5795-VCL (Del. Ch.) at 45–46, internal citations omitted.
37 See for example *In re Abbott Laboratories Derivative Shareholders Litigation*, 325 F.3d 795, 804 (7th Cir. 2003).
38 In *re SAIC Inc. Derivative Litigation*, 948 F. Supp. 2d 366 (S.D.N.Y. 2013) (aff'd in *Welch v. Havenstein*, No. 13–2648-cv, 2014 WL 322055 (2d Cir. Jan. 30, 2014)), the District Court acknowledged that the magnitude and duration of the underlying misconduct may be probative of whether directors had actual or constructive knowledge of wrongdoing and that there may be exceptional circumstances in which news coverage of the company's misconduct is so pervasive that it created a 'reasonable inference' of knowledge as no director could credibly claim to have missed it (although, in that case, reports in such small publications as *CityLimits* and *IEEE Spectrum Risk Factor* did not reach that standard of pervasiveness).
39 *Louisiana Municipal Police Retirement System et al v. Pyott et al* ('the *Botox Derivative Case*') C.A. No. 5795-VCL (Del. Ch.) (at 81), the Court quotes Chancellor Allen's observation in the Caremark judgment that: '[A] *Caremark* theory "is possibly the most difficult theory in corporation law upon which a plaintiff might hope to win a judgment." But "difficult" does not mean "impossible".'
40 *In re Target Inc. Shareholder Derivative Litigation*, No. 14-cv-203 (D.C. Minnesota), Motion to Dismiss granted 7 July 2016; *In re The Home Depot, Inc. Shareholder Derivative Litigation*, No.1:15-CV-2999-TWT (D.C. Northern District of Georgia), Motion to Dismiss granted 30 November 2016; *In re Wyndham Worldwide Corporation* Civil Action *Shareholder Derivative Litigation*, No. 2:14-CV-01234 (SRC) (D.C. New Jersey), Motion to Dismiss granted 20 October 2014.

41 *In re The Wendys Company Shareholder Derivative Complaint*, CASE NO.: 1:16-cv-1153 (D.C. Southern District of Ohio), complaint filed 8 December 2016.

42 *ASIC v. Rich* (2003) 44 ACSR 341, [35]; *ASIC v. Rich* (2009) 75 ACSR 1, [7201], citing *Commonwealth Bank of Australia v. Friedrich* (1991) 5 ACSR 15, 123; *ASIC v. Vines* (2005) 55 ACSR 617, [1067]; *Daniels v. Anderson* (1995) 37 NSWLR 438, 505.

43 *ASIC v. Healey & Ors* [2011] FCA 717 (*Centro*), [16], [143] and [162]. See also *ASIC v. Rich* (2009) 75 ACSR 1, [7205–6].

44 *Wyong Shire Council v. Shirt* (1980) 146 CLR 40, 47, applied in *ASIC v. Rich* (2009) 75 ACSR 1, [7231, 7236] and *ASIC v. Vines* (approved by the Court of Appeal in *Vines v. ASIC* (2007) 25 ACLC 448); *ASIC v. Ingleby* (2012) 91 ASCR 66, 69. For a general discussion of the application of the duty of due care and diligence under section 180 of the Corporations Act to the governance of climate-related risks, see Hutley and Hartford-Davis 2016.

45 See generally *Centro* [2011] FCA 717, [16], [143] and [162]. See also *ASIC v. Rich* (2009) 75 ACSR 1, [7205–6].

46 Ibid.

47 *Daniels v. Anderson* (1995) 37 *NSWLR* 438, 502, applied in *Centro* [2011] FCA 717, 646, [125]. Similarly, the director's conduct will be judged in the context of their *actual* responsibilities within the organisation in addition to their statutory responsibilities and those formalised in the company constitution or by board resolution: *Shafron v. ASIC* (2012) 286 ALR 612; *ASIC v. Rich* (2009) 75 ACSR 1, 614.

48 *Centro* [2011] FCA 717, [16], [143] and [162]. See also *ASIC v. Rich* (2009) 75 ACSR 1, [7203].

49 *Alcoa of Australia Retirement Plan Pty Ltd v. Frost* [2012] VSCA 238, Nettle JA at [47–48], in relation to the determination of a fund member's entitlement to TPD benefits. Section 56(3) of the SIS Act specifically contemplates that trustee directors should seek advice, and be indemnified out of the assets of the trust in doing so In the words of Deputy President Forgie in *Re VBN and APRA*: 'As essential as professional advice is, the trustees' obligation goes beyond merely seeking, accepting and following professional advice . . . the trustee [must] use their own acumen, knowledge and judgment in weighing all the relevant factors, including professional advice'. *VBN and Ors and Australian Prudential Regulation Authority and Anor* [2006] AATA 710; (2006) 92 ALD 259 (25 July 2006), 469.

50 *Finch v. Telstra*, at 254.

51 See for example *Tuftevski v. Total Risks Management Pty Ltd* [2009] NSWSC 1021, where a question arose as to what was required by way of enquiry on the part of a trustee in the context where the trustee had received material adverse to the employee's claim. Smart AJ held [at 16]: 'In my opinion bona fide enquiry and genuine decision making where these are required constitute an integral part of performing a fiduciary obligation. . . . The process followed by the Trustee . . . must involve deciding a question of fact in good faith and giving it real and genuine consideration. This often cannot be done without conducting some investigation and making relevant inquiries'.

52 *Centro* [2011] FCA 717.

53 Whether or not the directors' reliance on the advice of experts or employees was 'reasonable' is a question of fact in each case: *Permanent Building Society (in liq) v. Wheeler* (1994) 14 ACSR 109; 12 ACLC 674; *Vrisakis v. ASC* (1993) 9 WAR 395; 11 ACSR 162 at 215; 11 ACLC 763.

54 *In Re HIH Insurance Ltd (in prov liq); Australian Securities and Investments Commission v. Adler* (2004) 41 ACSR 72; 20 ACLC 576; [2002] NSWSC 171; BC200200827, at [451].

55 *Australian Securities and Investments Commission v. Citrofresh International Ltd (No 2)* (2010) 77 ACSR 69; 28 ACLC 10–002; [2010] FCA 27 at [54]–[59].

56 *Permanent Building Society (in liq) v. Wheeler* (1994) 14 ACSR 109; 12 ACLC 674; see also *Vrisakis v. ASC* (1993) 9 WAR 395; 11 ACSR 162 at 215; 11 ACLC 763.

57 *ASIC v. Healey & Ors* [2011] FCA 717.
58 *Micra Contracts Ltd (in Liquidation), Re* [2016] BCC 153, 160–161.
59 *Micra Contracts Ltd (in Liquidation), Re* [2016] BCC 153, 161.
60 See for example *Re Brian D Pierson (Contractors) Ltd* [2001] 1 BCLC 275.
61 [1999] 1 BCLC 433 at 489.
62 See for example *Weavering Capital (UK) Limited v. Dabhia and Platt* [2013] EWCA Civ 71.
63 *Re Bradcrown Ltd* [2002] BCC 428 at 439.
64 *Aronson v. Lewis*, 473 A.2d 805, 812 (Del.1984) (citing *Kaplan v. Centex Corp.*, 284 A.2d 119, 124 (Del. Ch. 1971)), overruled on other grounds by *Brehm v. Eisner*, 746 A.2d 244 (Del.2000); *Espinoza v. Dimon* 797 F.3d 229 (2015).
65 *Cede & Co. v. Technicolor, Inc.*, 634 A.2d 345, 361 (Del. 1993); *Steiner v. Meyerson*, 1995 WL 441999 (Del. Ch. 1995), at 5; and *Walt Disney*, 907 A.2d 693, at 747 (quoting *Sinclair Oil Corp. v. Levien*, 280 A.2d 717, 720 (Del.1971); *Unocal Corp v. Mesa Petroleum Co*, 493 A.2d 946, 954 (Del.1985).
66 See generally Jacobs2015; *Cede & Co. v. Technicolor, Inc.*, 634 A.2d 345, 367 (Del. 1993); *Smith v. Van Gorkom*, 488 A.2d 858, 873 (Del. 1985); *Aronson v. Lewis*, 473 A.2d 805, 812 (Del. 1984). See also *In re Walt Disney Derivative Litigation* 907 A.2d 693, at 747 (Del. Ch. 2005).
67 *McPadden v. Sidhu*, 964 A.2d 1262, 1273–74 (Del. Ch. 2008); *Rabkin v. Philip A. Hunt Chem. Corp.*, 547 A.2d 963, 970 (Del. Ch. 1986). See generally discussion in Lubben 2006. The Delaware standard of care may even be higher than that of gross negligence under common law precepts – see *Benihana of Tokyo, Inc. v. Benihana, Inc.*, 891 A.2d 150, 192 (Del. Ch. 2005) (quoting *Tomczak v. Morton Thiokol, Inc.*, No. 7861, 1990 WL 42607, at *12 (Del. Ch. Apr. 5, 1990)).
68 *Van Gorkon*, at 881 and 872: 'Under the business judgment rule there is no protection for directors who have made "an unintelligent or unadvised judgment'. *Mitchell v. Highland-Western Glass, Del.Ch., 167 A. 831, 833 (1933)*' and, at 873: 'We think the concept of gross negligence is also the proper standard for determining whether a business judgment reached by a board of directors was an informed one'.
69 *Rich ex rel. Fuqi Int'l, Inc. v. Yu Kwai Chong*, 66 A.3d 963, 979 (Del.Ch.2013) ('[T]he business judgment rule has no role where directors have either abdicated their functions, or absent a conscious decision, failed to act'. [internal quotation marks omitted]).
70 *Cede & Co. v. Technicolor, Inc.*, 634 A.2d 345, 371, 367 (Del. 1993), citing Aronson v. Lewis, 473 A.2d 805, 812 (Del.1984).
71 *Cede & Co. v. Technicolor, Inc.*, 634 A.2d 345, 368 (Del. 1993); *Smith v. Van Gorkom*, 488 A.2d 858, 873 (Del. 1985); *Aronson v. Lewis*, 473 A.2d 805, 812 (Del. 1984).
72 *Smith v. Van Gorkom*, 488 A.2d 858, 875 (Del. 1985).
73 *Cede & Co. v. Technicolor, Inc.*, 634 A.2d 345, 368 (Del. 1993); *Smith v. Van Gorkom*, 488 A.2d 858, 873 (Del. 1985); *Aronson v. Lewis*, 473 A.2d 805, 812 (Del. 1984).
74 In *In re Gaylord Container Corp. Shareholders' Litig.*, 753 A.2d 462, 479 (Del. Ch. 2000) the court held that the board's 'reliance on a reputable law form to advise it regarding its opinions supports a conclusion that the board acted on an informed basis'.
75 *Cede & Co. v. Technicolor, Inc.*, 634 A.2d 345, 368 (Del. 1993); *Smith v. Van Gorkom*, 488 A.2d 858, 873 (Del. 1985); *Aronson v. Lewis*, 473 A.2d 805, 812 (Del. 1984). See also discussion in Jacobs 2015, 145.
76 *Graham v. Allis-Chalmers Mfg. Co.*, 188 A.2d 125, 130 (Del. 1963) ('[D]irectors of a corporation in managing the corporate affairs are bound to use that amount of care which ordinarily careful and prudent men would use in similar circumstances'.) *In re Walt Disney Derivative Litigation* 907 A.2d 693, at 749 (Del. Ch. 2005).
77 *Smith v. Van Gorkom*, 488 A.2d 858, 875 (Del. 1985).
78 *Cede & Co. v. Technicolor, Inc.*, 634 A.2d 345, 369 (Del. 1993).
79 *Cede & Co. v. Technicolor, Inc.*, 634 A.2d 345, 368 (Del. 1993).

80 Specifically, §102(b)(7) of the Delaware General Corporation Law provides '(b) . . . the certificate of incorporation may also contain . . . (7) A provision eliminating or limiting the personal liability of a director to the corporation or its stockholders for monetary damages for breach of fiduciary duty as a director, provided that such provision shall not eliminate or limit the liability of a director: (i) For any breach of the director's duty of loyalty to the corporation or its stockholders; (ii) for acts or omissions not in good faith or which involve intentional misconduct or a knowing violation of law; (iii) under § 174 of this title; or (iv) for any transaction from which the director derived an improper personal benefit'.

81 In *Smith v. Van Gorkom* 48 A.2d 858 (Del. 1985) the Delaware Supreme Court found the defendant directors 'fail[ed] to inform themselves of all information reasonably available to them and relevant to their decision to recommend the . . . merger'. Per *Cinerama, Inc. v. Technicolor, Inc.*, 663 A.2d 1156, 1166 n.18 (Del. 1995) 'The statute was, in fact, a legislative response to this Court's liability holding in *Van Gorkom*'. See also *Malpiede v. Townson*, 780 A.2d 1075, 1095 (Del. 2001); Yeager 2015, 1388.

82 *In re Cornerstone Therapeutics Inc. Stockholder Litigation and Leal v. Meeks*, 115 A.3d 1173 (Del. 2015).

83 Under Australian law, see *ASIC v. Australian Property Custodian Holdings Ltd (recs and mgrs apptd) (in liq) (controllers apptd) (No 3)* [2013] FCA 1342 at [571]; applied in *Sharp v. Maritime Super Pty Ltd* [2013] NSWSC 389 at [33]. In the UK, see *Re Continental Assurance Company of London plc* [2007] 2 BCLC 287 at [399] per Park J: 'The duty is not to ensure that the company gets everything right. The duty is to exercise the reasonable care and skill up to the standard which the law expects of a director of the sort of company concerned, and also up to the standard capable of being achieved by the particular director concerned'; *Howard Smith Ltd v. Ampol Petroleum Ltd* [1974] AC 821 at 832; *Micra Contracts Ltd (in Liquidation), Re* [2016] BCC 153. Under Delaware law, see for example *Brehm v. Eisner* 746 A.2d 244, 264 (Del. 1998).

84 Under UK law, see *Overend, Gurney & Co v. Gibb and Gibb* (1872) LR 5 HL 480 at 487, 495; *Lagunas Nitrate Co v. Lagunas Syndicate* [1899] 2 Ch 392 at 435; *Re National Bank of Wales Ltd* [1899] 2 Ch 629, CA; *Re Brazilian Rubber Plantations and Estates Ltd* [1911] 1 Ch 425.

85 *ASIC v. Flugge* [2016] VSC 779.

86 For example, in *Madoff Securities International Ltd (in liquidation) v. Raven* [2013] WL 5338134 at para. 265, the UK High Court held that a failure to exercise reasonable care and skill could arise from a director's failure to turn their minds to the question whether a particular transaction was in the best interests of their company. See also discussion of Australian legal principles in Loechel, Hodgkinson and Moffat 2013, 473; and re US law in Smith and Morreale 2007, 497.

87 Under Australian law, see *Centro* [2011] FCA 717, [16], [143] and [162]; *ASIC v. Rich* (2009) 75 ACSR 1, [7203]; in the UK, see *Secretary of State for Trade and Industry v. Baker (No 5) (Re Barings)* (No 5) [1999] 1 BCLC 433 at 489: '(i) Directors have, both collectively and individually, a continuing duty to acquire and maintain a sufficient knowledge and understanding of the company's business to enable them properly to discharge their duties as directors'; under Delaware law, see *Cede & Co. v. Technicolor, Inc.*, 634 A.2d 345, 368 (Del. 1993); *Smith v. Van Gorkom*, 488 A.2d 858, 873 (Del. 1985); *Aronson v. Lewis*, 473 A.2d 805, 812 (Del. 1984).

88 In respect of Australian law, see Hutley and Hartford-Davis, *id.*, [41]; US law see *Van Gorkon*, 872; *Mitchell v. Highland-Western Glass*, Del.Ch., 167 A. 831, 833 (1933).

89 Moran v. Household Int'l, Inc., 490 A.2d 1059, 1075 (Del. Ch. 1985), *aff'd*, 500 A.2d 1346 (Del. 1985).

90 See *Van Gorkom*, 488 A.2d at 872.

91 *Smith v. Van Gorkom*, 488 A.2d 858, 873 (Del. 1985).

92 *Re Bradcrown Ltd* [2002] BCC 428 at 439; *Weavering Capital* [2013] EWCA Civ 7.

93 *ASIC v. Healey & Ors* [2011] FCA 717, [569], [580] and [582].

94 See for example under Australian law: *ASIC v. Hellicar* [2012] HCA 17; *Shafron v. ASIC* [2012] HCA 18; *ASIC v. Macdonald (No 11)* [2009] NSWSC 287; *ASIC v. Macdonald (No 12)* [2009] NSWSC 714; *Morley v. ASIC* [2010] NSWCA 331; *James Hardie Industries NV v. ASIC* [2010] NSWCA 332 (collectively, the 'James Hardie cases').

95 For example, in the Australian case of *ASIC v. Citrofresh International Ltd (No 2)* (2010) 77 ACSR 69; [2010] FCA 27 at [54]–[59] misleading disclosures were prepared in reliance on the advice of two consultants who were not experts in the relevant subject matter, nor otherwise held technical or scientific qualifications or experience that may have justified such reliance.

96 *Permanent Building Society (in liq) v. Wheeler* (1994) 14 ACSR 109; 12 ACLC 674.

97 *ASIC v. Healey & Ors* [2011] FCA 717, [175].

98 Under Delaware law, the 'duty to monitor' is an incident of the duties of good faith and loyalty rather than diligence or prudence, as discussed in Part 2.

99 See for example *Chen v. Howard-Anderson*, 87 A.3d 648 (Del. Ch. 2014).

100 *Australian Securities and Investments Commission v. Cassimatis (No 8)* [2016] FCA 1023; *Australian Securities and Investments Commission, in the matter of Padbury Mining Limited v. Padbury Mining Limited* [2016] FCA 990; *Australian Securities and Investments Commission, in the matter of Sino Australia Oil and Gas Limited (in liq) v. Sino Australia Oil and Gas Limited (in liq)* [2016] FCA 934.

101 Hutley and Hartford-Davis, *id.*, [51].

References

Books and articles

Allen, W. T., et al. 2001. Function Over Form: A Reassessment of Standards of Review in Delaware Corporation Law. *Business Law*, 56, 1287, 1302–1303.

Anam, A. 2012. A Critical Analysis of the UK Company Law Corporate Objective: Purposive, Practical and Possible: Longitudinal Corporate Objective to Remedy the Enlightened Shareholder Value Approach of the *Companies Act 2006*. *Unpublished, SSRN*, June 28. Available at: http://papers.ssrn.com/sol3/papers.cfm?abstract_id=2117591

Bainbridge, S. M. 2012. *Corporate Governance After the Financial Crisis*. New York: Oxford University Press.

Bainbridge, S. M., et al. 2008. The Convergence of Good Faith and Oversight. *UCLA Law Review*, 55, 559.

Barker, S., Baker-Jones, M., Fagan, E. and Barton, E. 2016. Climate Change and the Fiduciary Duties of Pension Fund Trustees – Lessons From the Australian Law. *Journal of Sustainable Finance & Investment*, 6(3), 211–244.

Barrett, P. and Philips, M. 2016. Can Exxon Mobil Be Found Liable for Misleading the Public on Climate Change? *Bloomberg Businessweek*, September 7. www.bloomberg.com/news/articles/2016-09-07/will-exxonmobil-have-to-pay-for-misleading-the-public-on-climate-change

Brown, J. R. Jr. and Gopalan, S. 2009. Opting Only In: Contractarians, Waiver of Liability Provisions, and the Race to the Bottom. *Indiana Law Review*, 42, 285.

Bruner, C. M. 2013. Is the Corporate Duty of Care a "Fiduciary" Duty? Does It Matter? *Wake Forest Law Review*, 48, 1027.

Collins, P. 2014. The Best Interests Duty and the Standard of Care for Superannuation Trustees. *Australian Library Journal*, 88(9), 632.

Easterbrook, F. and Fishel, D. 1991. *The Economic Structure of Corporate Law*. Cambridge, MA: Harvard University Press.

Edelman, J. 2014. The Role of Status in the Law of Obligations. In Gold, A. S. and Miller, P. B. (eds.), *Philosophical Foundations of Fiduciary Law*. Oxford: Oxford Scholarship Online.

Egan, B. 2016. Fiduciary Duties of Governing Persons of Business Entities. *38th Annual Conference on Securities & Business Law*, University of Texas, Dallas, February 12.

Freeman, R. E. 1984. *Strategic Management: A Stakeholder Approach*. Boston: Pittman.

Freeman, R. E. 2010. *Stakeholder Theory: State of the Art*. Cambridge: Cambridge University Press.

Friedman, M. 1962. *Capitalism and Freedom*. Chicago: University of Chicago Press.

Gelter, M. 2017. Mapping Types of Shareholder Law Suits Across Jurisdictions. In Erickson, J., Griffith, S., Webber, D. and Winship, V. (eds.), *Research Handbook on Shareholder Litigation. Fordham Law Legal Studies Research Paper No. 3011444; ECGI – Law Working Paper No. 363/2017*. Available at: https://ssrn.com/abstract=3011444

Gerner-Beuerle, C., Paech, P. and Schuster, E. P. 2013. *Study on Directors' Duties and Liability*. LSE Enterprise. Available at: http://ec.europa.eu/internal_market/company/docs/board/2013-study-analysis_en.pdf

Guyatt, D. 2015. *Climate Change Investment Solutions: A Guide for Asset Owners*. Report for the Global Investor Coalition on Climate Change, April 22, 2015. Available at: www.iigcc.org/publications/publication/climate-change-investment-solutions-a-guide-for-asset-owners

Hamermesh, L. A. 2000. Why I Do Not Teach Van Gorkom. *Georgia Law Review*, 24, 477.

Hargovan, A. and Harris, J. 2013. For Whom the Bell Tolls: Directors "Duties to Creditors After Bell". *Sydney Law Review*, 35, 433.

Hill, C. A. and McDonnell, B. 2012. Fiduciary Duties: The Emerging Jurisprudence. In Hill, C. A. and McDonnell, B. (eds.), *Research Handbook on the Economics of Corporate Law*. Cheltenham, UK and Northampton, MA: Edward Elgar Publishing, Chapter 8.

Jacobs, Justice J. B. 2015. Fifty Years of Corporate Law Evolution: A Delaware Judge's Retrospective. *Harvard Business Law Review*, 5, 141.

Jensen, M. C. 2001. Value Maximisation, Stakeholder Theory and Corporate Objective Function. *Journal of Applied Corporate Finance*, 8.

LaCroix, K. Data Related Derivative Suit Filed Against Wendy's. *The D&O Diary*, December 19. Available at: www.dandodiary.com/2016/12/articles/cyber-liability/data-breach-related-shareholder-derivative-lawsuit-filed-wendys/

Lafferty, W. M., Schmidt, L. A. and Wolfe Jr., D. J. 2012. A Brief Introduction to the Fiduciary Duties of Directors Under Delaware Law. *Penn State Law Review*, 116(3), 837.

Liddell, G. 2015. Fiduciary Duty and Climate Change. *Investment Operations & Custody*, May 24. Available at: http://ioandc.com/fiduciary-duty-and-climate-change/ [Accessed October 17, 2017]

Loechel, B., Hodgkinson, J. and Moffat, K. 2013. Climate Change Adaptation in Australian Mining Communities: Comparing Mining Company and Local Government Views and Activities. *Climate Change*, 119, 465.

Loughrey, J. 2013. The Director's Duty of Care and Skill and the Financial Crisis. In Loughrey, J. (ed.), *Directors' Duties and Shareholder Litigation in the Wake of the Financial Crisis*. Cheltenham, UK: Edwards Elgar, Chapter 1, p. 460.

Lubben, S. J. and Darnell, A. J. 2006. Delaware's Duty of Care. *Delaware Journal of Corporate Law*, 31, 589.

Magnier, V. 2017. *Comparative Corporate Governance*. Cheltenham, UK: Edward Elgar Publishing.

Marshall, S. and Ramsay, I. 2012. Stakeholders and Directors' Duties: Law, Theory and Evidence. *UNSW Law Journal*, 35(1), 291.

Miller, G. P. 2010. A Modest Proposal for Fixing Delaware's Broken Duty of Care. *Columbia Business Law Review*, 319.

Morwood, J. (ed.). 2001. *Pocket Oxford Latin Dictionary*. Oxford: Oxford University Press.

Pan, E. J. 2010. The Duty to Monitor Under Delaware Law: From *Caremark* to *Citigroup*. *Director Notes*, No. 4, February, p. 2.

Poon, A. 2017. An Examination of New York's Martin Act as a Tool to Combat Climate Change. *Boston College Environmental Affairs Law Review*, 44(1), 115.

Richardson, B. 2012. Fiduciary and Other Legal Duties. In Baker, H. K. and Nofsinger, J. (eds.), *Socially Responsible Finance and Investing: Financial Institutions, Corporations, Investors, and Activists*. New York: John Wiley & Sons, Chapter 5.

Shepherd, C. and Ridley, A. 2015. *Company Law*. Oxford/New York: Routledge.

Smith, J. A. and Morreale, M. 2007. The Fiduciary Duties of Directors and Officers. In Gerrard, M. B. (ed.), *Global Climate Change and U.S. Law*. New York: American Bar Association.

Stathers, R. and Zavos, A. 2015. Responding to Climate Change Risk in Portfolio Management. *Schroders*, February. Available at: www.schroders.com/staticfiles/Schroders/Sites/global/pdf/Portfolio-Climate-Change-Risk-April-2015.pdf [Accessed September 15, 2017].

Teele-Langford, R. 2013. Solving the Fiduciary Puzzle – the Bona Fide and Proper Purposes of Company Directors. *Australian Business Law Review*, 41, 127.

Teele-Langford, R. 2016. Corporate Culpability, Stepping Stones and Mariner – Contention Surrounding Directors' Duties Where Companies Breach the Law. *Company & Securities Law Journal*, 34, 75.

Thornton, R. 2008. Ethical Investments: A Case of Disjointed Thinking. *Cambridge Law Journal*, 396.

Velasco, J. 2015. A Defense of the Corporate Law Duty of Care. *The Journal of Corporation Law*, 40(3), 647.

Waitzer, E. and Sarro, D. 2014. Fiduciary Society Unleashed: The Road Ahead for the Financial Sector. *The Business Lawyer*, August 9, pp. 1081–1116.

Yeager, C. A. 2015. At Least Somewhat Exaggerated: How Reports of the Death of Delaware's Duty of Care Don't Tell the Whole Story. *Georgetown Law Journal*, 103(5), June, 1387–1407.

Cases and learned opinions

Alcoa of Australia Retirement Plan Pty Ltd v. Frost [2012] VSCA 238

Aronson v. Lewis, 473 A.2d 805, 812 (Del.1984)

ASIC, in the matter of Padbury Mining Limited v. Padbury Mining Limited [2016] FCA 990

ASIC, in the matter of Sino Australia Oil and Gas Limited (in liq) v. Sino Australia Oil and Gas Limited (in liq) [2016] FCA 934

ASIC v. Australian Property Custodian Holdings Ltd (recs and mgrs apptd) (in liq) (controllers apptd) (No 3) [2013] FCA 1342

ASIC v. Cassimatis (No 8) [2016] FCA 1023

ASIC v. Citrofresh International Ltd (No 2) (2010) 77 ACSR 69

ASIC v. Flugge [2016] VSC 779

ASIC v. Healey & Ors [2011] FCA 717

ASIC v. Hellicar [2012] HCA 17

ASIC v. Ingleby (2012) 91 ASCR 66

ASIC v. Macdonald (No 11) [2009] NSWSC 287

ASIC v. Macdonald (No 12) [2009] NSWSC 714

ASIC v. Rich (2009) 75 ACSR 1

ASIC v. Vines (2005) 55 ACSR 617

Bell Group Ltd (in liq) v. Westpac Banking Corporation (No 9) (2008) 70 ACSR 1

Benihana of Tokyo, Inc. v. Benihana, Inc., 891 A.2d 150 (Del. Ch. 2005)

Bhullar v. Bhullar [2003] EWCA Civ 424

Birdi v. Specsavers Optical Group Ltd [2015] EWHC 2870 (Ch)

Bishopsgate Investment Management Ltd (in liquidation) v. Maxwell (No 2) [1994] 1 All ER 261

Boardman v. Phipps [1967] 2 AC 46 at 124

Breen v. Williams (1996) 186 CLR 1

Brehm v. Eisner, 746 A.2d 244 (Del.2000)

Bristol and West Building Society v. Mothew [1998] Ch 1

Cede & Co. v. Technicolor, Inc., 634 A.2d 345, 362 (Del. 1993)

Chan v. Zacharia (1984) 154 CLR 178

Charitable Corp. v. Sutton, 2 Atk. 400, 406, 26 Eng. Rep. 642, 645 (Ch. 1742)

Chen v. Howard-Anderson, 87 A.3d 648 (Del. Ch. 2014)

Cinerama, Inc. v. Technicolor, Inc., 663 A.2d 1156, 1166 n.18 (Del. 1995)

Commonwealth Bank of Australia v. Friedrich (1991) 5 ACSR 15

Daniels v. Anderson (1995) 37 NSWLR 438

Espinoza v. Dimon 797 F.3d 229 (2015)

Extrasure Travel Insurances Ltd v. Scattergood [2002] EWHC 3093 (Ch)

Gesoff v. IIC Indus., Inc., 902 A.2d 1130, 1145 (Del. Ch. 2006)

Graham v. Allis-Chalmers Mfg. Co., 188 A.2d 125 (Del. 1963)

Guth v. Loft, Inc., 5 A.2d 503 (Del. 1939)

Howard Smith Ltd v. Ampol Petroleum Ltd [1974] AC 821

Hirsche v. Sims [1894] AC 654

Hospital Products Ltd v. United States Surgical Corporation [1984] HCA 64; (1984) 156 CLR 41

In re Abbott Laboratories Derivative Shareholders Litigation, 325 F.3d 795, 804 (7th Cir. 2003)

In re Caremark Int'l Inc. Deriv. Litig., 698 A.2d 959 (Del. Ch. 1996)

In re Citigroup Inc. S'holder Derivative Litig., 964 A.2d 106 (Del. Ch. 2009)

In re Cornerstone Therapeutics Inc. Stockholder Litigation and Leal v. Meeks, 115 A.3d 1173 (Del. 2015)

In re HIH Insurance Ltd (in prov liq); Australian Securities and Investments Commission v. Adler (2004) 41 ACSR 72

In re Gaylord Container Corp. Shareholders' Litig., 753 A.2d 462 (Del. Ch. 2000)

In re General Motors Company Derivative Litigation Consolidated C.A. No. 9627-VCG

In re Goldman Sachs Grp., Inc. S'holder Litig., C.A. No. 5215-VCG (Del. Ch. Oct. 12, 2011)

In re Massey Energy Co., C.A. No. 5430-VCS, 2011 BL 14964 (Del. Ch. May 31, 2011)

In re SAIC Inc. Derivative Litigation, 948 F. Supp. 2d 366 (S.D.N.Y. 2013)

In re Target Inc. Shareholder Derivative Litigation, No. 14-cv-203 (D.C. Minnesota)

In re the Home Depot, Inc. Shareholder Derivative Litigation, No.1:15-CV-2999-TWT (D.C. Northern District of Georgia)

In re the Wendys Company Shareholder Derivative Complaint, CASE NO.: 1:16-cv-1153 (D.C. Southern District of Ohio), complaint filed December 8, 2016.

Weinberger v. UOP Inc., 457 A.2d 701 (Del. 1983)

Welch v. Havenstein, No. 13-2648-cv, 2014 WL 322055 (2d Cir. Jan. 30, 2014)

Wyong Shire Council v. Shirt (1980) 146 CLR 40

Hutley, N., SC and Hartford-Davis, S. (2016) *Climate Change and Directors' Duties.* Memorandum of Opinion for the Centre for Policy Development and Future Business Council, October 7. Available at: www.futurebusinesscouncil.com/fiduciary_duties_media-release/ [Accessed August 16, 2017]. The author of this chapter was an instructing solicitor on that brief.

Statutes, treaties and other regulatory instruments

Australian Stock Exchange Corporate Governance Council (ASXCGC). 2010. *Corporate Governance Principles and Recommendations*

Companies Act 2006 (UK)

Corporations Act 2001 (Cth)

Delaware General Corporation Law

REST 3d TRUSTS § 2

Securities & Exchange Commission Act 1934

Securities & Exchange Commission (SEC). 2010. 17 CFR Parts 211, 231 and 241 Commission Guidance Regarding Disclosure Related to Climate Change; Final Rule. *Interpretive Guidance, Federal Register*, 75(25), February 8.

Standards Australia. *Australian/New Zealand Standard: Risk Management, Principles & Guidelines*, AS/NZS ISO 31000:2009.

United Nations Framework Convention on Climate Change (UNFCCC). 2015. Adoption of the Paris Agreement. *Conference of the Parties*, Paris, December 12. Available at: http://unfccc.int/resource/docs/2015/cop21/eng/l09r01.pdf [Accessed August 16, 2017].

Press releases

ExxonMobil. 2015. ExxonMobil to Hold Media Call on New York Attorney General Subpoena. *News Release*, November 5.

ExxonMobil. 2016. ExxonMobil Earns $2.7 Billion in Third Quarter of 2016. *Press Release*, October 28. Available at: http://news.exxonmobil.com/press-release/exxonmobil-earns-27-billion-third-quarter-2016

Moody's Investors Service. 2017. Significant Credit Risks Arise for Oil and Gas Companies in Energy Transition. *Press Release*, April 26. Available at: www.moodys.com/research/Moodys-Significant-credit-risks-arise-for-oil-and-gas-industry—PR_365728 [Accessed September 19, 2017].

New York Attorney-General (NYAG). 2016. A.G. Schneiderman Secures Unprecedented Agreement With Peabody Energy to End Misleading Statements and Disclose Risks Arising From Climate Change. *Press Release*, November 9. Available at: https://ag.ny.gov/press-release/ag-schneiderman-secures-unprecedented-agreement-peabody-energy-end-misleading

Robbins Geller Rudman & Dowd. 2016. Robbins Geller Rudman & Dowd LLP Files Class Action Suit Against ExxonMobil Corporation. *PR Newswire*, November 7, 2016. Available at: www.prnewswire.com/news-releases/robbins-geller-rudman-dowd-llp-files-class-action-suit-against-exxon-mobil-corporation-300358768.html

Reports

Amado, J.-C. and Adams, P. 2012. *Value Chain Climate Resilience: A Guide to Managing Climate Impacts on Companies and Communities*. Report prepared for Partnership for Resilience and Environmental Preparedness (PREP), Montreal, July.

Association for Sustainable and Responsible Investment in Asia (ASRIA) and Chubb Insurance Group (Chubb). 2015. *Climate Governance in Asia: Considerations for Corporate Directors and Officers*.

AXA Group. 2017. *Climate Change: Investment Risk Analysis*. Available at: https://www-axa-com.cdn.axa-contento-118412.eu/www-axa-com%2F36c0571a-d585-43a0-ac57-3f39e4c389ba_climatechange_report_investmentriskanalysis_va_28.08.17-b.pdf [Accessed September 19, 2017]

Bank of England Prudential Regulation Authority (BoEPRA). 2015. *The Impact of Climate Change on the UK Insurance Sector*, September.

BlackRock. 2016. *Adapting Portfolios to Climate Change: Implications and Strategies for All Investors*. BlackRock Investment Institute Global Insights, September. Available at: www.blackrock.com/investing/literature/whitepaper/bii-climate-change-2016-us.pdf [Accessed September 19, 2017].

Boston Common Asset Management. 2015. *Are Banks Prepared for Climate Change? Impact Report 2015*, October.

Carbon Tracker and the Grantham Research Institute. 2013. *Unburnable Carbon 2013: Wasted Capital and Stranded Assets*.

Ernst & Young (EY). 2017. *Climate Risk Barometer*, July. Available at: www.ey.com/Publication/vwLUAssets/Climate_Risk_Disclosure_Barometer_2017/$FILE/ey-climate-risk-disclosure-barometer-2017.pdf [Accessed October 17, 2017]

French Treasury (in collaboration with the Banque de France and the Autorité de Contrôle Prudentiel et de Résolution). 2017. *Assessing Climate Change–Related Risks in the Banking Sector*. Synthesis of the project report submitted for public consultation with regard to Article 173 (V°) of the 2015 French Energy Transition Act, Paris, February. Available at: www.tresor.economie.gouv.fr/File/433465

Intergovernmental Panel on Climate Change (IPCC). 2014. Climate Change 2014 Synthesis Report. *Summary for Policy Makers*, 10.

International Energy Agency (IEA). 2015. Energy and Climate Change. *World Energy Outlook: Special Briefing for COP21*. Available at: www.iea.org/media/news/WEO_INDC_Paper_Final_WEB.PDF [Accessed August 16, 2017]

International Energy Agency (IEA). 2017. *Perspectives for the Energy Transition – Investment Needs for a Low-Carbon Energy System*. Report prepared for the German Government as input to the G20 Presidency, March 20. Available at: www.energiewende2017.com/wp-content/uploads/2017/03/Perspectives-for-the-Energy-Transition_WEB.pdf

Kay, J. 2012. *The Kay Review of UK Equity Markets and Long-Term Decision Making*. Final Report to UK Department for Business, Innovation & Skills, July.

Norges Bank Investment Management. 2017. *Climate Change Strategy: Expectations to Companies*. Available at: www.nbim.no/globalassets/documents/climate-change-strategy-document.pdf?id=5931 [Accessed September 19, 2017]

Schroders Investment Management. 2017. Climate Change: Redefining the Risks. *Insights*, September. Available at: www.schroders.com/getfunddocument?oid=1.9.2813957 [Accessed September 19, 2017]

S&P Dow Jones Indices. 2017. *The Carbon Scorecard*, May 9. Available at: www.trucost.com/publication/the-carbon-scorecard/ [Accessed May 10, 2017]

Standard & Poor's Ratings Services. 2015. Climate Risk: Rising Tides Raise the Stakes. *Insights*, December. Available at: www.spratings.com/documents/20184/984172/Insights+Magazine+-+December+2015/cff352af-4f50-4f15-a765-f56dcd4ee5c8 [Accessed September 19, 2017]

Sullivan, R., Martindale, W., Feller, E. and Bordon, A. 2015. *Fiduciary Duty in the 21st Century*. Global Compact Report, United Nations, September.

Sustainability Accounting Standards Board (SASB). 2016. *Climate Risk Technical Bulletin*, TB001-10182016, October.

Task force on Climate-related Financial Disclosures (TCFD). 2017. *Final Recommendations*. Report to the G20 Financial Stability Board, June 29.

TCFD. 2017a. *TCFD Recommendations Report Annex: Implementing the Recommendations of the TCFD*, June 29. Available at: www.fsb-tcfd.org/wp-content/uploads/2017/06/FINAL-TCFD-Annex-062817.pdf [Accessed August 16, 2017]

Two Degrees Investing Initiative (2Dii) and MinterEllison. 2017. *The Carbon Boomerang: Climate Litigation Risk in the Context of the Transition to a Low-Carbon Economy*. Report to the European Union (H2020), September.

United Nations Environment Programme (UNEP) and Columbia Law School Sabin Center for Climate Change Law (Sabin Center). 2017. *The Status of Climate Change Litigation – a Global Review*, May. Available at: http://wedocs.unep.org/handle/20.500.11822/20767 [Accessed July 15, 2017]

Vanguard. 2017. *Investment Stewardship 2017 Annual Report*. Available at: https://about.vanguard.com/investment-stewardship/annual-report.pdf [Accessed 19 September 2017]

Speeches

Australian Prudential Regulation Authority (APRA). 2017. *Australia's New Horizon: Climate Change Challenges and Prudential Risk*. Speech by Executive Board Member Geoff Summerhayes to the Insurance Council of Australia Annual Forum 2017, Sydney, February 17.

Financial Reporting Council (FRC). 2016. *Climate Disclosure Standards Board's – Comply or Explain: Review of FTSE 350 Companies*. Presentation by CEO Stephen Haddrill, January 28.

10 Climate change

What implications for central banks and financial regulators?

Sandra Batten, Rhiannon Sowerbutts and Misa Tanaka[1]

1. Introduction

In the United Kingdom, the Bank of England is responsible for maintaining the stability of the financial system. The Bank's Financial Policy Committee (FPC) is charged with a primary objective of identifying, monitoring and taking action to remove and reduce systemic risks with a view to protecting and enhancing the resilience of the UK financial system. The Bank's Prudential Regulation Authority (PRA) is responsible for promoting the safety and soundness of individual financial institutions through the prudential regulation and supervision of around 1,700 banks, building societies, credit unions, insurers and major investment firms. The Bank therefore monitors the risk exposures and resilience of individual financial institutions, as well as how the interactions between financial institutions influence the stability of the financial system as a whole.

The Bank of England, as well as a few other central banks,[2] is examining how asset stranding caused by climate change and the transition to a low-carbon economy might affect the stability of the financial system. This chapter examines the channels via which climate change and policies to mitigate climate change could affect central banks' ability to meet their financial stability objectives. It also considers the potential role of central banks and financial regulators in assessing and mitigating climate-related financial risks.

2. Impact of climate change on financial stability: key transmission channels

There are two main types of climate-related risks that can affect the value of assets held by the financial sector: physical risks, which arise from climate change itself, and transition risks, arising from the transition to a low-carbon economy.[3] This section explains these concepts and outlines the channels via which these could affect the stability of the financial system.

2.1 Physical risks

Physical risks can be defined as those risks that arise from the interaction of climate-related hazards (including hazardous events and trends) with the vulnerability of exposure of human and natural systems, including their ability to adapt. According to IPCC (2014), climate change-related risks from extreme events, such as heat waves, heavy precipitation, and coastal flooding, are already "moderate".[4] These risks will be higher with 1°C of additional warming relative to the 1986–2005 period, and risks associated with some types of extreme events (e.g. extreme heat) increase progressively with further warming.[5]

2.1.1 Insured versus uninsured losses

The manifestation of climate-related physical risks – for example via natural disasters that are influenced by climate change – can potentially result in loss of human lives, as well as in severe damages to properties and the productive capacity of the economy. Climate-related catastrophes can therefore result in large financial losses. The allocation of these losses and the impact of the losses on the financial system and the macroeconomy will depend on the extent of insurance coverage. As shown in Figure 10.1, *insured* losses arising from climate-related natural disasters will propagate to the financial sector via the reaction of insurers to their initial losses. But *uninsured* losses could delay reconstruction, reduce the value of collateral securing bank loans (e.g. properties) and weaken the balance sheets of affected borrowers (e.g. corporations and households) and thus could ultimately cause losses for banks. As we explain in more detail in what follows, the total impact on the financial system could end up being larger than the initial losses resulting from a natural catastrophe that are borne by financial institutions if there are financial frictions that propagate the initial shock.

Data from Munich RE suggest that, on average, only 23% of the losses from the world's largest natural catastrophes (in terms of inflation-adjusted overall losses, including those unrelated to climate change) occurring during 1980 to 2016 had been insured, while only 51% of the largest meteorological loss events had been insured (see Annex 1, Tables 10.A1–10.A2). Their data also show that, of those natural disasters that were related to weather, hurricanes in North America led to the largest losses, while losses from floods and winter storms in Europe were considerably lower (see Annex 1, Tables 10.A2–10.A4).

2.1.2 Impact of insured losses on the balance sheets of insurers

If insured losses resulting from an event or a series of events are sufficiently large and concentrated, they could lead to distress or failure of insurance companies. For example, Hurricane Andrew in 1992 resulted in the insolvency of several insurance companies. The failure and distress of insurance companies in turn could affect financial stability if they lead to disruptions to critical insurance services and systemically important financial markets, such as securities lending and funding transactions (French and Vital 2015). Large-scale fire sales of assets by distressed insurers could reduce asset prices, which could adversely affect the balance sheets of other financial institutions, such as banks.

To date, weather-related catastrophes have not led to large-scale failures of insurance firms or systemwide financial instability in advanced economies.[6] What

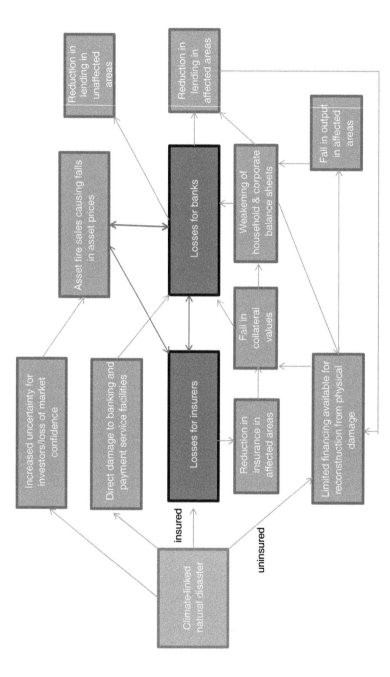

Figure 10.1 A transmission map from a natural disaster to financial sector losses and the macroeconomy

has been more common, however, is collective withdrawal of insurers from covering risks that they consider to have become uninsurable (Chartered Insurance Institute 2009). Less severely, insurers may simply respond by raising premiums for covering similar risks. The reduced insurance coverage could in turn reduce the collateral values of properties in affected areas (and, potentially, also unaffected areas that face similar risks), which is a form of "asset stranding". The reduced collateral values could in turn tighten the borrowing constraints of households and corporations. Thus, even if losses are largely insured and financing for reconstruction is immediately available, a severe weather-related catastrophe could affect the banking sector and the real economy in the medium term (Figure 10.1).

In advanced economies, the public sector has often stepped in to avoid this impact, either to assume these risks directly or to support the creation of privately funded entities to assume them. For example, the 1992 Hurricane Andrew led to the creation of the state-run Citizens Property Insurance Corp, which provides "the insurance of last resort" for home and business owners in Florida. In the United Kingdom, Flood Re was established by the insurance industry in agreement with the government in April 2016 to offer a reinsurance mechanism for flood risk and thus enable household insurers to offer affordable flood insurance to UK households with domestic properties facing higher levels of flood risk. Its operations are funded through a levy collected from UK household insurers.[7] Flood Re, however, does not cover flood risks to business premises, second homes, buy-to-let properties and any property built after 1 January 2009.

2.1.3 Impact of uninsured losses on the balance sheets of banks

Insurance is a key mechanism via which losses arising from natural disasters are spread across time and people. Thus, while withdrawal of insurers from covering weather-related risks would help protect the insurance industry from losses, this does not necessarily represent an efficient outcome for the financial system or the economy as a whole. *Ex ante*, an excessively high price for catastrophe insurance could lead to underinsurance, which in turn could reduce collateral values. The reduction in collateral values could in turn reduce lending to inefficiently low levels in the presence of borrowing constraints. For example, Garmaise and Moskowitz (2009) show that a poorly functioning catastrophe market leads to about 20% less bank financing of catastrophe-susceptible commercial real estate *ex ante*.

Ex post, underinsurance could magnify the economic impact of a natural disaster by constraining the financing of the post-disaster reconstruction that contributes positively to GDP (a "flow" measure). The resulting delay in reconstruction could also reduce the collateral values securing the loans – such as the properties securing mortgage or small business loans – thus further tightening the financing constraints of affected households and corporations. Indeed, von Peter et al. (2012) find that it is the uninsured losses that drive the negative impact on GDP after a natural disaster, while insured losses have insignificant impact in both the short and long run.

In the United Kingdom, more than 85% of loans to individuals and 75% of loans to small and medium-sized enterprises (SMEs) were secured on property (as of 2014). The UK's Environmental Agency (2009) also suggested that around 5.2 million of properties in England, or one in six properties, are already at risk of flooding, while the Met Office (2011) highlighted that climate change is likely to increase the risk of both fluvial and coastal flooding in the United Kingdom. Thus, floods and other natural disasters could potentially have a negative impact on the value of the collateral securing these loans, especially if the collateralised properties are uninsured.[8]

The post-disaster reduction in collateral values is likely to be larger the less the risk of such disasters was reflected in property prices *ex ante* and the more insurers pull out from covering properties in the affected regions *ex post*. In the United Kingdom, there is some evidence that flood risks are generally not reflected in property prices until floods actually occur. For example, Lamond's (2009) study of the flood event in 2000 found that being designated as a high flood risk area has no effect on property prices. An actual flooding, however, has a temporary (three-year) effect on property values. Lamond (2009) reports that less than half of the respondents reported that they were fully aware of the flood risk to their property at purchase, and for transacted property about one-third were alerted to the risk status of their potential purchase by insurance premiums.

Households' and corporations' balance sheets could be further weakened if output and employment fall in affected areas due to slow reconstruction, which is more likely when the affected parties suffer large uninsured losses and fiscally funded aid is limited. For example, a survey of firms conducted by the Federal Reserve Bank of New York (2014) after Superstorm Sandy (2012) found that almost a third of the affected firms had no insurance, and only a few had business disruption or flood insurance. Losses also came from sources which are harder to insure: 59% of firms reported losses from decreased customer demand, in contrast to 29% reporting damage to or loss of assets, which is easier to insure. The impact on firm balance sheets was considerable: half of the firms covered storm-related financing needs with personal resources, while others increased debt levels. One year after the disaster, 9 out of 10 of the affected firms reported persistent financing needs to cover operating expenses or to reposition their business.

A reduction in collateral values and a weakening of household and corporate balance sheets in turn could increase the loss-given-default (LGD) and the probability of default (PD) of loans, thus could adversely affect the banking system (Figure 10.1). There is some empirical evidence that supports the hypothesis that natural disasters affect the soundness of banks and that the structure of the financial system influences the losses borne by banks. For example, Klomp (2014) finds evidence that, for a sample of 160 countries in the period 1997 to 2010, meteorological and geophysical disasters (hydrological disasters including floods; meteorological disasters concerning storms and hurricanes; geophysical disasters including earthquakes, tsunamis and volcanic eruptions; and climatic disasters including extreme temperatures, droughts and wildfires) increase the likelihood of bank default. This effect, however, is mitigated in countries with rigorous financial regulation and supervision, and highly developed economies in which banks tend to have well-diversified asset portfolios and borrowers are typically better insured. In a separate study using US data on property damages from hurricanes, earthquakes and other natural disasters during 1976 to 2010, Lambert et al. (2015) also found that disaster damages in banks' business regions significantly increase the probability of their failure in the medium term, that is about five to nine years after the disaster damage. The authors conjecture that public financial aid and insurance pay-outs, as well as borrower savings could cushion the impact of a disaster on banks in the short term, but not in the medium term when support from these sources are depleted. Landon-Lane et al. (2009) find evidence that, for some regions and periods in the United States, droughts were associated with farm mortgage foreclosures and bank stress, but climate-related bank stress has become less important since 1940 due to adaptation of both farmers and banks.

Finally, major natural disasters abroad could also affect domestic banks, particularly if the resulting economic disruptions, fall in tax revenues and rise in fiscal expenditures lead to a sharp increase in sovereign default risk. An analysis by Standard and Poor's (2014b) suggests that the countries that are most vulnerable to climate change are emerging-market countries, mostly in Africa and Asia, and that sovereigns with low credit ratings tend to be more vulnerable compared to those with high ratings.

2.1.4 Impact on the credit flow to the real economy and financial markets

If banks suffer losses on their capital as a result of a natural disaster and cannot raise new capital immediately, then they could reduce lending to both affected and unaffected areas in order to improve their regulatory capital ratios. The resulting reduction in credit supply could in turn exacerbate the fall in the collateral values and further damage the balance sheets of households and corporations, potentially deepening the post-disaster downturn (Figure 10.1).

A natural disaster could potentially also "crowd out" bank lending in unaffected areas, as credit demand increases in affected areas when households and corporations seek to fund the reconstruction of damaged homes and buildings by supplementing insurance payments through bank credit; and banks operating in these areas could be constrained in increasing credit supply, especially if they have suffered losses on their capital due to the disaster. Cortes and Strahan (2015) examine how banks in the US reallocate capital when credit demand increases in areas affected by a natural disaster and show that bank lending in other markets declines by about 50 cents per dollar of additional lending in the area which experienced the disaster. Banks were also found to increase sales of more liquid loans and increase deposit rates to attract funds.

Major natural disasters could potentially also trigger a sharp increase in precautionary demand for liquidity by financial institutions, households and corporations, for example due to disruptions in banking services directly caused by disasters (e.g. due to closures of bank branches and ATMs in areas affected by the disaster) and the increased uncertainty facing households and financial market participants in the immediate aftermath of a disaster. A surge in hoarding of safe, liquid assets, such as cash and government bonds, could potentially destabilise the financial system and the economy in the absence of central bank intervention to supply liquidity.[9] The existing literature also points to the possibility that major natural disasters could lead to long-term changes in risk preferences of affected people, which could have longer-term impact on financial market dynamics.[10]

2.2 Transition risks

Transition risks can be defined as the risks of economic dislocation and financial losses associated with the transition to a lower-carbon economy. As we discuss in what follows, a smooth transition to a low-carbon economy is possible if the expectation of a future policy tightening on carbon emission induces an early and orderly shift of private investment towards low-carbon technologies. Moreover, not making a transition implies that the physical risks from climate change are likely to increase over time. Nevertheless, it is possible that a late and abrupt policy tightening on carbon emission could lead to a loss in value – or "stranding" – of carbon-intensive investment. The aggregate impact could be substantial given the size of the sectors affected: for example, oil and gas sectors alone account for 14% of FTSE 100 index (as at 28 February 2017).

A substantial reduction in CO_2 emission can be achieved without a large sacrifice in GDP growth if it is possible to increase energy efficiency (i.e. reduce energy intensity of GDP)[11] and reduce carbon intensity of energy, as summarised by the Kaya identity:

$$\text{Carbon emissions} = \text{Population} \times \frac{\text{GDP}}{\text{Population}} \times \frac{\text{Energy used}}{\text{GDP}} \times \frac{\text{Carbon}}{\text{Energy used}}$$

Transition to a low-carbon economy would therefore require investments to shift from high-carbon energy production technologies towards low- and ultimately zero-carbon energy production. If investments in low-carbon energy production do not take place in sufficiently large scale and the policy on carbon emission is abruptly tightened, then the transition to a low-carbon economy could be associated with sharp falls in asset prices, such as those of fossil fuels and firms that depend heavily on their use (Carney 2015).[12]

Next, we set out a simple framework to conceptualise the transition to a low-carbon economy as a multiple-equilibrium problem, and examine empirical evidence on the pricing of the transition risk in financial markets.

2.2.1 Transition risk as a multiple-equilibrium problem

Consider a very simple stylised "game" between the government and the electricity companies in determining investment in low-carbon electricity generation, for example investment in carbon dioxide capture and storage (CCS). CCS can capture CO_2 before it is released in the atmosphere and store it underground, thus providing low-carbon electricity generation when applied to power stations using fossil fuels.

At time T, private electricity companies decide whether to invest in CCS, which costs i_T for each company. At time T+1, the government chooses to "shut down" unabated fossil-fuel fired power plants if the benefit B_{T+1} of doing so, in terms of preventing the adverse impact on climate, exceeds the costs C_{T+1} in terms of the increased cost of electricity for the population. The cost to the government of shutting down unabated electricity production at T+1, however, depends on the amount of electricity that can be generated by low-carbon alternatives, for example renewables and coal- and gas-fired power plants with CCS. Thus, we assume that the more investment takes place in low-carbon electricity production at time T, the lower will be the cost of shutting down high-carbon electricity production at T+1: so $C_{T+1}(I_T)$ is decreasing in I_T, where I_T is the *aggregate* investment in low-carbon electricity production at time T.

The private return from investing in low-carbon electricity production at time T depends on whether private electricity companies (and their investors) expect the government to shut down unabated electricity production at time T+1. The private investors know that the government will shut down unabated electricity production at T+1, if $C_{T+1}(I_T) < B_{T+1}$, which occurs if I_T rises above a critical threshold I^*_T, which is defined by the condition $C_{T+1}(I^*_T) = B_{T+1}$. Thus, if a sufficiently large number of companies invest in low-carbon electricity production, then they will expect the government to shut down the unabated electricity production facilities in the future.

Suppose that the government decides to shut down the unabated electricity production facilities at T+1 (Table 10.1, column 2). We assume that those electricity companies that had invested in CCS at time T can obtain a "high" price, P_H, per unit of fossil fuel R converted into electricity, minus the abatement cost A: thus, their net profit will be $(P_H - A)R - i_T$, which we assume to be positive. By contrast, those companies that had not invested in CCS at time T will be shut down and hence obtain zero profits: in this case, capital in unabated fossil-fuel power plants

Table 10.1 Stylised payoffs of electricity companies under different scenarios about climate change policy

	Government shuts down unabated electricity production at T+1 (low emission)	Government continues to allow unabated electricity production at T+1 (high emission)
Invest in CCS at T	$(P_H - A)R - i_T > 0$ low-carbon equilibrium	$(P_L - A)R - i_T < 0$ low-carbon investment becomes loss making
Don't invest in CCS at T	0 some fossil fuels and unabated power plants become stranded	$P_L R > 0$ high-carbon equilibrium

and fossil fuel reserves, R, that would have been used for power generation, will become "stranded".

Suppose now that the government decides to keep unabated power plants open at T+1 (Table 10.1, column 3). In this case, those companies that had invested in CCS at time T can only obtain a 'low' price, P_L, due to the availability of abundant electricity supply from unabated power plants. We assume that, in this case, those companies that had invested in CCS at time T will earn negative profits: $(P_L - A)$ $R - i_T < 0$. By contrast, those companies that had not invested in CCS will obtain a profit of $P_L R$ by selling unabated electricity.

In this setup, the electricity companies' investment choice in CCS is subject to "strategic complementarity", where the return from investing in the technology depends on whether others also invest. If everyone invests in CCS at T such that the aggregate investment exceeds I^*_T, then the cost of transitioning to a low-carbon economy for the government is reduced sufficiently such that it becomes credible for the government to shut down unabated power plants at T+1. This in turn creates incentives for private electricity companies to invest in low-carbon technology: the result is an orderly transition to a "low-carbon" equilibrium, in which fossil fuels can continue to be used for power generation as a result of CCS being in operation.[13] By contrast, if nobody invests in CCS at T, then the cost of shutting down all the unabated fossil-fuel powered plants at T+1 becomes too high and hence the government's commitment to transition to a low-carbon economy becomes "time inconsistent", or not credible, leaving the economy stuck at a "high-carbon" equilibrium (Figure 10.2).

However, a disorderly transition is possible if, for example, the government's policy on carbon emission were to tighten abruptly – for example, due to a sudden change in popular attitude towards climate change, or a technological breakthrough in low-carbon energy generation, which increases the benefits of transition, B_{T+1}. In a disorderly transition scenario, the value of fossil fuels and firms that depend on high-carbon energy production could fall sharply: in the stylised example in Table 10.1, the value of the electricity company without CCS would fall from $P_L R$ to zero. Such disorderly adjustments in asset prices could lead to corporate defaults and distress and hence trigger financial instability if the affected companies are highly leveraged. Figure 10.3 shows that the major oil companies have varying degrees of indebtedness, but several of them are becoming increasingly more levered.

The simple framework here underscores the value of transparent, predictable policy on carbon emission in anchoring private investors' expectations. In particular, a pre-commitment of policy tightening on carbon emission strengthens private investors' incentives to invest in low-carbon technologies, thus mitigating the risk of asset stranding and making an orderly transition to a low-carbon economy more likely. Such a pre-commitment could, for example, take the form of a pre-announced path for a carbon price which helps to internalise some of the externalities associated with carbon emission. But even a less well-defined commitment, such as the 2015 Paris Agreement, might help coordinate private

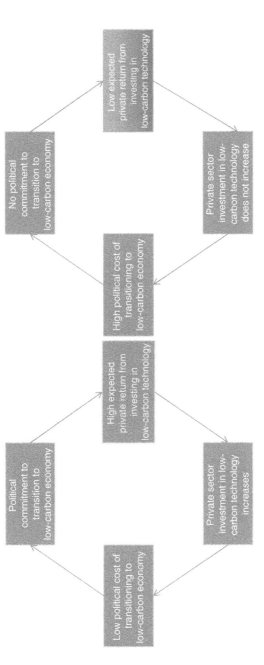

Figure 10.2 "Low-carbon-emission" and "high-carbon-emission" equilibria

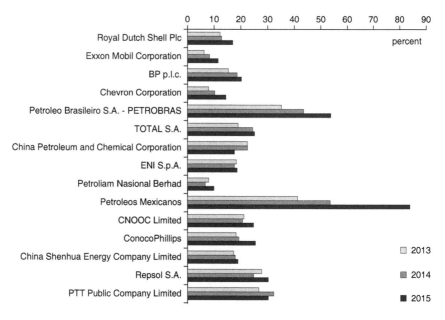

Figure 10.3 Debt-to-asset ratios of major oil companies, 2013–2015

Note: The ratio is calculated as short-term plus long-term debt as a percentage of total assets. The 2015 debt ratios for ENI S.p.A, Petroliam Nasional Berhad and Petróleos Mexicanos were estimated by assuming that their short-term debt levels in 2015 were the same as in 2014, as these were missing.

Sources: Moody's and authors' calculations

investments towards low-carbon technologies if investors perceive this to be a credible signal for future tightening of policy on carbon emission.[14]

2.2.2 To what extent is the transition risk reflected in asset prices?

There is evidence that some institutions have already started divesting from high-carbon assets, such as fossil fuel companies, and that this is already having some market impact. A movement to divest from fossil fuels started in US universities and religious institutions. By the end of 2016, 688 institutions and more than 58,000 individuals across the world with US$5 trillion in assets have pledged to divest from fossil fuel companies.[15] This movement to reduce investment in high-carbon assets has not been confined to asset managers. In May 2015, Bank of America announced plans to reduce its financial exposure to coal companies. Since then, other for-profit financial institutions, including JP Morgan, Wells Fargo, Morgan Stanley, Crédit Agricole, Citibank, Allianz and Aegon have made similar announcements regarding their financial exposures to the coal sector.

By using standard event study methodology it is possible to examine the market reaction to specific events, which could be associated with a change in market

expectations about the profitability in investing in carbon-intensive assets. To estimate the impact we look at changes in the market valuation of the firm's equity
measured by abnormal returns (returns above and beyond those expected under
normal market activity and movement, that is residual returns after stripping out
market returns) following the event. For this exercise we examine the effect on all
energy firms on the spectrum from coal companies to renewable energy firms.[16]
To find and date events, we search for news stories in major newspapers or energy
specific investment press mentioning the words "carbon bubble",[17] "unburnable
carbon" and "fossil fuel divestment", and use data from climate organisations
which track divestment announcements. Although we have more than 50 different events between January 2008 and January 2016, many of them happened
close together, and so we excluded any event which happened within five days of
another event from the analysis. We also test major significant events, such as the
Paris Agreement, individually. Detailed discussion of the methodology is found
in Annex 2.

Figure 10.4 illustrates the contrasting cumulative abnormal returns experienced
by a petroleum refining company (CVR Energy) and a wind turbine manufacturer
(Nordex) in the immediate aftermath of the announcement of the Paris Agreement
on 12 December 2015. More generally, we find that these events had a negative
but statistically insignificant effect on the abnormal returns for oil and gas companies but a positive and significant effect for renewable energy companies.

There are a number of reasons the events might not have had a significant impact
on the market values of fossil fuel companies. First, investors could be uncertain
about both the future course of climate-related policies and their impact on the
value of fossil fuel companies. Second, investors concerned about the transition

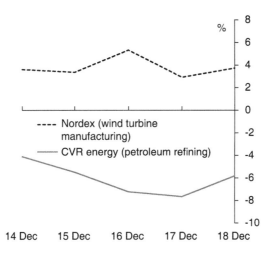

Figure 10.4 Cumulative abnormal returns after the Paris Agreement

Sources: Thomson Reuters Datastream, Bloomberg Finance L.P. and authors' calculations

risk might choose to divest from fossil fuels over several years rather than liqui-dating their portfolios immediately based on specific news. Altogether, the results suggest tentatively that, although some investors are beginning to incorporate expected changes in energy policy into their assessment of firms, in general this has not been producing large and sudden movements in equity prices.

3. Risk assessment: quantifying physical and transition risks

In informing their decisions about possible responses, financial regulators will need to assess and quantify risks arising from climate-related physical and tran-sition risks. It has been suggested that stress tests could be used to examine the extent to which the financial system is exposed to climate-related risks (e.g. Gar-man and Fox-Carney 2015; ESRB 2016; Farid et al. 2016). A stress test examines the potential impact of a hypothetical adverse scenario on the health of the finan-cial system and individual institutions within it. Stress tests allow policy makers to assess the resilience of the financial system and individual institutions to a range of adverse shocks and, if needed, take measures to ensure that financial institutions are resilient and can continue to supply credit to the real economy even under stress.

Conducting a climate-related stress test would require (a) formulating a coher-ent "tail risk" stress testing scenario which could have a major impact on the stability of the financial system; (b) identifying sectors that are most exposed to financial loss in that scenario; (c) identifying available data and additional data that need to be collected; and (d) modelling the transmission mechanism of shocks across the financial system. This section explains key considerations for designing such a stress test.

3.1 Stress testing against physical risks

A key challenge in conducting a climate-related stress test lies in identifying a relevant scenario in which the financial sector is expected to suffer a large finan-cial loss. As stress tests can only examine the resilience of the financial system to particular adverse scenarios, the scenario design will be a key determinant of the informativeness of any climate-related stress tests. Although UK weather-related events have thus far caused losses that are small relative to weather-related events abroad, such as hurricanes (see Annex 1, Tables 10.A1–10.A4), it may be reason-able to conduct a stress test if it is possible to identify, based on climate science which takes into account the impact of future changes in climate, a plausible UK scenario which could give rise to large economic losses – for example one that involves substantial and long-lasting physical damages to key infrastructures, production facilities, London's financial centre and other heavily populated met-ropolitan areas.[18]

It is also possible that UK banks and insurers are more likely to suffer large losses from extreme weather events abroad. For example, Lloyd's (2015) has pub-lished a climate-related global stress scenario which involves a sharp reduction in food production across a number of countries. However, there are challenges associated in identifying a global stress scenario which is most relevant for the stability of the UK financial system, as climate change physical risk could manifest itself in a multitude of ways and locations.[19] Moreover, the behaviour of foreign governments and financial institutions is likely to be a key determinant of the impact of an extreme weather event abroad on the stability of the UK financial system. More generally, designing a credible systemwide stress test for global climate-related physical risks remains a challenge given the uncertainties about the effects of climate change on weather events across the world and the transmission of weather-related disasters through the financial system and the economy.

Nevertheless, the disclosure of new information used in stress tests could help enable financial market participants to make their own assessments about climate-related risk exposure of particular institutions. For example, although many authorities have been criticised for conducting stress tests that lacked credibility, some have welcomed them on the grounds that they helped to release a large volume of information that enabled market participants to make their own assessments (Ahmed et al. 2011; Ong and Pazarbasioglu 2013; Candelon and Sy 2015).

To be informative, climate-related stress tests should aim to identify how the economic losses would be distributed and propagated within the financial system under a given scenario and not simply on the amount of insured losses that could be generated by a weather-related event. Such a stress test would also need to examine the possibility that the insurance and banking sectors might react to the initial shock in such a way as to magnify the impact on the economy, as described in Section 2.1. It is also important to ensure that any policy response to such stress test results does not induce a reduction in the supply of insurance against climate-related physical risks, as this may simply pass on the risks elsewhere in the financial system without necessarily increasing the stability of the financial system as a whole.

3.2 Stress testing against transition risks

Stress testing the financial system against transition risks is *conceptually* more straightforward. This requires constructing a technologically plausible scenario which is consistent with transforming the domestic and global economy within a pre-specified transition period in order for it to be consistent with the goal of maintaining the global warming to below 2 degrees in the long run. At the most basic level, the financial system could be stress-tested against a specific path of carbon price which could affect its exposure to non-financial corporations in several industries. This approach has the advantage of capturing the financial impact of internalising the carbon externalities on firms to which the financial sector is exposed without having to specify the policy used to implement it or prejudging the entities and sectors being affected. An alternative approach would be to use sector-level projections constructed by international organisations.

There may be *practical* challenges associated with such a stress test, however. First, leaving significant leeway for individual financial institutions in estimating how a specific climate policy scenario, for example a given increase in carbon price, could affect their financial exposures might be problematic in the absence of reliable portfolio-level information that allows regulators and investors to verify these estimates and compare across institutions. Thus, in the absence of such information, a stress test using a more tightly specified transition scenario, for example one that outlines the amount of losses in each industry, might be more informative.

Second and more importantly, regulators currently face significant data gaps in assessing the impact of a transition scenario on the financial sector. As noted by Battiston et al. (2017), exposure data at the level of individual financial institutions to do a full stress test of the financial system is unavailable for the Euro Area, even to financial authorities. Moreover, because bank loan data are not collected at sufficiently granular sectoral levels, it is not even possible to compute precisely the exposure of banks to the climate-relevant sectors via their loans. Based on an analysis using fairly broad sectoral aggregation, they conclude that a typical Euro Area bank would not default solely due to its exposures over loans to firms in the fossil and utilities sectors, but climate policies impacting (i) energy intensive and transport or (ii) the housing sector would imply increased volatility on a portion of assets representing respectively about 50 and 280% of banks' assets.

These considerations suggest that further progress on climate-related disclosures at company level could help inform such stress tests.

4. What role for central banks and financial regulators in mitigating climate-related risks for the financial sector?

Central banks and financial regulators could potentially play two types of roles in mitigating risks associated with asset stranding. First, these institutions could help ensure that the assessment of climate-related risks by private financial institutions is based on good models and data. Second, they can also ensure that financial institutions have the ability to absorb losses arising from climate-related risks. This section discusses both existing initiatives and possible areas for future work for central banks and financial regulators.

4.1 Encouraging more efficient pricing and distribution of catastrophe risks

Natural disasters are more likely to lead to distress or failures of insurance companies if they underestimate the risks *ex ante* and have insufficient capital as a result. The existing analyses suggest that the insurance industry may indeed be underestimating the impact of climate change on catastrophe risks. Standard and Poor's (2014a) argues that reinsurers might be underestimating their exposure to 1-in-10-year and 1-in-250-year catastrophe losses by an average of about 50%, using an illustrative scenario analysis to test the potential impact of climate change. Lloyd's (2014) suggests that, despite improvements since Hurricane Andrew, most catastrophe models – which are now used extensively by insurers and reinsurers, as well as governments, capital markets and other financial entities – still tend to rely heavily on historical data and do not necessarily incorporate climate change trends explicitly. More recently, however, some institutions have started to develop catastrophe models that incorporate the impact of climate change.[20]

But the issue is not just about the possible underestimation of the likelihood of particular types of events. Climate change may also change the correlation between individual risks – for example the extent to which European wind storms happen in clusters – and the assumptions made about these correlations affect the setting of insurance firms' capital requirements. Larger catastrophes could also affect multiple sectors and thus can result in correlated losses across business lines. The impact of climate change on these correlations is highly uncertain but could imply that benefits from diversification are reduced.

Greater collaboration between central banks, financial regulators and the scientific community could also result in better use of the scientific data to validate existing catastrophe risk models and to develop new models. This in turn could lead to more efficient pricing of catastrophe risks and greater insurance coverage of vulnerable populations. Better understanding and pricing of physical climate risks *ex ante* could in turn reduce the risk of asset stranding *ex post*, for example by reducing both the incentives and availability of finance for property developers to construct buildings in flood-prone areas. We note, however, that uncertainty about the wider repercussions of extreme weather events implies that certain risks – such as the likelihood that they trigger riots that could cause further damage – are inherently hard to model.

4.2 Effective disclosure of climate-related risks

In December 2015, the Financial Stability Board (FSB) set up an industry-led Task Force on Climate-related Financial Disclosures (TCFD) to make recommendations for consistent and voluntary company disclosures that will help financial market participants understand their climate-related risks. The Task Force published its final report in June 2017.[21] The disclosure framework is intended for all publicly listed companies across sectors and jurisdictions and covers four areas of governance, strategy, risk management and metrics and targets. Importantly, companies are encouraged to use scenario analysis to assess potential business, strategic and financial implications of climate-related risks and opportunities, and disclose them in their mainstream financial filings. The Task Force recommends that companies explicitly consider a 2-degree scenario, reflecting the international commitment under the Paris Agreement.

Disclosure is a tool which is mainly aimed at removing asymmetric information between the firm's management and investors. Investors may be interested in different types of climate-related disclosures depending on their objectives and concerns. For example, those investors that only care about the financial risks to which they are exposed may be interested primarily in disclosures about firms' forward-looking strategies to increase the robustness of their business models to a tighter policy on carbon emissions, changes in technology and societal attitude on carbon emissions.[22] By contrast, those investors that also care about the externalities caused by carbon emissions generated by firms in their portfolios for ethical reasons might also care about firms' current carbon emissions and their strategies for reducing them in the future.[23]

In general, the effectiveness of disclosure in improving market efficiency depends on whether other frictions are also present. If asymmetric information is the only friction in the market, then its removal through disclosure should enable market participants to price risks more accurately and to avoid investing in firms that they consider are causing large negative externalities. Well-designed climate-related disclosures should help investors to price risks associated with a tighter policy on carbon emissions. This in turn could encourage firms to adopt strategies that lower their exposures to such risks, for example by investing in products that are less carbon intensive. Thus, effective disclosure could facilitate orderly transition to a low-carbon economy if it manages to inform and influence the asset-allocation decisions of a large number of investors. It could also help inform policy institutions that can either influence or are affected by transition risks, including governments and central banks.

The existing literature points to a number of high-level considerations which must be taken into account in order to ensure that disclosure produces a more efficient outcome. First, the published information must be relevant to the investors' objectives in order for them to pay attention to it (Sowerbutts et al. 2013). For example, if only a subset of investors care about the externalities associated with carbon emissions by firms that they invest in, then the information about firms' carbon emissions might not necessarily influence the investment decisions of those that only care about financial risks.

Second, if multiple frictions are present, then 'the theory of the second best' might apply: in general, if there are several frictions in the market, then removing one friction could lead to worse outcomes.[24] In such a context, disclosure could induce firms to change their strategy to focus on improving the metric which is being disclosed rather than long-term economic efficiency. This highlights the importance of choosing the right metric: for example, encouraging firms to disclose only their current carbon emissions might incentivise them to invest in technologies that can reduce them in the near term rather than investing in technologies that could reduce emissions more substantially in the longer term.

Third, if the disclosed information is difficult to interpret and investors face differential costs in understanding it, then disclosure could end up making some investors better informed while leaving others uninformed, thus encouraging uninformed investors to demand a higher premium from investing in firms in order to avoid losing to better-informed investors (Easley and O'Hara 2004).[25] Disclosure of information that is hard to interpret could also encourage uninformed investors to hold less information-sensitive debt, and the resulting fall in the cost of debt relative to equity could encourage firms to take on greater leverage (Dang et al. 2009). This strand of literature suggests that climate-related disclosure needs to be designed in such a way to better inform a wide range of investors.

For some investors, the way financial institutions implement the FSB's disclosure recommendations may also matter. For example, retail investors may not pay any attention to climate-related risks in choosing financial products unless the information is presented in a way that is easy to find (e.g. on online investment platforms), easy to compare against and easy to act upon. While institutional investors are important, retail investors do matter in aggregate. For example, BCG estimates that, of the US$71.4 trillion of assets under management globally at end-2015, 40% were retail, and that this segment has been growing relative to the institutional segment. Retail interest in sustainable investment is increasing: the global sustainable investment market is estimated to have grown to US$22.9 trillion at the start of 2016, up 25% since 2014, while the share of retail assets in total sustainable investment in Canada, Europe and the United States is estimated to have increased from 13% to 26% during the same period.[26] The climate-related financial disclosures could therefore have a major impact on this segment if the disclosed information is presented in a simple and user-friendly format, which allows retail investors to understand, assess and compare the climate-related risks in alternative financial products.

To sum up, the existing literature suggests that climate-related disclosures are more likely to benefit a wider range of investors, and hence be more effective, if they are based on forward-looking information that is relevant for assessing financial risks and returns. To influence the decisions of a wide-range of investors, such information will have to be communicated in a manner that is simple to interpret. For example, firms could be encouraged to disclose their own estimates of how their market value would be affected by a given increase in carbon price, which would capture the impact of a tighter policy on carbon emissions. Such disclosure could be accompanied by publication of relevant hard, verifiable data (e.g. about ownership of assets that are heavily exposed to a tighter climate policy) and the assumptions used for estimating the impact of a higher carbon price (e.g. on demand for their output and input prices), as well as the value of their assets (e.g. the value of oil reserves in the case of an oil company), so as to help enable investors and analysts to scrutinise the calculations. Disclosure of such information by non-financial firms could also inform central banks and regulators in assessing the impact of transition risks on the financial system.

4.3 Mitigating prudential risks associated with stranded assets

The decision of financial institutions to fund activities that are intensive in CO_2 emissions can contribute to increasing the climate-related physical risks, albeit indirectly; and conversely, their financing of technologies that help reduce CO_2 emissions can contribute to a reduction of climate-related physical risks. This is a problem of *externalities*, as the financial institutions that fund these activities do not necessarily suffer the losses and gains resulting from changes in climate-related physical risks, most of which might occur in the future, and hence may not internalise these losses and gains when making the funding decisions. The standard ways of addressing such externalities include appropriate use of taxes and subsidies and legislation that directly targets the specific externalities.

It has been argued that macroprudential financial regulation should be used to encourage lending towards low-carbon sectors (e.g. Campiglio 2016). We think that prudential regulations are blunt instruments for dealing with climate-related externalities, and hence using them for the purpose of internalising these externalities could give risk to undesirable outcomes. For example, capital requirements for banks and insurers are designed to mitigate prudential risks, and hence adapting these to reflect externalities could undermine their primary purpose or could give rise to undesirable effects. On the one hand, relaxing regulations just to encourage particular types of lending, for example by reducing risk weights that are used in calculating the regulatory capital ratios below their prudentially sound levels, could jeopardise the safety and soundness of financial institutions.[27] On the other hand, tightening regulations on financial exposures to carbon-intensive firms could also have the unintended effect of increasing the cost of finance for those borrowers, thus reducing their ability to invest in emission-reducing technologies (e.g. CCS and renewables), unless exclusions can be applied to financing that is specifically earmarked for such investments. Thus, targeted policy measures are more likely to be effective in achieving climate-related objectives than adapting prudential regulations. Such policies might include appropriately priced carbon taxes on firms' activities, which could vary over time.

That said, a case can be made for prudential regulators to take measures to ensure that financial institutions have adequate capacity to absorb losses arising from asset stranding if prudential risks arising from asset stranding are found to be material. Any such decision would need to be backed by thorough rigorous risk assessment. Moreover, the regulatory tools need to be selected and calibrated carefully to avoid undesirable side effects, such as those discussed earlier.

5. Conclusion

This chapter has outlined two main ways in which climate change and climate policies impact the financial stability objectives of central banks. First, a weather-related natural disaster could trigger financial instability and a macroeconomic downturn if it causes severe damage to the balance sheets of households, corporations, banks and insurers (*physical risks*). The economic impact of a given natural disaster is likely to be less severe if the relevant risks are priced in financial contracts *ex ante* and the financial system has distributed them efficiently, for example via insurance and reinsurance.

Second, a sudden, unexpected tightening of carbon emission policies could lead to a disorderly re-pricing of carbon-intensive assets (*transition risks*). This has a potential for generating balance sheet losses for financial institutions that hold these assets and, in extremis, financial instability. An orderly transition to a low-carbon economy is possible and is likely to be facilitated by transparent and predictable policies on carbon emissions that encourage an early re-direction of private investment towards low-carbon technologies.

Further work is needed to assess and quantify the magnitude of prudential risks arising from both of these sources, but there are several barriers for detailed risk assessment, including (i) the scientific uncertainty over the impact of climate change on physical risks in the medium term, (ii) uncertainty over the direction of climate-related policies and (iii) data gaps. Those financial regulators which are mandated to focus on prudential and financial stability risks may not see the case for using financial regulations to mitigate the impact of these risks on the financial sector without clear evidence of material financial stability risks, especially when financial regulations are not the best tool to address these risks, for reasons outlined earlier.

Nevertheless, we think there are at least two areas in which central banks and financial regulators could contribute in mitigating the financial risks associated with climate change and climate-related policies. First, central banks could collaborate with other financial regulators and the scientific community to encourage better use of the scientific data to test existing catastrophe risk models and to develop new models. Better understanding and pricing of physical climate risks *ex ante* could in turn reduce the risk of asset stranding *ex post*, for example by reducing both the incentives and availability of finance for developers to construct in disaster-prone areas. This in turn is likely to mitigate financial stability risks arising from climate-related natural catastrophes.

Second, central banks and regulators can judge whether climate-related disclosure by industries are succeeding in reducing the build-up of climate-related financial stability risks. Such disclosure is likely to be more effective if it can ultimately be communicated in a manner that is forward looking, relevant for financial risks and simple to understand – for example, how a given change in carbon price will affect the value of the firm. Over time, effective disclosure could also help inform the central banks' assessment of financial stability risks arising from the transition to a low-carbon economy.

Annex 1

Losses from past natural disasters, 1980–2016

Table 10.A1 Five costliest natural loss events, ordered by inflation-adjusted overall losses, 1980–2016

Date	Event	Affected areas	Overall losses (US$m, 2016 values)	Insured losses (US$m, 2016 values)	Insured losses to overall losses (percent)	Fatalities
11 Mar 2011	Earthquake, tsunami	Japan: Honshu, Miyagi, Sendai, Aomori, Tohoku, Fukushima, Mito, Ibaraki, Tochigi, Utsunomiya, Iwate, Morioka, Yamagata, Chiba, Tokyo	162,000	30,900	19.1	15,880
25–30 Aug 2005	Hurricane Katrina, storm surge	United States: LA, New Orleans, Slidell, MS, Biloxi, Pascagoula, Waveland, Gulfport, Bay St. Louis, Hattiesburg, McComb, AL, FL	154,000	74,300	48.2	1,720
12 May 2008	Earthquake	China: Sichuan, Mianyang, Beichuan, Wenchuan, Shifang, Chengdu, Guangyuan, Ngawa, Ya'an, Ziyang, Chongqing, Yunnan, Maoxian, Meishan, Suining, Garzê, Neijiang, Gansu, Shaanxi	107,000	380	0.4	86,445
17 Jan 1995 23–31 Oct 2012	Earthquake Hurricane Sandy, storm surge	Japan: Hyogo, Kobe, Osaka, Kyoto United States, Cuba, Haiti, Bahamas, Canada, Jamaica, Dominican Republic, Puerto Rico	89,800 71,600	2,700 30,500	3.0 42.6 22.7	6,430 207

Source: Munich RE NatCat SERVICE (as of August 2017); http://natcatservice.munichre.com/topten/1?filter=eyJ5ZWFyRnJvbSI6MTk4MCwieWVhclRvIjoyMDE2IQ%3D%3D&type=1

Table 10.A2 Five costliest meteorological loss events, ordered by inflation-adjusted overall losses, 1980–2016

Date	Event	Affected areas	Overall losses (US$m, 2016 values)	Insured losses (US$m, 2016 values)	Insured losses to overall losses (percent)	Fatalities
25–30 Aug 2005	Hurricane Katrina, storm surge	United States: LA, New Orleans, Slidell, MS, Biloxi, Pascagoula, Waveland, Gulfport, Bay St. Louis, Hattiesburg, McComb, AL, FL	154,000	74,300	48.2	1,720
23–31 Oct 2012	Hurricane Sandy, storm surge	United States, Cuba, Haiti, Bahamas, Canada, Jamaica, Dominican Republic, Puerto Rico	71,600	30,500	42.6	207
23–27 Aug 1992	Hurricane Andrew	United States, Bahamas	45,700	29,100	63.7	66
6–14 Sep 2008	Hurricane Ike	United States, Cuba, Turks and Caicos Islands, Dominican Republic, Haiti	41,100	20,700	50.4	168
7–21 Sep 2004	Hurricane Ivan, storm surge	United States, Cayman Islands, Grenada, Jamaica, Saint Vincent and the Grenadines, Trinidad and Tobago, Saint Lucia, Barbados, Cuba, Dominican Republic, Haiti	28,700	15,000	52.3	120
					51.4	

Source: Munich RE NatCat SERVICE (as of August 2017); http://natcatservice.munichre.com/topten/1?filter=eyJ5ZWFyRnJvbSI6MTk4MCwieWVhclRvIjoyMDE2fQ%3D%63D&type=1

Table 10.A3 Five costliest meteorological loss events in Europe, ordered by inflation-adjusted overall losses, 1980–2016

Date	Event	Affected areas	Overall losses (US$m, 2016 values)	Insured losses (US$m, 2016 values)	Insured losses to overall losses (percent)	Fatalities
26 Dec 1999	Winter Storm Lothar	France, Germany, Switzerland, Belgium, Italy	15,400	8,400	54.5	113
25–26 Jan 1990	Winter Storm Daria	United Kingdom, Germany, Netherlands, France, Belgium, Denmark, Luxembourg, Poland, Ireland, Norway, Finland, Sweden	10,100	7,700	76.2	85
15–16 Oct 1987	Winter Storm 87J	United Kingdom, France, Norway, Spain	9,100	5,400	59.3	18
18–20 Jan 2007	Winter Storm Kyrill	Germany, United Kingdom, Netherlands, Belgium, Austria, France, Czech Republic, Poland, Belarus, Denmark, Slovenia, Switzerland, Ukraine	7,800	4,500	57.7	49
25–27 Feb 1990	Winter Storm Vivian	Germany, United Kingdom, Belgium, France, Netherlands, Austria, Norway, Luxembourg, Switzerland, Denmark, Sweden, Finland, Ireland	4,300	3,400	79.1	51

Source: Munich RE NatCat SERVICE (as of August 2017); http://natcatservice.munichre.com/topten/1?filter=eyJ5ZWFyRnJvbSI6MTk4MCwieWVhclRvIjoyMDE2fQ%3D%3D&type=1

Table 10.A4 Five costliest hydrological loss events, ordered by inflation-adjusted overall losses, 1980–2016

Date	Event	Affected areas	Overall losses (US$m, 2016 values)	Insured losses (US$m, 2016 values)	Insured losses to overall losses (percent)	Fatalities
1 Aug – 15 Nov 2011	Flood, landslide	Thailand: North, Sukhothai, Phichit, Phitsanulok, Nakhon Sawan, Uthai Thani, Kumpangpetch, Tak, Central, Chai Nat, Sing Buri, Ang Thong, Phra Nakhon Si Ayuttaya, Chainat, Lopburi, Saraburi, Suphan Buri, Nakhon Pahom, Pathumthani, Nonthaburi, Samutsakhon, Northeast, Ubon, Ratchathani, Khon Kaen, Srisaket, Roi-et, Surin, Mahasarakham, Kalasin, East, Chacheongsao, Nakhon Nayok, Prachinburi, South, Krabi, Phang Nga, Bangkok	39,900	14,800	37.1	813
27 Jun – 15 Aug 1993	Flood	United States: MS, MO, IA, IL, ND, IN, MN, WI, KS, NE, SD	34,900	2,200	6.3	48
Jun – Sep 1998	Flood (Jangtze River)	China: Jiangxi, Anhui, Hubei, Hunan, Chongqing, Sichuan, Yunnan, Jiangsu, Zheijiang, Guangdong, Fujian, Guangxi	28,600	540	1.9	3,600
12–22 Aug 2002	Flood, flash flood	Germany, Austria, Czech Republic, Hungary, Switzerland, Slovakia	24,400	5,300	21.7	39
24 Jul – 18 Aug 1995	Flood	Korea, Democratic People's Republic of:	23,600	n/a	n/a	68

Source: Munich RE NatCat SERVICE (as of August 2017); http://natcatservice.munichre.com/topten/1?filter=eyJ5ZWFyRnJvbSI6MTk4MCwieWVhclRvIjoyMDE2fQ%3D%3D&type=1

Annex 2

Event study methodology

We apply a standard event study to examine the market reaction to a number of climate-/"carbon bubble"–related events. An event study aims to examine behaviour for a sample of firms experiencing a common event – in this case a climate-related news event – that may affect the valuation of firms where a large part of their business is to produce energy.

To determine whether a date is an 'event' we search Lexis Nexis for "carbon bubble", "burnable carbon" and "fossil fuels divestment". We restrict our search to news stories appearing in major newspapers such as the *New York Times*, *Wall Street Journal*, *The Times*, the *Financial Times*, *Guardian* and *The Telegraph* and also to specialist energy periodicals. Where two stories have a high degree of similarity we take the first appearance of that story as a date. When news events appear within five days of each other it is difficult to disentangle the events and the later event is not examined nor is it to calculate normal returns. Although we have more than 50 different events during January 2011 to January 2016, this exclusion means we end up with 34 events in total. We also do a separate test for the single event of the COP21 agreement.

We examine energy firms in France, Germany, UK and the United States and the relevant benchmark indexes for each country from 4 January 2011–15 January 2016. This covers all firms on the energy sector from coal firms to renewable-energy firms. Equity price data was obtained from Datastream and benchmark data from Bloomberg Finance L.P.

To estimate normal returns we use a very simple market model for our baseline specification, where:

$$return_{it} = \alpha + \beta return_{mkt,t} + \eth_t$$

Due to the large number of clustered events it is difficult to find a long period of time without an event, and so we use all days which are not within five days of an event for our estimation window.

In our baseline specification we use an event window of 0 to +5 days to estimate cumulative abnormal returns, although we also check that our results are robust to using other estimation windows.

Our null hypothesis is that cumulative abnormal returns (CAR) over the event window are zero and our test statistic is CAR divided by an estimate of its standard deviation. As all the events are clustered in time this renders the independence assumption for the abnormal returns in the cross-section incorrect, biasing the estimated standard deviation downwards and biasing any test statistic upwards. As a result, we use the standard deviation of the equity's returns in non-event periods to calculate the benchmark test statistic. However, because the climate change events should – in theory – be associated with increased uncertainty for the firms affected, using non-event period variance may understate the true variance of returns during the period. As a result we compute an alternative test statistic using the variance of returns in the estimation window.

Notes

1 The views expressed in this chapter are those of the authors and cannot be taken to represent those of the Bank of England or to state Bank of England policy. This chapter should therefore not be reported as representing the views of the Bank of England or members of the Monetary Policy Committee, Financial Policy Committee or Prudential Regulation Committee.

2 See, for example, the European Systemic Risk Board (2016).

3 Bank of England (2015) and Carney (2015) have noted that "liability risk" could potentially also affect the insurance industry. Parties that have suffered loss and damage arising from physical or transition risk from climate change could seek to recover losses from others who they believe might have been responsible. If such claims are upheld, those parties against whom the successful claims are made either will have to bear the losses themselves or could seek to pass on some or all of the losses to their liability insurance providers. This chapter does not discuss this risk, as it is not directly related to asset stranding.

4 IPCC (2014) classifies the level of additional risk due to climate change into "undetectable", "moderate", "high" and "very high". The strength of scientific evidence linking climate change to the likelihood of specific types of hazards is variable. For example, IPCC (2014) suggests that there is reasonably strong evidence linking climate change to a decrease in cold temperature extremes, an increase in warm temperature extremes (e.g. heat waves), an increase in extreme high sea levels (e.g. storm surges) and an increase in the number of heavy precipitation events in a number of regions. By contrast, evidence linking climate change to frequency and magnitude of fluvial floods, droughts and tropical cyclone activity is either more limited or less robust and varies across regions, although links have been made in specific cases (e.g. Schaller et al. 2016).

5 Increasing warming also increases the risk of triggering "tipping points" – such as thawing of permafrost, release of methane and collapse of land-based polar ice sheets – which could have profound, irreversible consequences (Stern 2013).

6 Bank of England (2015) noted that the use of catastrophe risk modelling, portfolio diversification, alternative risk transfer and short-term contracts would suggest general insurers are reasonably well equipped to manage the current level of direct physical risks.

7 In agreeing to set up Flood Re, the insurance industry obtained a commitment from the government that it will continue minimum levels of investment in flood defence and maintenance over the 25-year period. See www.floodre.co.uk/ for further details on Flood Re.

8 Although most mortgage providers generally require buildings insurance as a condition for granting a mortgage, they do not necessarily require cover for specific hazards, such as floods, to be in place.

9 For example, after the Great East Japan Earthquake in March 2011 – which remains the largest natural disaster since 1980 based on total losses – the Bank of Japan had to offer record amounts of liquidity (BoJ 2011).

10 Evidence on the impact of natural disasters on risk preference is mixed. Some studies suggest that exposure to natural disasters leads to an increase in observed risk aversion (see Cassar et al. 2011; Cameron and Shah 2015). Other studies, however, find a decrease in risk aversion and an increase in risky behaviours such as gambling and drinking (see Ingwersen 2014; Eckel et al. 2009; and Hanaoka et al. 2015). Bernile et al. (2017) find that CEOs who experience natural disasters without suffering extremely negative consequences lead firms to behave more aggressively, whereas CEOs who witness the extreme downside of natural disasters behave more conservatively.

11 The reduction in energy intensity of GDP can be achieved in a number of ways, including via (i) changes in energy consumption behaviour and lifestyles, (ii) changes in economic incentives to consume energy and (iii) the low-cost availability of energy-efficient technology.

12 Policies aimed at reducing carbon emissions can either target a given quantity of emissions (through a cap-and-trade system such as the EU Emission Trading Scheme – ETS) or their price (through carbon taxes).

13 Van Vuuren et al. (2011) notes that, by 2100, the total fossil fuel energy use is projected to rise above the levels used in 2000 under all RCPs, including in RCP 2.6, which is likely to keep the warming below 2°C due to the assumed deployment of CCS technologies.

14 There is a possibility that a pre-commitment of policy tightening on carbon emission (e.g. via a carbon tax that increases over time) could incentivise fossil fuel producers to extract fossil fuels (e.g. oil) at a faster rate before policy is tightened further (e.g. Sinclair 1994). This incentive could be mitigated by the low elasticity of oil demand, which implies that increased oil supply could lead to a collapse of oil and other fossil fuel prices.

15 Arabella Advisors (2016).

16 The sector includes all the firms in the exploration and production, integrated oil and gas, oil equipment and services, pipelines, renewable energy equipment and alternative fuels sectors.

17 Carbon bubble is the notion that the companies that are dependent on fossil fuel-based energy production could be considered as overvalued when the possibility that some fossil fuel reserves may become unusable or "stranded" if the global warming is to be kept within certain limits.

18 For example, Climate UK (2012) notes that, while London is well protected against tidal flooding through the Thames Barrier, it is vulnerable to surface water flooding, which could increase in frequency if climate change leads to heavier rainfalls, which could overcome the drainage system.

19 For more information and examples of the significant climate anomalies and weather events around the world, see the NOAA annual Global Climate Report (NOAA 2016).

20 See, for example, RMS: www.rms.com/blog/2014/06/24/rms-and-risky-business-modeling-climate-change-risk/

21 Available at: www.fsb-tcfd.org/publications/

22 The first type of investors is likely to care about firms' current and past carbon emissions only if they think the risk of these firms being successfully sued for causing climate change is sufficiently high.

23 For disclosure aimed at climate-conscious investors, see, for example, the proposal by Oxford Martin School (2015).

24 Goldstein and Sapra (2014), for example, show that disclosure requirements could encourage the firm management to choose less productive assets, which are simpler for market participants to understand.
25 Thakor (2015) also shows that mandatory disclosure of soft strategic information may make firms more fragile, as it could generate disagreements amongst short-term debt holders and induce them to "run" or to not finance projects.
26 Global Sustainable Investment Alliance (2017).
27 A private-sector firm which specialised in such lending, based on reduced capital risk weights – an entirely plausible outcome – would have insufficient capital to be prudentially safe and sound. Such lending could, however, be made by an entity with a state guarantee.

References

Ahmed, E., Appeddu, A., Bowler, M., Holinka, T., Licari, J. M., Loiseau-Aslanidi, O. and Witton, Z. 2011. Europe Misses Again on Bank Stress Tests. *Regional Financial Review*, Moody's Analytics, July.

Arabella Advisors. 2016. *The Global Fossil Fuel Divestment and Clean Energy Investment Movement*, December.

Bank of England. 2015. *The Impact of Climate Change on the UK Insurance Sector: A Climate Change Adaptation Report by the Prudential Regulation Authority*. Available at: www.bankofengland.co.uk/pra/documents/supervision/activities/pradefra0915.pdf

Bank of Japan. 2011. *Responses to the Great East Japan Earthquake by Payment and Settlement Systems and Financial Institutions in Japan*. Payment and Settlement Systems Department.

Battiston, S., Mandel, A., Monasterolo, I., Schuetze, F. and Visentin, G. 2017. A Climate Stress-Test of the Financial System. *Nature Climate Change*, 7, 283–288.

Bernile, G., Bhagwat, V. and Rau, P. R. 2017. What Doesn't Kill You Will Only Make You More Risk-Loving: Early-Life Disasters and CEO Behavior. *Journal of Finance*, 72, 167–206.

Cameron, L. and Shah, M. 2015. Risk-Taking Behavior in the Wake of Natural Disasters. *Journal of Human Resources*, 50(2), 484–515.

Campiglio, Emanuele. 2016. Beyond Carbon Pricing: The Role of Banking and Monetary Policy in Financing the Transition to a Low-Carbon Economy. *Ecological Economics*, 121, 220–230.

Candelon, B. and Sy, A. N. R. 2015. How Did Markets React to Stress Tests? *IMF Working Paper* 15/75.

Carney, M. 2015. *Breaking the Tragedy of the Horizon – Climate Change and Financial Stability*. Speech at Lloyd's of London, September 29. Available at: www.bankof england.co.uk/publications/Documents/speeches/2015/speech844.pdf

Cassar, A., Healy, A. and von Kessler, C. 2011. Trust, Risk and Time Preferences After a Natural Disaster: Experimental Evidence From Thailand. *Working Paper*.

Chartered Insurance Institute. 2009. *Coping With Climate Change: Risk and Opportunities for Insurers*. Available at: www.cii.co.uk/knowledge/policy-and-public-affairs/articles/coping-with-climate-change/22989

Climate UK. 2012. *A Summary of Climate Change Risks for London*. Available at: http://climatelondon.org.uk/wp-content/uploads/2012/01/CCRA-London.pdf

Cortes, K. and Strahan, P. 2015. Tracing Out Capital Flows: How Financially Integrated Banks Respond to Natural Disasters. *Federal Reserve Bank of Cleveland Working Paper*, No. 14–12.

Dang, T., Gorton, G. and Holmstrom, B. 2009. Opacity and the Optimality of Debt for Liquidity Provision. *Working Paper*.

Easley, D. and O'Hara, M. 2004. Information and the Cost of Capital. *Journal of Finance*, 59(4), 1553–1583, 8.

Eckel, M., El-Gamalb, A. and Wilson, R. K. 2009. Risk Loving After the Storm: A Bayesian-Network Study of Hurricane Katrina Evacuees. *Journal of Economic Behavior & Organization*, 69, 110–124.

Environmental Agency. 2009. *Flooding in England: A National Assessment of Flood Risk*. Available at: www.gov.uk/government/uploads/system/uploads/attachment_data/file/292928/geho0609bqds-e-e.pdf

European Systemic Risk Board. 2016. Too Late, Too Sudden: Transition to a Low-Carbon Economy and Systemic Risk. *Reports of the Advisory Scientific Committee*, No. 6, February.

Farid, M., Keen, M., Papaioannou, M., Parry, I., Pattillo, C., Ter-Martirosyan, A. and Other IMF Staff. 2016. After Paris: Fiscal, Macroeconomic, and Financial Implications of Climate Change. *IMF Staff Discussion Note*, SDN 16/01.

Federal Reserve Bank of New York. 2014. *Superstorm Sandy: Update From Businesses in Affected Areas*. Available at: www.newyorkfed.org/medialibrary/interactives/fall2013/fall2013/files/key-findings-sandy.pdf

French, A. and Vital, M. 2015. Insurance and Financial Stability. *Bank of England Quarterly Bulletin*, 2015Q3.

FSB Task Force on Climate-Related Financial Disclosures. 2017. *Final Report: Recommendations of the Task Force on Climate-Related Financial Disclosures*. June 15. Available at: www.fsb-tcfd.org/publications/

Fuss, S., Canadell, J. G., Peters, G. P., Tavoni, M., Andrew, R. M., Ciais, P., Jackson, R. B., Jones, C. D., Kraxner, F., Nakicenovic, N. and Le Quéré, C. 2014. Betting on Negative Emissions. *Nature Climate Change*, 4(10), 850–853.

Garmaise, M. and Moskowitz, T. J. 2009. Catastrophic Risk and Credit Markets. *Journal of Finance*, LXIV(2), 657–707.

Garman, J. and Fox Carney, D. 2015. *Known Unknowns: The Hidden Threats That Climate Risks Pose to British Prosperity*. Institute for Public Policy Research. Available at: www.ippr.org/files/publications/pdf/known-unknowns-hidden-threats-climate-risks-nov2015.pdf?noredirect=1

Global Sustainable Investment Alliance. 2017. *2016 Global Sustainable Investment Review*.

Goldstein, I. and Sapra, H. 2014. Should Banks' Stress Test Results Be Disclosed? An Analysis of the Costs and Benefits. *Foundations and Trends(R) in Finance*, 8(1), 1–54.

Hanaoka, C., Shigeoka, H. and Watanabe, Y. 2015. Do Risk Preferences Change? Evidence From Panel Data Before and After the Great East Japan Earthquake. *NBER Working Paper 21400*.

Ingwersen, N. 2014. Impact of a Natural Disaster on Observed Risk Aversion. *Working Paper*.

Intergovernmental Panel on Climate Change. 2014. *Climate Change 2014 Synthesis Report*.

International Energy Agency. 2013. *Technology Road Map: Biofuels for Transport*. Paris: International Energy Agency.

Keen, B. D. and Pakko, M. R. 2010. Monetary Policy and Natural Disasters in a DSGE Model. *Federal Reserve Bank of St. Louis Research Division Working Paper* 2007-025D.

Klomp, J. 2014. Financial Fragility and Natural Disasters: An Empirical Analysis. *Journal of Financial Stability*, 13(C), 180–192.

Lambert, C. Noth, F. and Schüwer, U. 2015. How do banks react to catastrophic events? Evidence from Hurricane Katrina. *SAFE Working Paper Series 94*. Research Center SAFE – Sustainable Architecture for Finance in Europe, Goethe University Frankfurt.

Lamond, J. 2009. *Flooding and Property Values*. Available at: http://cwhsurveyors.co.uk/downloads/flooding-and-property-values.pdf

Landon-Lane, J., Rockoff, H. and Steckel, R. H. 2009. Droughts, Floods and Financial Distress in the United States. *NBER Working Paper*, No. 15596.

Lane, M. and Mahul, O. 2008. Catastrophe Risk Pricing: An Empirical Analysis. *World Bank Policy Research Working Paper*, No. 4765.

Lloyd's. 2014. *Catastrophe Modelling and Climate Change*. Available at: www.lloyds.com/~/media/lloyds/reports/emerging%20risk%20reports/cc%20and%20modelling%20template%20v6.pdf

Lloyd's. 2015. *Food System Shock*. Emerging Risk Report.

Meinshausen, M., Meinshausen, N., Hare, W., Raper, S. C., Frieler, K., Knutti, R., Frame, D. J. and Allen, M. R. 2009. Greenhouse-Gas Emission Targets for Limiting Global Warming to 2 °C. *Nature*, 458(7242), 1158–1162.

Met Office. 2011. *Climate: Observations, Projections and Impacts*. Available at: www.metoffice.gov.uk/media/pdf/t/r/UK.pdf

National Oceanic and Atmospheric Administration (NOA). 2016. *Global Climate Report – Annual 2016*. Available at: https://www.ncdc.noaa.gov/sotc/global/201613

Ong, L. L. and Pazarbasioglu, C. 2013. Credibility and Crisis Stress Testing. *IMF Working Paper* 13/178.

Oxford Martin School. 2015. *Working Principles for Investment in Fossil Fuels*. Available at: www.oxfordmartin.ox.ac.uk/downloads/reports/Net_Zero_Working_Principles.pdf.

Schaller, N., Kay, A. L., Lamb, R., Massey, N. R., van Oldenborgh, G. J., Otto, F. E., Sparrow, S. N., Vautard, R., Yiou, P., Ashpole, I. and Bowery, A. 2016. Human Influence on Climate in the 2014 Southern England Winter Floods and Their Impacts. *Nature Climate Change*, 6, 627–634. doi: 10.1038/NCLIMATE2927.

Sinclair, P. J. N. 1994. On the Optimal Trend of Fossil Fuel Taxation. *Oxford Economic Papers*, New Series, Vol. 46, Special Issue on Environmental Economics, October, pp. 869–877.

Sowerbutts, R., Zimmerman, P. and Zer, I. 2013. Banks' Disclosure and Financial Stability. *Bank of England Quarterly Bulletin*, 2013 Q4.

Standard and Poor's. 2014a. *Climate Change Could Sting Reinsurers That Underestimate Its Impact*. Available at: www.globalcreditportal.com/ratingsdirect/renderArticle.do?articleId=1356905&SctArtId=260148&from=CM&nsl_code=LIME&sourceObjectId=8706036&sourceRevId=1&fee_ind=N&exp_date=20240902-15:44:53&sf4482828=1#

Standard and Poor's. 2014b. *Climate Change Is a Global Mega-Trend for Sovereign Risk*. Available at: www.globalcreditportal.com/ratingsdirect/renderArticle.do?articleId=1318252&SctArtId=236925&from=CM&nsl_code=LIME&sourceObjectId=8606813&sourceRevId=1&fee_ind=N&exp_date=20240514-20:34:43

Stern, N. 2013. The Structure of Economic Modeling of the Potential Impacts of Climate Change: Grafting Gross Underestimation of Risk onto Already Narrow Science Models. *Journal of Economic Literature*, 51(3), 838–859.

Surminski, S. and Eldridge, J. 2014. Flood Insurance in England – an Assessment of the Current and Newly Proposed Insurance Scheme in the Context of Rising Flood Risk. *Centre for Climate Change Economics and Policy Working Paper*, No. 161, *Grantham Research Institute on Climate Change and the Environment Working Paper*, No. 144.

Swiss Re. 2014. *Liability Claims Trends: Emerging Risks and Rebounding Economic Drivers*. No. 4/2014.

Task Force on Climate-related Financial Disclosures. 2015. *Final Report - Recommendations of the Task Force on Climate-related Financial Disclosures*. Available at: https://www.fsb-tcfd.org/publications/final-recommendations-report/

Thakor, A. V. 2015. Strategic Information Disclosure When There Is Fundamental Disagreement. *Journal of Financial Intermediation*, 24(2), 131–153.

van Vuuren, D. P., Edmonds, J., Kainuma, M., Riahi, K., Thomson, A., Hibbard, K., Hurtt, G. C., Kram, T., Krey, V., Lamarque, J. F. and Masui, T. 2011. The Representative Concentration Pathways: An Overview. *Climatic Change*, 109, 5–31.

von Peter, G., von Dahlen, S. and Saxena, S. 2012. Unmitigated Disasters? New Evidence on the Macroeconomic Cost of Natural Catastrophes. *BIS Working Papers* No. 394.

11   Diversifying stranded asset risks by investing in "green"

Mobilising institutional investment in green infrastructure

Christopher R. Kaminker[1]

1. Introduction

1.1 Objective and organising framework

The objective of this chapter is to provide a survey of the role of institutional investors in financing green infrastructure. While institutional investors are increasingly evaluating and deploying strategies for green finance and investment in recognition of the opportunities presented by a transition to a lower-carbon economy, another important consideration is how investors view "climate risk". A growing body of literature examines how investors might better assess 'stranded assets risk' (Caldecott 2011; Gurria 2013; Bank of England 2015) originating through physical, liability and transition channels (Carney 2015), and 'rebalance or tilt' their portfolios towards green infrastructure to hedge against these risks.

As such, this chapter endeavours to highlight drivers of green finance and investment, including relevant examples in which the public sector has worked with institutional investors to support their involvement in green finance, in the context of an investment environment characterised by increasing attention to climate-related financial risk and stranded assets. Following an introductory section (1), the main body of the chapter is divided into three further sections:

1   A review of institutional investment in green infrastructure (focused on sustainable energy) that is occurring "organically", where government sets an "investment-grade" enabling environment and creates the demand for investment but does not deploy some form of a risk mitigant or transaction enabler to mobilise institutional investors;
2   A stock taking of institutional investment in green infrastructure where the public or official sector has worked to increase the supply of capital through deploying a risk mitigant or transaction enabler to facilitate an investment in green infrastructure;
3   A summary with implications for further research.

1.2 Green infrastructure investment needs and related financing and investment sources

Estimates suggest that approximately USD 89 trillion in infrastructure investment across transport, energy and water systems will be needed in the next 15 years – or USD 5.93 trillion annually, on average (NCE 2015) – in a "high-carbon" scenario (Figure 11.1). This is significantly higher than the approximately USD 3 trillion invested in all types of infrastructure today (McKinsey 2016). However, the incremental costs of making infrastructure investments "low-carbon" rather than "high carbon" are estimated by NCE (2015) to be only 4.5% (i.e. USD 4 trillion over the next 15 years, or USD 0.27 trillion per year on average). Green infrastructure[2] typically involves higher up-front investments than traditional infrastructure but comes with a wider set of returns and benefits.[3]

This suggests that investment for green infrastructure will need to take place at a far greater scale over coming decades to achieve the aims of the Paris Agreement and the Sustainable Development Goals. The scale of this investment is so large that it will, inevitably, have to rely in large part on mobilising private capital. Public finance can and does play a critical role to "jump start", mobilise and guide investment, but transformational change will require large-scale private-sector engagement (OECD 2015a). Examination of these issues so far has often been centred on the financing of climate change mitigation and adaptation and how to close the financing gap to fund the needed low-carbon investments.

Strategies for closing the financing gap need to consider (a) a policy regime that establishes price incentives and policy coherence and (b) the significant financial, regulatory and structural constraints faced by traditional sources of financing for

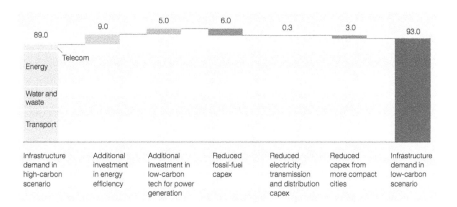

Figure 11.1 Up-front capital costs to meet global infrastructure demand

Note: Global demand for infrastructure services, 2015–2030, USD trillion (constant 2010 $, indicative figures)

Source: NCE (2015)

green infrastructure – governments, corporate actors (e.g. utilities, project developers and others) and the banking sector.

The global financial crisis and responses to it led to a transformation of the financial landscape, with changes in behaviour by the banking sector in particular. Long-term financing by banks has declined as they de-risk (deleverage) globally, although it is beginning to revitalise in some areas (Pooler 2014). In the capital markets, a range of factors including ambiguous macroeconomic prospects and declining forecasted returns for equity investments in publicly traded companies have had adverse effects on demand for long-term equity capital (OECD 2015a). In addition to constraints in the banking sector, other traditional sources of finance such as corporate actors also face their own constraints (OECD 2015a).

Despite these constraints, the banking sector remains a key provider of investment financing, but it likely will not be able to compensate for constraints among other traditional sources and fill the massive financing gap for sustainable infrastructure on its own. For instance, the People's Bank of China (PBoC) estimates that China will need to invest at least RMB 2 trillion (USD 320 billion) per year in green sectors in order to meet the environmental targets under the 13th Five Year Plan (2016–2020). Public fiscal resources, however, can cover no more than 15% of these investments (Green Finance Task Force 2015).

A related and broader issue is whether the financial system can enable capital reallocation consistent with the "green" transition and for the long run, that is by providing financing for companies and industries that protect and improve the environment and shifting financing away from fossil fuel industries and environmentally harmful activities (Boissinot et al. 2016; Wehinger and Nassr 2016 forthcoming). It is only through such a re-allocation that the infrastructural foundations of the global economy can be rewired to be consistent with keeping the global temperature increase to well below 2°C, as called for under the Paris Agreement.

1.3 The role of institutional investors

In this context, much attention has been focused on the potential for institutional investors – including pension funds, insurance companies, investment funds and sovereign wealth funds – to significantly increase their investments in green infrastructure. For instance, McKinsey (2016) estimates that institutional investors could provide USD 1 trillion to USD 1.5 trillion in additional private capital for sustainable projects – up to half of the current annual infrastructure investment gap. But that will happen only if a range of structural challenges and market barriers currently adding costs and restricting returns is removed and if policies are put in place to ensure adequate returns to meet institutional investors' liabilities.

In a low-interest-rate environment, and if governments provide a sound enabling environment, green infrastructure projects could be attractive to institutional investors. In many cases institutional investors have to invest for the long term in order to fund liabilities that are multi-generational in nature. As a subset of green infrastructure, sustainable energy projects offer many of the attributes of "core" infrastructure assets and have a number of unique characteristics which can appeal to institutional investors and are not monetised in internal-rate-of-return calculations. For instance, institutional investors require stable and predictable cash flows to meet their liabilities. These liabilities can be met in part through direct investments in sustainable energy assets, which can provide steady, long-term, inflation-linked income streams, due in part to low operating expenses and stable contracts for revenue. These income streams also have low correlations to the returns of other investments (Kaminker et al. 2015; OECD 2016b).

Despite these factors favouring green infrastructure investment, the broader context in which institutional investors make their capital allocation decisions has tended to limit their investments in these types of "real assets". Their decision-making process for allocating capital among different types of instruments and asset classes is complex and varies significantly across institutions and geographies. Institutional investors have varying risk appetites, liability profiles, investment preferences, illiquidity tolerances and other constraints, which will determine the extent to which they will seriously consider investments in green infrastructure. Moreover, institutional investors will not make an investment just because it is "green". Their primary concern is the risk-adjusted financial performance of the asset (Kaminker et al. 2015). Their willingness to finance major investment projects in any given country will be heavily influenced by perceptions of the country's sovereign risk, investment climate, policy settings and institutions.

Institutional investors managed USD 92.6 trillion in assets in 2013 in OECD countries (projected to grow to USD 120 trillion by 2019) and USD 10 trillion in emerging markets and developing countries (Kaminker et al. 2015; OECD/Bloomberg Philanthropies 2015).[4] Continued growth in funds under management is occurring in most markets. The main exposure of institutional investors to green infrastructure so far has been through indirect investments,[5] via holdings of the debt and equity of listed corporations active in the green infrastructure industry (OECD/Bloomberg Philanthropies 2015). Such indirect investments can be important for supporting sustainable energy projects in particular, as more than half of the capital directed to sustainable energy in 2015 came from corporate on-balance sheet financing (BNEF 2016). However, the scope for institutional investors to increase their indirect sustainable energy infrastructure investment is constrained by their willingness to purchase new debt and equity issued from corporations, which depends on institutional investors' perception of risk-adjusted return opportunities and the state of corporations' balance sheets (Kaminker et al. 2015). Furthermore, indirect investment – unlike direct investment in projects – does not necessarily translate into investments in projects and contribute to addressing the infrastructure investment gap.

While there are expanding pockets of activity in direct green infrastructure investment in projects by institutional investors, as illustrated in the examples provided in this report, these types of investments have been minimal compared to the scale of their assets. Looking just at large pension funds surveyed by the OECD, direct equity investment in unlisted infrastructure projects[6] of all types accounted for only 1% of their asset allocation in 2015, and green infrastructure accounted for only a fraction of that 1% (OECD 2016a).

1.4 Barriers to institutional investment in green infrastructure and challenges

The regulatory environment in which institutional investors operate and the risk-return profile of investments will determine whether institutional capital can be mobilised to support infrastructure development – and whether the infrastructure in question is "green". Policy makers can take actions to create an investment environment in which investors have lower risk perceptions and there are significant reductions in the cost of capital, which is fundamental to reducing the costs of green infrastructure.

The OECD has produced a significant amount of analysis discussing the barriers to institutional investors' investment in infrastructure in general and sustainable energy infrastructure in particular.[7] Kaminker et al. (2015) studied a collection of reasons for limited investment by institutional investors in sustainable energy projects specifically. It found that investors with fiduciary responsibilities generally look to policy makers to foster investment certainty and improve the risk-adjusted returns available from sustainable energy and that many institutional investors have yet to conclude that sustainable energy investments offer a sufficiently attractive risk-adjusted financial return. Standing in the way of increased investment are a number of potential obstacles, some that apply to infrastructure generally, others that are specific to sustainable energy. The report summarised these issues into four categories:

1   Weak, uncertain or counterproductive environmental, energy and climate policies.
2   Regulatory policies with unintended consequences.
3   A lack of suitable financial vehicles with attributes sought by institutional investors.
4   A shortage of objective data and skills to assess transactions and underlying risks and returns.

In addition to these barriers affecting institutional investment in green infrastructure in developed countries, there exist further barriers that are unique to emerging economies and developing countries. These are the countries that have large projected electricity demand, which implies colossal future infrastructure build. The mismatch between investment opportunities and risks and the need to address investment barriers is particularly evident in emerging and developing economies. Examples of further barriers affecting green infrastructure investment in these countries include (i) options to mitigate regulatory, currency and corruption risk are generally less available to investors and more costly than in developed countries, (ii) investment contracts are not standardised across countries, making due diligence more time consuming and expensive and (iii) international arbitration is often not an option, leaving disputes to be solved in local courts.

A more comprehensive set of barriers in developed as well as emerging economies and developing countries is provided in Kaminker et al. (2015) and World Bank/IMF/OECD (2015). After examining these barriers in depth,

Kaminker et al. (2015) proposed high-level policy recommendations and policy considerations for governments to facilitate institutional investors' investment in sustainable energy infrastructure (as a subset of green infrastructure), building on findings from previous G20/OECD reports.

1.5 Climate risk

The preceding discussion focuses on factors impacting how institutional investors view the opportunity presented by investment in sustainable energy and other green infrastructure. Another consideration that could impact green infrastructure investment as well as investment in emissions-intensive projects and activities is how investors view climate risk. In the wake of the Paris Agreement, investors can be expected to perceive increased regulatory risks around unabated fossil fuel–related investments and the potential for lower returns from such investments. Such changes in perceptions may be triggered by the expectation of increasingly stringent carbon pricing and climate change mitigation policy and by an evolving investor governance and disclosure landscape. Climate change itself, policies and technological changes in response to climate change and green finance all create risks that have various implications for the financial sector and institutional investors (Wehinger and Nassr 2016 forthcoming). As described by Bank of England (2015) and Carney (2015), among these are "physical risks" from climate change that mostly affect the insurance industry[8] but can extend to other sectors (e.g. banks' mortgage loan portfolio can be exposed)[9]. Related are "liability risks" for corporations that may be held responsible for climate change-related losses or damages and from which affected parties may seek compensation.

There are also risks linked to policy and technological responses to environmental challenges including climate change, which can affect the financial sector and institutional investors. These and related "transition risks" generally result from the adjustment process towards a cleaner and lower-carbon economy that can prompt a reassessment of asset values (Dietz et al. 2016), as their ability to generate returns is impaired and they face pre-mature write-downs or even conversion to liabilities, thus there is a potential for these assets to become stranded ("stranded assets") (CTI 2011; Caldecott et al. 2014). These risks mainly affect lenders and (equity) investors in projects concerned, but the re-pricing of assets may have effects that can go beyond the institutions or the sector in which it occurs, including broader economic effects (including for sovereigns and their ratings) and potentially impacts on financial stability (Dietz et al. 2016; Bank of England 2015; Carney 2015).

Despite growing awareness of climate-related risks to the financial sector and institutional investors in particular, the understanding of these risks is still incomplete (and may remain so) due to their complexity (ESRB 2016). Climate-related physical risk management in the insurance and re-insurance sectors is relatively sophisticated, but in other sectors and with regard to other sources of risks (i.e. transition risks), the work is still at an earlier stage in terms of data availability and quality, tools and methodologies as well as capacities devoted to environmental issues impacting the financial sector (FDF 2016). Enhanced transparency and disclosure of climate-related and environmental risk exposures across the corporate and financial sectors could help not only to improve understanding and analysis of the risks but also to improve the decision making of borrowers, lenders and investors alike. This could contribute to improved risk pricing and could support a more orderly transition to a low-carbon economy, allowing financial market actors to take a view on current as well as future risks and adjust investment strategies, improve long-run decision making and foster long-term investment by institutional investors (Wehinger and Nassr 2016 forthcoming).

For such reasons, disclosures with a focus on carbon exposures and their risks should become standard in the non-financial as well as the financial sectors. Efforts to improve disclosure are being undertaken at the OECD (OECD 2015a), as well as by the FSB's Task Force on Climate-related Financial Disclosures (TCFD) (FSB 2016). The NGO CDP has also been very active on disclosure issues. It requests "information on the risks and opportunities of climate from the world's largest companies on behalf of 827 institutional investor signatories with a combined US$100 trillion in assets".

2. Strengthening the demand for green institutional investment to develop organically

For institutional investors which manage a very large share of national savings, a fundamental pre-condition for investing in green infrastructure is the establishment of appropriate domestic framework conditions, which provide the clear price signals, predictability and policy coherence that investors need. While simple enough in principle, such a framework often proves difficult to achieve in practice, as retroactive policy changes, weak carbon pricing, fossil fuel subsidies and unintended effects of non-climate–related (e.g. financial and investment) regulations can undermine policies that are otherwise supportive of the low-carbon transition.

OECD/IEA/ITF/NEA (2015) and OECD (2016b) both find that even though technology costs are falling fast, policy and market obstacles still constrain overall growth in investment in renewable energy, limiting the pipeline of bankable projects and affecting the risk–return profile of investments. In addition to insufficiently ambitious climate mitigation policies, the misalignment of other policies and regulations with respect to climate goals can also act to hinder investment. Such misalignments may occur across the general investment environment, for instance in the areas of investment policy, competition policy and electricity market design, trade and financial markets policy (OECD/IEA/ITF/NEA 2015).

2.1 A survey of institutional investment activity and demand for green investment

In locations where sufficient preconditions are in place and other aspects of the enabling environment create circumstances in which investment demand is generated, investment will be more likely. Indeed, despite the overall low levels of investment in infrastructure compared to the size of the institutional investor market, investment demand for green and sustainable infrastructure is strong and growing, and investment activity is ramping up.

While no unified and systematic database exists for tracking stocks and flows of investments in green infrastructure by institutional investors, a number of estimates are available from different sources, and methodologies or templates for tracking and reporting investments are emerging. For instance, the Asset Owners Disclosure Project (AODP 2016) estimates that the stock of "low-carbon investments" across a range of asset classes by institutional investors was valued at USD 138 billion in 2016. On an individual and proportional basis, the UK Environment Agency Pension Fund holds the highest rank in the survey with 26.4% of AuM invested in low-carbon investments. At the national level, the Netherlands tops the country table for low-carbon investments on both an absolute and proportional basis – with an aggregate of USD 39 billion invested in low carbon, representing 3.4% of the total AuM in the country. This survey uses a reporting taxonomy for eligible investments elaborated by the Low Carbon Investment Registry, which in turn reports entries by institutional investors tallying to USD 50 billion. These figures could be considered as lower bounds to the stock of investments, given that they only describe investments by those who choose to report them.

The OECD's Large Pension Fund Survey (OECD 2016a) found that of the 26 pensions and reserve funds that reported[10] sector allocations in their infrastructure portfolios, nine reported exposure to renewable energy totalling USD 1.4 billion of investments, compared with USD 25 billion of non–renewable-energy–sector investments and USD 27 billion of transport investments. Using a wider definition, funds reported "green" investment through a variety of channels, with exposure to green equities, green bonds, and in alternative investments such as real estate, private equity and infrastructure. The aforementioned Swedish pension fund AP2 reported 9% of its total portfolio was invested in green assets. Dutch pension fund ABP and the New Zealand Superannuation Fund both reported 6.7% of their total portfolios were invested in green assets. These funds were leaders in the overall survey population in terms of green investment – most funds reported much lower or no exposure to green investments. The largest allocation of an infrastructure portfolio to renewables reported was 19% (PFA, Denmark), while the smallest reported was less than 1% of total infrastructure investment (OMERS, Canada).

In addition, some institutional investors are poised to significantly increase investment in this area. Goldman Sachs (2015) finds that in the last few years, institutional investors have begun to recognise that successful low-carbon technologies benefit from a mix of policy support, market acceptance, technical advances and cost reductions. For certain green infrastructure sectors (e.g. LEDs, onshore wind, solar PV and hybrid and electric vehicles) these dynamics combine to create a virtuous (self-reinforcing) cycle. Table 11.1 summarises a wide assortment of existing institutional investor commitments, targets and allocations to "green finance", all actions taken in the last three years. Once again, a mixture of terms is used for defining the nature of the green financing actions, with 24 different terms used across the 38 actions.

In September 2014, a coalition of three pension funds (CalSTRS, APG and PensionDanmark) pledged to increase low-carbon investments across all asset classes

Table 11.1 Institutional investor commitments, targets and allocations

Actor	Sector	Commitment	Allocation (latest available)
Aggregate			
Institutional investors	Sustainably managed assets	n/r	USD 21.4 trillion (2014)
Institutional investors	European renewable energy equity	n/r	EUR 26 bn or 37% of aggregate deal value
Institutional investors where public action deployed	Green infrastructure	n/a	USD 8 bn (2016)
Portfolio Decarbonisation Coalition	Low or lower-carbon assets	USD 100 bn by COP21	USD 600 bn (2015) – already 6x the target
Montreal Carbon Pledge	Disclosure of carbon footprint	USD 500 bn	USD 3 trillion (2015) – already more than 6x the target
Asset Owners Disclosure Project	Low-carbon investments	n/r	USD 138 bn or 0.4% of index AuM (2016)
Institutional investors in the Netherlands	Low-carbon investments	n/r	USD 39 bn (3.4% of total NL index AuM – 2016)
Low Carbon Investment Registry	Low-carbon assets	n/r	USD 50 bn
Industry			
OECD Large Pension funds	Renewable energy projects	n/a	USD 1.4 bn
Coalition of CalSTRS, APG and PensionDanmark	Low-carbon investments across all asset classes	USD 31 bn by 2020	USD 29 bn (2015)
Insurance industry (the SRI Initiative: ICMIF and IIS)	Green investments/climate-smart investments	Double the 2012 amount (USD 42 bn) to USD 84 bn by 2015, and increase by 10x to USD 420 bn by 2020	USD 109 bn (July 2015), already in excess of the 2015 target
Catalytic Finance Initiative	Clean energy projects	USD 10 bn by 2022	USD 1.5 bn (2015)
Cubico Fund (OTPP, PSP Investments, Santander)	Water and renewables projects	USD 2 bn	USD 2 bn
Aligned Intermediary (University of California Regents, TIAA CREF, NZ Super, OPTrust)	Climate infrastructure (clean energy, water, waste)	USD 1 bn	n/a

Individual

Pension funds			
PensionDanmark	Renewable energy projects	10% unlisted equity	EUR 2.5 bn
PFA Pension	Renewable energy projects	n/r	19% of infrastructure portfolio
PFZW	Sustainable investments	EUR 16 bn by 2020	USD 4 bn (2015)
UK Environment Agency Pension Fund	Low-carbon investments		26.4% of AuM (calculate USD figure)
AP2	Green assets	n/r	9% of total portfolio
AP2	Green bond strategic asset allocation	1% of portfolio	SEK 4.2 bn (USD 500 million) (2016)
ABP	Green assets		6.7% of portfolio
NZ Super	Green assets		6.7% of portfolio
New York State Common Retirement Fund	Sustainable investment	USD 5 bn (incl. launch of a USD 2 bn low-emission index)	USD 1.5 bn (2015)
Insurance companies			
Allianz	Renewable energy projects	EUR 4 bn	EUR 3 bn
AXA	Green investments	EUR 3 bn by 2020	
SwissRe	Climate risk and resilience coverage	USD 10 bn by 2020	USD 1.5 bn (2015)
Aviva	Low-carbon infrastructure	GBP 500 million per year to 2020	
Asset managers			
BNP Paribas Investment Partners	Low-carbon assets		EUR 14 bn (2015)
Endowments			
University of California	Breakthrough Energy Coalition	USD 1.25 bn over 2016–2020	
Family offices			
Threshold Group	Impact investment		USD 1 bn

(*Continued*)

Table 11.1 (Continued)

Actor	Sector	Commitment	Allocation (latest available)
Other investors and financial institutions			
Divest-Invest (140 foundations and other investors)	Public pledge to divest portfolio of fossil assets and re-invest at least 5% in "clean energy and climate solutions"[1]	USD 12 billion in total assets that have committed at least 5% – and in many cases over 10% of redirected investment	Actual amount of funds divested and re-invested difficult to track due to varying degrees of disclosure
Citigroup	Green financing	USD 100 bn	
Bank of America	Low-carbon business	Increase from current USD 50 bn to USD 125 bn by 2025	
Wells Fargo	Greener economy	USD 30 bn by 2020	
Goldman Sachs	Clean energy	USD 150 bn by 2025	
Re-Invest 2015: Banks and non-banking financial companies	Renewable energy investment in India	INR 712 bn (USD10.7 bn)	INR 295 bn (USD 4.4 bn) (March 2016)
Google	Renewable energy projects	USD 2.5 bn	

1 The details of the commitment are: "1) Stop any new investments in the top 200 fossil fuel companies. 2) Drop coal, oil and gas from our investment portfolio by divesting from the top 200 fossil fuel companies. 3) Invest at least 5 percent of our portfolio into climate solutions defined as renewable energy, energy efficiency, clean technology and clean energy access".

Source: Kaminker (2016)

to USD 31 billion by 2020 and had already reached USD 29 billion by the end of 2015. Among insurance companies, the SRI Initiative launched in 2014 commits its participants to doubling their USD 42 billion of "green, climate-smart investments" in 2012 to USD 84 billion by 2015, and increasing the 2012 figure by a further 10 times to USD 420 billion by 2020. By July 2015 the figure had already reached USD 109 billion, well in excess of the 2015 target. A plethora of other institutional investor initiatives geared at sustainable finance were showcased in the margins of COP 21 including, inter alia, the Portfolio Decarbonisation Coalition, the Montreal Carbon Disclosure Pledge, the Divest-Invest Pledge and the Aligned Intermediary.

2.2 Institutional investors have driven the growth of a green bond market

Institutional investors have driven the growth of a market for green bonds, investing in the majority of issuances while working to improve the market's structure and green integrity (Kaminker 2017). Bonds are a core component of pension funds' and insurance companies' portfolios,[11] and bonds with long tenors are potentially a good fit with institutional investors' long-term liabilities, allowing for asset–liability matching. Green bonds fit within the investment portfolios of mainstream institutional investors and can reconcile latent and emerging demand from institutional investors for sustainability-themed, ESG-screened investments. The green bond "label" serves as a discovery mechanism for institutional investors and helps to lower search costs associated with identifying green opportunities in a figurative ocean of fixed-income opportunities (Kaminker 2016).

As shown in Figure 11.2, annual issuance of green bonds increased to USD 95 billion in 2016. Data from the 2016 survey of large pension funds (LPFs) and public pension reserve funds (PPRFs) (OECD 2016a) reported an increase in allocations to green bonds in 2014 and 2015, partly due to an uptick in issuance and available supply, but also increased investor interest. In response to the greater availability of green bonds (see Tables 11.2 and 11.3), a dozen institutional investors have made commitments or targets for green bond investments in excess of USD 15 billion to date, and 14 dedicated green bond funds have emerged (with 9 launched in 2015 alone). In 2016, Swedish pension fund AP2 established a standalone green bond portfolio, arguing the market has "achieved a maturity and size" to justify the fund's implementing a separate investment strategy and classifying its green bond holdings as a distinct asset class. In the margins of COP21, asset owners, investment managers and individual funds managing more than USD 11.2 trillion of assets signed a statement in support of the green bond market.

In the emerging market for labelled and unlabelled green bonds, bonds have mainly been used for refinancing (and recycling lending) and for funding on-balance-sheet activity (for existing and forthcoming projects) by corporations, MDBs and sub-sovereign, municipal and agency issuers. The market has also featured asset-backed securities and project bonds – two bond categories that could (and would need to) play a much larger role in a 2-degree policy scenario, provided the right policies are in place (Kaminker 2017).

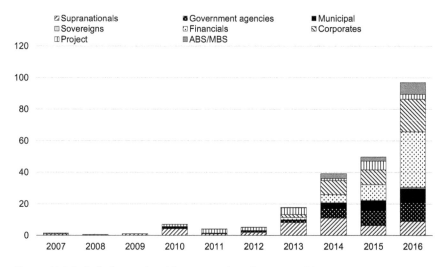

Figure 11.2 Labelled green bond issuance and market composition

Note: "SSA" includes supranational, sub-sovereign and agency issuers such as development banks, local funding authorities, export credit agencies etc. "Corporate" includes sectors such as utilities/energy, financials, consumer discretionary and staples, technology, industrials and others. This figure includes project bonds that are "tagged green" on the Bloomberg Terminal which are not included in other lists such as that of the Climate Bonds Initiative. Note also that 2016 figures include all Chinese green bonds issued in line with the People's Bank of China green catalogue, although some of these do not meet international investor expectations of green bonds due to the inclusion of "clean coal".

Source: Kaminker (2017), citing SEB analysis provided to OECD, based on Bloomberg data

2.3 The case of renewable energy investment by institutional investors in the EU

A growing number of institutional investors have identified renewable energy assets in Europe as a source of inflation-linked, long-term and stable cash flows. This increased appetite can be attributed to a number of factors including the presence of policy support mechanisms that create revenue stability (e.g. feed-in-tariffs). An enduring low-interest-rate environment with low-yielding government bonds has led some pension funds and insurers to invest in renewable energy directly, citing their fiduciary obligation to identify stable attractive returns with low correlations to other asset classes (e.g. PensionDanmark has allocated EUR 2.5 billion to renewables, and Allianz owns 63 wind farms and seven solar parks worth EUR 3 billion).

Recent data from OECD's *2016 Business and Finance Outlook* confirms the growing prominence of institutional investors in renewable energy in Europe (OECD 2016b). In 2010, utilities financed 62% of equity in wind energy projects in Europe, while institutional investors had financed only 6% (Figure 11.3). By 2015, utility finance had decreased to 39%, while the share of institutional

Table 11.2 Institutional commitments or targets for green bond investment

Green bond commitments or targets

Actor	Sector	Commitment	Comments
Credit Agricole	Bank	EUR 2 bn	Target by end of 2017
Barclays	Bank	GBP 2 bn	Increased from 1 bn target
KfW	Public Financial Institution	EUR 1 bn	Within 4 years
HSBC	Bank	USD 1 bn	No time frame
Zurich	Insurer	USD 2 bn	No time frame
Actiam	Asset manager	EUR 1 bn	No time frame
AXA	Insurer	EUR 1 bn	No time frame
Aviva	Insurer	Increase holdings	No time frame
Deutsche Bank	Bank	EUR 1 bn	No time frame
California State Treasury	Public Financial Institution	USD 1.1 bn	No time frame
Bangladesh Central Bank	Central Bank	Some of its foreign currency reserves	No time frame
AP2	Pension Fund	1% of portfolio allocation	No time frame
AP4	Pension Fund	Strong commitment and significant allocation to green bonds	No time frame
Total		**EUR 12bn +**	

Source: Kaminker (2016)

Table 11.3 Green bond funds manage EUR 1.66 billion

Actor	Focus	Assets under management
Storebrand	Green bond fund	EUR 500 million
Foresight	Unlabelled green bond fund	EUR 200 million
Humanis	Green bond fund ("HGA Obligations Vertes")	EUR 105 million
SEB	Green bond fund	EUR 55 million
Mirova	Green bond fund	EUR 62.55 million
Calvert	Green bond fund	EUR 61.29 million
Erste Asset Management	Responsible bond global impact fund	EUR 41.6 million
Raiffeisen Capital Management	Green bond fund	EUR 35 million
Allianz	Green bond fund	EUR 20 million
State Street	Green bond fund	EUR 20.34 million
Columbia Threadneedle	Social bond fund	USD 20 million
NN Investment Partners	Euro green bond fund	EUR 20 million
Nikko AM	World Bank green bond fund	SGD 16.46 million
Total	**EUR 1.16 billion (as of May 2016)**	

Source: Kaminker (2016)

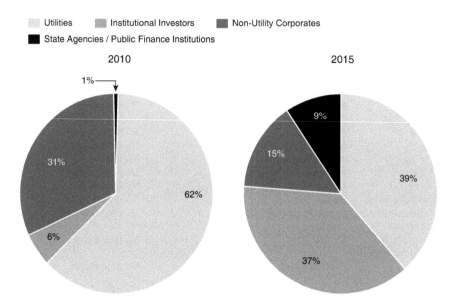

Figure 11.3 Change in equity mix in wind energy projects in Europe, 2010 and 2015

Note: Figures correspond to shares of total equity in sample

Source: BNEF (2016), OECD calculations

investors increased to 37%, making up for part of the difference. The increase of equity provision by institutional investors in the sample[12] can be traced mainly to the acquisition of brownfield assets or portfolios for onshore wind deals. Pension funds and insurers were not involved in any greenfield onshore wind-power transactions included in the 2015 sample. This suggests that institutional investors look to the onshore wind sector mainly for the acquisition of existing projects.

Results from a database maintained by HgCapital focused just on renewable energy in the EU show that institutional investors (broadly defined) have allocated more than EUR 25 billion in equity in European projects that have a combined debt and equity investment in excess of EUR 70 billion. Institutional equity investment in EU renewables grew with a 60% CAGR from EUR 2 billion in 2012 to EUR 8.7 billion in 2015.

According to HgCapital (2016), the number of active institutional investors in renewable energy increased from fewer than 10 in 2004 to more than 75 in 2016, with direct investment (as opposed to investment through funds) by pension funds, insurance companies and listed "yieldco" or investment trust funds the fastest-growing sources of new capital. In the UK and Germany, with perceived stable regulatory regimes, institutional investor equity increased as a percentage of total equity investment in EU renewables from 1% in 2007 to 17.5% by the end of 2015.

In terms of institutional investment in EU renewables, according to HgCapital (2016) operating projects or projects that have completed construction are overwhelmingly favoured by institutional investors, accounting for nearly 80% of all institutional equity capital invested in renewable energy projects since 2011. The number of investors that will invest in completed projects has risen over the last four years, with more than 70 active investors. Around 20 institutional investors take construction risk, and fewer than 10 currently support project development. Direct project equity accounts for 89% of institutional capital invested in renewables since 2004 and 93% since 2011.

Data from HgCapital (2016) also describe an emerging ecosystem of investment in EU renewables. It is one in which private equity funds, dedicated renewable energy fund specialists and large strategic developers such as Nordic utilities take the early-stage risks in developing, building and de-risking projects. Once de-risked, these projects become attractive investments for pension funds, insurance companies, listed yieldcos and generalist infrastructure funds who are seeking stable but lower yields.

In this context, institutional investors are playing a role in recycling capital from the balance sheets of utilities through the sales of project stakes or refinancing. Banks, private equity funds, project developers and utilities can then redeploy the proceeds into the development and construction of new projects (OECD 2016b). Similarities have been drawn to the commercial real estate sector, where private equity–type funds – which are prepared to take on greater risks in exchange for higher returns – develop, build and lease out new properties, which are then sold on as cash flowing investments to pension funds, real estate investment trusts and other long-term investors (HgCapital 2016).

3. Catalysing the supply of green institutional capital: a stock taking of approaches

While some of these investment figures and pledges may seem large on an absolute basis, they are minute compared to the scale of institutional assets under management and the scale of the investment demand and financing gap for green and sustainable infrastructure. Further, the individual allocations and pledge levels and activity cited in the previous sections are largely exceptions to the rule that institutional investment in green infrastructure projects has been limited to a very small percentage of the portfolio.

The last five recommendations from Kaminker (2016) focused on a further element of a strong domestic policy framework, creating the supply-side conditions for scaling up green infrastructure investment by institutional investors. These actions are centred on the establishment of specific policies, instruments, funds, risk mitigants and transaction enablers for mobilising institutional investment. There is an important role for governments in both reducing barriers to investment and supporting the development of investment channels, such as green bonds, funds and direct investment, which can hold the key to scaling up institutional investment in green infrastructure.

3.1 Research methodology

The categories of public-sector actions considered in this chapter are informed by the empirical framework laid forth in Kaminker et al. (2015), which used a base of 70 examples of institutional investment in sustainable energy (companies and projects) to develop a framework that classifies investments according to different types of financing instruments and investment funds and highlights the risk mitigants" and "transaction enablers" that governments along with public financial institutions can use to mobilise institutionally held capital.

The scope and data collected (in the "stock-taking" research) covers green infrastructure sectors for which there are existing examples of and information on investment by institutional investors, where the public or official sector was present in the investment transaction (the "deal") using some form of intervention to enable or facilitate these transactions and mobilise private financial capital. The specifications and format used for the stock-taking research are given in Box 11.1.

Box 11.1   Attributes included in stock taking

Under each sector, examples of "deals" were included in the form of micro case studies containing key information on the following attributes:

- Physical asset descriptor (e.g. Solar PV installation, [x] MW in [y] Location)
- Channel and financial structure (e.g. direct equity investment; [x] USD)
- Institutional investor (e.g. [name]; public pension fund)
- Stage of the project cycle in which investor participated if appropriate (e.g. construction, operation, refinancing, multiple)
- Role and nature of public-sector action (e.g. [public financial institution name]; credit enhancement)

Risk mitigants include an array of targeted interventions generally aimed at reducing, re-assigning or re-apportioning different investment risks using a variety of mechanisms. Transaction enablers facilitate institutional investment in sustainable energy infrastructure projects by reducing the transaction costs associated with these investments while also mitigating risk in some cases. A partial list of risk mitigants and transaction enablers is shown in the two right-hand columns of Figure 11.4. Additional examples and definitions are provided in Tables 11.1 and 11.2, and a more complete discussion is provided in Kaminker et al. (2015).

3.2 Results of the stock-taking research

3.2.1 Geography

The research resulted in 33 case studies collected (shown in Table 11.4), which were then divided into eight categories of green infrastructure assets in the database.

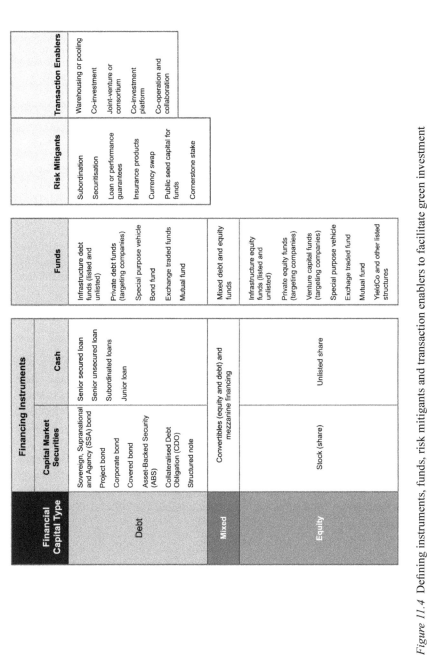

Figure 11.4 Defining instruments, funds, risk mitigants and transaction enablers to facilitate green investment

Source: Kaminker et al. (2015)

Table 11.4 Green infrastructure sectors covered in stock taking

Sector and sub-sector	Number of deals	Deal names
Sustainable energy (power generation and storage) Technologies in sample include: onshore and offshore wind, solar PV and concentrated PV, solar thermal, geothermal, small-scale hydro, bioenergy, fuel cells	18	GIB Offshore Wind Fund, Greencoat UK Wind, Lake Turkana Wind, Albion Community Power, Crescent Dunes Solar, Bloom Energy, Off Grid Electric Tanzania, Hawaii GEMS, Pampa Wind, ReNew Wind, Hindustan Solar, Tiwi MakBan Geothermal, Montalto di Castro Solar, NTR Wind Fund, Ararat Australia Wind, Cestas Solar, Seine Rive Gauche Wind, Gemini Wind
Green-enabling infrastructure (offshore wind interconnectors)	3	Greater Gabbard OFTO, Gwynt y Mor OFTO, Duddon Sands OFTO
Energy-efficiency projects (in commercial and residential buildings)	3	Cheltenham Hospital, IDB Efficiency ABS, NY WHEEL
Low-carbon mobility	2	Quebec Electric Rail, EV Charging China
Green buildings	1	Hines Poland Fund
Agriculture and forestry	1	AATIF
Water and sanitation	1	Consorcio Agua Azul
Mixed green infrastructure	4	GEEREF, Kommuninvest Aggregator, CT Green Bank C-PACE, Asia Climate Partners
Total	**33**	

Source: Kaminker (2016)

In total, the case studies included 67 examples of the use of risk mitigants and transaction enablers. Investments were logged in 17 countries. It is important here to note that this study is illustrative only, and there would be similar cases in countries not named here. G20 countries hosted the majority of investments observed including multiple deals in Australia, Canada, China, France, India, Italy, Mexico, South Africa, the UK and the United States.

Examples of institutional investment outside of the G20 were also found, for instance in wind projects in Kenya and Uruguay, a water utility plant project in Peru, a geothermal project in the Philippines, a pan-Asian fund, a pan-African fund and a fund targeting countries eligible for Official Development Assistance.

3.2.2 Physical assets

More than half of the deals (18) were in the sustainable energy sector. Within the other half of the sample, six deals involved energy efficiency and green-enabling infrastructure such as off-shore wind interconnectors (three each), and two involved low-carbon mobility. Four deals featured multiple types of green infrastructure. The stock taking was not intended to be comprehensive and was supposed to be limited to selected examples to provide a picture of the range of approaches used. Nevertheless, a fairly thorough search of readily available public information was undertaken. The distribution of samples across the categories reflected the amount of identifiable (and publicly available) institutional investor activity in each sector, with very few examples to be found for some sectors.

For instance, in the green buildings, agriculture and forestry and water and sanitation sectors, only one example could be identified per sector. While assessing and explaining the paucity of examples in certain sectors is beyond the scope of this research, the lack of data in itself is a finding which would be worthwhile to investigate in future research.

3.2.3 Stage of project life cycle

The majority of case studies in the sample focused on construction-stage project investment. This finding is at odds with others showing that the vast majority of "organic" institutional investment in renewable energy (i.e. investments occurring without direct specific public intervention) is centred on lower-risk operational assets. Based on this trend, governments appear to be targeting their public intervention at the construction stage, perhaps to address a perceived financing gap specific to the construction stage.

3.2.4 Public- and official-sector actors

The results of the research suggest that there are in fact many ways in which governments are already working to help mobilise institutional investment in green infrastructure using a variety of approaches. A range of public or official sector actors was involved across the case studies. Six deals featured more than one actor, with the Gemini Wind deal featuring four (EIB and three export credit agencies). Six multilateral development banks (ADB, AfDB, EBRD, EIB, IDB and IFC/WBG) were involved in 12 deals (36%).

Given the relatively recent establishment of public green investment banks (GIBs), it is notable that five such institutions, located in three countries, were involved across one-quarter (eight) of the deals (UK GIB, Australia CEFC, NY Green Bank, Connecticut Green Bank, Hawaii GEMS). A recent OECD report (OECD 2016b) examines the role of GIBs, which are publicly capitalised entities established specifically to facilitate private investment in domestic low-carbon, climate-resilient infrastructure[13] and other green sectors such as water and waste management. These dedicated green investment entities have been established at national level, state level, county level and city level. GIBs have been added to the ranks of other public financial institutions, including MDBs and bilateral development finance institutions, which are mobilising private investment in sustainable energy and other green infrastructure using interventions to mitigate risks and enable transactions. Other OECD reports focus on the activities of public financial institutions in this area (Miyamoto and Chiofalo 2015; Cochran et al. 2014).

Seven public financial institutions (including national development banks, export credit agencies and a local funding agency) were involved in nine deals (27%). These included actors from six countries: Belgium, Canada, Denmark, Germany, India, Italy and Sweden (ONDD, EDC, EKF, KfW, IIFCL, SACE, and Kommuninvest). Two government-sponsored "blended capital" funds made investments captured in the dataset (Danish Climate Investment Fund and the Africa Agriculture and Trade Investment Fund). The Green Climate Fund was involved with a deal as well, despite only recently becoming operational.

A full third of the deals (11) featured actors related to seven sovereign governments and their ministries or agencies (Danish government; French Treasury; German Federal Ministry for Economic Cooperation and Development; Ireland Strategic Investment Fund; Japan International Cooperation Agency; UK Department for Business, Innovation and Skills; and the US Department of the Treasury, Department of Energy, and Agency for International Development). Sub-sovereign governmental actors in Canada and the United States were also involved in two deals (Government of Quebec and the Delaware Strategic Fund).

3.2.5 Institutional investors involved

Institutional investors were by definition involved in all of the case studies. As distinct from the "organic" institutional investment that is described in Section 2, this research focused on deals that featured some type of public- or official-sector intervention that occurred alongside capital provision by pension funds, insurers and investment managers (that predominantly manage institutional capital). Private equity funds and other forms of investment vehicles that do not disclose their investors are beyond the scope of the research. Half of the deals featured "undisclosed institutional investors", whose presence in the deal was mentioned publicly but the actors were not named. Total institutional capital committed across the 33 case studies is approximately USD 8 billion.

Pension funds were the most active type of institutional investor, with 17 different actors named out of a total of 27 institutional investors whose participation in the deals was disclosed publicly. Notably, five Canadian pension funds (AIMCo, CDPQ, PSP Investments, OPTrust and OTPP) were involved in transactions domestically as well as in Australia, the UK and the United States. Other institutional investors identified in the sample were from Australia (AMP), Denmark (PBU, PensionDanmark and PKA); France (Mirova); Germany (Allianz, Euler Hermes and KGAL); Japan (Nipponkoa Insurance); New Zealand (NZSuper); Sweden (AMF Pensionsförsäkring, AP3 and AP4); the UK (Aviva, Greater Manchester Pension Fund, Legal & General, LPFA and Strathclyde Pension Fund); the United States (CalSTRS, UN JSPF and the Packard and Calvert foundations).

3.3 Risk mitigants in the stock-taking research

The 44 risk mitigants logged across the 33 deals include an array of targeted interventions generally aimed at reducing, re-assigning or re-apportioning different investment risks using a variety of mechanisms. By providing coverage for risks which are new and are not currently covered by financial actors or are simply too costly for investors, risk-mitigating tools increase the attractiveness and acceptability of sustainable energy projects for institutional investors that are particularly risk averse (e.g. pension funds). These are laid out in a typology and summary shown in Table 11.5.

Risk mitigants targeted at credit enhancement (an intervention that improves the chances that financing will be repaid) were deployed 23 times across the sample. The most common technique is the partial credit guarantee, which accounted for more than half (13) of credit enhancements. Otherwise, five instances of subordination, three revenue guarantees and two loan guarantees were observed.

Public investment as a form of risk mitigant was used 21 times, with cornerstone stakes being the most widespread (10). Cornerstone stakes are public investments made in a structure early in the investment process so as to increase chances of success and to play a demonstration role to attract other investors. These were followed by grants (six), the "blending" of concessional and institutional capital to take (four) and one example of a seeding fund with public capital.

3.4 Transaction enablers in the stock-taking research

Transaction enablers facilitate institutional investment in green infrastructure projects by reducing the transaction costs associated with these investments or creating new channels and also mitigating risk in some cases. As most institutional investors have limited experience with direct investment in green infrastructure projects, the cost associated with identifying, executing and managing investments is often prohibitive.

Transaction enablers were used 19 times in the sample (see Table 11.6 for a typology). Warehousing (pooling small transactions) and securitisation (transforming illiquid assets into tradable securities) were the focus of six transactions. There were six further examples of co-investment and syndication by public actors alongside institutional investors. Public–private partnerships were used on four occasions, and there were three instances of public actors deploying conduit structures to leverage the capacity and capabilities of a larger or more specialised public institution to access normally unavailable channels.

Nearly a third of the 33 deals made use of a risk mitigant as well as a transaction enabler. For example, the Africa Agriculture and Trade Investment Fund involved three risk mitigants including a credit enhancement (subordination) and two public investments (a cornerstone stake and blending), alongside a partnership transaction enabler. On the other hand, CT Green Bank C-PACE featured one risk mitigant (subordination) and four transaction enablers (pooling, warehousing, securitisation and conduit). The Gemini Wind transaction was notable again for its usage of three different partial credit guarantees, as well as subordination and co-investment techniques.

Table 11.5 A typology and summary of risk mitigants deployed

Risk mitigant	Short description of public- or official-sector intervention	Deal example (name)	Sector	Financing channel	Actor that deployed risk mitigant	Institutional investor involved
Credit enhancement[1]	*A credit enhancement is any intervention that improves the chances that financing will be repaid. It is a form of public investment that results in a contingent liability.*					
Layered fund subordination	Taking a subordinated position in a fund to give priority to private investors with regard to claims on assets.	GIB Offshore Wind Fund	Sustainable energy	Intermediated unlisted project equity	UK Green Investment Bank	Strathclyde Pension Fund, undisclosed Sovereign Wealth Fund
		AATIF (Africa Agriculture and Trade Investment Fund)	Sustainable agriculture	Intermediated private equity fund	KfW & German Federal Ministry for Economic Cooperation and Development (BMZ)	Undisclosed institutional investors, Deutsche Bank
Partial credit guarantee	Guaranteeing payments for the principal and interest on debt issuance up to certain percentage.	Hindustan Solar	Sustainable energy	Listed project bond	IIFCL, ADB	Yes Bank and other institutional investors
		Energy Efficiency Securitization by the IABD	Energy efficiency	ABS	IADB	Undisclosed institutional investors
		Greater Gabbard offshore transmission link	Sustainable energy	Listed project bond	EIB, EC	Numerous undisclosed institutional investors

Loan guarantee	A legally binding agreement under which the guarantor agrees to pay any or the entire amount due on a loan instrument in the event of non-payment by the borrower.	Crescent Dunes Solar CSP	Sustainable energy	Direct investment in unlisted equity of a project developer	US Department of Energy	Public Sector Pension Investment Board (Canada) and Ontario Teachers' Pension Plan
Revenue guarantee	Guaranteeing certain cash flows for a project.	Consorcio Agua Azul	Sustainable water	Direct investment in listed project bonds	Government of Peru	Undisclosed local pension funds
		Cestas Solar	Sustainable energy	Direct equity co-investment in asset	French Treasury	Mirova, KKB, ACofi, Omnes
Public investment	*Any form of direct public investment or presence in any deal structure.*					
Cornerstone stake	An investment in an offering that occurs early in the investment process so as to increase chances of success and to play a demonstration role to attract other investors.	Lake Turkana wind farm	Sustainable energy	Intermediated unlisted equity investment in project	Danish government, DCIF (a government-owned fund)	DCIF, Danish pension funds
		Cheltenham General Hospital	Energy efficiency	Intermediated unlisted equity investment in project	UK Green Investment Bank	Aviva Investors
		Hines Poland Sustainable Income Fund	Green buildings	Intermediated private equity fund	EBRD	Undisclosed "foreign institutional investor"

(Continued)

Table 11.5 (Continued)

Risk mitigant	Short description of public- or official-sector intervention	Deal example (name)	Sector	Financing channel	Actor that deployed risk mitigant	Institutional investor involved
Blending	Strategic mixing of concessional, non-concessional and for-profit financing to attract risk-capital.	Albion Community Power	Sustainable energy	Direct investment in unlisted equity of a pure-play corporate	UK Green Investment Bank	The Greater Manchester Pension Fund, Strathclyde Pension Fund
Grant	Concessional funds allocation.	Off-grid electric Tanzania	Sustainable energy	Unlisted debt investment intermediated through a debt vehicle	US Agency for International Development	The Packard Foundation, Ceniarth, Calvert Foundation.
Fund seeding	Public investment to help establish private equity funds that specialise in green projects.	GEEREF	Sustainable energy and energy efficiency	Equity: unlisted intermediated fund of funds	EIB	At least 8 private equity funds with institutional investor limited partners

1 Other forms of credit enhancement are possible but were not observed in this deal sample. These include, for instance loan loss reserves and insurance, interest rate buy-downs and debt service reserves.

Source: Kaminker (2016)

Table 11.6 A typology and summary of transaction enablers deployed

Transaction enabler type	Short description	Deal example (name)	Sector	Financing channel	Actor that deployed the transaction enabler	Institutional investor involved
Securitisation	A technique whereby illiquid or small-scale assets are transformed into securitised products.	Energy efficiency securitisation in Mexico	Energy efficiency	Unlisted debt investment, intermediated	IDB	Numerous institutional investors
Warehousing, pooling	Bundle together smaller projects to get them to a commercial scale that is attractive for institutional investors.	Off Grid Electric	Sustainable energy	Unlisted debt investment, intermediated	Off Grid Electric set up a debt investment vehicle	The David and Lucile Packard Foundation and other family offices
		Greencoat UK Wind	Sustainable energy	Intermediated listed project equity	Greencoat UK Wind (a listed infrastructure fund)	Numerous institutional investors
Co-investment, joint ventures, partnerships, consortiums and loan syndication	Institutional investors partner up with other investors to invest in an asset.	Ararat Australia Wind	Sustainable energy	Unlisted direct project debt financing (loan) project	Australia Clean Energy Finance Corporation	OPSEU Pension Trust
		NY WHEEL (Warehouse for Energy Efficiency Loans)	Energy efficiency	Direct unlisted debt investment in project company structure	NY Green Bank	Undisclosed Institutional Investors, Citigroup
Co-operation and collaboration	Informal sharing of knowledge and resources between actors.	Electric public transport system in Québec	Low-carbon mobility	Unlisted equity investment	LISEA (a concession company created for this project), EIB	Caisse de dépôt et placement du Québec
Conduit aggregation	Leveraging a larger or more specialised public institution to access normally unavailable channels.	Kommuninvest aggregator	Mixed green finance	Intermediated, listed SSA green bond	Kommuninvest (Swedish Local Funding Authority)	Ap3, AP4, CalSTRS, UN Joint Staff Pension Fund
		CT Green Bank C-PACE	Sustainable energy	Intermediated, unlisted non-rated pooled project bonds	Connecticut Green Bank	Undisclosed institutional investors

Source: Kaminker (2016)

3.5 *Mapping channels used by investors in the stock-taking research*

As described in Kaminker et al. (2015), a variety of investment channels are potentially available to institutional investors for accessing green infrastructure, and different channels may be more appropriate when taking into account certain decisions that are routinely made. For example, large institutional investors evaluate prospective investments based on decisions to make the investment directly ("in-house") or to create a contract with an intermediary ("out-source") to make the investment on their behalf. Channels can provide exposure to listed or unlisted debt or equity, a single project asset or company or can bundle multiple smaller-scale projects together. Kaminker et al. (2015) developed a "matrix frame" to visualise the different channels for investment. Some of the deals from the stock-taking research are plotted on such a frame in Figure 11.5.

In terms of the investment channel used on the equity side (accounting for half of the deals), the most frequent routes to access green infrastructure by institutional investors were unlisted investments in projects made via intermediated funds (eight deals or 25% of the sample), followed by unlisted investments made directly in projects (four deals, or 13%). There were also two examples each of unlisted direct investments in corporations and listed, intermediated investments in projects.

On the debt side, by far the most frequent channel used a project bond structure, accounting for 41% (13) of all deals. There were 10 examples (31% of the sample) of direct investment in a listed project bond structure and a further three investments in listed project bonds. Of the project bonds, three-quarters benefited from credit-enhancement techniques; with 60% (eight) credit enhanced through some form of partial credit guarantee. Finally, there were two other examples of debt financing (not in the form of a bond) included in the sample: a subordinated loan as part of the Gemini wind transaction and an unlisted debt fund.

4. Summary and implications for future research

Overall, this chapter endeavoured to identify both areas in which organic investment is occurring and approaches where the public sector is working to overcome barriers to institutional investment, with a view for laying the foundation for further research and analysis. A first step in determining future avenues for potentially fruitful research is to examine where the original analysis had to draw its boundaries. As such, several areas lay beyond the scope of this report and could usefully be addressed in future research.

While the original report focused for the most part on direct project investment, an analysis of the role of institutional investors in financing corporate investment would be useful to understand how much of the financing gap these sources can realistically fill. Green corporate investment by institutional investors could be useful to examine from several perspectives, from early-stage venture capital and growth capital financing to passive listed equities strategies (e.g. low-carbon index strategies). A deeper inspection of the role of institutions in partnering with

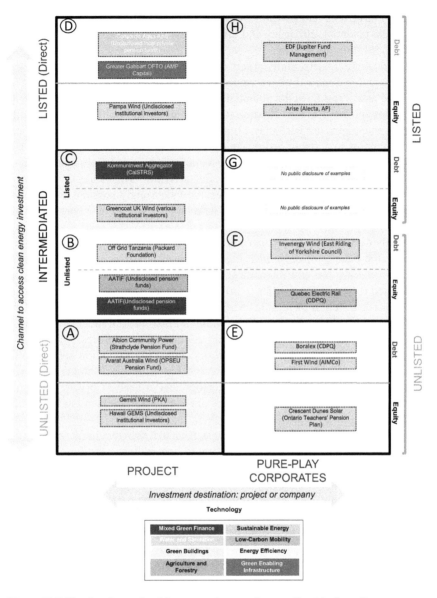

Figure 11.5 Plotting the stock-taking research examples on a "matrix frame"
Source: Kaminker (2016)

corporations on project investments through the project financing cycle and their role in capital recycling could similarly be useful.

As a key corollary point, as these different channels for green investment develop and mature, it will be important to gain a more complete and granulated understanding of the financial and performance characteristics of the different types of structures and investment options. These insights will be essential to gauge the potential, efficiency and effectiveness for hedging stranded asset risk across portfolios and sectors.

For example, issuers, underwriters and others such as the World Bank Group, HSBC and *The Economist* have argued that green bonds are a 'natural hedge' for stranded assets and have the potential to offset climate risk exposure in investor portfolios and serve as a destination for capital divested from fossil fuels. Whilst there is potential to use pure-play, project and asset-backed securities green bonds as instruments to actively hedge against climate policy risks in a portfolio that includes emissions-intensive assets, in practice, most green bonds are secured on the balance sheet of issuers with diversified activities. This is clearly an area in need of further research, which will become increasingly possible as the green bond market grows and matures to include larger amounts of recourse-to-asset bonds.

Another area that was beyond the scope of this research was to assess and explain the paucity of examples in certain green infrastructure sectors. While the stock taking was not intended to be comprehensive and was supposed to be limited to selected examples to provide a picture of the range of approaches used, the distribution of samples across the categories turned out to reflect the amount of identifiable (and publicly available) institutional investor activity in each sector, with very few examples to be found in some places. For instance, in the green buildings, agriculture/forestry and water/sanitation sectors, only one example could be identified per sector. Future research could more systematically examine these important sectors also in need of private capital to understand the role of institutional investors and what barriers might be specific to them.

The results of the 33 mini case studies suggest that there are in fact many ways in which governments are already working to help mobilise institutional investment in green infrastructure using a variety of approaches. Nearly a third of the deals made use of a risk mitigant as well as a transaction enabler, and six deals featured more than one actor. Future research could examine some of the more innovative deals using a more comprehensive and methodical case study approach to understand what factors were essential in mobilising institutional capital. Assessing empirically the efficiency and effectiveness of different types of risk mitigants and transaction enablers could also hold significant promise for future research, provided the data were of sufficient quality to undertake such a study.

With respect to individual actors, drawing on related OECD work (OECD 2016d), this report also describes some instances in which "green investment banks" (GIBs) have sought to engage institutional investors. In recent years, at least a dozen special-purpose GIBs have been established. These are domestically focused public institutions that use limited public capital to leverage or crowd-in private capital, including from institutional investors, for sustainable energy infrastructure investment. Given the relatively recent establishment of GIBs, it is notable that five such institutions, located in three countries, were involved across one-quarter (eight) of the deals. As such, future research could examine the specific role that GIBs play in catalysing institutional capital.

Another finding of the stock taking concerned the specific channel used. The most frequent channel to access green infrastructure across the sample was via a project bond structure (the majority not labelled as green), accounting for 41% (13) of all deals. Of these project bonds, three-quarters benefited from credit-enhancement techniques, with the majority credit enhanced through some form of partial credit guarantee. This is consistent with findings from a recent OECD report (Kaminker 2017) on green bonds, which examines the potential for project bonds, among others, to support green infrastructure finance. Given the prevalence of this specific channel, future research could examine these deals in depth and options for scaling up credit enhancement mechanisms for project bonds. Given that institutional investment activity has increased during a low-interest-rate environment, key macroeconomic drivers for demand could be important to explore in depth, especially in the context of the ongoing global "search for yield" by institutional investors. Such research could also be geared at improving the understanding on prospects for long-term returns from green infrastructure investing by different types of institutional investor.

To date the majority of "organic" institutional investment in green infrastructure projects has occurred predominantly in OECD countries. A separate and very important question is how institutional investors approach green infrastructure investments in emerging markets and developing economies (EMDEs). A quarter (eight) of the deals took place in EMDEs, and three further deals involved mandates that extend to EMDEs. Studying the elements that needed to come together to make these deals work and overcome barriers would be important to determine which interventions hold the most promise for catalysing investment in EMDEs.

It follows that it will be very important to explore how institutional investors can interact with international climate finance mechanisms targeted at emerging economies and developing countries. An examination of the role of institutional investors in the emerging international "climate finance" architecture was outside the scope of this analysis, but these issues currently arise in discussions around international climate finance and fund mechanisms (see for instance the work of the Global Innovation Lab for Climate Finance).

Emerging from the research and analysis is a much broader point related to systemwide implications. If the right enabling environment and policy tools are coupled with financial sector innovation, there is an opportunity to significantly mitigate climate and stranded asset risk in institutional investor portfolios (which will ultimately benefit their beneficiaries) while also improving overall financial stability. These same framework conditions will also serve to drive accelerating flows of capital towards the low-carbon transition. Focusing research attention on these issues, including through convergence of both academic and practitioner communities, will become increasingly vital in years ahead to ensure that the most efficient and effective approaches rise to the top.

Acknowledgements

This chapter is an extract and update from a report (Kaminker 2016) that was originally provided by the Organisation for Economic Co-operation and Development (OECD) as a contribution to the G20 Green Finance Study Group. The author of this chapter as well as the original report is Christopher Kaminker (University of Oxford and Skandinaviska Enskilda Banken, formerly of the OECD), under the supervision of Robert Youngman, Simon Buckle (OECD Environment Directorate) and André Laboul (OECD Directorate for Financial and Enterprise Affairs).

The author is thankful in particular to Hideki Takada and Bérénice Lasfargues (OECD Environment Directorate) for their valuable research assistance, to Nick Robins (UNEP/G20 Green Finance Study Group Secretariat) and Robert Youngman for their guidance, comments and encouragement and to Andrew Prag (Directorate for Financial and Enterprise Affairs), Kaori Miyamoto (OECD Development Co-operation Directorate) and Ben Caldecott (University of Oxford) for their expert review. The author is grateful to the following who provided substantive input to the report in the form of case studies and data: Jeremy Burke (UK Green Investment Bank), Sarah Davidson (NY Green Bank), Bert Hunter (Connecticut Green Bank), the Japanese Ministry of Finance, Gildas Lamé (French Ministry of Finance), Nannan Lundin (Prime Minister's Office, Sweden), Tristan Knowles (Australia Clean Energy Finance Corporation), Tom Murley (HgCapital) and Joel Paula (OECD).

The original work benefitted from review and comments provided by the Greening Institutional Investors sub-group of the G20 Green Finance Study Group, co-chaired by the People's Bank of China and the Bank of England, as well as the OECD/G20 Taskforce on Institutional Investors and Long-Term Financing. The OECD/G20 Taskforce comprises government delegates to the OECD Insurance and Private Pensions Committee (IPPC) and its Working Party on Private Pensions (WPPP), as well as the OECD Committee on Financial Markets (CMF), the International Organisation of Pension Supervisors (IOPS) and other G20 government delegates.

Notes

1   Christopher Kaminker, University of Oxford (christopher.kaminker@ouce.ox.ac.uk) & Skandinaviska Enskilda Banken (christopher.kaminker@seb.se).
2   For the purposes of this text, the term "green infrastructure" includes (1) "low-carbon and climate-resilient" infrastructure projects, which either mitigate greenhouse gas emissions or support adaptation to climate change or both and (2) "sustainable energy infrastructure", as defined in Kaminker (2016).
3   Estimates of additional investment requirements typically do not consider returns on investment through lower operating costs due to energy savings from efficiency investments or lower fuel costs in the case of renewable energy replacing fossil energy. They also do not consider other benefits such as lower health costs. One study (Kennedy and Corfee-Morlot 2012) estimates that shifting to low-carbon and climate-resilient (LCR) infrastructure could result in systemic change that only slightly raises or even lowers overall investment costs. Investing in sustainable energy also makes economic sense.

The IEA (2014) presents evidence that the USD 44 trillion in additional investment needed to decarbonise the energy system in line with their "2 degree scenario" by 2050 is more than offset by more than USD 115 trillion in fuel savings – resulting in net savings of USD 71 trillion.

4 Total assets of institutional investors in 2013 amounted to USD 92.6 trillion maximum. Note that there is a double counting issue with this number, as mutual funds manage some assets from pension funds and insurance companies. Total assets of institutional investors (excluding investment funds) amounted to USD 57.7 trillion in 2013. This lower figure excludes assets of investment funds that are managed alongside pension and insurance funds.

5 Indirect infrastructure investments are investments in companies which are involved in the infrastructure industry either as manufacturers, operators or providers of on-balance-sheet financing or via intermediaries such as private equity funds targeting corporate investments, as distinct from direct investments in infrastructure projects.

6 This should be contrasted with the more routine type of institutional investment made in corporate stocks and bonds.

7 See for instance the G20/OECD Policy Note on pension fund financing for green infrastructure and initiatives (OECD 2012)

8 The financial management of these impacts is a key challenge and has been covered in work of the OECD; see Wolfrom and Yoko-Arai (2016).

9 There may be implications for banks where there is significant underinsurance of climate risks as uninsured losses from climate change-related extreme events could create financial stress for bank clients, e.g. uninsured or underinsured households forced to default on mortgages or other consumer credit as a result of disaster losses (Wehinger and Nassr 2016; Wolfrom and Yoko-Arai 2016).

10 The survey reviewed trends in assets and asset allocation by 99 large pension funds (LPFs) and public pension reserve funds (PPRFs), which in total managed USD 10.3 trillion in assets, one-third of the total worldwide assets held by this class of institutional investor.

11 OECD pension funds and insurance companies in 2013 invested on average 53% and 64%, respectively, of their portfolio in bonds (simple average) (Kaminker 2016).

12 The data on investment, including new-build and acquisition transactions, is compiled from the BNEF database of clean energy projects. The sample for 2010 includes 70 projects (57 new builds; 13 acquisitions), and the sample for 2015 includes 44 projects (29 new builds; 15 acquisitions). The total disclosed transaction value of the deals included in the sample was USD 11.7 billion in 2010 and USD 14.9 billion in 2015. The aggregated transaction value of greenfield projects stood at USD 10.8 billion in 2010 and USD 11 billion in 2015. The volume of total equity invested has decreased from USD 6.6 billion in 2010 to USD 6.1 billion in 2015. The institutional investor category includes pension funds, insurance companies, private equity and infrastructure funds.

13 Low-carbon and climate-resilient (LCR) infrastructure projects either mitigate greenhouse gas emissions or support adaptation to climate change or both (OECD 2016b).

References and further readings

AODP. 2016. *Global Climate Index*. Available at: www.AODProject.Net

B20. 2014. *Driving Growth and Jobs*. B20 Policy Recommendations to the G20, Sydney. Available at: www.b20australia.info.

Bank of England. 2015. *The Impact of Climate Change on the UK Insurance Sector – a Climate Change Adaptation Report by the Prudential Regulation Authority*, September. Available at: www.bankofengland.co.uk/pra/Documents/supervision/activities/pradefra0915.pdf

BNEF. 2016. *Global Trends in Renewable Energy Investment 2016*. Available at: http://about.bnef.com/press-releases/global-trends-in-renewable-energy-investment-2016/

Boissinot, J., Huber, D. and Lame, G. 2016. Finance and Climate: The Transition to a Low-Carbon and Climate-Resilient Economy From a Financial Sector Perspective. *OECD Journal: Financial Market Trends*, 2015(1). doi: http://dx.doi.org/10.1787/fmt-2015-5jrrz76d5td5

Caldecott, B. 2011. *Why High-Carbon Investment Could be the Next Sub-Prime Crisis*. Available at: https://www.theguardian.com/environment/2011/jul/12/high-carbon-investment

Caldecott, B., McDaniels, J. and Derricks, G. 2014. *Summary of Proceedings*. Stranded Assets Forum, Waddeson Manor, March 14–15. Available at: www.smithschool.ox.ac.uk/research/stranded-assets/.

Carney, M. 2015. *Breaking the Tragedy of the Horizon – Climate Change and Financial Stability*. Speech given by Mark Carney, Governor of the Bank of England, Chairman of the Financial Stability Board at Lloyd's of London, September 29. Available at: www.bankofengland.co.uk/publications/Pages/speeches/2015/844.aspx.

Clark, G. L. and Monk, A. H. B. 2013a. The Scope of Financial Institutions: In-Sourcing, Outsourcing and Off-Shoring. *Journal of Economic Geography*, 13(2), 279–298. Available at: http://joeg.oxfordjournals.org.

Clark, G. L. and Monk, A. H. B. 2013b. Transcending Home Bias: Institutional Innovation Through Cooperation and Collaboration in the Context of Financial Instability. *SSRN Electronic Journal*, 1–18. Available at: www.ssrn.com.

Climate Policy Initiative (CPI). 2013. *The Challenge of Institutional Investment in Renewable Energy*. Available at: http://climatepolicyinitiative.org/wp-content/uploads/2013/03/The-Challenge-of-Institutional-Investment-in-Renewable-Energy.pdf.

Cochran, I., Hubert, R., Marchal, V. and Youngman, R. 2014. Public Financial Institutions and the Low-Carbon Transition: Five Case Studies on Low-Carbon. Infrastructure and Project Investment. *OECD Environment Working Papers*, No. 72, OECD Publishing, Paris. Available at: https://www.oecd-ilibrary.org/docserver/5jxt3rhpgn9t-en.pdf?expires=1522760710&id=id&accname=guest&checksum=DA1873C624764588F01C054AB8D662A0.

CTI. 2011. Unburnable Carbon – Are the World's Financial Markets Carrying a Carbon Bubble? *Carbon Tracker Initiative*. Available at: www.carbontracker.org/wp-content/uploads/2014/09/Unburnable-Carbon-Full-rev2-1.pdf.

Dietz, S., Bowen, A., Dixon, C. and Gradwell, P. 2016. 'Climate Value at Risk' of Global Financial Assets. *Nature Climate Change*, advance on. Available at: http://dx.doi.org/10.1038/nclimate2972

ESRB. 2016. *Too Late, Too Sudden: Transition to a Low-Carbon Economy and Systemic Risk*. European Systemic Risk Board (ESRB), ASC Report No. 6, February.

FDF. 2016. *Report on the GFSG – Private Sector Workshop "Modeling and Assessing Environmental Risks"*, Berne, Switzerland, May 11–12, Swiss Federal Department of Finance (FDF).

FSB. 2016. *Phase I Report of the Task Force on Climate-Related Financial Disclosures*. Financial Stability Board, March. Available at: www.fsb-tcfd.org/wp-content/uploads/2016/03/Phase_I_Report_v15.pdf.

G20/OECD. 2012. *G20/OECD Policy Note on Pension Fund Financing for Green Infrastructure and Initiatives*. Available at: www.oecd.org/finance/private-pensions/S3%20G20%20OECD%20Pension%20funds%20for%20green%20infrastructure%20-%20June%202012.pdf.

G20/OECD. 2013. *G20/OECD High-Level Principles of Long-Term Investment Financing by Institutional Investors*. Available at: www.oecd.org/finance/private-pensions/G20-OECD-Principles-LTI-Financing.pdf.

G20/OECD. 2014a. *G20/OECD Report on Effective Approaches to Support Implementation of the G20/OECD High Level Principles on Long-Term Investment Financing by Institutional Investors*. Report to G20 Finance Ministers and Central Bank Governors, September. Available at: www.oecd.org/daf/fin/private-pensions/G20-OECD-Report-Effective-Approaches-LTI-Financing-Sept-2014.pdf.

G20/OECD. 2014b. *G20/OECD Checklist on Long-Term Investment Financing Strategies and Institutional Investors*, September. Available at: www.oecd.org/daf/fin/private-pensions/G20-OECD-Checklist-LTI-Financing-Strategies-Institutional-Investors.pdf.

G20/OECD. 2016. *Guidance Note on Diversification of Financial Instruments for Infrastructure and SMEs*. Available at: www.oecd.org/daf/fin/private-pensions/G20-OECD-Guidance-Note-Diversification-Financial-Instruments.pdf.

Goldman Sachs. 2015. *The Low Carbon Economy: GS SUSTAIN Equity Investor's Guide to a Low Carbon World, 2015–25*. Goldman Sachs Equity Research. Available at: www.goldmansachs.com/our-thinking/pages/new-energy-landscape-folder/report-the-low-carbon-economy/report.pdf

Green Finance Task Force. 2015. *Establishing China's Green Financial System*. Available at: www.unep.org/newscentre/default.aspx?DocumentID=26802&ArticleID=34981

Gurria, A. 2013. *The Climate Challenge: Achieving Zero Emissions*. Lecture by the OECD Secretary-General, Mr. Angel Gurría. London, 9 October 2013. Avaliable at: http://www.oecd.org/env/the-climate-challenge-achieving-zero-emissions.htm

HgCapital. 2016. *Institutional Investment Database*, Murley, T., ed.

IEA. 2014. *Medium-Term Renewable Energy Market Report 2014*. Paris: OECD/IEA Publishing. http://dx.doi.org/10.1787/renewmar-2014-en.

Kaminker, C. 2016. *Progress Report on Approaches to Mobilise Institutional Investment for Green Finance: An OECD contribution to the G20 Green Finance Study Group*. Paris: OECD Publishing. Available at: www.oecd.org/cgfi/resources/Progress_Report_on_Approaches_to_Mobilising_Institutional_Investment_for_Green_Infrastructure.pdf

Kaminker, C. 2017. *Mobilising Bond Markets for a Low-Carbon Transition*. Paris: OECD Publishing. http://dx.doi.org/10.1787/9789264272323-en

Kaminker, C., et al. 2013. Institutional Investors and Green Infrastructure Investments: Selected Case Studies. *OECD Working Papers on Finance, Insurance and Private Pensions*, No. 35, OECD Publishing, Paris. http://dx.doi.org/10.1787/5k3xr8k6jb0n-en

Kaminker, C., et al. 2015. Mapping Channels to Mobilise Institutional Investment in Sustainable Energy: An OECD Report for G20 Finance Ministers and Central Bank Governors. In Kaminker, C. (ed.), *Green Finance and Investment*. Paris: OECD Publishing. doi: http://dx.doi.org/10.1787/9789264224582-en

Kennedy, C. and Corfee-Morlot, J. 2012. Mobilising Investment in Low Carbon, Climate Resilient Infrastructure. *OECD Environment Working Papers*, No. 46, OECD Publishing, Paris. http://dx.doi.org/10.1787/5k8zm3gxxmnq-en.

McKinsey. 2016. *Financing Change: How to Mobilize Private Sector Financing for Sustainable Infrastructure*. McKinsey & Company Center for Business and Environment, January.

Miyamoto, K. and Chiofalo, E. 2015. Official Development Finance for Infrastructure: Support by Multilateral and Bilateral Development Partners. *OECD Development Co-operation Working Paper*, No. 25, OECD Publishing, Paris. Available at: https://www.oecd-ilibrary.org/docserver/5jrs3sbcrvzx-en.pdf?expires=1522760432&id=id&accname=guest&checksum=CC4D59DFBBB6B3C01D9CBF4C51F30200.

NCE. 2014. *Infrastructure Investment Needs of a Low-Carbon Scenario*. Global Commission on the Economy and Climate. Available at: http://newclimateeconomy.report/2015/wp-content/uploads/2016/04/Infrastructure-investment-needs-of-a-low-carbon-scenario.pdf.

NCE. 2015. *Seizing the Global Opportunity: Partnerships for Better Growth and Better Climate*. Global Commission on the Economy and Climate. Available at: http://new climateeconomy.report/2015/wp-content/uploads/2014/08/NCE-2015_Seizing-the-Global-Opportunity_web.pdf.

OECD/Bloomberg Philanthropies. 2015. Green Bonds: Mobilising the Debt Capital Markets for a Low Carbon Transition. In Kaminker, C. (ed.), *OECD Policy Perspectives Series*. Paris. Available at: www.oecd.org/environment/cc/Green%20bonds%20PP%20[f3]%20[lr].pdf

OECD/IEA/ITF/NEA. 2015. *Aligning Policies for a Low-Carbon Economy*. Paris: OECD Publishing. http://dx.doi.org/10.1787/9789264233294-en.

OECD. 2015a. *Climate Change Disclosure in G20 Countries: Stocktaking of Corporate Reporting Schemes*. Paris: OECD Publishing. Available at: www.oecd.org/investment/corporate-climate-change-disclosure-report.htm.

OECD. 2015b. *OECD Business and Finance Outlook 2015*. Paris: OECD Publishing. http://dx.doi.org/10.1787/9789264257573-en

OECD. 2016a. *Annual Survey of Large Pension Funds and Public Pension Reserve Funds: Report on Pension Funds' Long-Term Investments*. Paris: OECD Publishing. Available at: www.oecd.org/daf/fin/private-pensions/2015-Large-Pension-Funds-Survey.pdf.

OECD. 2016b. *OECD Business and Finance Outlook 2016*. Paris: OECD Publishing. http://dx.doi.org/10.1787/9789264257573-en

OECD. 2016c. *Investment Governance and the Integration of ESG Factors*. Paris: OECD Publishing.

OECD. 2016d. *Green Investment Banks: Scaling Up Private Investment in Low-Carbon, Climate-Resilient Infrastructure, Green Finance and Investment*. Paris: OECD Publishing. http://dx.doi.org/10.1787/9789264245129-en

Pooler, M. 2014. EU Banks Back in Infrastructure Loan Zone. *Financial Times*, May 24. Available at: www.ft.com/cms/s/0/2d625268-e0ef-11e3-a934-00144feabdc0.html

PRI. Forthcoming. *Greening Institutional Investment, Principles for Responsible Investment*.

Wehinger, G. and Nassr, I. K. 2016. Green Financing: Challenges and Opportunities in the Transition to a Clean and Climate-Resilient Economy. *OECD Journal: Financial Market Trends*, 2016(2), 63–78.

Wolfrom, L. and Yoko-Arai, M. 2016. Financial Instruments for Managing Disaster Risks Related to Climate Change. *OECD Journal: Financial Market Trends*, 2015(1). http://dx.doi.org/10.1787/fmt-2015-5jrqdkpxk5d5

World Bank/IMF/OECD. 2015. *Capital Market Instruments to Mobilize Institutional Investors to Infrastructure and SME Financing in Emerging Market Economies*. Report for the G20. Available at: www.oecd.org/g20/topics/development/WB-IMF-OECD-report-Capital-Markets-Instruments-for-Infrastructure-and-SME-Financing.pdf.

12 Stranded assets as economic geography

The case for a disciplinary home?

Ben Caldecott

1. Introduction

Given the speed at which it has become an important topic, the academic literature on stranded assets is still surprisingly under-developed, primarily because of the comparatively long peer review and publication process for journals. Researchers, scholars, and practitioners have often opted for the publication of working papers, research notes, speeches, government white papers, and reports to disseminate their work as quickly as possible so they can influence a fast-moving discourse.

This means that the stranded assets literature from the early first half of the 2010s is heavily dependent on the 'grey literature'. This leaves it susceptible to criticism, despite research showing that although published research is more likely to contain results from larger samples, methodological rigor does not appear to differ between the published and the grey literatures (Conn et al. 2015).

Fortunately, this is now well on the way to being rebalanced, with work on stranded assets increasingly being published in the peer-reviewed academic literature (for example, see Caldecott 2017; McGlade and Ekins 2015; Jakob and Hilaire 2015; Caldecott and Mitchell 2014) and in the process of being produced within a number of disciplines and sub-disciplines, from macroeconomics (Batten et al. 2016; Campiglio et al. 2015) through to finance (Campiglio 2016; Battiston et al. 2016) and law (Barker et al. 2016). This diversity and the appeal of the topic to a wide range of disciplines and sub-disciplines are important. They create the opportunity for the topic to be interpreted in different ways and applied to different contexts, potentially enabling the linking up of these disparate strands of work in the future, which may support multi-disciplinary collaboration.

While it means that the topic may be able to draw on the widest possible range of expertise, this approach has a concomitant risk – that as an emerging topic it is spread too thinly and then fails to establish itself properly. As such, there is a strong rationale for stranded assets to find a disciplinary home. This needs to be a discipline or sub-discipline that can help it to both develop firmer foundations and explore new areas by providing ideas, concepts, and methodologies that can be usefully employed in answering some of the research questions identified throughout this volume. It also needs to be a discipline supportive of producing research that interacts with and speaks to a range of 'real-world' audiences and one that is suitably adaptable so as to encourage multi-disciplinary research.

Economic geography is a strong candidate as a disciplinary home for stranded assets. The sub-discipline can both contribute to the development of stranded assets as a scholarly endeavour and itself benefit from interacting with a topic that intersects with some of the most pressing contemporary issues related to environmental sustainability. It is also my contention that economic geography is better suited as a disciplinary home for stranded assets than either environmental economics or environmental geography, which are two obvious alternatives. While both have important contributions to make – the latter particularly in terms of understanding the nature of environment-related risks and the former in terms of understanding the costs of environmental externalities for society – economic geography is better placed to engage with the wide range of research questions that the topic of stranded assets generates. Similarly, management and finance as disciplines have significant contributions to make, especially in relation to how corporations manage these issues and how financial institutions price environment-related risk but have little to contribute in terms of other areas of concern, such as how stranded assets may or may not exacerbate spatial disparities and inequalities. Economic geography, as we shall see in the next section, has a sufficiently wide gamut of interests, theory, and empirical data to engage more successfully over a sustained period of time on the topic and across multiple research themes related to stranded assets.

2. Economic geography

Economic geography is a sub-discipline both of geography and of economics. Clark et al. (2000) bounds economic geography as being 'concerned with the spatial configuration of firms, industries, and nations within the emerging global economy in all its manifestations' (Clark et al. 2000, p. vii). Scott (2000) argues for something similarly broad and place-related:

> [economic geographers] have generally and rather insistently focused on questions involving the spatial and locational (or, in another vocabulary, the urban and regional) foundations of economic life, and it is the remarkable collection of insights assembled under these signs that may be designated as 'economic geography'.
>
> (Scott 2000, p. 19)

There are significant differences between economic geography as practised by economists and economic geography as practised by geographers (Clark 1998). Geographical economics has been much more narrowly focused on international trade theory, so-called new economic geography. In the new economic geography the goal is to devise a modelling approach that lets one discuss the economies of regions or countries within the context of a national or international economy in general equilibrium (Krugman 2000, 1996, 1993, 1991). Clark (1998) is critical of the 'stylized facts' that dominate intellectual reasoning within new economic geography, such as industry regions and increasing returns to scale. Many other economic geographers are critical of geographical economics as practised by Krugman and his fellow economists (for example, see Scott 2006), not least because their work mirrors neoclassical location theory orthodoxies of the 1950s and 1960s that were previously discredited by economic geographers (see Hudson 2006).

Economic geography as practised by geographers is less easily defined than geographical economics and has undergone a number of significant periods of change. Scott (2000) identifies its rise as a sub-discipline within geography in the 1950s. The rise of Fordist mass production and a modern consumer society due to the long post-war boom fuelled complex spatial disparities that generated exciting research questions for geographers and economists (Scott 2000).

One important strand of this early work was 'regional science', which was an expression of dissatisfaction with mainstream economics as a 'wonderland of no spatial dimensions' (Isard 1956, p. 25). Regional science combined elements of economics with elements of geography and attempted to 'rewrite neoclassical competitive equilibrium theory in terms of spatial coordinates' (Scott 2000, p. 21).

This early theme of plugging all-too-obvious gaps in neoclassical economics continued with 'behavioural economic geography'. This attempted to show that individual decision makers were influenced by the quantity and quality of the information available, as well as their ability to use the information, and how this could shed light on locational and geographic decisions (Pred 1967). The concepts of learning and perception in behavioural economic geography were added by Cox and Golledge (1969). For anyone familiar with the contemporary discourse on behavioural economics (for example, see Thaler and Sunstein 2008), this behavioural strand of economic geography feels incredibly prescient. It is perhaps these early predilections that also help explain why economic geographers have been so critical of the new economic geography and geographical economists, with their reliance on 'over-simplifications, abstractions, and stylised facts'.

As the post-war boom gave way to the oil shocks, stagflation, and the collapse of manufacturing industries in North America and Europe, economic geography responded by reinterpreting questions in terms of Marxist political economy (Scott 2000). Harvey (1973) sought to demonstrate how the forces of capitalism create geographies, in particular how capitalist production leads to uneven development and spatial divisions of labour that foster inequality (Scott 2000; Sheppard 2006). Over the 1970s and early 1980s economic geographers consequently tackled a wide range of urban and regional problems, particularly poverty, unemployment, deindustrialisation, and regional decline (Scott 2000).

The popularity within economic geography of Marxist political economy, with its emphasis on grand structural processes, resulted in a backlash from the late 1970s onwards. The political and intellectual baggage of Marxist approaches were being abandoned not only in economic geography but across the social sciences. In economic geography there was a growing recognition 'that the social and cultural contexts – within which market mechanisms are embedded – are crucial to the functionality of markets' (Sheppard 2006, p. 15). These social and cultural contexts, deprioritised in Marxist political economy, rose to the fore; 'uniqueness and difference had now turned into points of analytic interest rather than mere background noise, and with the affirmation of their investigative significance, any notion of theoretical totalization became correspondingly anathema' (Scott 2000, p. 21). This was accompanied by the rise of gender and not just class as a topic of significance for economic geographers (for example, see Massey 1984).

Economic geography then moved to focus on particular localities and concentrated on understanding the internal and external pressures that they faced, not least in the context of economic decline and industrial restructuring (Scott 2000). The resurgence of regional economies as a result of 'post-Fordist' industries then became of significant interest, for example Silicon Valley for high-technology manufacturing (for example, see Saxenian 1994) and the City of London for financial services (for example, see Thrift 1994). Vertical disintegration, inter-industrial transactional networks, and local labour markets with increasing returns effects were the main factors driving forward such post-Fordist regional economic development (Scott 1986).

With the end of the Cold War and markedly increased interconnectedness and international trade came a growing interest in the causes and consequences of economic globalisation, including in terms of the international division of labour (for example, Taylor and Thrift 1982), multinational corporations (for example, Dicken 1986), 'hypermobility' and the 'end' of geography (for example, Amin and Robins 1990; O'Brien 1992), innovation (for example, Simmie 1997), and social regulation and persistent local inequality (for example, Peck 1996; Peck and Tickell 1994).

Functional integration by sectors and corporations across economies, supported by different scales of related regulation from the regional to the national and international, has catalysed the globalisation of finance and money (Scott 2000). In the geography of finance – a part of economic geography – scholars became interested in both the connection between finance and industry and 'the development of finance as a set of institutions distinct from the production of goods and services' (Clark and Wójcik 2007, p. 3). The former group focused on financial institutions as allocators of capital between companies, sectors, regions, and countries, as well as how the real economy was being shaped by the power of interests within global finance (Clark and Wójcik 2007). The latter group explore how financial institutions beyond banks and insurance companies, for example pension funds and asset managers, have developed and driven the globalisation of finance (for example, see Clark and Wójcik 2007; Clark 1998, 2003, 2007).

Economic geography has evolved from a focus in the post-war period on location and regional research interested in optimisation and spatial hierarchies, particularly in North America and Western Europe, into a sub-discipline grappling with some of the most interesting questions facing societies internationally – from inequality and unemployment through to globalisation and innovation. Even from this condensed survey of the literature, it is clear that the sub-discipline has responded to the great events and trends, which have in turn become important research questions for economic geographers. Economic geography has also shifted from the great theory-driven methodological approaches (for example, Marxist political economy) to more nuanced and empirically driven research that dynamically informs and interacts with theoretical innovation (Clark 2007). This makes economic geography grounded and responsive to developments and concerns in the real world and less susceptible to poorly substantiated stylised facts and theoretical abstractions. We can see this tendency to focus on the big issues facing contemporary policy makers and decision makers in recent work focused on understanding the causes and implications of the global financial crisis (for example, see Wójcik and MacDonald-Korth 2015; Wojcik 2013).

But despite economic geography's positive tendency to speak to contemporary concerns, it seems that the sub-discipline has largely failed to engage seriously on environmental questions (Dicken 2004). Looking at the economic geography literature, it is indeed surprising how little has been written on environmental topics. They appear only in passing and recently in only a very limited number of contexts, for example: (i) how environmental regulation shapes firms' location decisions (Tole and Koop 2011); (ii) the emergence of new environmental markets, specifically carbon markets in Europe and the financial geography of these developments (Knox-Hayes 2009); and (iii) the spatial adoption of renewable energy technologies (Graziano and Gillingham 2015). While these are important contributions, they are not particularly broad or deep wells of literature in economic geography, at least not yet. Environment-related questions, including the ones that economic geographers have so far decided to take on, are given a much more comprehensive treatment across the different sub-disciplines of economics. Environmental economics is itself a significant sub-discipline within economics.

Realising that this neglect is an anomaly given that this should be natural terrain for a discipline intimately concerned with location and context and that it is one of the most pressing issues for a wide range of actors – from firms to governments to investors – a number of economic geographers came together to propose a new 'environmental economic geography' (EEG) in the mid-2000s (Gibbs 2006; Angel 2006; Hayter 2008; Bridge 2008). There has been a debate about what EEG should be focused on, what theories and concepts it could draw on, and how it should be bounded.

Bridge (2008) argues convincingly that EEG should focus on 'the difference that "environment" makes to processes we have traditionally considered to be (purely) economic' (Bridge 2008, p. 78). This is very much in the spirit of work on stranded assets to date. Other proponents of EEG have been content to be less discerning and simply bound it as research grounded in economic geography that addresses any element of the 'biophysical world' (Bridge 2008; Angel 2006). The debate has yet to be settled and unfortunately it appears that EEG has not yet succeeded in rising to the original challenge – of making the environment a topic of significant contemporary concern to economic geographers. There remains a very obvious gap between what economic geography is contributing to environmental questions and what it can and should be contributing.

3. A mutually beneficial relationship

There is a strong case for economic geography to become a disciplinary home for stranded assets. It can play to economic geography's strengths and help to correct some of its weaknesses, particularly in relation to the environment. It can also build on or even rejuvenate some of economic geography's oldest recurring themes and support the development of some of its newest research areas.

Economic geography's healthy scepticism of neoclassical economics and stylised facts, as well as its long-standing appreciation of behaviour and cognition, means that it is well positioned to examine the reasons stranded assets can happen and why this matters. To an economic geographer it is obvious that novel risks would be hard to comprehend and integrate into decision making due to individual, cultural, and organisational biases and misaligned incentives. In contrast, in the world of the neoclassical economist, perfect information means there can be no stranded assets and that markets are already pricing in this information effectively (see Helm 2015).

The consistent focus of economic geographers on spatial disparities, inequalities, and the rise and fall of different firms, sectors, regions, and countries means that the sub-discipline should naturally be interested in how stranded assets could cause or change these processes. Understanding these issues and how they can be effectively managed to the benefit of society also requires deep historical and international perspectives – something the discipline can readily offer.

The topic of stranded assets has been so far preoccupied with the financial implications of asset stranding – both from a macroeconomic and microeconomic perspective. In particular, it has focused on how different types of financial institutions can manage these issues, especially in terms of changes to practice, governance, and regulation, and what it might mean if they do not. The geography of finance's focus on the globalisation of finance and empirical work to understand processes and behaviours within finance can also be productively utilised to shed light on questions related to stranded assets.

In each of these areas stranded asset–related work has begun, but it lacks the coherence of a disciplinary home. Economic geography has an opportunity to be such a home, and there are several reasons economic geographers might want to invest the time in making this happen.

First, as discussed, economic geography can and should do better in relation to environmental concerns and should aspire to 'own' an environmental issue that is not already dominated by another discipline or sub-discipline. Stranded assets could finally give EEG the opportunity to live up to its potential.

Second, as many economic geographers have noted (Bridge 2008; Gibbs 2006; Sheppard 2006; Hanson 2006; Dicken 2004; Scott 2000; Clark et al. 2000), economic geography has been historically weak at influencing and informing policy. As we have seen, stranded assets has already achieved significant policy salience and as a topic is generating some very important policy questions at different levels – from the regional to the international. These policy issues are also gaining public recognition – something that economic geography could do well to piggyback on. In effect, embracing stranded assets could help to solve the 'missing geographers' problem identified by Dicken (2004).

Third, stranded assets requires a multi-disciplinary or even a 'trans-disciplinary' approach, and economic geography is suited to this endeavour (Pike 2007). Other disciplines, in particular economics, have too much baggage to do this effectively. Economic geography's attractiveness rests on its strength through difference and ability to synthesise (Bagchi-Sen and Lawton Smith 2006; Bridge 2008; Pike 2007), and stranded assets plays to these strengths.

4. Conclusion

This chapter makes the case for economic geography as the disciplinary home for stranded assets. Economic geography can both contribute to the development of stranded assets as a scholarly endeavour and itself benefit from interacting with a topic that intersects with some of the most pressing contemporary issues related to environmental sustainability. It can help stranded assets to both develop firmer foundations and explore new areas by providing relevant ideas, concepts, and methodologies that can be usefully adapted. Importantly, it is a discipline supportive of producing research that interacts with and speaks to a range of practitioner audiences and one that is suitably adaptable so as to encourage multi-disciplinary research.

This proposition should be attractive to economic geographers. Stranded assets has the virtue of fitting into a number of current and recurring themes within economic geography. Economic geography must do better in relation to environmental topics, and stranded assets can provide EEG the opportunity to live up to its much-vaunted potential. Stranded assets can also help economic geography reach new audiences and address the 'missing geographers' problem.

Economic geography's healthy scepticism of neoclassical economics and stylised facts, as well as its long-standing appreciation of behaviour and cognition, means that it is well positioned to examine the reasons stranded assets can happen and why this matters. The consistent focus of economic geographers on spatial disparities, inequalities, and the rise and fall of different firms, sectors, regions, and countries means that the sub-discipline has a lot to offer in terms of understanding how stranded assets could cause or change these processes. In addition, the geography of finance's focus on the globalisation of finance and empirical work to understand processes and behaviours within finance can also be productively utilised to shed light on questions related to stranded assets and financial institutions.

While the growing diversity and appeal of stranded assets means the topic can draw on a wide range of disciplines, this approach has a concomitant risk – that it is spread too thinly and then fails to establish itself properly. This is arguably the most significant risk to the future development and longevity of stranded assets as a topic of both 'real-world' interest and sufficient academic rigour.

References

Amin, A. and Robins, K. 1990. Industrial Districts and Regional Development: Limits and Possibilities. In *Industrial Districts and Inter-Firm Cooperation in Italy*. Geneva: International Institute for Labour Studies, pp. 185–219.

Angel, D. P. 2006. Towards an Environmental Economic Geography. In Bagchi-Sen, S. and Lawton Smith, H. (eds.), *Economic Geography: Past, Present and Future*. London: Routledge.

Bagchi-Sen, S. and Lawton Smith, H. 2006. *Economic Geography Past, Present and Future*. London: Routledge.

Barker, S., et al. 2016. Climate Change and the Fiduciary Duties of Pension Fund Trustees – Lessons From the Australian law. *Journal of Sustainable Finance & Investment*, 6(3), 211–244. Available at: www.tandfonline.com/doi/full/10.1080/20430795.2016.120 4687 [Accessed October 24, 2016].

Batten, S., Sowerbutts, R. and Tanaka, M. 2016. *Let's Talk About the Weather: The Impact of Climate Change on Central Banks*. London. Available at: www.bankofengland.co.uk/research/Pages/workingpapers/default.aspx [Accessed June 19, 2016].

Battiston, S., et al. 2016. A Climate Stress-Test of the EU Financial System. *SSRN*.

Bridge, G. 2008. Environmental Economic Geography: A Sympathetic Critique. *Geoforum*.

Caldecott, B. (ed.). 2017. Stranded Assets and the Environment. *Journal of Sustainable Finance & Investment*, Special Issue, 7, 1.

Caldecott, B. and Mitchell, J. 2014. Premature Retirement of Sub-Critical Coal Assets: The Potential Role of Compensation and the Implications for International Climate Policy. *Seton Hall Journal of Diplomacy and International Relations*, Fall/Winter 2014.

Campiglio, E. 2016. Beyond Carbon Pricing: The Role of Banking and Monetary Policy in Financing the Transition to a Low-Carbon Economy. *Ecological Economics*, 121, 220–230.

Campiglio, E., Godin, A. and Kinsella, S. 2015. The Economic Implications of the Transition to a Low—Carbon Energy System: A Stock—Flow Consistent Model. *1st Global Conference on Stranded Assets and the Environment, Smith School of Enterprise and the Environment, University of Oxford*.

Clark, G. L. 1998. Stylized Facts and Close Dialogue: Methodology in Economic Geography. *Annals of the Association of American Geographers*, 88(1), 73–87.

Clark, G. L. 2003. *European Pensions & Global Finance*. Oxford: Oxford University Press.

Clark, G. L. 2007. Beyond Close Dialogue: Economic Geography as if it Matters. In *Politics and Practice in Economic Geography*. London: SAGE Publications Ltd, pp. 187–198.

Clark, G. L., Feldman, M. P. and Gertler, M. S. 2000. *The Oxford Handbook of Economic Geography*. Oxford: Oxford University Press.

Clark, G. L. and Wójcik, D. 2007. *The Geography of Finance: Corporate Governance in the Global Marketplace*. Oxford: Oxford University Press.

Clark, P. 2015. Shell's Arctic Pullout Fuels "Stranded Assets" Debate. *The Financial Times*. Available at: www.ft.com/cms/s/0/1c72d562-65d8-11e5-9846-de406ccb37f2.html#axzz478e7pYTE.

Conn, V. S., et al. 2015. Grey Literature in Meta-Analyses. *Nursing Research*, 52, July, 256–261.

Cox, K. R. and Golledge, R. G. 1969. Editorial Introduction: Behavioral Models in Geography. In Cox, K. R. and Golledge, R. G. (eds.), *Behavioral Problems in Geography: A Symposium*. San Francisco: Department of Geography, Northwestern University.

Dicken, P. 1986. *Global Shift: Industrial Change in a Turbulent World*. New York: Harper and Row.

Dicken, P. 2004. Geographers and "Globalization": (Yet) Another Missed Boat? *Transactions of the Institute of British Geographers*, 29(1), 5–26.

Gibbs, D. 2006. Prospects for an Environmental Economic Geography: Linking Ecological Modernization and Regulationist Approaches. *Economic Geography*, 82(2), April 2016, 193–215.

Graziano, M. and Gillingham, K. 2015. Spatial Patterns of Solar Photovoltaic System Adoption: The Influence of Neighbors and the Built Environment. *Journal of Economic Geography*, 15(4), 815–839.

Hanson, S. 2006. Think Back, Thinking Ahead: Some Questions for Economic Geographers. In Bagchi-Sen, S. and Lawton Smith, H. (eds.), *Economic Geography: Past, Present and Future*. London: Routledge.

Harvey, D. 1973. *Social Justice in the City*. London: Edward Arnold.

Hayter, R. 2008. Environmental Economic Geography. *Geography Compass*, 2(3), 831–850.

Helm, D. 2015. Stranded Assets – a Deceptively Simple and Flawed Idea. *Energy Futures Network*, (15).

Hudson, R. 2006. The "New" Economic Geography. In Bagchi-Sen, S. and Lawton Smith, H. (eds.), *Economic Geography: Past, Present and Future*. London: Routledge.

Isard, W. 1956. *Location and Space-Economy*. New York: Wiley.

Jakob, M. and Hilaire, J. 2015. Climate Science: Unburnable Fossil-Fuel Reserves. *Nature*, 517(7533), 150–152.

Knox-Hayes, J. 2009. The Developing Carbon Financial Service Industry: Expertise, Adaptation and Complementarity in London and New York. *Journal of Economic Geography*, 9, 749–777.

Krugman, P. 1991. Increasing Returns and Economic Geography. *Journal of Political Economy*, 99(3).

Krugman, P. 1993. *Geography and Trade*. Cambridge, MA: MIT Press.

Krugman, P. 1996. Urban Concentration: The Role of Increasing Returns and Transport Costs. *International Regional Science Review*, 19(1), 5–30.

Krugman, P. 2000. Where in the Word Is the "New Economic Geography"? In Clark, G. L., Feldman, M. P. and Gertler, M. S. (eds.), *The Oxford Handbook of Economic Geography*. Oxford: Oxford University Press.

Massey, D. 1984. *Spatial Divisions of Labour: Social Structures and the Geography of Production*. London: Macmillan.

McGlade, C. and Ekins, P. 2015. The Geographical Distribution of Fossil Fuels Unused When Limiting Global Warming to 2 [deg]C. *Nature*, 517(7533), 187–190.

O'Brien, R. 1992. *Global Financial Integration: The End of Geography*. London: Pinter.

Peck, J. 1996. *Work-Place: The Social Regulation of Labor Markets*. New York: Guildford.

Peck, J. and Tickell, A. 1994. Searching for a New Institutional Fix: The After-Fordist Crisis and the Global- Local Disorder. In Amin, A. (ed.), *Post-Fordism: A Reader*. Oxford: Blackwell, pp. 280–315.

Pike, A. 2007. Economic Geography: Past, Present and Future. In Bagchi-Sen, S. and Lawton Smith, H. (eds.), *Journal of Economic Geography*, 7(2), 220–222.

Pred, A. 1967. Behavior and Location: Foundations for a Geographic and Dynamic Location Theory. *Lund Studies in Geography Series B*, (27).

Saxenian, A. 1994. *Regional Advantage: Culture and Competition in Silicon Valley and Route 128*. Cambridge, MA: Harvard University Press.

Scott, A. J. 1986. High-Technology Industry and Territorial Development: The Rise of the Orange County Complex, 1955–1984. *Urban Geography*, (7), 3–45.

Scott, A. J. 2000. Economic Geography: The Great Half-Century. In Clark, G. L., Feldman, M. P. and Gertler, M. S. (eds.), *The Oxford Handbook of Economic Geography*. Oxford: Oxford University Press.

Scott, A. J. 2006. A Perspective of Economic Geography. In Bagchi-Sen, S. and Lawton Smith, H. (eds.), *Economic Geography: Past, Present and Future*. London: Routledge.

Sheppard, E. 2006. The Economic Geography Project. In Bagchi-Sen, S. and Lawton Smith, H. (eds.), *Economic Geography: Past, Present and Future*. London: Routledge.

Simmie, J. (ed.). 1997. *Innovation Networks and Learning Regions?* London: Jessica Kingsley.

Taylor, M. and Thrift, N. 1982. Models of Corporate Development and the Multinational Corporation. In *The Geography of Multinationals*. New York: St Martin's Press, pp. 14–32.

Thaler, R. H. and Sunstein, C. R. 2008. *Nudge: Improving Decisions About Health, Wealth, and Happiness*. New York: Penguin.

Thrift, N. 1994. On the Social and Cultural Determinants of International Financial Centres. In Corbridge, S., Thrift, N. and Martin, R. (eds.), *Money, Power and Space*. Oxford: Blackwell.

Tole, L. and Koop, G. 2011. Do Environmental Regulations Affect the Location Decisions of Multinational Gold Mining Firms? *Journal of Economic Geography*, 11(1), 151–177.

Wójcik, D. 2013. The Dark Side of NY-LON: Financial Centres and the Global Financial Crisis. *Urban Studies*, 50(13), 2736–2752.

Wójcik, D. and MacDonald-Korth, D. 2015. The British and the German Financial Sectors in the Wake of the Crisis: Size, Structure and Spatial Concentration. *Journal of Economic Geography*, 15(5), 1033–1054.

13 Next steps for stranded assets and the environment

Ben Caldecott

1. Research opportunities

While much has been written on stranded assets in a relatively short period of time, there remain significant gaps in the literature concerning what drives asset stranding and under what circumstances. Perhaps the most glaring imbalance in the literature generally has been the continued focus on listed upstream fossil fuel producers, particularly international oil and gas companies listed on the New York and London stock exchanges. These companies own less than 5% of total global oil and gas reserves versus the disproportionate amount held by states through national oil companies and other state-owned enterprises (Stevens 2016).

Upstream oil and gas production is just one of many sectors of the global economy that merits analysis and research on stranded assets. Studies have attempted to rebalance away from this focus on upstream energy to downstream (see Chapter 6 and Caldecott and McDaniels 2014b; Caldecott et al. 2015; Caldecott, Kruitwagen et al. 2016) and midstream (Marks 2016), as well as to focus on sectors outside energy, such as agriculture (Rautner et al. 2016; Morel et al. 2016; Caldecott et al. 2013), food (Howard et al. 2014), residential property (see Chapter 7 and Muldoon-Smith 2015), and shipping (Prakash et al. 2016). Sectors in which there are as yet unrealised opportunities for stranded assets-related research include transport, manufacturing, tourism, commercial property, and fisheries, among others.

This sector imbalance in the current literature is combined with a geographical one. Much of the work on stranded assets has focused on sectors in Australia, Canada, China, Western Europe, the Middle East, and the United States (Caldecott, Harnett et al. 2016). There is comparatively little work looking at these issues in Africa, the Caribbean, Central Asia, Eastern Europe, Latin America, South Asia, or Southeast Asia (Caldecott, Harnett et al. 2016). This is a significant omission given the exposure of many of these regions to environment-related risk factors, the presence of extensive fossil fuel resources that may become unburnable, and the particular challenges and opportunities facing lower-income and emerging economies.

In addition to these sectoral and geographical discrepancies, there are significant gaps in the literature on the environment-related risks that could strand assets. The risks that are perhaps best understood, and where the most work has been done to quantify and measure impacts spatially and temporally with good degrees of confidence, have been in relation to physical environmental change. For example, research to understand physical climate impacts, such as precipitation, flooding, heat waves, and other extreme weather events is significantly more mature in comparison to research focused on societal forms of environment-related risk, such as policy and regulation, norms, and litigation. So while we have sophisticated models that are used to dynamically estimate future flood risk, we have nothing nearing this capability in relation to estimating how regulation will impact sectors of the economy.

This divide in the breadth and depth of capabilities between the physical and the societal has two main origins. First, research on physical environmental change has been going on for much longer, arguably since the 1800s (for example Tyndall 1863), while research on societal responses to such changes is much more recent (see Chapter 1). Further contributing to this is the fact that societal environment-related risks inevitably follow from physical ones, as there is a lag time between impacts being felt and understood and societies responding to them.

Second, physical processes are observable and measurable, and consequently causal relationships are more readily established. As such, future outcomes can be estimated and quantified, whereas attempting to understand how societies singularly and plurally respond to anything, let alone environmental change, is fraught with difficulty. There is also a disciplinary gap between scientists and physical geographers on the one hand and social scientists and human geographers on the other. The former are bound together by common modern scientific methods, whereas the latter straddle a far wider range of approaches and perspectives, some of which are in direct conflict with one another.

Enhancing our understanding of societal environment-related risks is a priority and one that the topic of stranded assets has taken on directly – after all, the topic emerged from a concern with such risks (e.g. unburnable carbon and the carbon bubble). Another opportunity is bringing together physical and societal environment-related risks into the same framework. While stranded assets has also explicitly attempted to do this (see Figure 13.1 in Chapter 1) it has been constrained by a lack of research attempting to understand the relationships and correlations between the physical and the societal and between different types of societal risk (see Caldecott, Dericks et al. 2016). For example, how does an increased frequency of extreme weather events impact social norms; how does that affect the likelihood of successful climate litigation; and how could this then change regulation that aims to support renewable energy deployment? Stranded assets are in large part going to be the result of these chains of causality, but little is known about how they emerge and how this might differ between different jurisdictions with different political, legal, and cultural traditions. It is self-evident that developing a better understanding of these issues will require a multidisciplinary approach.

Temporary versus permanent asset stranding is also a gap in the literature (Caldecott, Harnett et al. 2016; Caldecott and McDaniels 2014a). This is the distinction between an asset that is devalued due to falling commodity prices or mothballed until market conditions improve and an asset that is closed down, dismantled, and no longer operational. The distinction is of particular importance to civil society and policy makers, where there is an interest in permanently stranding polluting infrastructure in order to achieve environmental outcomes (Caldecott, Harnett et al. 2016). There is also the related issue of residual value, even from a permanently stranded asset, for example the value of materials or chattels that can be resold. Caldecott and McDaniels (2014) identified how stranded gas-fired power stations in Europe have had their turbines removed and then exported to other jurisdictions – an example of such residual value being captured. Accountancy as both a profession and a discipline has much to contribute here, and existing accounting rules and standards can be used to determine the relevant boundaries between them when appropriately interpreted (Caldecott et al. 2014; Association of Chartered Certified Accountants and Carbon Tracker Initiative 2013). These concepts are not new; nonetheless, they are largely absent from the current literature on stranded assets.

The mirror to residual value is sunk costs, which are costs that cannot be eliminated, even by total cessation of production (Baumol and Willig 1981). In classical economic theory sunk costs are excluded from future business decisions, because the cost will be the same regardless of the outcome of a decision. In practice, the evidence suggests that sunk costs are regularly included in decision making (see Chapter 4). Through behavioural experiments, Kahneman and Tversky (1979) set out how loss aversion leads to the 'sunk cost fallacy', which is the tendency to continue with activities already invested in even if such activities are not economically rational. Sunk costs and their potential to influence decision making in the context of stranded assets is another rich seam currently absent in the literature – the notable exception being Chapter 4 in this volume. The role of loss aversion in exacerbating the problem of stranded assets by encouraging companies and investors to 'throw good money after bad' could be a significant problem that needs careful and urgent attention.

Another distinction largely absent from the current literature is in relation to the differences between physical (or tangible) and non-physical (or intangible) assets. Most of the literature has focused on the stranding of physical assets, largely ignoring the latter. Ansar et al. (2013) is one of the few examples of work that examines how the stigmatisation of firms can affect reputational assets and the ability of firms to retain human capital. Caldecott and Rook (2015) also look at how investment consultants could strand their reputational and relational assets by not appropriately integrating sustainable finance theory and practice into the advice they provide asset owners. Non-physical assets – such as brands, relationships, intellectual property, organisational capital, research pipelines, software, and human capital – require a much more substantial treatment in the stranded assets literature. This is particularly the case given that investment in non-physical assets exceeds that in physical assets in many developed countries, a trend that appears to accelerate as economies become more developed (OECD 2012).

Perception of environment-related risk, and the behaviours that may or may not result from different perceptions, is of central importance to stranded assets and should be a topic of interest to researchers and practitioners alike. If environment-related risks were observed, their materiality understood, such factors properly integrated into decision making, and then acted on, stranded assets would be a much less knotty problem. But such risks are often not observed, let alone understood or acted on. Even when environment-related risks are observed, material, and understood and options exist to act on and manage such risks, institutions and individuals may still not act. This tendency results in mispricing and the misallocation of resources, including by governments, companies, and financial institutions.

There are likely to be many reasons for this. Kay (2012) refers to endemic short-termism in financial markets, and Carney (2015) echoes this with his 'tragedy of the horizon'. Remuneration incentives, principal–agent problems, governance arrangements, organisational culture, liquidity requirements, misinterpretations of fiduciary duty, and diffuse shareholder ownership have all been cited as factors that contribute to the de-prioritising of the long term in favour of the short term (Caldecott and Rook 2015). Efforts to address these factors and extend the horizons of decision making will probably make addressing stranded assets easier, particularly as many environment-related risks are likely to become more acute over time, with a subset only materialising in a significant way over the medium to long term.

However, there could be issues specific to environment-related risks that make them more challenging to grapple with than other risks. There are a number of reasons to think that this could be a possibility: the environment-related risks in question are largely novel; understanding them is complex and often requires an multidisciplinary approach that straddles the physical and social sciences; contemporary and historical data is sparse; and many of the risks are non-linear (Caldecott 2015). Unlike some other risks that governments, companies, and investors face, there is also a lack of viable options to hedge risk, and when these exist, they are relatively illiquid and immature (Caldecott 2015).

If correct, these hypotheses would have significant implications. Extending time horizons may not be sufficient to properly integrate environment-related risks into decision making. Such risks may require further foregrounding for decision makers, and this may make regulatory responses, as opposed to voluntary ones, much more appropriate. This is an area that merits further consideration, particularly given the current focus on voluntary actions to support the integration of environment-related risks into decision making, such as the Task Force on Climate-related Financial Disclosures (see Chapter 8 and TCFD 2016).

Another hypothesis that requires further research is the idea that asset stranding caused by environment-related factors is likely to be more significant and places more value at risk than previous periods of 'intensive' stranding seen in the transition periods between techno-economic paradigms. How did societies manage previous periods of intensive stranding, and are there lessons that can be divined from these experiences? These are important questions for situating stranded assets within economic history and theories of economic growth and development. They are questions that would benefit from engagement with economic historians, who are yet to interact with the current discourse on stranded assets – Chapter 2 in this volume being the one exception so far.

Stranded assets has been appropriated in unexpected ways too. For example, it has been used as a catalyst to help reconceive protected areas (PAs) as productive spatial assets (Caldecott and Jepson 2014; Jepson et al. 2015, 2017). The reframing of PAs in this way and the implication that such PA assets can become stranded is being tested among nature conversation scholars and practitioners as a way of more effectively restating the case for PAs (Caldecott and Jepson 2014; Jepson et al. 2015, 2017). It could also have significant implications for PA management planning and the ability of PAs to attract investment and better manage risk (Caldecott and Jepson 2014; Jepson et al. 2015, 2017). There could be opportunities for the concept of stranded assets to be used in other areas not originally envisaged, and this should inform how those working on stranded assets seek to engage with other disciplines.

These opportunities for further stranded assets–related research could better connect our understanding of physical and societal environment-related risk, improve our knowledge of perception and behaviour, expand the scope of work into new sectors and geographies, and put stranded assets into a historical perspective. This is a significant future research programme that needs to be properly situated to be successfully realised.

Reflecting on this, Chapter 12 makes the case for economic geography as the disciplinary home for stranded assets. The sub-discipline can both contribute to the development of stranded assets as a scholarly endeavour and itself benefit from interacting with a topic that intersects with some of the most pressing contemporary issues related to environmental sustainability. It can help stranded assets to both develop firmer foundations and explore new areas by providing ideas, concepts, and methodologies that can be usefully employed in answering the research questions identified in the book. Importantly, it is a discipline supportive of producing research that interacts with and speaks to a range of practitioner audiences and one that is suitably adaptable so as to encourage multidisciplinary research.

While the growing diversity and appeal of stranded assets means the topic can draw on a wide range of disciplines, this approach has a concomitant risk – that it is spread too thinly and then fails to establish itself properly. This is arguably the most significant risk to the future development and longevity of stranded assets as a topic of both 'real-world' interest and sufficient academic rigour.

2. Final reflections

This project has generated significant and novel contributions to an important topic. Beyond the direct contributions of the chapters and the production of the volume, the project has made other contributions. First and foremost, it has helped to galvanise a growing network of practitioners and researchers internationally to engage with stranded assets and apply the concept to a range of research problems. This is hugely encouraging and is now, I hope, self-sustaining.

Second, through research that forms part of the volume and the broader corpus of work on stranded assets produced since 2010, change appears to have materialised in the real world – environment-related risks that were not considered before are now being considered, and at the margin, this will have helped to shift resources away from polluting activities and towards more sustainable ones. This work will have had a role in speeding up the consideration of such issues by an array of key decision makers.

Third, we hope through the use of this volume as an advanced primer by scholars, researchers, and practitioners, new cohorts will become interested in the topic, begin work in related areas, or apply some of the ideas set out in this volume to their work and activities.

Finally, this volume through its individual contributions has partially answered some pressing questions but has also raised many more. Answers to these could help societies successfully manage environmental change and the transition to environmental sustainability. But answers of satisfactory quality will be less likely unless more research on stranded assets is done and that this research is of the highest quality. The contributors to this volume are part of this endeavour, but many more scholars, researchers, and practitioners at different stages in their careers and with different perspectives are needed as part of the journey. This is critical for the next phase of work on stranded assets and if the topic is to extend successfully into new spatial, temporal, behavioural, and cultural domains. This development is important if we are to understand and then integrate stranded assets into real-world decision making – a necessary condition for a cleaner, safer, and more productive future.

References

Ansar, A., Caldecott, B. and Tibury, J. 2013. Stranded Assets and the Fossil Fuel Divestment Campaign: What Does Divestment Mean for the Valuation of Fossil Fuel Assets? *Smith School of Enterprise and the Environment, University of Oxford*, October.

Association of Chartered Certified Accountants & Carbon Tracker Initiative. 2013. *Carbon Avoidance? Accounting for the Emissions Hidden in Reserves*.

Baumol, W. J. and Willig, R. D. 1981. Fixed Costs, Sunk Costs, Entry Barriers, and Sustainability of Monopoly. *The Quarterly Journal of Economics*, 96(3), 405. Available at: http://qje.oxfordjournals.org/lookup/doi/10.2307/1882680 [Accessed September 10, 2016].

Caldecott, B. 2015. *Why Stranded Assets Matter and Should Not Be Dismissed*. Available at: https://theconversation.com/why-stranded-assets-matter-and-should-not-be-dismissed-51939.

Caldecott, B., Dericks, G., et al. 2016. *Stranded Assets: The Transition to a Low Carbon Economy*. Lloyd's of London Emerging Risk Report.

Caldecott, B., Dericks, G. and Mitchell, J. 2015. Stranded Assets and Subcritical Coal. *Smith School of Enterprise and the Environment, University of Oxford*.

Caldecott, B., Harnett, E., et al. 2016. *Stranded Assets: A Climate Risk Challenge*. A. Rios (ed.). Washington, DC: Inter-American Development Bank.

Caldecott, B., Howarth, N. and McSharry, P. 2013. Stranded Assets in Agriculture: Protecting Value from Environment-Related Risks. *Smith School of Enterprise and the Environment, University of Oxford.* Available at: www.smithschool.ox.ac.uk/research-programmes/stranded-assets/Stranded Assets Agriculture Report Final.pdf.

Caldecott, B. and Jepson, P. 2014. Towards a Framework for Protected Area Asset Management. *Smith School of Enterprise and the Environment, University of Oxford.*

Caldecott, B., Kruitwagen, L., et al. 2016. Stranded Assets and Thermal Coal: An Analysis of Environment-Related Risk Exposure. *Smith School of Enterprise and the Environment, University of Oxford*, pp. 1–188.

Caldecott, B. and McDaniels, J. 2014a. *Financial Dynamics of the Environment: Risks, Impacts, and Barriers to Resilience.* Oxford: Smith School of Enterprise and the Environment, Universityh of Oxford.

Caldecott, B. and McDaniels, J. 2014b. Stranded Generation Assets: Implications for European Capacity Mechanisms, Energy Markets and Climate Policy. *Smith School of Enterprise and the Environment, University of Oxford.* Available at: www.smithschool. ox.ac.uk/research-programmes/stranded-assets/Stranded Generation Assets – Working Paper – Final Version.pdf.

Caldecott, B., McDaniels, J. and Dericks, G. 2014. Summary of Proceedings: 1st Stranded Assets Forum, Waddesdon Manor, March 14–15. *Smith School of Enterprise and the Environment, University of Oxford.* Oxford: Smith School of Enterprise and the Environment, University of Oxford.

Caldecott, B. and Rook, D. 2015. Investment Consultants and Green Investment: Risking Stranded Advice? *Smith School of Enterprise and the Environment, University of Oxford.*

Carney, M. 2015. Breaking the Tragedy of the Horizon – Climate Change and Financial Stability. *Bank of England.* Available at: www.bankofengland.co.uk/publications/Pages/speeches/default.aspx [Accessed July 11, 2016].

Howard, S., Murray, V. and Driscoll, M. 2014. Stranded Assets in the Food Manufacturing Sector – Nutrition: An Emerging Threat or Opportunity? *Forum for the Future.*

Jepson, P., et al. 2015. A Framework for Protected Area Asset Management. *Smith School of Enterprise and the Environment, University of Oxford.*

Jepson, P., et al. 2017. Protected Area Asset Stewardship. *Biological Conservation*, 212, 183–190. Available at: www.sciencedirect.com/science/article/pii/S0006320716304979 [Accessed October 22, 2017].

Kahneman, D. and Tversky, A. 1979. Prospect Theory: An Analysis of Decision Under Risk. *Econometrica*, 47(2), 263. Available at: www.jstor.org/stable/1914185?origin=crossref [Accessed September 10, 2016].

Kay, J. 2012. *The Kay Review of UK Equity Markets and Long-Term Decision Making.*

Marks, A. 2016. Avoiding Gridlock: Policy Directions for a Decentralised Electricity System. *Center for Policy Development.*

Morel, A., et al. 2016. Stranded Assets in Palm Oil Production: A Case Study of Indonesia About the Sustainable Finance Programme. *Smith School of Enterprise and the Environment, University of Oxford.*

Muldoon-Smith, K. 2015. Energy Performance Legislation and Stranded Assets in Commercial Real Estate. *Unpublished TBC.*

OECD. 2012. Corporate Reporting of Intangible Assets: A Progress Report.

Prakash, V. et al. 2016. Revealed Preferences for Energy Efficiency in the Shipping Markets. *Carbon War Room and UCL Energy Institute Paper*, August.

Rautner, M., Tomlinson, S. and Hoare, A. 2016. Managing the Risk of Stranded Assets in Agriculture and Forestry. *Chatham House Research Paper*.

Stevens, P. 2016. International Oil Companies: The Death of the Old Business Model. *Chatham House Research Paper*, May.

Task Force on Climate-Related Financial Disclosures. 2016. *Phase I Report of the Task Force on Climate-Related Financial Disclosures*. Available at: www.fsb-tcfd.org/wp-content/uploads/2016/03/Phase_I_Report_v15.pdf [Accessed August 7, 2016].

Tyndall, J. 1863. *Heat as a Mode of Motion*. New York: D. Appleton and Company. Available at: https://archive.org/details/heatconsideredas00tynduoft.

Index

Note: Page numbers in *italics* indicate figures and in **bold** indicate tables on the corresponding pages.

For Product Safety Concerns and Information please contact our EU
representative GPSR@taylorandfrancis.com
Taylor & Francis Verlag GmbH, Kaufingerstraße 24, 80331 München, Germany

www.ingramcontent.com/pod-product-compliance
Ingram Content Group UK Ltd.
Pitfield, Milton Keynes, MK11 3LW, UK
UKHW021020180425
457613UK00020B/1006